Pray without Ceasing

Prayer for Morning & Evening

In Cooperation with the
INSTITUTE *for* LITURGICAL MINISTRY
at Maria Stein Center

Pray without Ceasing

Prayer for Morning & Evening

Joyce Ann Zimmerman, C.PP.S.
Kathleen Harmon, S.N.D. de N.
Jean-Pierre Prévost, S.M.M.
Delphine Kolker, C.PP.S.

A Liturgical Press Book

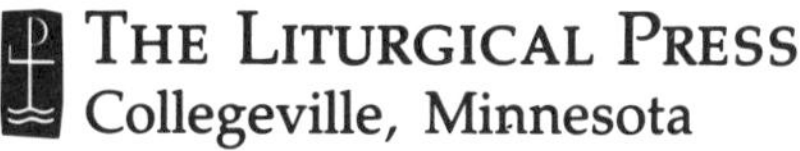

THE LITURGICAL PRESS
Collegeville, Minnesota

Artwork by Cordelia Gast, C.PP.S.

1 2 3 4 5 6 7 8 9

Library of Congress Cataloging-in-Publication Data

Pray without ceasing : prayer for morning and evening / Joyce Ann Zimmerman . . . [et al.].

p. cm.

"Intended for any Christian who wishes to enter into the daily rhythm of the Paschal mystery"—Introd.

"In cooperation with the Institute for Liturgical Ministry at Maria Stein Center."

Includes index of Psalms.

ISBN 0-8146-2294-1

1. Church year—Prayer-books and devotions—English. 2. Catholic Church—Prayer-books and devotions—English. 3. Bible. O.T. Psalms—Meditations. I. Zimmerman, Joyce Ann. 1945- .

BX2170.C55P65 1993

264′.024—dc20 93-32055

CIP

CONTENTS

INTRODUCTION

Long ago, Paul reminded the Thessalonians to "rejoice always, pray without ceasing, give thanks in all circumstances; for this is the will of God in Christ Jesus for you" (1 Thess 5:15-18, NRSV). To our modern ears, this may sound like an impossible ideal. Yet, there it is: bold, unadorned, unmitigated. Pray without ceasing.

From earliest times, the Church has taken seriously our need for continuous prayer. Especially by gathering at evening and morning—those special times of the day marked by sunset and sunrise, natural symbols for the rhythm of the dying and rising of Jesus Christ—do we pray ourselves into the very Mystery we are and live. For this reason, these times of the day have been marked by communal prayer with a defined structure that draws us into the Paschal Mystery.

Many have sometimes had a mistaken notion that the Liturgy of the Hours is for ordained priests and those men and women religious obliged by their constitutions to pray it. Although limited to a small segment of the Church for many centuries, this communal prayer at morning and evening—that which is officially called the "Liturgy of the Hours"—is really the prayer of the whole Church. Actually, the prayer at morning and evening is a daily prayer mandated by our baptismal call and commitment. To be immersed in the dying and rising of Christ by our Baptism is to assume its expression in the daily rhythm of our lives. To pray at morning and evening is the natural, Christian thing to do.

Communal prayer has taken many forms since the founding Christians began praying together. Sometimes more celebrative including much music, movement, and exuberance; sometimes more contemplative including simple recitation, richness of the Word, and quiet rest: in either case, the prayer seeks to draw Christians to a deeper experience and appreciation of the Spirit who works in our lives to make Jesus Christ present to all and in all. Besides style of celebration, time has blessed this daily prayer with rich accretions that have abundantly fed Christians' hunger for God. Whether with respect to style of praying or elements that make up the prayer, one thing remains constant: communal prayer capturing the dynamic rhythm of psalmody and intercessions deeply roots us for living the Paschal Mystery.

Style and Content of the Prayer

Even though certain forms of the Liturgy of the Hours have developed as a means for instruction and edification, morning and evening prayer are primarily times for praise and thanksgiving. To this end, *Pray without Ceasing* has a more simple structure than the official Roman rite for the Liturgy of the Hours; the reason for this is to make the prayer more accessible to a larger number of people. It is important that we restore prayer at morning and evening as the *prayer of the Church* and not continue our present malaise of allowing it to be the prayer of only a small segment of the whole. *Pray without Ceasing*, although an adaptation of the official Roman rite, is intended for any Christian who wishes to enter into the daily rhythm of the Paschal Mystery.

There is a long-standing precedent for adapting the style and content of prayer at morning and evening to accommodate the needs of particular groups. Many religious congregations do so even today. So *Pray without Ceasing* is simply following in these venerable footsteps. It attempts to capture the dynamic rhythm of the Paschal Mystery in its style at the same time that it retains a primary characteristic of praise and thanksgiving through the structure of its content.

Two marked styles shape the prayer offered in this volume. The weekdays are more contemplative; the structure is simple, the psalms are recited. This affords ample time to enter quietly into the prayer and experience its power. Weekends are noticeably festive; the structure is more elaborate and much of the prayer is sung. Thus, each weekend is a "mini Easter Triduum," so to speak, and the very celebration style reflects this. Likewise, the solemnities—those special festivals that are so strikingly connected to the yearly unfolding of the Paschal Mystery—are more festive than the feasts.

The content is divided into a fourfold structure. An opening hymn (or Light Service in the case of festive evening prayer) serves to focus the assembled community. The conclusion—blessing and dismissal—sends us forth to labor or rest in the knowledge of our firmly-established relationship with God. We have chosen to conclude the blessing with the Sign of the Cross using the traditional formula. Those communities who understand "Father" as a gender-specific reference to God rather than a metaphoric one could substitute a different blessing formula. The structural heart of the prayer, of course, is psalmody and intercessory prayer. These two structural elements play against each other, drawing us into praise and thanksgiving.

The psalms help us to be caught up in the timelessness of God's realm; they are a treasury of the expression of human and divine relationships. These ancient songs/prayers cover the whole gamut of human emotions as they capture Israel's—and our—relationship to God and each other. The biblical psalter consists of 150 psalms, and one ideal is to use all of them in a given course of time. This is the choice of the Roman rite of the Liturgy of the Hours, which uses almost all of these 150 psalms in the course of four weeks. Another option—borne out in ancient practice—is to limit the number of psalms to those more appropriate for the particular time of day and those that bring out the daily rhythm of the Paschal Mystery. Accordingly, *Pray without Ceasing* only uses forty-five psalms, arranged in a two-week series that opens onto the festivity of the weekend mini-Triduum. Further, each day has a leitmotif that draws us surely into the rhythm of the Paschal Mystery and toward Sunday as the climax of all our celebrations of prayer: Monday, loss of the sanctuary and longing for God; Tuesday, trust and protection; Wednesday, dependence on God and the fragility of humanity; Thursday, God's largess; Friday, our sinfulness and the triumph of the cross; Saturday, waiting and eager anticipation; Sunday, Resurrection.

At the same time that we pray the psalms, we are also reminded of our dependence on God as we make known our needs during intercessory prayer. Both the morning invocations—prayers addressed to the risen Christ whom we are celebrating—and the evening petitions—intentions calling forth from us profound dependence—are written in litany form. This ancient structure suggests that even our expression of needs is a litany of praise and thanksgiving for God's wondrous deeds on our behalf.

Ideally, prayer at morning and evening is communal prayer. Realistically, many of us find ourselves in situations where this prayer takes place without the supporting voices of others. Even though as baptized members of the Body of Christ we are never really "alone," our actual circumstances are often such that we have no one else present when we pray. *Pray without Ceasing* was written to serve the needs of both groups and individuals. Hopefully, all of us can join our voices to those of others in a Church that prays without ceasing.

Using *Pray without Ceasing*

Praying can be such a simple joy. But when we must find our way around a complexly structured prayer, some of that joy is curbed. This volume uses a simple structure of prayer, and even its format is easy to follow. No *ordo* (directions for when to pray what) is needed. The user only must know the number of the week in Ordinary Time or the place in the festal season.

Ordinary Time is arranged in a two-week series. Thus, during the odd-numbered weeks of Ordinary Time, pray from Week 1; during the even-numbered weeks of Ordinary Time, pray from Week 2. That's all there is to it! The festal seasons are arranged similarly. If the user knows what week it is (easily found by consulting any Catholic calendar), that person knows what to pray. The festal seasons have much repetition built into their pattern. This repetition promotes familiarity with texts that only occur during one brief period of the liturgical year. Additionally, the repetition allows us time to savor the flavor of the festal seasons, encouraging a deeper penetration into the mysteries and riches that mark a particular season.

The Contents listing at the beginning of the volume gives an overview of the included prayers and also serves as a page guide for locating these prayers. Listed are the entries for Ordinary Time as well as those prayers for the festal seasons, and the solemnities and feasts from the Table of Liturgical Days of the General Roman Calendar are arranged chronologically. Exceptions to this are those solemnities and feasts that are integral to a festal season (for example, the three feasts immediately following Christmas Day are printed with the Advent-Christmas-Epiphany prayers). We have omitted propers for the memorials listed on the Table of Liturgical Days in order to encourage an unbroken celebration of the rhythm of the Paschal Mystery as it unfolds during the festal seasons and the major festivals. Two prayers for festive days not found on the General Roman Calendar are included, one for Thanksgiving Day and one for any civic holiday.

Most of the prayers are complete, so "flipping" to another section of the volume is kept to a minimum. No prayer requires more than a single shift to another section of the prayerbook. Music is included to encourage the singing of those elements that are more properly sung. However, we laid out the text in such a way that the music would not be visually intrusive thus interfering with recitation of the prayer. We printed music for the Benedictus and Magnificat only for MONDAY 1. The melodies are quickly learned, so the bold type indications for cadences (note changes) are sufficient for these canticles to be sung easily even when the notes are not there.

Two other resources are necessary for praying this format of prayer at morning and evening. One or more hymn books are needed for the opening hymns (choice determined by the available books and repertoire of the user) and scriptural texts are needed for proclaiming the Word of God.

Alternatives for Celebration

Pray without Ceasing is not intended to be an invariable, but an adaptable prayer. Users are encouraged to adjust it for local needs as much as is helpful. In this way the prayer is both universal and personal.

Opening Hymn. Some people are accustomed to beginning prayer at morning and evening with "O God, come to my assistance. O God, make haste to help me." This may certainly be added and it may be a good substitute for the hymn if one is praying alone.

The choice of the hymn takes into consideration the time of day (morning or evening prayer) and the leitmotif for each day (see above). It is not necessary—and may not even be desirable—to constantly change hymns. If a group finds a cycle of hymns that works for them, stick with it. Change is built in for solemnities or feasts and during festal seasons. Familiarity is ordinarily an important feature of this prayer. It is neither the time nor the place to be constantly learning new music.

Psalmody. The psalms are arranged to be either recited (during weekdays and on feasts) or sung (on weekends and solemnities). If at all possible, this variable degree of festivity should be respected.

When the psalms are recited, a more meditative, contemplative mood prevails. The psalms are arranged by sense lines determined by the Hebrew hemistiches (that is, the combination of stressed and unstressed Hebrew syllables that determines the length of lines in the Hebrew Masoretic text). Punctuation aids the recitation. The praying group is to strive to recite the psalms "with one voice" raised in praise and thanksgiving to God. Feeling together the "pulse" of the stressed and unstressed syllables aids in this "one voice" praying. The short lines provide natural places for breathing stops.

Recitation parts are determined by the "voices" contained in the psalms themselves as well as by obvious shifts in mood in the text. Solo voices (one person reciting) are noted for most passages written in the first person singular ("I" or "me"); choir parts are noted for passages that are collective in voice. In some cases, the psalms contain obvious refrains or acclamations, which lend themselves nicely to be recited by "All."

When the voicing of a psalm begins with "All," it may take some practice for a community to "breathe" together so everyone comes in on the same breath. Especially challenging are those psalms that begin with a single Alleluia. Until a community has learned to pray easily with one voice, it may be helpful for the prayer leader (or solo voice) to speak the word or line in question as a solo part, with the community repeating the Alleluia or joining in the second line of the strophe.

The variation in voices serves to bring out the meaning and movement within the text. Some have commented that the solo voices foster lack of participation, for the assembly is simply "listening" to someone else pray. Actually, the solo voices invite a deeper entry into the text so that participation as transformation can occur. The contrasts in voices help delineate the movement in the text.

Our strophes (stanzas) are often not the customary four lines. We chose to let shifts in voices, adversatives, and other such poetic conventions determine the strophes.

We have included simple psalm tones (recitation notes and cadences) with the sung psalms for weekends and solemnities. Of course, other favorite sung settings of the psalms may be substituted. Preferably, the psalms are sung by a cantor with the assembly singing the antiphon at the various shift points in the psalms as indicated in the text. If no cantor is available, the psalms may also be sung in choir, alternating between two sides with everyone singing the antiphons.

Whether recited or sung, the psalms are prayed in such a way as to bring out the movement in each psalm. Psalms start someplace, and take us somewhere else. Part of the power of the prayer is to move into this journey in our relationships with God and each other. Some reflective time after each psalm is helpful to key into this movement. The psalm prayers which are included with the sung settings of the psalms help us to experience their movement. A brief reflection time between the singing of a psalm and its psalm prayer is appropriate; thus, the psalm prayer acts as a kind of "collect" for the community prayer.

The Word of God and gospel canticle (Benedictus or Magnificat) are structurally included with the psalmody because they also are from Sacred Scripture and because they complete and complement the leitmotif of the psalmody itself. The choice of Scripture selection is left to the discretion of the users. One suggestion is to draw on the daily/Sunday lectionary: the first lectionary selection is suitable for evening prayer and the Gospel for morning prayer. For those communities for whom daily Mass is part of their regular prayer cycle, the choice of lectionary readings helps connect prayer at morning and evening with Eucharist as well as affords more time to proclaim and pray them. It is hardly mere repetition. Another suggestion is to engage in the ancient practice of *lectio continua* in which a particular book of Scripture is read over a given period of time. This is especially rich during the festal seasons.

One simple sung setting for each gospel canticle is given. Others are available and surely may be substituted. Our translation of the gospel canticles capitalizes on a style that is similar to Hebrew psalmody. Particularly noticeable is the use of parallelism—lines, and sometimes even whole strophes, that are parallel.

Intercessions. Our intercessions are all written in litany form in order to lead us to praise and thanksgiving at the same time that we make known our needs. The morning intercessions are invocations addressed directly to Christ since morning praise is a resurrection prayer celebrating his risen life and presence in the community. They clearly underscore the special praise feature of prayer at the beginning of the day. The evening intercessions are petitions consisting of a stated intention. It is always appropriate during intercessory prayer to pause briefly between the announcing of the invocation or petition and the assembly's response (our typographic use of ellipses [...] indicates suggestions for these pauses). Note, too, that the final petition for evening prayer is always for the deceased; this is quite in keeping with a "dying" leitmotif of evening prayer.

Each of the intercessions has a sung setting given in the text. We encourage their singing, even if no trained cantor is present. The litany character of these prayers suggests that they be sung. If they are recited, however, it would be better for the prayer leader to simply begin with the first invocation or petition, followed by the assembly's response. It gets tedious if the prayer leader says the response which is then repeated by the assembly.

Rubrics. We deliberately omitted any rubrical notes in the prayer text because we presume *Pray without Ceasing* will be used in many different pastoral situations. We encourage each group to decide what works best for them. In general, we suggest standing for the opening hymn or Light Service, for the psalm prayers, for the Intercessions, and for the concluding blessing and sign of peace/dismissal. Be seated for the psalms (it is also fitting to kneel during Psalm 141) and for the Word of God (unless a Gospel is proclaimed, and then standing is recommended). Incense may be used during Psalm 141; in this case it symbolizes our purification and our prayers rising to God. Incense is also appropriate during the Gospel Canticles; during this time the order for incensing might include the Paschal Candle, altar, Cross, book of Scriptures, presider, and the assembly.

About this Psalm Translation

Our project of writing an adaptation of the Liturgy of the Hours began from a desire to experience better the daily rhythm of prayer. Soon, however, it became clear that the psalm translations that were available would not serve our purpose. Two issues predominated: Hebrew poetry and inclusive language.

Hebrew Poetry. The psalms are ancient poetic compositions, most of which were probably originally composed as sung liturgical texts. Unfortunately, we have no extant music to help us know how they were sung. This, indeed, is a great loss. But we do have numerous textual indications of the beauty and depth of Hebrew poetry. We tried to capture its spirit in our English translation. We paid particular attention to three Hebraic poetic devices: parallelism, adversatives (contrasts), and chiasms.

At first glance, parallelism seems to be simple repetition of words or phrases in the psalms. But at closer scrutiny, Hebrew poetic parallelism always takes us deeper into a text. An idea is stated, then repeated; but the images of the repetition, although close to the first idea, actually add to it and bring us to a new place. Parallelism helps us maintain a balance of thought, all the time contributing to a pleasing poetic meter and rhythm. Adversatives or contrasts clue us into shifts in the movement of the text. Adversatives might be indicated by contrasts in verb tenses (usually a play between the present and the past) or poetic images. These startle us into new ways of looking at familiar ideas or bring us to reversals in thought or action. Finally, chiasms are cross-patterned structures of repeated images or concepts that contribute to a pleasing rhythm and draw us to make comparisons.

The final editing of the translation took into serious account the fact that this is a *prayer text* that is meant to be *recited or sung aloud*. In some cases—especially for the sung texts—word order was changed so the cadences were smoother in the English. The punctuation and short lines respecting the Hebrew hemistiches also aid praying with one voice.

The psalms were written in simple language; our translation tries to respect that. Words are few and direct. It should be remembered, though, that Hebrew poetry—indeed, all poetry—is multivalent; that is, hidden meanings must be teased out of the text. These hidden meanings unlock the door to the timelessness and universality that is constitutive of all poetry. Good poetry never wears. The psalms, too, will never wear. This is why they can be prayed over and over again and always lead us to new meanings.

Inclusive Language. This is a most problematic area because it means so many different things to different people. What is satisfying to one group may be quite offensive to another. We realize that—although our ideal is to render our text truly inclusive—our decisions about translation necessarily involved value judgments that may or may not be acceptable. When the text clearly refers to both men and women, we rendered the translation so. Those were the easy decisions. Other areas are more problematic.

The language about God is especially difficult. We chose not to take liberties with the text by substituting other images. When the Hebrew tetragrammaton is used (YHWH), we translated it as "LORD" (using upper case letters) out of respect for the Jewish custom of not pronouncing the holy name. When the Hebrew word *adonai* is used, we translated it "Lord" (using lower case letters). Although these words have undue masculine overtones for some people, to strike them from the psalms is to alter radically the rhythm of the verses and overuse other names for God. We never refer to God with a masculine pronoun; in most cases we were able to avoid using the passive voice.

We substituted gender-neutral terms for other language that carries patriarchal freight. For example, when God is called "king," we translated it "Sovereign." When David is referred to as the king, we retained the term. When the text means all kings, we translated it "rulers." We translated "princes" as "nobles." In each case demanding a decision about rendering the text inclusive, the context, poetry, and faithfulness in translation were our guiding posts.

Our translation and prayer texts are hardly perfect. That would be asking the impossible. We do hope they are faithful to the spirit of the Word of God and the tradition of praying daily the Paschal Mystery. We hope they lead others who perhaps have never committed themselves to this kind of daily prayer to experience this great prayer of the Church. We hope these prayers nudge committed believers in the direction to "pray without ceasing."

Acknowledgments

This project was born from numerous challenges by people I contact through my courses and pastoral workshops to develop a prayer that would call persons daily to the riches of God's presence. Only they can really judge whether we have succeeded. I am grateful to them for their encouragement.

Of course, this prayerbook would never have happened without the other three project team members; they have willingly found time in already very full schedules to complete this work. They responded to my request for collaboration with enthusiasm, commitment, and proficiency. I have enjoyed working with them. Much of the work was initially completed by each project team member working alone in her/his own area of expertise. Kathleen Harmon composed all the music and set it up for printing; Jean-Pierre Prévost generated the basic, literal translation of the Hebrew Masoretic text into English; Delphine Kolker monitored the text for its literary quality; I composed the texts for the prayers, intercessions, blessings, and dismissals, and prepared the camera-ready copy for printing. We met together as an editorial committee to work out the final translation of the psalms and to discuss decisions regarding other areas of the text. The strengths of the completed version are due to their professional competence and spiritual depth; I alone bear the responsibility for any errors or weaknesses.

I am grateful for the support my Congregation, the Sisters of the Precious Blood of Dayton, Ohio has given me. Joyce Langhals, C.PP.S., President, and Nancy Raley, C.PP.S., Vice-president have advised and encouraged me and saw the end even before I did. Let them know that I am grateful. The participants in the Liturgy in a Formative Environment (L.I.F.E. 91, 92, 93) programs offered at Maria Stein Center each summer have prayed this together and made invaluable suggestions. To all of them I am indebted. Michael Naughton, O.S.B., Director of The Liturgical Press, has been enthusiastic and supportive of the project since seeing a manuscript early on, and has made invaluable suggestions for bringing this prayerbook to publication. To the many others who have walked with us on this journey: Thank you.

Prayer at morning and evening has an inherent power to change people. I find it an awesome and unique responsibility to offer this book of prayer. May those who pray it know the nearness of their God. May we all pray without ceasing.

Joyce Ann Zimmerman, C.PP.S.

Ordinary Time

MORNING HYMN

PSALMODY

Psalm 84 *To the choirmaster. On the gittith. By the Qorahites. Psalm.*

Solo 1 How lovable are your tents,
O LORD of hosts.
My soul longs—indeed faints—
for the courts of the LORD.
My heart and my flesh sing for joy
to the living God.
Even the sparrow finds a home
and the swallow a nest for herself
where she sets her young
next to your altars,
O LORD of hosts,
my Sovereign and my God.
Blessed are those who dwell in your house;
they will continue to praise you.

Selah (pause).

All Blessed is the one whose strength resides in you.
Those whose hearts are set on pilgrimage
make the valley of tears a place of fountains
as they travel through it.
Even the early rain covers it with blessings.
They walk with ever greater strength:
the God of gods will be seen in Zion.

Solo 1 O LORD God of hosts,
hear my prayer;
listen, O God of Jacob.

Selah (pause).

All See our shield, O God,
and consider the face of your Messiah.
For one day in your courts is better
than a thousand elsewhere.

Solo 1 I would rather stand at the threshold
of the house of my God,
than live in the tents of the wicked.
For the LORD is a sun and a shield;
God is grace and glory.
The LORD gives,
and does not refuse any good
to those who walk in integrity.

All O LORD of hosts,
blessed is the one
who trusts in you.

Psalm 5 *To the choirmaster. For the flutes. Psalm of David.*

Solo 1 Give ear to my words, O LORD,
perceive my groaning.
Be attentive to the sound of my cry,
my Sovereign and my God,
for to you I pray.
O LORD, in the morning
hear my voice.
In the morning I prepare for you
and I keep watching.

Choir 1 For you are not a God delighting in wickedness,
nor does evil daunt you.
Mockers cannot stand
before your eyes.
You hate all makers of emptiness,
and you will destroy speakers of deceit.
People of bloodshed and fraud,
the LORD abhors.

Solo 1 But I, in the abundance of your steadfast love,
shall come to your house.
With awe I shall prostrate myself in your holy temple.
O LORD, guide me in your justice
because of my adversaries;
straighten your way before me.

Choir 2 Nothing right comes from their mouths:
their insides are rotted,

their throats are open tombs,
their tongues are forked.
Prove them wrong, O God;
let them fall by their own counsels.
For their many transgressions,
drive them away
since they have rebelled against you.

All All who take refuge in you shall rejoice;
forever they will shout for joy.
You will lay protection over them
and all those who love your name
will exult in you.
For you bless the righteous, O LORD;
as with a shield of delight you will crown them.

Word of God

Benedictus

Joyce Ann Zimmerman, C.PP.S. Kathleen Harmon, S.N.D. de N.

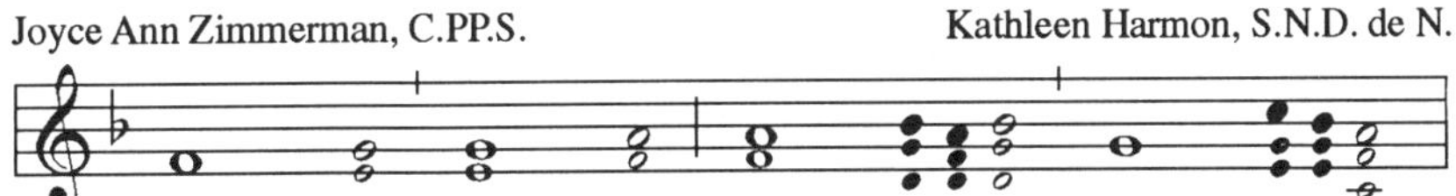

Blessed be the Lord God of **Israel**,
who visited and redeemed the **people**,
who raised up for us a **mighty** savior
from the house of **ser**vant David.

Just as the Lord spoke through the mouths of the holy prophets of **old**—
salvation comes out of the hands of our enemies and those who **hate** us,
that, with our ancestors, we might perform **works** of mercy,
remembering the holy covenant **sworn** to Abraham—

so does the Lord deliver us from the hands **of** our enemies,
that we might serve without fear before **the** Lord,
worshiping in **ho**liness
and in righteousness **all** our days.

And you also, child, will be called a prophet of God Most **High**:
for you will go before the Lord to prepare a **way**,
bringing people knowledge of salvation by for**giveness** of sins;
because of the deep and tender mercy **of** our God.

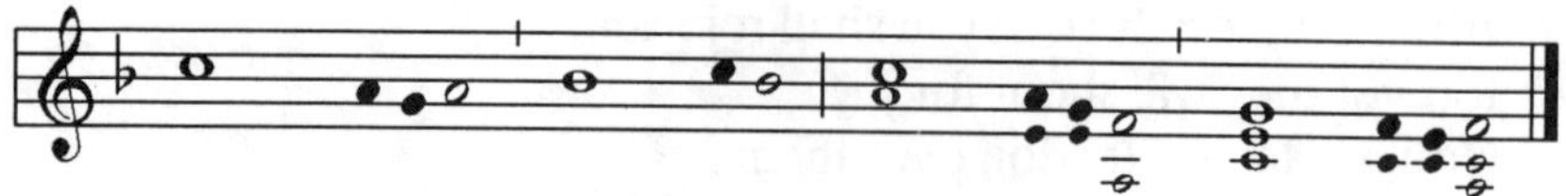

Whereby a light rising from on high will **vis**it us
to appear to those in darkness and in a shadow **of** death,
to guide our feet along a **straight**, sure path
into a **way** of peace.

INTERCESSIONS

Invocations

Cantor, then Assembly:

O Jesus Christ, **risen** presence a**mong** us ...
O Jesus Christ, **strength** of our new **day** ...
O Jesus Christ, **joy** of all who **trust** in you ...
O Jesus Christ, **hear** our prayer of **praise** ...
O Jesus Christ, **turn** our tears to **joy** ...
O Jesus Christ, **draw** us to your**self** ...
O Jesus Christ, **be** a refuge for those in **need** ...
O Jesus Christ, **lead** us along your straight **paths** ...
O Jesus Christ, **protect** us that we may exult in **you** ...
O Jesus Christ, **bless** the just ones with **love** ...
O Jesus Christ, **shield** your people from **harm** ...

Our Father ...

Prayer
Good and gracious God,
you have been present to us
in the loveliness of your dwelling place:
even as we long to dwell with you forever,
be with us now as we labor to bring your presence
to all those we meet in the ordinary circumstances of our lives.
We pray through Jesus Christ. **Amen.**

CONCLUSION

Blessing
May almighty God cover us with a shield of delight and bless us
in the name of the Father, and of the Son, and of the Holy Spirit. **Amen.**

Dismissal
Go forth and live your day uprightly in God. **Thanks be to God.**

MONDAY 1 Evening Prayer

EVENING HYMN

PSALMODY

Psalm 131 *Song of ascents (pilgrimages). Of David.*

Solo 1 O LORD, my heart has not boasted
and my eyes have not pretended.
Nor have I engaged in things too great
and too wondrous for me.

Solo 2 Have I not calmed
and quieted my soul?
Like a weaned child against a mother,
like a weaned child within me, so is my soul.

All Put your hope, O Israel, in the LORD,
from now and forever.

Psalm 92 *Psalm. Song for the day of the Sabbath.*

All It is good to give thanks to the LORD,
to sing to your name, O Most High;
to recount your steadfast love in the morning
and your faithfulness during the night,
with the lute, the lyre,
and the sound of the harp.

Solo 1 For you have given me joy, O LORD,
by your work;
about your handiwork, I will shout with joy.

All How great are your works, O LORD!
Your plans are very profound.
The foolish do not know them,
and the stupid do not understand.
In their blossoming, the wicked are like grass;
all makers of emptiness flourish
only to perish forever and ever.

Solo 2 But you, O LORD, are exalted forever.
Behold, your enemies, O LORD,
behold, your enemies will perish.
All makers of emptiness will be scattered.

Solo 1 But you have exalted my strength like that of the wild ox,
anointing me with fresh oil.
My eyes have beheld my enemies
and my ears have heard those who rise against me.

Solo 2 The righteous will flourish like a palm tree,
and rise like a cedar in Lebanon.
Planted in the house of the LORD,
in the courts of our God, they will flourish.
Even in old age they will give fruit—
they will be fresh and full of sap—
recounting that the LORD is upright.
God is my rock, in whom there is no iniquity.

Word of God

Magnificat

Joyce Ann Zimmerman, C.PP.S. Kathleen Harmon, S.N.D. de N.

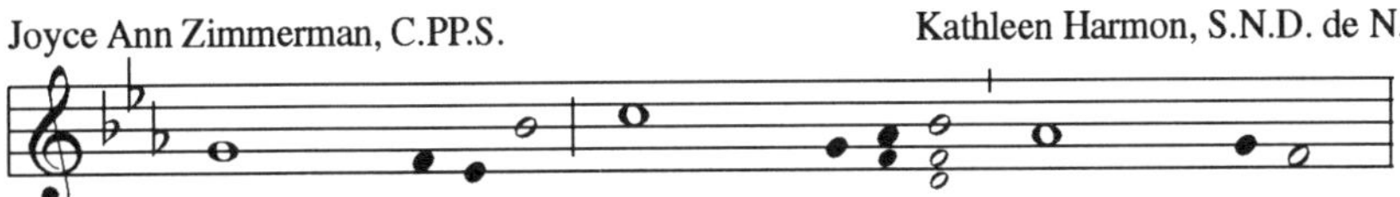

My soul does magni**fy** the Lord!
I delight in **God** my savior
who looked kindly **on** lowliness.

Now all ages will **call** me blessed
for the Mighty One **did** great things.
Holy is **God's** name;
mercy is from age to age for **those** in awe!

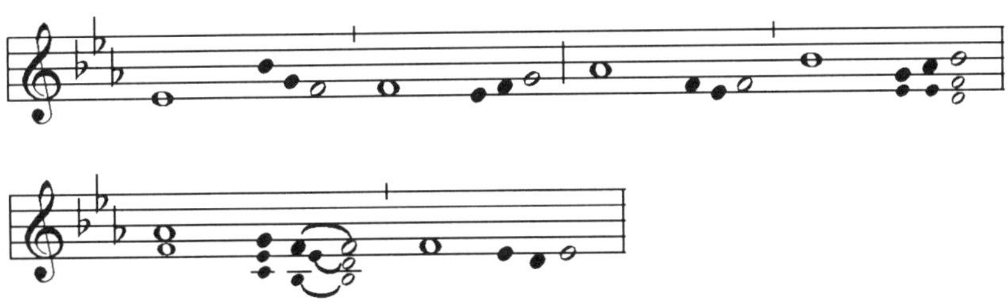

The Lord's strong arm did **migh**ty deeds:
confused the proud in **their** smug hearts;
toppled sovereigns **from** their thrones,
and exalted **hum**ble ones;
filled the hungering with **good** things,
and sent the rich **a**way empty.

The Lord helped servant **Is**rael
to re**mem**ber mercy,
as was spoken to Ab**ra**ham
and his descendants for**ev**ermore!

INTERCESSIONS

Petitions

Cantor, then Assembly:
KH
We lift our hearts to God.
Cantor:

For hu**mil**ity ...
For calm and **qui**et ...
For hope and conso**la**tion ...
For **thank**fulness ...
For **faith**fulness ...
For gladness in work well **done** ...
For growth in **jus**tice ...
For fruitfulness in old **age** ...
For up**right**ness ...
For those who have died this **day** ...

Our Father ...

Prayer
Gentle God,
your great works are the source of our strength:
be with us this night and refresh us
so we will be ready to live the Good News of your Son
when we rise to greet a new day,
living in your love forever and ever. **Amen.**

CONCLUSION

Blessing
May God keep us safe from all harm this night and bless us
in the name of the Father, and of the Son, and of the Holy Spirit. **Amen.**

Dismissal
Go in peace to rest in God. **Thanks be to God.**

TUESDAY 1 Morning Praise

MORNING HYMN

PSALMODY

Psalm 113

All Alleluia!

Choir 1 Give praise, servants of the LORD;
praise the name of the LORD.
Let the name of the LORD be blessed
from now on and forever.
From the rising of the sun to its setting,
let the name of the LORD be praised.
The LORD is exalted above all nations;
God's glory is greater than the heavens.

All Who is like the LORD our God,
enthroned above?

Choir 2 Who looks down to watch over
the skies and the earth?
Who raises the weak from dust
and the poor from ashes,
to return them to the company of nobles,
the nobles of the people?
Who brings home the sterile woman,
now a rejoicing mother of many children?

All Alleluia!

Psalm 3 *Psalm of David. In his flight from Absalom his son.*

Solo 1 O LORD, how many are my adversaries!
Many are rising against me;
many are saying to my soul:
"There is no salvation
for you in God."

Selah (pause).

Solo 2 But you, O LORD,
are a shield over me,
my glory and the one lifting my head.
With my voice to the LORD I will cry,
and God will answer me from the holy mountain.

Selah (pause).

Solo 1 I lie down and sleep;
I wake up
for the LORD sustains me.
I shall not fear the multitudes of people
positioning themselves
around and against me.

Solo 2 Arise, O LORD;
save me, my God,
for you strike all my enemies on the cheek
and you shatter the teeth of the wicked.

All From the LORD, salvation!
Upon your people, blessing!

Selah (pause).

Word of God

Benedictus

Blessed be the Lord God of **Israel**,
who visited and redeemed the **people**,
who raised up for us a **mighty** savior
from the house of **ser**vant David.

Just as the Lord spoke through the mouths of the holy prophets of **old**—
salvation comes out of the hands of our enemies and those who **hate** us,
that, with our ancestors, we might perform **works** of mercy,
remembering the holy covenant **sworn** to Abraham—

so does the Lord deliver us from the hands **of** our enemies,
that we might serve without fear before **the** Lord,
worshiping in **ho**liness
and in righteousness **all** our days.

And you also, child, will be called a prophet of God Most **High**:
for you will go before the Lord to prepare a **way**,
bringing people knowledge of salvation by for**giveness** of sins;
because of the deep and tender mercy **of** our God.

Whereby a light rising from on high will **vis**it us
to appear to those in darkness and in a shadow **of** death,
to guide our feet along a **straight**, sure path
into a **way** of peace.

INTERCESSIONS

Invocations

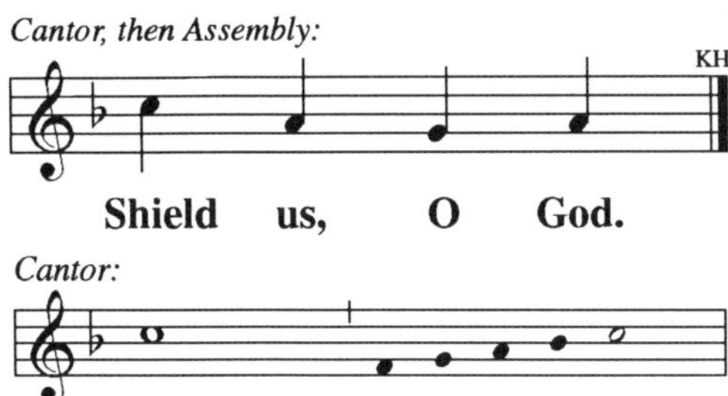
Cantor, then Assembly:
KH
Shield us, O God.
Cantor:

Risen Christ, **glo**ry of our God,
Risen Christ, **support** of all the nations,
Risen Christ, **joy** of all creation,
Risen Christ, **bless**ing for the faithful,
Risen Christ, **ans**wer for those in need,
Risen Christ, **com**fort for the fearful,
Risen Christ, **sa**vior here among us,

Our Father ...

Prayer
O God who guards and protects,
your name is worthy of all praise
and your glory lifts up the lowly:
be with us today as a shield that surrounds us,
and help us to trust

that you guide us in right ways
and protect us from all evil.
We pray through Jesus Christ. **Amen.**

CONCLUSION

Blessing
May almighty God protect us and bless us
in the name of the Father, and of the Son, and of the Holy Spirit. **Amen.**

Dismissal
Go forth to live your day with confidence in God. **Thanks be to God.**

TUESDAY 1 Evening Prayer

EVENING HYMN

PSALMODY

Psalm 39 *To the choirmaster. To Yedoutûn. Psalm of David.*

Solo 1 I said,

Solo 2 "I will watch my ways
so as not to sin with my tongue.
I will watch over my mouth with a bridle
so long as the wicked are in my presence."

Solo 1 I was dumb and silent,
deprived of happiness.
My pain kept growing;
my heart was boiling within me.
In my eagerness, a fire was burning.
I spoke with my tongue:

Solo 2 "Let me know, O LORD, my end.
What is the extension of my days?
Let me know how frail I am.
Behold, you have given me only handbreadths for my days,
and my lifetime is as nothing before you."

Selah (pause).

All Surely all human beings stand like a breath.
Human beings mill about like shadows,
vainly piling up riches
without knowing for whom.

Solo 2 "And now, O Lord, what do I hope for?
My hope is in you.
Deliver me from all my transgressions.
Do not make me the scorn of the fool.
I remained silent, I did not open my mouth,
but you have made me speak.
Do not strike me;
by the blow of your hand I am destroyed."

All When you rebuke human beings for sin,
you instruct them;
you dissolve like a moth what is precious to them.
Surely all human beings are like a breath.

Selah (pause).

Solo 2 "Listen to my prayer, O LORD,
and to my cry.
To my tears, be not insensitive.
For I am nothing but a guest with you,
a settler like all my ancestors.
Turn your eyes from me and let me be comforted,
before I depart and am no more."

Psalm 86 *A prayer of David.*

Solo 1 Turn your ear, O LORD,
and answer me,
for I am poor and needy.
Keep my soul
for I am faithful.
Save your servant who trusts in you;
you are my God.
Have pity on me, O Lord,
for I cry to you all day long.

Bring joy to the soul of your servant,
as I lift up my soul to you, O Lord.

All For you are good, O Lord, and forgiving,
abounding in steadfast love for all those who cry to you.

Solo 1 Give ear, O LORD, to my prayer;
be attentive to the voice of my supplications.
I cry to you in the day of my distress,
and you answer me.
There is no one like you, O Lord, among the gods,
and there is nothing like your achievements.
All the nations that you have made
will come and worship in your presence, O Lord,
and give glory to your name.

All For you are great and work wonders;
you alone are God.

Solo 1 Teach me, O LORD, your ways,
and I shall walk in your truth.
Gather together my heart for the reverence of your name;
I will thank you, O Lord my God, with all my heart.
Let me give glory to your name forever.
For your steadfast love for me is great:
you have delivered my soul from the depths of Sheol.
O God, the arrogant have risen up against me,
and a council of violent people have sought my life,
for they have not kept you in mind.

All But you, O Lord, are a merciful and gracious God,
slow to anger and rich in steadfast love and truth.

Solo 1 Turn to me and be gracious to me;
give your strength to your servant.
Bring salvation to the offspring of your servant.
Make me a sign of goodness,
that those who hate me shall see and be put to shame.
Because you are the LORD,
you help me and comfort me.

Word of God

Magnificat
My soul does magni**fy** the Lord!
I delight in **God** my savior
who looked kindly **on** lowliness.

Now all ages will **call** me blessed
for the Mighty One **did** great things.
Holy is **God's** name;
mercy is from age to age for **those** in awe!

The Lord's strong arm did **migh**ty deeds:
confused the proud in **their** smug hearts;
toppled sovereigns **from** their thrones,
and exalted **hum**ble ones;
filled the hungering with **good** things,
and sent the rich **a**way empty.

The Lord helped servant **Is**rael
to re**mem**ber mercy,
as was spoken to Ab**ra**ham
and his descendants for**e**vermore!

INTERCESSIONS

Petitions

Cantor, then Assembly:

Cantor:

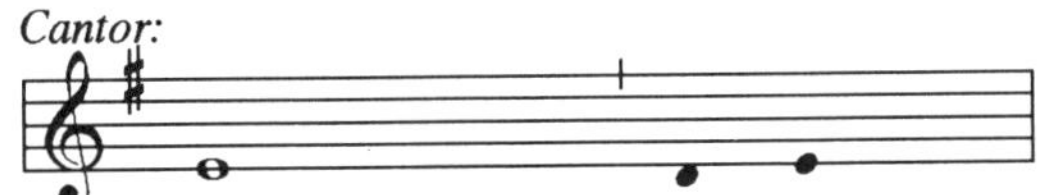

For those who speak idly ... **we** plead,
For those who are frail and in shadow ... **we** plead,
For those who are scorned ... **we** plead,
For those who are in turmoil ... **we** plead,
For those who despair ... **we** plead,
For those who are poor and needy ... **we** plead,
For those who are sad and downtrodden ... **we** plead,
For those with divided heart ... **we** plead,
For those who have died this day ... **we** plead,

Our Father ...

Prayer
Loving God,
your faithful presence has guarded us this day:
we come before you this evening
with hearts filled with confidence in you.
Increase our trust
that we may rest peacefully in you forever and ever. **Amen.**

CONCLUSION

Blessing
May our loving God guard us this night and bless us
in the name of the Father, and of the Son, and of the Holy Spirit. **Amen.**

Dismissal
Go to rest, confident in the steadfast presence of God. **Thanks be to God.**

WEDNESDAY 1 Morning Praise

MORNING HYMN

PSALMODY

Psalm 8 *To the choirmaster. On the gittith. Of David.*

All O LORD our Lord,
how magnificent is your name
over all the earth!

Choir 1 You set your glory above the skies.
From the mouths of babes and infants,
you have established strength against your adversaries
to still the enemy and avenger.

Solo 1 If I look at your skies,
the work of your fingers,
the moon and stars that you have set in place,

What are mortals that you remember them?
And human beings that you care for them?

Choir 2 But you have made them slightly less than a god,
and with glory and radiance you crown them.
You made them rule over the work of your hands.
You have placed everything under their feet—
sheep and cattle, all together,
and even the beasts from the fields,
the birds of heaven
and the fish from the sea,
all that crosses along the paths of the seas.

All O LORD our Lord,
how magnificent is your name
over all the earth!

Psalm 90 *Prayer. Of Moses, the man of God.*

Choir 1 O Lord, you have been a refuge for us
from generation to generation.
Before the mountains were born
and before you formed the earth and the universe,
you are God from eternity to eternity.

Choir 2 You return mortals to dust,
and then you say, "Come back, O humans."
For a thousand years in your eyes
are like the day of yesterday that has gone by,
or like a vigil in the night.
You sweep mortals away in their sleep,
but in the morning they will be
like the grass that flourishes.
In the morning grass is bright and flourishes
but at night it fades and dries out.

Choir 1 For we have been consumed by your anger
and we have been terrified by your zeal.
You have set our iniquities before you,
our hidden sins in the light of your face.
All our days pass away in your anger,
our years end up like a sigh.
The days of our lives are seventy years,

perhaps eighty if we are very strong.
Still most of them are toil and emptiness,
for our lives soon pass away—
quickly we vanish!

Choir 2 Who knows the power of your anger,
and that your wrath equals the reverence due you?
So teach us to count our days
and let wisdom come to our hearts.

Choir 1 Turn back, O LORD! How long?
Bring comfort to your servants.
Fill us in the morning with your steadfast love,
that we may sing and rejoice all our days.
Gladden us as many days as you have humbled us,
those years we experienced evil.

Choir 2 Let your work be visible to your servants,
and your splendor to their offspring.
Let the favor of the Lord our God be over us,
and the work of our hands be a strength over us.

All O may the work of our hands be a strength over us!

Word of God

Benedictus
Blessed be the Lord God of **Israel**,
who visited and redeemed the **people**,
who raised up for us a **mighty** savior
from the house of **ser**vant David.

Just as the Lord spoke through the mouths of the holy prophets of **old**—
salvation comes out of the hands of our enemies and those who **hate** us,
that, with our ancestors, we might perform **works** of mercy,
remembering the holy covenant **sworn** to Abraham—

so does the Lord deliver us from the hands **of** our enemies,
that we might serve without fear before **the** Lord,
worshiping in **ho**liness
and in righteousness **all** our days.

And you also, child, will be called a prophet of God Most **High**:
for you will go before the Lord to prepare a **way**,
bringing people knowledge of salvation by for**giveness** of sins;
because of the deep and tender mercy **of** our God.

Whereby a light rising from on high will **visit** us
to appear to those in darkness and in a shadow **of** death,
to guide our feet along a **straight**, sure path
into a **way** of peace.

INTERCESSIONS

Invocations

Cantor, then Assembly:
KH
Your fav - or rests ov - er us.
Cantor:

Saving Christ, your **glory** shines over **all** creation ...
Saving Christ, your care **crowns us** with glory ...
Saving Christ, your **majesty** invests **us** with honor ...
Saving Christ, your **works** re**flect** your splendor ...
Saving Christ, you **formed** us to find **refuge** in you ...
Saving Christ, you **teach** us to **count** our days ...
Saving Christ, you **offer us** wise hearts ...
Saving Christ, you bring **comfort to** your servants ...
Saving Christ, you **satisfy** us with your **stead**fast love ...
Saving Christ, you **bless us** with strength ...

Our Father ...

Prayer
God of the universe,
you speak to us in all of creation
and call to us most surely in the depths of our hearts:
help us to recognize your righteous wrath
and to gain your favor by listening to you today
in our work, in our leisure, and in one another.
We pray through Jesus Christ. **Amen.**

CONCLUSION

Blessing
May the creator God
who formed our humanity in the divine image bless us
in the name of the Father, and of the Son, and of the Holy Spirit. **Amen.**

Dismissal
Go forth to live this day, mindful that we are images of God. **Thanks be to God.**

WEDNESDAY 1 Evening Prayer

EVENING HYMN

PSALMODY

Psalm 36 *To the choirmaster. In honor of David, the servant of the Lord.*

Solo 1 The deceitful words of the wicked
enter my heart.
No fear of God
confronts their eyes;
in their own eyes they are flattered
when they admit their guilt and hate.
The words of their mouths speak emptiness and deceit;
they have ceased to discern how to do good.
Even when resting they contemplate emptiness;
they stand on a way that is not good
and do not despise evil.

All O LORD, in heaven is your steadfast love;
your truth rises to the firmament.

Choir 1 Your justice is like the highest mountains,
your judgment is like a great abyss.
Humankind and beast, you save, O LORD.

All How precious is your steadfast love, O God!

Choir 2 Humankind takes refuge
in the shade of your wings.
They are gratified with oil in your house,
and you inebriate them with the torrent of your delights.

All For with you is the source of life;
in your light, we see light.

Solo 1 Extend your steadfast love to those who know you,
and your justice to upright hearts.
Let not the foot of the arrogant touch me,
nor the hand of the wicked lead me astray.
The makers of emptiness fell,
they stumbled and could not rise.

Psalm 79 *Psalm of Asaf.*

Choir 1 O God, nations have invaded your heritage.
They have profaned your holy temple;
they have reduced Jerusalem to ruins.
They have given the corpses of your servants
as food for the birds of the skies;
the flesh of your faithful, to the beasts of the land.
They have poured out their blood like water
all around Jerusalem,
and there is no one to bury them.
We are the laughingstock of our neighbors,
the mockery and the scorn of those around us.

All Until when, O LORD?
Will you be angry forever?
Will your indignation burn like fire?

Choir 2 Pour out your anger onto the nations
who have not recognized you,
and against empires
who have not prayed in your name.
For they have eaten up Jacob,
they have destroyed your pasture.

Choir 1 Do not remember against us our sins of the past.
Quickly, let your mercy come to meet us,
for we have grown extremely weak.

Help us, O God of our salvation,
on account of the glory of your name.

Choir 2 Why would the nations say,
"Where is their God?"
Make clear among the nations and to us
the vindication of the blood of your servants that was shed.
Let the groaning of captives come before you;
by your strong arm,
preserve those doomed to death.
Let the disdain by which our neighbors
have scorned you, O Lord,
turn against them deep in their hearts,
seven times over.

All But we are your people,
your flock, and your pasture.
We will give thanks to you forever;
from age to age,
we will tell your praise.

Word of God

Magnificat
My soul does magni**fy** the Lord!
I delight in **God** my savior
who looked kindly **on** lowliness.

Now all ages will **call** me blessed
for the Mighty One **did** great things.
Holy is **God's** name;
mercy is from age to age for **those** in awe!

The Lord's strong arm did **might**y deeds:
confused the proud in **their** smug hearts;
toppled sovereigns **from** their thrones,
and exalted **hum**ble ones;
filled the hungering with **good** things,
and sent the rich **a**way empty.

The Lord helped servant **Is**rael
to re**mem**ber mercy,

as was spoken to Ab**ra**ham
and his descendants for**e**vermore!

INTERCESSIONS

Petitions

Cantor, then Assembly:

That we may acknowledge our emptiness and deceit ... **we** pray,
That we may overcome fear ... **we** pray,
That we may know God's steadfast love ... **we** pray,
That we may find refuge from harm ... **we** pray,
That we may be met with mercy ... **we** pray,
That we may be preserved from evil ... **we** pray,
That we may give thanks always and everywhere ... **we** pray,
That those who have died today may live forever ... **we** pray,

Our Father ...

Prayer
O God,
your steadfast love and fidelity
have guided us through this day
and strengthened us to overcome weakness:
may we rest in the peace of your perfect creation
now and always. **Amen.**

CONCLUSION

Blessing
May God protect us from all evil and bless us
in the name of the Father, and of the Son, and of the Holy Spirit. **Amen.**

Dismissal
Go to rest in peace. **Thanks be to God.**

THURSDAY 1 Morning Praise

MORNING HYMN

PSALMODY

Psalm 63 *Psalm of David. While he was in the desert of Judah.*

Solo 1 O God, you are my God, I seek you;
my soul thirsts for you.
My flesh longs for you
in a dry and wasted land,
deprived of water.

Solo 2 So in the sanctuary I have contemplated you
to see your might and your glory.
Because your steadfast love is better than life,
my lips will praise you.
So I will bless you all my life;
in your name I will raise my hands.
As with milk and rich food,
my soul is filled;
my mouth gives praise with joyful lips.
I remember you upon my bed,
pondering you throughout the night.
For you were a help for me;
in the shade of your wings I keep singing.
My soul clings to you;
your right hand upholds me.

Solo 1 But let those who seek my destruction
be cast into the depths of the earth.
Let them be given over to the power of the sword;
let them become a prey for jackals.

All Then the king shall rejoice in God.
All those who swear by God will be praised,
for the mouths of liars will be shut.

Psalm 126 *Song of ascents (pilgrimages).*

Choir 1 When the LORD accompanied
those who returned to Zion,
we were like dreamers.
Then our mouth
was filled with laughter
and our tongue with joy.
Then it was said among nations:
"The LORD has done great
deeds among these people."

All The LORD has done great
deeds among us.
Now we rejoice.

Choir 2 Return our captives, O LORD,
like torrents in the Negeb.
Those who sow in tears
harvest with shouts of joy.
Indeed, the one who goes out weeping,
carrying the bag of seed,
comes back joyful,
carrying the sheaves.

Word of God

Benedictus
Blessed be the Lord God of **Israel**,
who visited and redeemed the **people**,
who raised up for us a **mighty** savior
from the house of **ser**vant David.

Just as the Lord spoke through the mouths of the holy prophets of **old**—
salvation comes out of the hands of our enemies and those who **hate** us,
that, with our ancestors, we might perform **works** of mercy,
remembering the holy covenant **sworn** to Abraham—

so does the Lord deliver us from the hands **of** our enemies,
that we might serve without fear before **the** Lord,
worshiping in **ho**liness
and in righteousness **all** our days.

And you also, child, will be called a prophet of God Most **High**:
for you will go before the Lord to prepare a **way**,
bringing people knowledge of salvation by for**giveness** of sins;
because of the deep and tender mercy **of** our God.

Whereby a light rising from on high will **vis**it us
to appear to those in darkness and in a shadow **of** death,
to guide our feet along a **straight**, sure path
into a **way** of peace.

INTERCESSIONS

Invocations

Cantor, then Assembly:
KH
We thirst for you, O God.

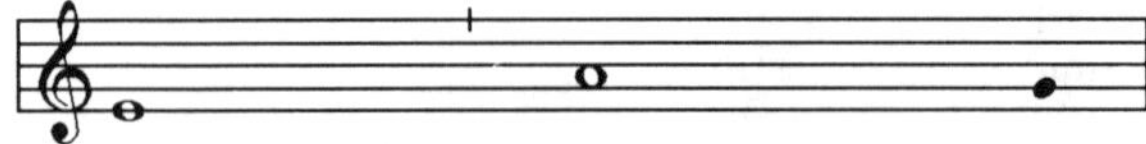
Cantor:

O loving Savior, **unleash** your might and your **glory**,
O loving Savior, **satisfy** us with a rich **feast**,
O loving Savior, **keep** us in the shade of your **wings**,
O loving Savior, **uphold** us by your right **hand**,
O loving Savior, **refresh** us with enlivening **dreams**,
O loving Savior, **fill** us with **laughter**,
O loving Savior, **harvest** in us your **joy**,
O loving Savior, **be** our Bread of **Life**,
O loving Savior, **be** our Cup of Salva**tion**,

Our Father ...

Prayer
O God of our salvation,
you brought forth your holy people
to settle in a land flowing with milk and honey:
be with us this day
as we labor to make your abundant blessings known.
We pray through Jesus Christ. **Amen.**

CONCLUSION

Blessing
May the God of freedom loosen all weariness from us and bless us
in the name of the Father, and of the Son, and of the Holy Spirit. **Amen.**

Dismissal
Go forth to sow the seeds of God's presence. **Thanks be to God.**

THURSDAY 1 Evening PRAYER

EVENING HYMN

PSALMODY

Psalm 85 *To the choirmaster. By the Qorahites. Psalm.*

Choir 1 You have cherished your land, O Lord;
you have returned the captives of Jacob.
You have taken away the guilt of your people,
forgiving all their sins.

Selah (pause).

Choir 2 You have taken away all your wrath;
you have turned away from the heat of your anger.

All Bring us back, O God of our salvation,
and put away your displeasure with us.

Choir 1 Will you be angry with us forever?
Will you maintain your anger
from generation to generation?
Will you not return and revive us
so that your people rejoice in you?

All Make us see, O Lord, your steadfast love
and give us your salvation.

Solo 1 Let me hear what God will say.
The Lord speaks words of peace

to the people and to the faithful.
But let them not turn back to folly.

Choir 2 Surely salvation is near
for those who revere God,
that glory may dwell in our land.
Steadfast love and truth have met;
justice and peace have kissed each other.
Truth will spring up from the ground,
and justice will look down from heaven.

All The LORD will also give prosperity,
and the land will yield its fruit.
Justice will go forth
to set the way for God's steps.

Psalm 75 *To the choirmaster. "Do not destroy." Psalm of Asaf. Song.*

All We give thanks to you, O God,
we give thanks,
for your wonders proclaim
the nearness of your name.

Solo 1 "Yes, at the appointed time
I will judge in equity.
The earth and all its inhabitants may vacillate,
but I hold firm its pillars.

Selah (pause).

I said to the arrogant, 'Be not arrogant,'
and to the wicked, 'Do not raise your pride.
Do not raise your might on high;
do not speak with pride and haughtiness.'"

All For judgment comes neither from the east nor the west,
neither from the wilderness nor the mountains.
But it is God who judges:
one to cast down, another to raise up.
A cup is in the hand of the LORD,
full of mixed and fermented wine.
God pours it out.

The wicked will drink it even to the dregs;
all the wicked of the earth will drink.

Solo 2 But I will rejoice forever,
I will play music to the God of Jacob.
I will shatter all the pride of the wicked,
but the dignity of the righteous will be extolled.

Word of God

Magnificat
My soul does magni**fy** the Lord!
I delight in **God** my savior
who looked kindly **on** lowliness.

Now all ages will **call** me blessed
for the Mighty One **did** great things.
Holy is **God's** name;
mercy is from age to age for **those** in awe!

The Lord's strong arm did **might**y deeds:
confused the proud in **their** smug hearts;
toppled sovereigns **from** their thrones,
and exalted **hum**ble ones;
filled the hungering with **good** things,
and sent the rich **a**way empty.

The Lord helped servant **Is**rael
to re**mem**ber mercy,
as was spoken to Ab**ra**ham
and his descendants for**e**vermore!

INTERCESSIONS

Petitions

Cantor, then Assembly:
KH
We long for sal - va - tion.
Cantor:

That the land may produce abundant food for all **the** world ...
That all may hear **God** speak ...
That peace **may** prosper ...
That glory may dwell in **our** land ...
That justice **may** reign ...
That all people may proclaim God's won**drous** deeds ...
That God's judgments be **re**membered ...
That all may drink of our Sav**ior's** cup ...
That all who have died this day may be **ex**tolled ...

Our Father ...

Prayer
O good and bounteous God,
you have favored us with forgiveness and mercy:
restore us to the graciousness of your presence now and always. **Amen.**

CONCLUSION

Blessing
May our bounteous God
anoint us with the fullness of grace and bless us
in the name of the Father, and of the Son, and of the Holy Spirit. **Amen.**

Dismissal
Go and be refreshed during the night. **Thanks be to God.**

FRIDAY 1 Morning Praise

MORNING HYMN

PSALMODY

Psalm 51 *To the choirmaster. Psalm of David. In the coming to him of Nathan the prophet, after David had been with Bathsheba.*

ANTIPHON

Be gracious to **me**, O God,
in your **stead**fast love.
According to the abundance **of** your mercy
blot out my **trans**gressions. ANTIPHON

Cleanse me completely **from** my guilt
and purify me **from** my sin.
For my transgressions I do **rec**ognize,
and my sin stands always **be**fore me.

Against you alone **have** I sinned,
and what is evil in your eyes **I** have done.
Thus you may be declared just in your ways,
  and pure **in** your judgments.
Indeed, I was born guilty,
  already a sinner when my mother **con**ceived me. ANTIPHON

Surely in truth **you** delight,
and deep within my self you will **teach** me wisdom.
Cleanse me from my sin with hyssop and I **will** be pure,
wash me and I shall be brighter **than** snow.

Let me hear glad**ness** and joy,
let the bones you **broke** exult.
Turn your face **from** my sins
and blot out all my iniq**ui**ties. ANTIPHON

Create in me a pure **heart**, O God,
and renew within me **a** firm spirit.
Do not dismiss me **from** your presence,
and do not take away from me your ho**ly** spirit.

Give me back the joy of **your** salvation,
and let a willing spirit lie **o**ver me.
I will teach transgres**sors** your ways,
and sinners will turn back **to** you. ANTIPHON

Deliver me from bloodshed, O God,
  God of **my** salvation,
and my tongue will **sing** your justice.

O Lord, **open** my lips,
and my mouth will tell **your** praise.

For you take no pleasure in **sac**rifice,
and you would not accept an offering were **I** to give it.
The perfect sacrifice for God is a **brok**en spirit.
A broken and humble heart,
  O God, you will not **de**spise. ANTIPHON

In your kindness bring prosperi**ty** to Zion;
rebuild the walls of Je**ru**salem.
Then you can delight in sacrifices of justice,
  burnt and complete **of**ferings;
then bulls can be offered on **your** altars. ANTIPHON

Psalm Prayer
Merciful God,
your steadfast love sustains us even in our transgressions:
wash us brighter than snow
and restore us to your favor now and forever. **Amen.**

Word of God

Benedictus
Blessed be the Lord God of **Israel**,
who visited and redeemed the **people**,
who raised up for us a **migh**ty savior
from the house of **ser**vant David.

Just as the Lord spoke through the mouths of the holy prophets of **old**—
salvation comes out of the hands of our enemies and those who **hate** us,
that, with our ancestors, we might perform **works** of mercy,
remembering the holy covenant **sworn** to Abraham—

so does the Lord deliver us from the hands **of** our enemies,
that we might serve without fear before **the** Lord,
worshiping in **ho**liness
and in righteousness **all** our days.

And you also, child, will be called a prophet of God Most **High**:
for you will go before the Lord to prepare a **way**,
bringing people knowledge of salvation by for**giveness** of sins;
because of the deep and tender mercy **of** our God.

Whereby a light rising from on high will **vis**it us
to appear to those in darkness and in a shadow **of** death,
to guide our feet along a **straight**, sure path
into a **way** of peace.

INTERCESSIONS

Invocations

Cantor, then Assembly in canon:

1.
2.
KH
Hear our prayer, O God.
one or two voices
Hear, O God.

Cantor:

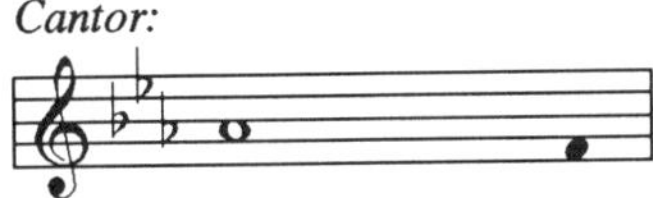

Jesus our Savior, **source** of mercy ...
Jesus our Savior, **source** of forgiveness ...
Jesus our Savior, **source** of compassion ...
Jesus our Savior, **source** of healing ...
Jesus our Savior, **source** of strength ...
Jesus our Savior, **source** of courage ...
Jesus our Savior, **source** of light ...
Jesus our Savior, **source** of life ...
Jesus our Savior, **source** of unity ...
Jesus our Savior, **source** of peace ...

Our Father ...

Prayer
Loving-kind God,
you show us mercy and compassion, truth and wisdom:
teach us always to do your holy will.
May our Friday penance restore to us a clean heart
that we may only hunger for you.
We pray through Jesus Christ our Savior. **Amen.**

CONCLUSION

Blessing
May God, the source of all mercy, bless us now and always
in the name of the Father, and of the Son, and of the Holy Spirit. **Amen.**

Dismissal
Go forth, and remain steadfast in our merciful God. **Thanks be to God.**

FRIDAY 1 Evening Prayer

EVENING HYMN

PSALMODY

Psalm 130 *Song of ascents (pilgrimages).*

ANTIPHON

Out of the depths, I cry to **you**, O LORD.
Lord, listen to **my** voice;
let your ears **be** attentive
to the voice of my supp**li**cations. ANTIPHON

If you, O LORD, were to keep in**iquities** in mind,
Lord, who **could** stand?
But with you **is** forgiveness,
and for that you are **re**vered. ANTIPHON

I wait for the LORD;
  my soul waits, and for God's **word** I hope.
My soul waits for **the** Lord
more than watchers **of** the morning
watch for **the** dawn. ANTIPHON

Let Israel hope **in** the LORD,
for steadfast love is found with the LORD
  and abundance of **re**demption.
It is the LORD who shall redeem **Is**rael
from all iniq**ui**ties. ANTIPHON

Psalm Prayer
Attentive God,
you hear our voice with unfailing kindness:
forgive us our wanderings from the path
of your redeeming love now and always. **Amen.**

Psalm 138 *Of David.*

ANTIPHON

KH
I give you thanks, O God; with my
whole heart I sing your praise.

I give you thanks with **all** my heart;
instead of other gods, I **sing** to you.
I bow down toward the **ho**ly sanctuary,
and I give thanks to your name
  on account of your steadfast love **and** your truth.

For you have ex**alted** your promise
even a**bove** your name.
On the day I cried, you **an**swered me;
you renewed cour**age** within me. ANTIPHON

Let all the rulers of the earth give thanks to you, O LORD,
  for they have heard the **words of** your mouth.
Let them sing about the ways of the LORD,
  for great is the **glory of** the LORD.
Although exalted,
  the LORD looks up**on** the lowly,
but recognizes the proud only **from** a distance. ANTIPHON

When I walk in the midst of distress,
you revive me against the **anger of** my enemies.
You stretch out your hand,
and your **right** hand saves me;
the LORD will do every**thing** for me.
O LORD, your steadfast love is forever.
Do not forsake the work **of** your hands. ANTIPHON

Psalm Prayer
Exalted God,
your name is above all others:
hear the thanksgiving prayer of your humble people
and increase our strength of soul
that we may preserve our life forever and ever. **Amen.**

Word of God

Magnificat
My soul does magni**fy** the Lord!
I delight in **God** my savior
who looked kindly **on** lowliness.

Now all ages will **call** me blessed
for the Mighty One **did** great things.
Holy is **God's** name;
mercy is from age to age for **those** in awe!

The Lord's strong arm did **might**y deeds:
confused the proud in **their** smug hearts;
toppled sovereigns **from** their thrones,
and exalted **hum**ble ones;
filled the hungering with **good** things,
and sent the rich **a**way empty.

The Lord helped servant **I**srael
to re**mem**ber mercy,
as was spoken to Ab**ra**ham
and his descendants for**e**vermore!

INTERCESSIONS

Petitions

Cantor, then Assembly in canon:

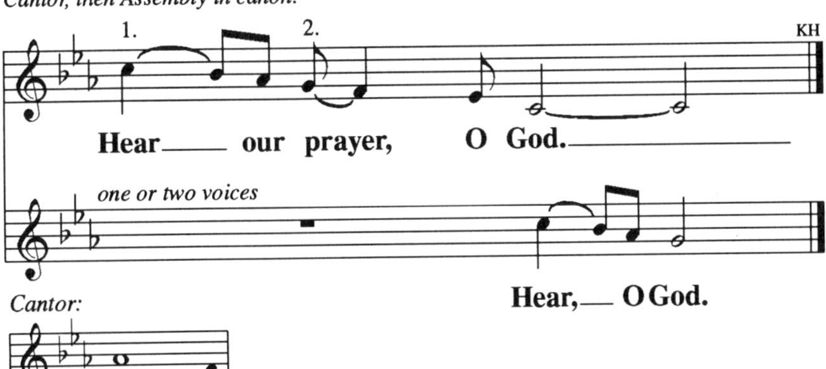
1.
2.
KH
Hear our prayer, O God.
one or two voices
Hear, O God.

Cantor:

For **help** ...
For for**give**ness ...
For **pa**tience ...
For **hope** ...
For re**demp**tion ...
For **mer**cy ...
For **strength** ...
For **cour**age ...
For de**liv**erance ...
For sal**va**tion ...
For **thank**fulness ...
For the faithful de**part**ed ...

Our Father ...

Prayer
Merciful God,
you are full of steadfast love
and ever faithful to your word of truth:
preserve us against all dangers
as we seek rest in you forever and ever. **Amen.**

CONCLUSION

Blessing
May the God of the Cross,
who conquered death and promised life,
grant us strength and conviction and bless us
in the name of the Father, and of the Son, and of the Holy Spirit. **Amen.**

Dismissal
Go to rest confidently in our saving God. **Thanks be to God.**

SATURDAY 1 Morning Praise

MORNING HYMN

PSALMODY

Psalm 65 *To the choirmaster. Psalm of David. Psalm.*

ANTIPHON

KH
You ans- wer us, O God, with awe- some deeds.

To you praise is due,
  O God **in** Zion,
and for you promises will be **ful**filled.
O you who listen to prayer,
  to you all flesh **shall** come.
When our transgressions—our deeds of iniquity—overcome us,
  you **for**give them. ANTIPHON

Blessed is the one you elect and **bring** near;
that one shall dwell in **your** courts.
Let us be filled with the goodness of **your** house,
the holiness of **your** temple.

With awesome deeds you answer us **in** justice,
O God of our **sal**vation,
protector of all the ends of **the** earth
and of the dis**tant** seas. ANTIPHON

Girded with might,
  you establish mountains **in** strength.
You still the roaring of the seas—
  the roaring of their waves—
  and the clamor **of** nations.
Because of **your** signs,
the inhabitants of the ends of the earth will stand **in** awe. ANTIPHON

You cause the breaking of morning and of evening
  to burst **with** joy.
You visit the earth and give it water;
  abundantly, you **en**rich it:
the river of God
  is replete **with** water.
You provide people with grain,
  for you designed **it** so.

Its furrows you water **a**bundantly,
and you make **them** smooth.
You soften it **with** showers,
and you bless **its** sprout. ANTIPHON

You crown the year with your bounty,
  and fertility springs in the wake of **your** chariot.
The pastures of the wilderness drip with water,
  and the hills are girded **with** joy.
Meadows are clothed with flocks,
  and valleys are covered **with** grain.
They shout, even more, **they** sing. ANTIPHON

Psalm Prayer
O God of creation and salvation,
you provide us with all good things
and sustain us by your care:
receive our morning prayer
for all praise is your due forever and ever. **Amen.**

Psalm 96

ANTIPHON
KH
Sing a new song, all the earth;
sing a new song all the earth.

Sing to the LORD a **new** song.
Sing to the LORD, all **the** earth.
Sing to **the** LORD,
bless **God's** name. ANTIPHON

From day to day proclaim the good news of sal**vation.**
Recount among the nations God's glory,
  God's marvels among **all** peoples.
For great is the LORD, highly to **be** praised
and revered above **all** gods.

For all the gods of the nations are as **nothing**,
but the LORD made **the** heavens.
Honor and splendor stand be**fore** God,
might and glory fill **the** temple. ANTIPHON

Give to the LORD, O families of **peoples.**
Give to the LORD glory **and** might.
Give to **the** LORD
the glory of **God's** name. ANTIPHON

Bring an offering and come into the **courts.**
Worship the LORD with ho**ly** splendor.
Dance in the sac**red** presence,
all **the** earth.

Say among the nations: "The LORD **reigns.**"
Surely God formed the universe
  so that it would **not** falter.
God **will** judge
the peoples **in** equity. ANTIPHON

Let the heavens re**joice**
and the earth **exult.**
Let the sea and its full**ness** roar.
Let the fields and all within them **be** glad. ANTIPHON

Then all the trees of the forest will shout with **joy**
in the presence of the LORD **who** comes.
For God comes to judge the earth,
  to judge the universe **with** justice
and with fidelity, **the** peoples. ANTIPHON

Psalm Prayer
O glorious and ever living God,
you are worthy of all praise:
we exalt you for your wondrous deeds.
Draw us into your presence
so that we may offer you
a fitting sacrifice of praise now and always. **Amen.**

Word of God

Benedictus
Blessed be the Lord God of **Israel**,
who visited and redeemed the **people**,
who raised up for us a **mighty** savior
from the house of **ser**vant David.

Just as the Lord spoke through the mouths of the holy prophets of **old**—
salvation comes out of the hands of our enemies and those who **hate** us,
that, with our ancestors, we might perform **works** of mercy,
remembering the holy covenant **sworn** to Abraham—

so does the Lord deliver us from the hands **of** our enemies,
that we might serve without fear before **the** Lord,
worshiping in **ho**liness
and in righteousness **all** our days.

And you also, child, will be called a prophet of God Most **High**:
for you will go before the Lord to prepare a **way**,
bringing people knowledge of salvation by for**giveness** of sins;
because of the deep and tender mercy **of** our God.

Whereby a light rising from on high will **visit** us
to appear to those in darkness and in a shadow **of** death,
to guide our feet along a **straight**, sure path
into a **way** of peace.

INTERCESSIONS

Invocations

Cantor, then Assembly:

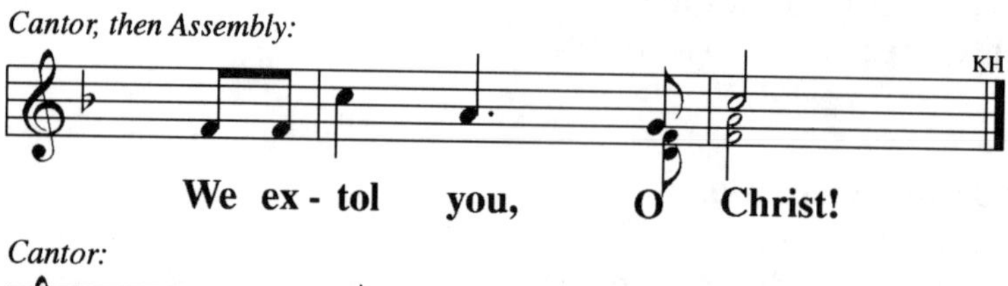

O living **Sav**ior, you **con**quer death,
O living **Sav**ior, you restore **us** to life,
O living **Sav**ior, you receive our **pro**mises,
O living **Sav**ior, you forgive **our** transgressions,
O living **Sav**ior, you favor us **with** prosperity,
O living **Sav**ior, you fill **us** with awe,
O living **Sav**ior, you call us **to** your presence,
O living **Sav**ior, you judge **us** with equity,
O living **Sav**ior, you bless us **with** your coming,

Our Father ...

Prayer
O redeeming God,
you shine the light of the risen Son upon us:
may that brightness guide us on our way today
as we look to the resurrection of your Son, Jesus Christ. **Amen.**

CONCLUSION

Blessing
Bow your heads and pray that almighty God bless us.
O God most holy: make your face shine on us today. **Amen.**
O Son most compassionate: look upon us with mercy. **Amen.**
O Spirit most loving: give us peace. **Amen.**
And may God bless us
in the name of the Father, and of the Son, and of the Holy Spirit. **Amen.**

Sign of Peace/Dismissal
Let us look upon the radiant face of others and offer a sign of peace.

SATURDAY 1 Evening Prayer

LIGHT SERVICE

Proclamation of the Light

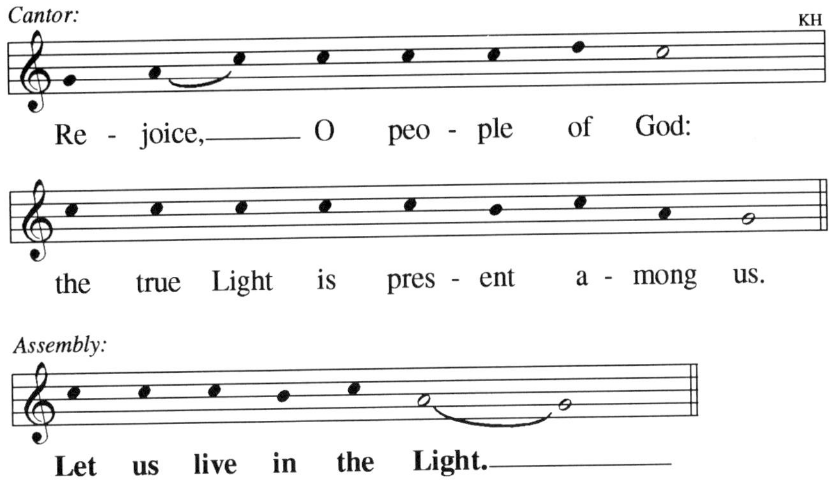
Cantor:
KH
Re - joice, O peo - ple of God:
the true Light is pres - ent a - mong us.
Assembly:
Let us live in the Light.

Evening Hymn

Thanksgiving for the Light

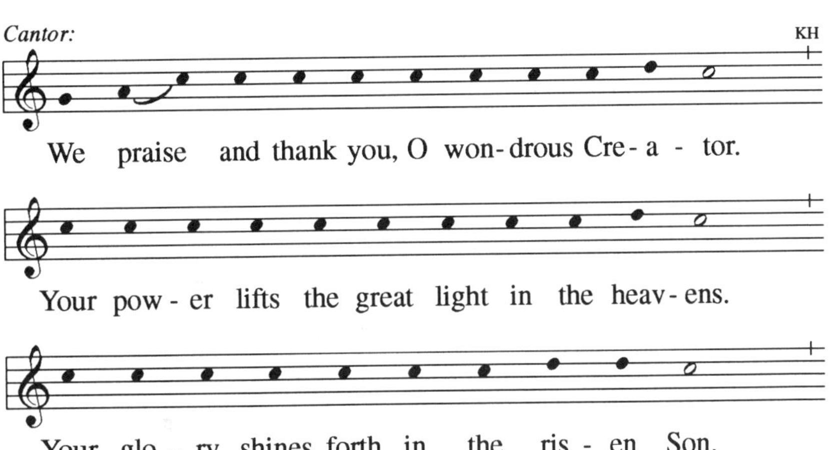
Cantor:
KH
We praise and thank you, O won- drous Cre - a - tor.
Your pow - er lifts the great light in the heav - ens.
Your glo - ry shines forth in the ris - en Son.

Your maj - es - ty lies o - ver all of cre - a - tion.
Your splen - dor clothes us with dig - ni - ty
and hon - or. Your good - ness o - ver-comes an - y
weak - ness. Your boun-ty sat - is - fies all hun - ger.
Your grace pro - claims our des - ti - ny.
Re - joice,___ O ho - ly peo - ple, in this great Light:
it is our sure sal - va - tion and glo - rious free - dom.
As our week - ly cel - e - bra - tion of res - ur - rec - tion draws near,
and dark - ness des - cends in qui - et rest, keep us
safe in this Light that nev - er fades. We praise and

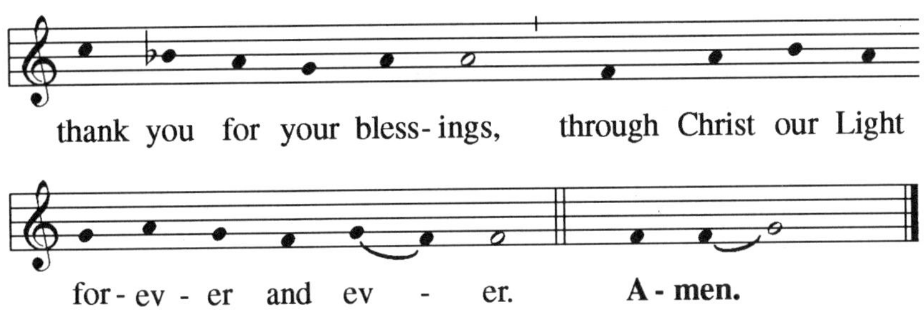
thank you for your bless- ings, through Christ our Light
for- ev - er and ev - er.
A - men.

PSALMODY

Psalm 141 *Psalm of David.*

ANTIPHON
KH
Let my prayer rise like in - cense.

O LORD, I cry **to** you:
"Hasten to me,
listen to my voice
when I cry **to** you."
Let my prayer rise
like incense in **your** presence,
the lifting up of my hands
like an evening **of**fering. ANTIPHON

Set, O LORD,
a guard over **my** mouth,
keep the door of **my** lips.
Do not incline my heart to any evil,
to performing wicked deeds
with those who work **ini**quity;
let me not partake **in** their feasting. ANTIPHON

When a just person strikes me, it is **a** favor;
and when I am corrected, it is like anoin**ting** oil.
May my head never **re**fuse it,
while my prayer stands firm against **ev**il doings.

Let wicked judges be smashed against **the** rock,
and they will understand that my words **were** measured.
Like plowed and broken furrows on **the** land,
their bones are shattered at the **mouth** of Sheol. ANTIPHON

But my eyes look to you,
  O LORD, **my** Lord.
In you I take refuge;
  do not pour out **my** life.
Keep me from the snare they have prepared for me
  and from the traps of those who cre**ate** emptiness.
Let the wicked fall into their nets
  while I a**lone** escape. ANTIPHON

Psalm Prayer
O merciful God,
you hear the voice of those who call to you:
as our evening prayer rises on incense,
so may our gaze turn toward you forever and ever. **Amen.**

Psalm 30 *Psalm of David. Song for the dedication of the temple.*

ANTIPHON

KH
I will ex- alt you, God: you have set me free.

I will ex**alt** you, O LORD,
for you have **set** me free
and have not allowed my enemies to re**joice** over me. ANTIPHON

O LORD my God,
  I have cried to you
  and **you** have healed me.
O LORD, you have brought my soul
  up from Sheol.
You have restored me to life,
  preventing me from going **down** the Pit. ANTIPHON

Sing to the LORD, O **faith**ful ones;
celebrate a memorial **to** God's holiness.
For we stand only an instant in God's anger,
  but a whole lifetime in **God's** delight.

In the evening come tears,
  but in the morning come **shouts** of joy.
So I said in my tranquility,
  "I will not **falter** forever."
O LORD, in your delight
  you have established might **as** my mountain.

When you hid your face,
  I was **ter**rified.
To you, O **LORD**, I cry
and to you, O Lord, I raise my **sup**plication.

What profit is there in my blood,
  in my going down **to** the Pit?
Does dust give you thanks,
  and **tell** your truth?
Listen, O LORD, and have mercy;
  O LORD, be a **help** to me. ANTIPHON

You have changed my **mourning** to dancing;
you have **loosened** my sackcloth
and girded **me** with joy.

So I **sing** your glory;
I **am** not silent.
O LORD my God,
  I will give thanks to **you** forever. ANTIPHON

Psalm Prayer
Glorious God of the day,
you overcome darkness and restore us to life:
draw us to your loving presence,
heal us of all alienation,
and hear our evening prayer of thanksgiving
for we extol and give thanks to you always and everywhere. **Amen.**

Word of God

Magnificat
My soul does magni**fy** the Lord!
I delight in **God** my savior
who looked kindly **on** lowliness.

Now all ages will **call** me blessed
for the Mighty One **did** great things.
Holy is **God's** name;
mercy is from age to age for **those** in awe!

The Lord's strong arm did **might**y deeds:
confused the proud in **their** smug hearts;
toppled sovereigns **from** their thrones,
and exalted **hum**ble ones;
filled the hungering with **good** things,
and sent the rich **a**way empty.

The Lord helped servant **Is**rael
to re**mem**ber mercy,
as was spoken to Ab**ra**ham
and his descendants for**e**vermore!

INTERCESSIONS

Petitions

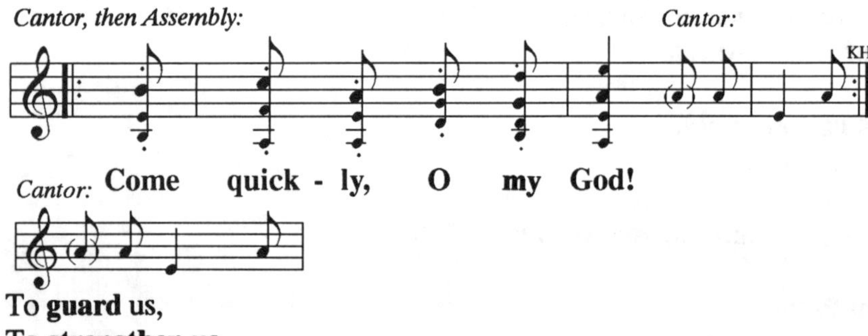
Cantor, then Assembly:
Cantor:
KH
Cantor:
Come quick - ly, O my God!

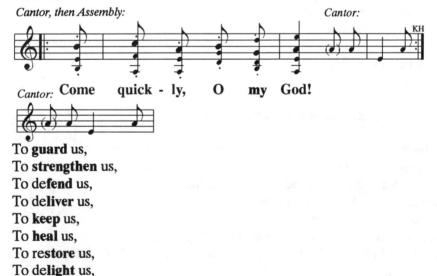

To **guard** us,
To **strengthen** us,
To de**fend** us,
To de**liver** us,
To **keep** us,
To **heal** us,
To re**store** us,
To de**light** us,
To en**rich** us,
To **bless** us,

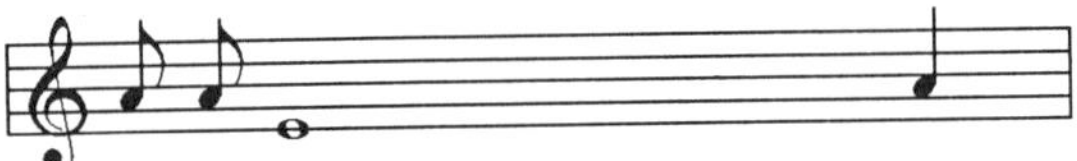

To **receive** those who have died this **day**,

Our Father ...

Prayer
Ever protector God and giver of life,
you sent your only Son
to gather your wandering children back
into your loving arms:
restore us to your holy courts
that we may praise you forever and ever. **Amen.**

CONCLUSION

Blessing
Bow your heads and pray that God bless us.
May God our creator nourish us as we await the fullness of resurrection. **Amen.**
May Jesus our brother lead us gently on the way. **Amen.**
May God the Spirit breathe within us while we wait with longing and patient endurance for the coming of our God. **Amen.**
And may God bless us
in the name of the Father, and of the Son, and of the Holy Spirit. **Amen.**

Sign of Peace/Dismissal
Let us offer one another a sign of the peace of Christ among us.

SUNDAY 1 Morning Praise

MORNING HYMN

PSALMODY

Psalm 95

ANTIPHON

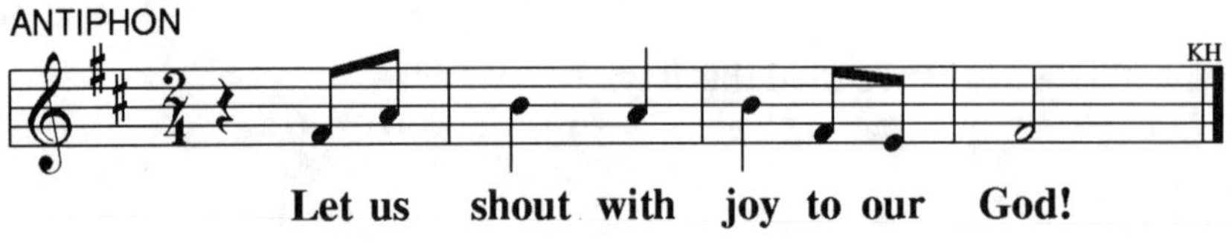

Come! Let us shout with joy **for** the LORD;
let us make noise for the rock of our **sal**vation.
Let us come into God's presence in **thanks**giving;
with songs, let us **cry** out. ANTIPHON

For the LORD is a great God
  and a great Sovereign a**bove** all gods,
in whose hands are hidden the secrets of the earth
  and the treasures of **the** mountains.
The sea belongs to God,
  the one **who** made it,
and whose hands, too, shaped the **dry** land. ANTIPHON

Come! Let us bow **and** kneel down,
let us kneel down in the presence of the LORD our maker,
  who is **our** God;
we are **the** people,
the pasture, and **the** flock. ANTIPHON

Today, may you listen to the **voice** of God:
"Harden not your hearts as **at** Meribah,
as on the day at Massah in the desert
  where your ancestors test**ed** me.
They tried me even though they had seen **my** works.

Forty years I was disgusted by that **gen**eration,
and I said: 'They are a people of twisted hearts,
  they did not recognize **my** ways.'
I swore indeed in **my** anger:
'They will not enter into my rest**ing**-place.'" ANTIPHON

Psalm Prayer
God of salvation,
you are our strength and sanctuary:
we bow down before your awe-inspiring majesty and creating power.
Draw your people to yourself
through your risen Son Jesus Christ. **Amen.**

Psalm 150

ANTIPHON

Praise God for **ho**liness;
praise God for the firmament **of** might.

Praise God for the mighty **deeds**;
praise God for unlimit**ed** greatness. ANTIPHON

Praise God with blast of **trumpet**;
praise God with lyre **and** harp.

Praise God with cymbal and **dance**;
praise God with strings **and** pipes. ANTIPHON

Praise God with resounding **drums**;
praise God with clamor**ous** drums.

Let all living **creatures**
praise **the** LORD. ANTIPHON

Psalm Prayer
O glorious God,
you are worthy of all praise:
may our whole being declare your marvels
and all creation sound a song of worship now and forever. **Amen.**

Word of God

Benedictus
Blessed be the Lord God of **Israel**,
who visited and redeemed the **people**,
who raised up for us a **mighty** savior
from the house of **ser**vant David.

Just as the Lord spoke through the mouths of the holy prophets of **old**—
salvation comes out of the hands of our enemies and those who **hate** us,
that, with our ancestors, we might perform **works** of mercy,
remembering the holy covenant **sworn** to Abraham—

so does the Lord deliver us from the hands **of** our enemies,
that we might serve without fear before **the** Lord,
worshiping in **ho**liness
and in righteousness **all** our days.

And you also, child, will be called a prophet of God Most **High**:
for you will go before the Lord to prepare a **way**,
bringing people knowledge of salvation by for**giveness** of sins;
because of the deep and tender mercy **of** our God.

Whereby a light rising from on high will **vis**it us
to appear to those in darkness and in a shadow **of** death,
to guide our feet along a **straight**, sure path
into a **way** of peace.

INTERCESSIONS

Invocations

Cantor, then Assembly:

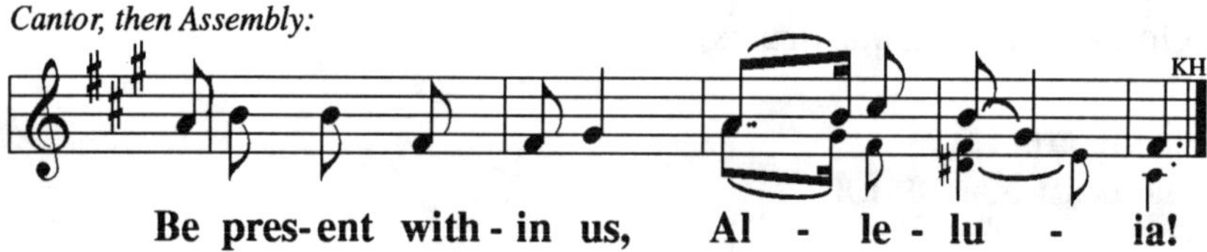

Cantor:

O risen Christ, **splen**did radiance **of** our God,
O risen Christ, **living** icon of **lo**ving covenant,
O risen Christ, **stead**fast rock of **our** salvation,

O risen Christ, **bril**liant joy of **a** new day,
O risen Christ, **sat**isfying refreshment **for** the weary,
O risen Christ, **un**ending celebration of **res**urrection,
O risen Christ, **true** promise of ever**last**ing life,
O risen Christ, **stead**fast hope **in** the Spirit,

Our Father ...

Prayer
God of the universe,
you create all things good and keep them in existence:
we stand before you in the radiant light of Jesus' resurrection.
Receive our morning prayer of praise
as a fitting reflection of our covenant with you.
Draw us to your presence
so that we might offer you praise and thanksgiving by our lives
now and always.
We pray through Jesus the risen Christ. **Amen.**

CONCLUSION

Blessing
Let us bow before our ever-creating God and ask for a blessing.
May the God of dawn bless us with risen life. **Amen.**
May the Son of justice bless us with unwavering courage. **Amen.**
May the Spirit of goodness bless us with glad thankfulness. **Amen.**
And may God bless us
in the name of the Father, and of the Son, and of the Holy Spirit. **Amen.**

Sign of Peace/Dismissal
Let us offer one another a sign of the presence
of our creative, redeeming, and loving God among us.

SUNDAY 1 Evening Prayer

LIGHT SERVICE

Proclamation of the Light

Cantor:
KH
Re - joice,___ O peo - ple of God:
the true Light is pres - ent a - mong us.
Assembly:
Let us live in the Light.___

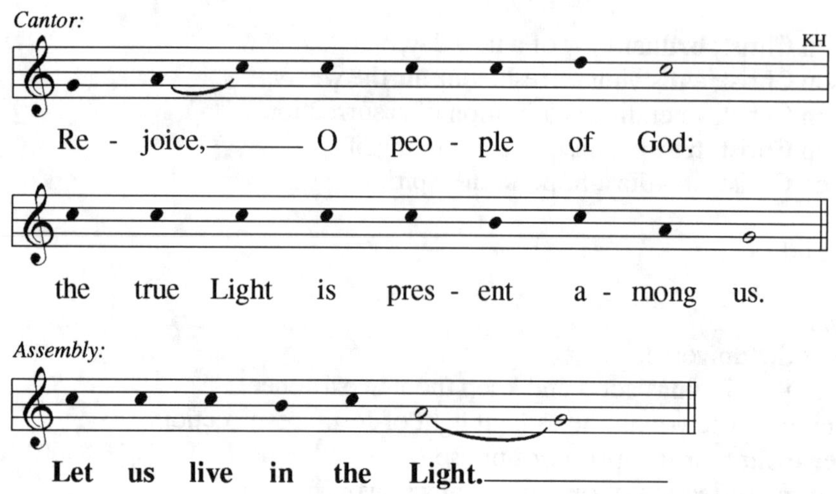

Evening Hymn

Thanksgiving for the Light

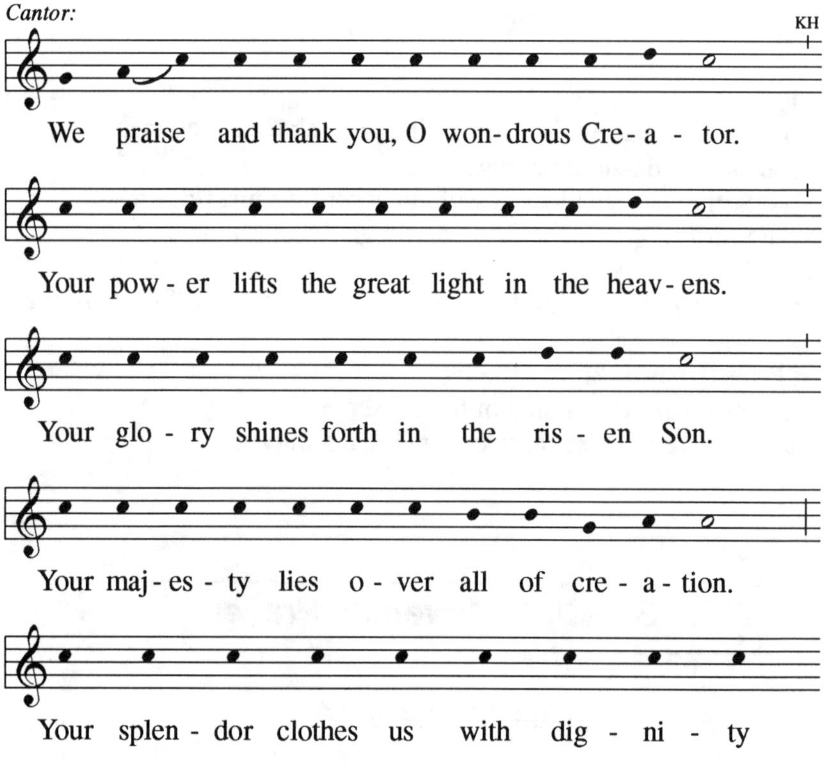

Cantor:
KH
We praise and thank you, O won-drous Cre - a - tor.
Your pow - er lifts the great light in the heav - ens.
Your glo - ry shines forth in the ris - en Son.
Your maj - es - ty lies o - ver all of cre - a - tion.
Your splen - dor clothes us with dig - ni - ty

and hon - or. Your good- ness o - ver-comes an - y
weak - ness. Your boun-ty sat - is - fies all hun - ger.
Your grace pro - claims our des - ti - ny.
Re - joice, O ho - ly peo - ple, in this great Light:
it is our sure sal - va - tion and glo - rious free - dom.
As our week-ly cel - e - bra - tion of res - ur - rec - tion draws to a
close, and dark-ness des-cends in qui - et rest, keep us
safe in this Light that nev - er fades. We praise and
thank you for your bless - ings, through Christ our Light
for - ev - er and ev - er. A - men.

PSALMODY

Psalm 141 *Psalm of David.*

ANTIPHON

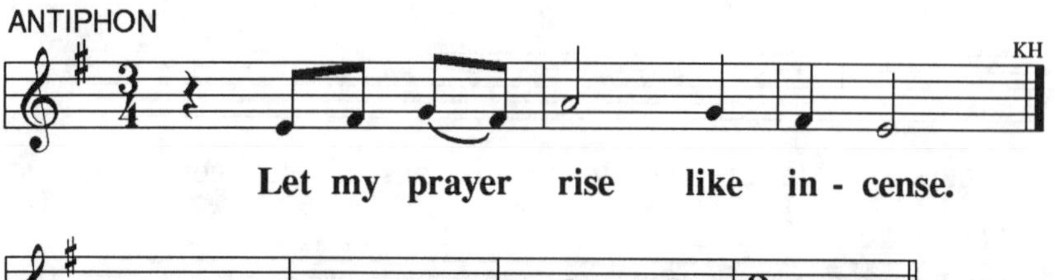
KH
Let my prayer rise like in - cense.

O LORD, I cry **to** you:
"Hasten to me,
listen to my voice
when I cry **to** you."
Let my prayer rise
like incense in **your** presence,
the lifting up of my hands
like an evening **of**fering. ANTIPHON

Set, O LORD,
a guard over **my** mouth,
keep the door of **my** lips.
Do not incline my heart to any evil,
to performing wicked deeds
with those who work **ini**quity;
let me not partake **in** their feasting. ANTIPHON

When a just person strikes me, it is **a** favor;
and when I am corrected, it is like anoin**ting** oil.
May my head never **re**fuse it,
while my prayer stands firm against **e**vil doings.

Let wicked judges be smashed against **the** rock,
and they will understand that my words **were** measured.
Like plowed and broken furrows on **the** land,
their bones are shattered at the **mouth** of Sheol. ANTIPHON

But my eyes look to you,
O LORD, **my** Lord.
In you I take refuge;
do not pour out **my** life.

Keep me from the snare they have prepared for me
  and from the traps of those who cre**ate** emptiness.
Let the wicked fall into their nets
  while I a**lone** escape. ANTIPHON

Psalm Prayer
O merciful God,
you hear the voice of those who call to you
with faith and love:
as our evening prayer rises to you on incense,
so may our gaze turn toward you now and always. **Amen.**

Psalm 67 *To the choirmaster. With stringed instruments. Psalm. Song.*

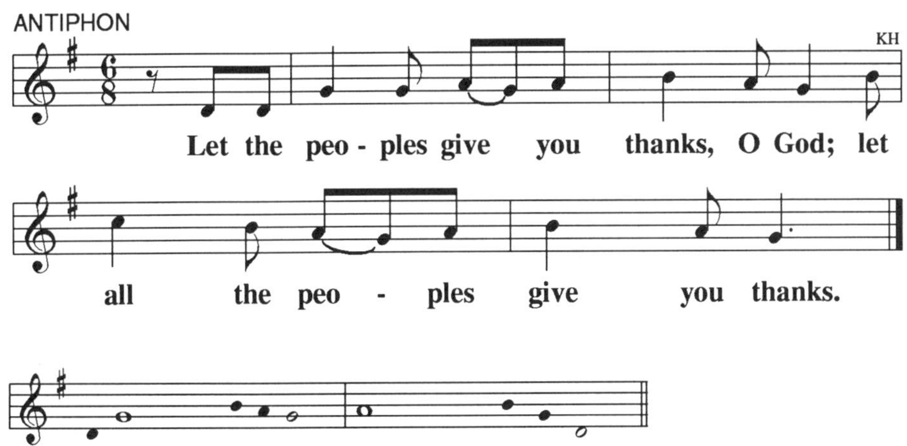
ANTIPHON
KH
Let the peo - ples give you thanks, O God; let
all the peo - ples give you thanks.

May God have mercy on us and **bless** us.
May God's face **shine** among us.

For your way is known **over** the earth,
and your salvation is known a**mong** all nations. ANTIPHON

May the nations rejoice and **shout** with joy,
for you judge the peoples rightly
  and the nations on the **earth** you guide. ANTIPHON

The earth has **given** its fruit.
May God, our God, **bless** us.

May God **bless** us,
and let all ends of the **earth** show reverence. ANTIPHON

Psalm Prayer
O gracious and powerful God,
you have blessed us with abundant gifts:
may all nations give thanks
and praise to your name forever and ever. **Amen.**

Word of God

Magnificat
My soul does magni**fy** the Lord!
I delight in **God** my savior
who looked kindly **on** lowliness.

Now all ages will **call** me blessed
for the Mighty One **did** great things.
Holy is **God's** name;
mercy is from age to age for **those** in awe!

The Lord's strong arm did **migh**ty deeds:
confused the proud in **their** smug hearts;
toppled sovereigns **from** their thrones,
and exalted **hum**ble ones;
filled the hungering with **good** things,
and sent the rich **a**way empty.

The Lord helped servant **Is**rael
to re**mem**ber mercy,
as was spoken to Ab**ra**ham
and his descendants for**e**vermore!

INTERCESSIONS

Petitions

Cantor, then Assembly:

Cantor:

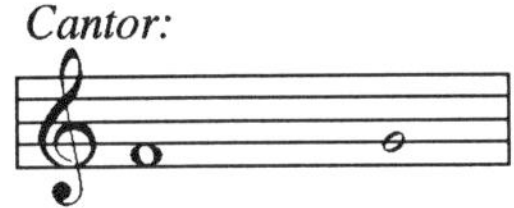

For the **Church** ...
For all **nations** ...
For civil **leaders** ...
For **cities** ...
For **farmlands** ...
For natural **resources** ...
For **children** ...
For **youth** ...
For the **oppressed** ...
For all those who died this **day** ...

Our Father ...

Prayer
O God,
you make us glad with the joy of your risen Son:
as we draw to a close our weekly celebration of redemption,
regard not our fickle ways and
guard us in the days to come
for we long to be in your sanctuary forever and ever. **Amen.**

CONCLUSION

Blessing
Let us bow before our redeeming God and ask for a blessing.
May the God who creates bless us with renewed strength. **Amen.**
May the God who saves bless us with fearless accountability. **Amen.**
May the God who anoints bless us with lasting courage. **Amen.**
And may God bless us
in the name of the Father, and of the Son, and of the Holy Spirit. **Amen.**

Sign of Peace/Dismissal
Let us strengthen one another with peace.

MONDAY 2 Morning Praise

MORNING HYMN

PSALMODY

Psalm 42 *To the choirmaster. Instruction. By the Qorahites.*

Solo 1 Like a deer longing
for streams of water,
so my soul longs
for you, O God.
My soul thirsts for God,
the living God.
When shall I come and see
the face of God?
My tears have been my food
day and night
while people said to me:
"Where is your God?"

Solo 2 These things I will remember
as I pour out my soul within me:
How I went along with the crowd,
moving in procession with them
up to the house of God,
with a cry of joy and thanksgiving.
We were a multitude keeping the feast.

All Why are you cast down my soul
and disturbed within me?
Put your hope in God—
my salvation and my God—
whom I will praise again.

Solo 1 My soul is cast down within me;
this is why I will remember you
from the land of Jordan and Mount Hermon,
from the land of Mizar.
Abyss cries out to abyss

at the thunder of your cataracts;
all your waves and billows have gone over me.

Solo 2 By day the LORD
commands the steadfast love,
and at night God's song is with me,
a prayer to the God of my life.
I will say to God, my rock:
"Why did you forsake me?
Why should I go wailing,
hard pressed by the enemy?"

Solo 1 My adversaries have been arrogant,
cutting a deep wound in my bones
by saying to me all day long,
"Where is your God?"

All Why are you cast down my soul
and disturbed within me?
Put your hope in God—
my salvation and my God—
whom I will praise again.

Psalm 43

Solo 1 Judge me, O God,
and plead my trial
against a nation unfaithful.
From people of deceit and iniquity, deliver me.

Solo 2 Since you are the God who is my fortress,
Why did you reject me?
Why should I wander in darkness,
hard pressed by the enemy?

Solo 1 Send your light and your truth;
they will guide me.
They will lead me to your holy mountain
and to your tents.

Solo 2 So I will come to the altar of God,
to God who makes me rejoice and dance;

with harp I will praise
God my God.

All Why are you cast down my soul
and disturbed within me?
Put your hope in God—
my salvation and my God—
whom I will praise again.

Word of God

Benedictus
Blessed be the Lord God of **Israel**,
who visited and redeemed the **people**,
who raised up for us a **mighty** savior
from the house of **ser**vant David.

Just as the Lord spoke through the mouths of the holy prophets of **old**—
salvation comes out of the hands of our enemies and those who **hate** us,
that, with our ancestors, we might perform **works** of mercy,
remembering the holy covenant **sworn** to Abraham—

so does the Lord deliver us from the hands **of** our enemies,
that we might serve without fear before **the** Lord,
worshiping in **ho**liness
and in righteousness **all** our days.

And you also, child, will be called a prophet of God Most **High**:
for you will go before the Lord to prepare a **way**,
bringing people knowledge of salvation by for**giveness** of sins;
because of the deep and tender mercy **of** our God.

Whereby a light rising from on high will **visit** us
to appear to those in darkness and in a shadow **of** death,
to guide our feet along a **straight**, sure path
into a **way** of peace.

INTERCESSIONS

Invocations

Cantor, then Assembly:
KH
We long for you, O God.

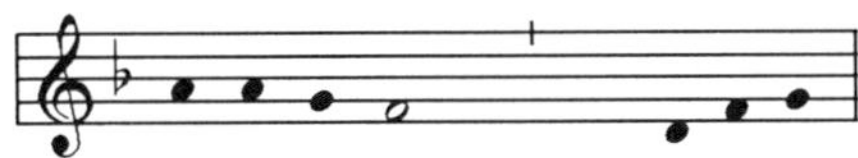
Cantor:

O living Christ, **in** our thirst ...
O living Christ, **in** our tears ...
O living Christ, **in** our darkness ...
O living Christ, **in our ali**enation ...
O living Christ, **in our** disquiet ...
O living Christ, **in** your call ...
O living Christ, **in** your steadfastness ...
O living Christ, **in your** deliverance ...
O living Christ, **in** your light ...
O living Christ, **in** your truth ...

Our Father ...

Prayer
O God of our desire,
you have been present to us in majesty and glory:
we long for that presence.
Lift up our downcast spirits,
that we may bring your light and truth
to all we meet this day.
We pray through Jesus Christ. **Amen.**

CONCLUSION

Blessing
May the God who eases all longing bless us
in the name of the Father, and of the Son, and of the Holy Spirit. **Amen.**

Dismissal
Go forth with a spirit willing to serve our God. **Thanks be to God.**

MONDAY 2 Evening Prayer

EVENING HYMN

PSALMODY

Psalm 123 *Song of ascents (pilgrimages).*

Solo 1 To you I lift up my eyes,
who dwell in heaven.

Choir 1 Behold, like the eyes of servants
look to the hand of their master,
like the eyes of a maid
look to the hand of her mistress,
so our eyes are lifted to the LORD our God
until mercy is bestowed upon us.

Choir 2 Have mercy on us, O LORD,
have mercy on us,
for we have been overwhelmed by contempt.
Our soul has been utterly filled
with the mockery of the indifferent
and the contempt of the arrogant.

Psalm 111

All Alleluia!

Choir 1 I will give thanks to the LORD with all my heart
in the council of the righteous and the assembly.

Choir 2 Great are the deeds of the LORD,
pondered by all who delight in them.

Choir 1 God's work is majesty and splendor,
and justice stands forever.

Choir 2 A memorial God has made of these wonders;
gracious and merciful is the LORD.

Choir 1 God has given food to those who show reverence,
remembering the covenant forever.

Choir 2 God has revealed to the people the power of these deeds
in giving them the nations for their heritage.

Choir 1 The deeds of God's hands are truth and justice;
the precepts of God are all trustworthy.

Choir 2 They are established forever and ever,
wrought in truth and equity.

Choir 1 God has sent deliverance to the people,
appointing the covenant forever;
holy and to be revered is God's name.

Choir 2 The beginning of wisdom is reverence for the LORD,
and its practice brings about clear understanding.

All The praise of God stands forever!

Word of God

Magnificat
My soul does magni**fy** the Lord!
I delight in **God** my savior
who looked kindly **on** lowliness.

Now all ages will **call** me blessed
for the Mighty One **did** great things.
Holy is **God's** name;
mercy is from age to age for **those** in awe!

The Lord's strong arm did **mighty** deeds:
confused the proud in **their** smug hearts;
toppled sovereigns **from** their thrones,
and exalted **hum**ble ones;
filled the hungering with **good** things,
and sent the rich **a**way empty.

The Lord helped servant **Is**rael
to re**mem**ber mercy,

as was spoken to Ab**ra**ham
and his descendants for**ev**ermore!

INTERCESSIONS

Petitions

Cantor, then Assembly:
KH
We lift up our eyes to God.

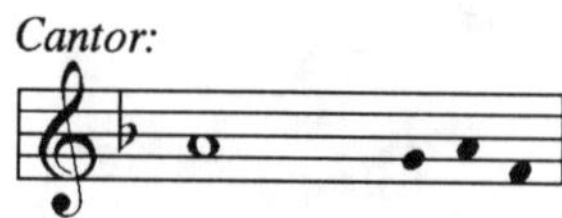
Cantor:

Turning to **God's** mercy ...
Scorning **the** wicked ...
Standing with **the** upright ...
Mindful of **the** covenant ...
Keeping **God's** precepts ...
Practic**ing** wisdom ...
Embracing un**der**standing ...
Rejoicing **in** faithfulness ...
Commending to God those who have **died** this day ...

Our Father ...

Prayer
Ever present God,
you sent Jesus to mediate the covenant:
forgive us for the times we have strayed
and send your Spirit to help us
to remain faithful now and always. **Amen.**

CONCLUSION

Blessing
May God keep us ever faithful and bless us
in the name of the Father, and of the Son, and of the Holy Spirit. **Amen.**

Dismissal
Go to rest this night in peace. **Thanks be to God.**

TUESDAY 2 Morning Praise

MORNING HYMN

PSALMODY

Psalm 27 *Of David.*

Solo 1 The LORD is my light and my salvation;
whom shall I fear?
The LORD is the stronghold of my life,
of whom shall I be afraid?

Solo 2 When evildoers approached
to devour me—
my adversaries and my enemies—
they stumbled and fell.
If an army encamps against me,
my heart shall not fear.
If war rises against me,
in this I trust:
One thing I ask from the LORD,
this only I will seek,
to dwell in the house of the LORD
all the days of my life,
to contemplate the favor of the LORD
and to meditate in God's sanctuary.

Solo 1 For God will hide me
in a shelter in the day of evil.
God will hide me in a secret chamber.
Upon a rock God will lift me up.

Solo 2 And now my head will be lifted above
my enemies who surround me.
And I will offer sacrifices in God's chamber,
sacrifices with wild jubilation.
I will sing and play music for the LORD.

Solo 1 Listen to my voice, O LORD, when I cry.
Have pity on me and answer me.

About you my heart has said:
"Seek God's face."
Your face, O LORD, I shall seek.

Solo 2 Do not hide your face from me;
do not send your servant back in anger.
You are my help.
Do not let me go, do not abandon me,
O God of my salvation.
Even if my father and my mother abandon me,
the LORD will receive me.

Solo 1 Teach me your way, O LORD,
and lead me on an upright path
because of my enemies.
Do not give me over to their wiles,
for false witnesses have risen against me,
breathing out violence.

Solo 2 If only I could be proved right
by seeing the goodness of the LORD
in the land of the living.

All Hope in the LORD!
Let your heart be strong and firm,
and hope in the LORD.

Psalm 125 *Song of ascents (pilgrimages).*

Choir 1 Those who trust in the LORD are like Mount Zion:
It will not fail; forever it will remain.

Choir 2 As Jerusalem is surrounded by mountains
so does the LORD surround the people,
from now and forever.
For the rule of the wicked will not weigh
upon the fate of the righteous,
because the righteous will not extend
their hands to crime.

Choir 1 Give prosperity, O LORD, to those who are good
and to those who are upright of heart.
But may the LORD drive away

those who turn aside to crooked ways,
the makers of emptiness.

All Peace be upon Israel!

Word of God

Benedictus
Blessed be the Lord God of **Israel**,
who visited and redeemed the **people**,
who raised up for us a **mighty** savior
from the house of **ser**vant David.

Just as the Lord spoke through the mouths of the holy prophets of **old**—
salvation comes out of the hands of our enemies and those who **hate** us,
that, with our ancestors, we might perform **works** of mercy,
remembering the holy covenant **sworn** to Abraham—

so does the Lord deliver us from the hands **of** our enemies,
that we might serve without fear before **the** Lord,
worshiping in **ho**liness
and in righteousness **all** our days.

And you also, child, will be called a prophet of God Most **High**:
for you will go before the Lord to prepare a **way**,
bringing people knowledge of salvation by for**giveness** of sins;
because of the deep and tender mercy **of** our God.

Whereby a light rising from on high will **visit** us
to appear to those in darkness and in a shadow **of** death,
to guide our feet along a **straight**, sure path
into a **way** of peace.

INTERCESSIONS

Invocations

Cantor, then Assembly:
KH
We shall not fear.

Cantor:

O risen Christ, you are **our** light ...
O risen Christ, you are **our** stronghold ...
O risen Christ, you are **our** shelter ...
O risen Christ, you are **our** confidence ...
O risen Christ, you are **our** salvation ...
O risen Christ, you are **our** path ...
O risen Christ, you are **our** strength ...
O risen Christ, you are **our** courage ...
O risen Christ, you are **our** trust ...
O risen Christ, you are **our** peace ...

Our Father...

Prayer
God of majesty,
you are the creator of all living things:
we praise you for your son Jesus
who is our light and our salvation.
Fill us with your Spirit,
so that in all our actions this day
we may seek only your face.
We pray through Jesus Christ. **Amen.**

CONCLUSION

Blessing
May God, our stronghold and source of confidence, bless us
in the name of the Father, and of the Son, and of the Holy Spirit. **Amen.**

Dismissal
Go forth this day to seek the face of God. **Thanks be to God.**

TUESDAY 2 Evening Prayer

EVENING HYMN

PSALMODY

Psalm 16 *A poem. Of David.*

Solo 1 Keep me, O God,
for I take refuge in you.
I say to the LORD:
"You are my Lord,
my happiness is only in you."

All As for idols in the land,
they are mighty only for those who delight in them.
People multiply these idols
after which they hurry.

Solo 2 But I will not offer them sacrifices of blood,
nor will I raise their names to my lips.
O LORD, my given portion and my cup,
you support my destiny
which has fallen for me in pleasant places,
nothing but a goodly heritage.

Solo 1 I bless the LORD who gives me counsel.
Even at night my heart instructs me.
I keep the LORD always before me.
Because God is at my right hand,
I shall not be moved.

Solo 2 Hence my heart rejoices
and my soul exults.
Even my body rests secure
because you do not abandon me to Sheol.
You do not allow your faithful
to experience the Pit.
You teach me the path of life.

All In your presence there is fullness of joy;
in your right hand, pleasures for eternity.

Psalm 116

Solo 1 I love the LORD
who has heard
the voice of my supplications.
For God has turned an ear to me
as I cry all my days.

Solo 2 Deadly chains have fettered me,
and the anguish of Sheol has reached up to me.
Distress and terror, I have encountered;
but I have called on the name of the LORD.
How long, O LORD?
Deliver my soul.

All The LORD is gracious and just;
our God is merciful.

Solo 1 The LORD is the protector of the innocent;
I was poor and God brought salvation to me.
Return, O my soul, to your rest,
for the LORD has done good to you.

Solo 2 For you have delivered my soul from death,
my eye from tears
and my foot from stumbling,
that I may walk in the presence of the LORD
in the land of the living.

Solo 1 Yes, I was right in saying,
"I am greatly afflicted."
In my agitation, I have said,
"Every human being is a liar."

Solo 2 What shall I return to the LORD
for all the bounty in my favor?
I will lift up the cup of salvation
and I will call on the name of the LORD.
Indeed, I will fulfill my promises to the LORD
in the presence of all the people.

All Precious in the eyes of the LORD
is the death of the faithful ones.

Solo 1 How long, O LORD?
For I am your servant,
I am your servant, the offspring of your handmaid.
You have loosened my bonds.

Solo 2 To you I will offer a sacrifice of thanksgiving
and I will call on the name of the LORD.
Indeed, I will fulfill my promises to the LORD
in the presence of all the people,
in the courts of the house of the LORD,
in your midst, O Jerusalem.

All Alleluia!

Word of God

Magnificat
My soul does magni**fy** the Lord!
I delight in **God** my savior
who looked kindly **on** lowliness.

Now all ages will **call** me blessed
for the Mighty One **did** great things.
Holy is **God's** name;
mercy is from age to age for **those** in awe!

The Lord's strong arm did **migh**ty deeds:
confused the proud in **their** smug hearts;
toppled sovereigns **from** their thrones,
and exalted **hum**ble ones;
filled the hungering with **good** things,
and sent the rich **a**way empty.

The Lord helped servant **Is**rael
to re**mem**ber mercy,
as was spoken to Abr**a**ham
and his descendants for**e**vermore!

INTERCESSIONS

Petitions

Cantor, then Assembly:

Cantor:

We plea **for** safety ... **and** cry out,
We seek refuge from distress **and** terror ... **and** cry out,
We beg **for** mercy ... **and** cry out,
We long to keep **from** stumbling ... **and** cry out,
We **need** counsel ... **and** cry out,
We des**ire** peace ... **and** cry out,
We yearn for **ful**fillment ... **and** cry out,
We hope for salvation for all who have died **this** day ... **and** cry out,

Our Father ...

Prayer
O saving God,
you are the source of life and holiness:
lead us through darkness on the path of light.
Guide us in righteousness now and forever. **Amen.**

CONCLUSION

Blessing
May the God of unfailing power
protect us this night with saving presence and bless us
in the name of the Father, and of the Son, and of the Holy Spirit. **Amen.**

Dismissal
Go to rest in the confidence of God's love. **Thanks be to God.**

WEDNESDAY 2 Morning Praise

MORNING HYMN

PSALMODY

Psalm 143 *Psalm of David.*

Solo 1 O LORD, hear my prayer;
in your faithfulness give ear to my supplications.
Answer me in your justice.

All Do not enter into judgment against your servant,
for no living creature is just before you.

Solo 1 For the enemy has pursued me,
crushed my life to the ground,
and made me sit in darkness with those long dead.
My spirit languishes within me;
within me my heart is devastated.

Solo 2 I remember the days of the past;
I ponder over all your deeds.
I meditate upon the work of your hands.
I stretch out my hands to you—
to you my soul is like parched land.

Selah (pause).

Solo 1 Quickly answer me, O LORD,
for my spirit fails.
Do not hide your face from me
or I resemble those who go down the Pit.
Let me hear in the morning of your steadfast love,
for in you I put my trust.

Solo 2 Let me know the way I should go,
for to you I lift up my soul.
Deliver me from my enemies, O LORD,
for in you I take refuge.

Solo 1 Teach me to do your will,
for you are my God.
Let your good spirit guide me
in the land of integrity.

Solo 2 For the sake of your name, O LORD, give me life.
In your justice, bring me out of distress.
In your steadfast love, cut off my enemies

and destroy all my adversaries,
for I am your servant.

Psalm 110 *Of David. Psalm.*

Solo 1 Thus says the LORD to my lord:
"Sit on my right
until I place your enemies
as a footstool for your feet."

Choir 1 Let the LORD send from Zion
the scepter of your strength.
Rule in the midst of your enemies.

Choir 2 Your people bring free offerings
on the day of your might
in holy splendor.
From the womb of dawn,
a dew of rejuvenation comes to you.

Solo 1 The LORD has promised
and will not repent:
"According to my word,
you are a priest forever, my king of justice."

Choir 1 The Lord is at your right,
who has smashed rulers on the day of wrath.
The Lord judges against the nations,
piling them with corpses.

Choir 2 The Lord has smashed heads
all over the land.
From a torrent the Lord drinks on the way,
and rises up in triumph.

Word of God

Benedictus
Blessed be the Lord God of **Israel**,
who visited and redeemed the **people**,
who raised up for us a **might**y savior
from the house of **ser**vant David.

Just as the Lord spoke through the mouths of the holy prophets of **old**—
salvation comes out of the hands of our enemies and those who **hate** us,
that, with our ancestors, we might perform **works** of mercy,
remembering the holy covenant **sworn** to Abraham—

so does the Lord deliver us from the hands **of** our enemies,
that we might serve without fear before **the** Lord,
worshiping in **ho**liness
and in righteousness **all** our days.

And you also, child, will be called a prophet of God Most **High**:
for you will go before the Lord to prepare a **way**,
bringing people knowledge of salvation by for**giveness** of sins;
because of the deep and tender mercy **of** our God.

Whereby a light rising from on high will **visit** us
to appear to those in darkness and in a shadow **of** death,
to guide our feet along a **straight**, sure path
into a **way** of peace.

INTERCESSIONS

Invocations

Cantor, then Assembly:

Cantor:

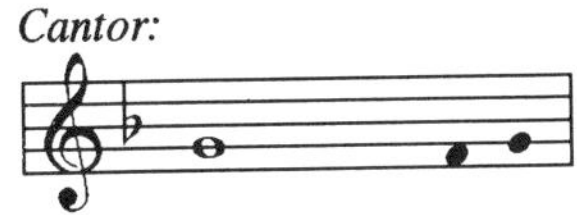

Hide not **from** us,
Give ear to our supp**li**cations,
Enter not into judgment **of** us,
Lift our languish**ing** spirits,
Speak to us of **your** love,
Teach us to walk in **your** ways,
Lead us on a **straight** path,
Preserve us for life **ever**lasting,
Receive our **free** offerings,

Our Father ...

Prayer
O God of redemption,
your mighty hand crushes the power of evil:
lead us in the ways of righteousness
that the power of your Gospel may reign over all the earth.
We pray through Jesus Christ. **Amen.**

CONCLUSION

Blessing
May the God of the nations protect us from all harm and bless us
in the name of the Father, and of the Son, and of the Holy Spirit. **Amen.**

Dismissal
Go forth armed with victory to overcome the powers of evil. **Thanks be to God.**

WEDNESDAY 2 Evening Prayer

EVENING HYMN

PSALMODY

Psalm 139 *To the choirmaster. Of David. Psalm.*

Solo 1 O LORD, you have searched me and you know:
you know when I sit and when I stand,
you discern my thought from a distance,
you search my path and my resting place,
and you are familiar with all my ways.
Even before there is any word on my tongue,
behold, O LORD, you know it completely.
You surround me behind and before,
you set your hand over me.
Such knowledge is too wonderful for me,
so lofty that I cannot reach it.

All Where can I go from your spirit?
And where can I flee from your face?

Solo 2 If I ascend to the heavens, you are there;
if I lie down in Sheol, behold, you are there.
If I rise with the wings of dawn
or lie down in the far end of the sea:
even there, your hand leads me
and your right hand seizes me.
If I say, "Surely darkness
will fall upon me
and night will replace the light around me,"
even darkness is not dark for you:
the night will shine like the day,
and darkness will be like light.

Solo 1 For you formed my inmost parts;
you weaved me in my mother's womb.
I give thanks to you because I was made
in an awesome and wonderful way.
Your works are wonderful,
well known to my soul.
My bones were not hidden from you
when I was made in secret,
woven in the depths of the earth.
Your eyes have seen my unformed matter.
In your book, the days to be formed were all written
before any one of them existed.

All How difficult for me are your thoughts!
How immeasurable, O God, their sum!
Were I to count them, they would be more than the sand.
Were I to end, I would still be with you.

Solo 2 If only, O God, you could kill the wicked,
then the bloodthirsty would turn away from me—
those who have spoken malice against you
and have risen up to destroy your cities.
Should I not, O LORD, hate those who hate you
and loathe those who rise up against you?
With pure hatred I hate them;
they have become my own enemies.

All Search me, O God, and know my heart;
examine me and know my thoughts.
See if any way in me is hurtful
and lead me into the way of eternity.

Psalm 9 *To the choirmaster. Muth lebben. Psalm of David.*

Solo 1 I will give thanks, O LORD, with all my heart.
I will tell of all your wonderful deeds.
I will rejoice, I will exult in you,
and I will play music for your name, O Most High.

Solo 2 When my enemies turned back
they stumbled and perished before you,
for you had taken up my case and my judgment.
You sat on the throne
as the one who judges with justice.
You rebuked nations;
you destroyed the wicked,
erasing their names
forever and ever.
The enemy has vanished
in ruins for eternity.
You destroyed cities—
even their memory has perished.

Choir 1 But the LORD remains enthroned forever,
making firm the throne of judgment.
God judges the world in justice
and the peoples in equity.

Choir 2 The LORD will be
a refuge for the poor,
a refuge in times of distress.
Those who know your name
will trust in you,
for you do not abandon those who seek you, O LORD.

Word of God

Magnificat
My soul does magnify the Lord!

I delight in **God** my savior
who looked kindly **on** lowliness.

Now all ages will **call** me blessed
for the Mighty One **did** great things.
Holy is **God's** name;
mercy is from age to age for **those** in awe!

The Lord's strong arm did **migh**ty deeds:
confused the proud in **their** smug hearts;
toppled sovereigns **from** their thrones,
and exalted **hum**ble ones;
filled the hungering with **good** things,
and sent the rich **a**way empty.

The Lord helped servant **Is**rael
to re**mem**ber mercy,
as was spoken to Ab**ra**ham
and his descendants for**e**vermore!

INTERCESSIONS

Petitions

Cantor, then Assembly:

Cantor:

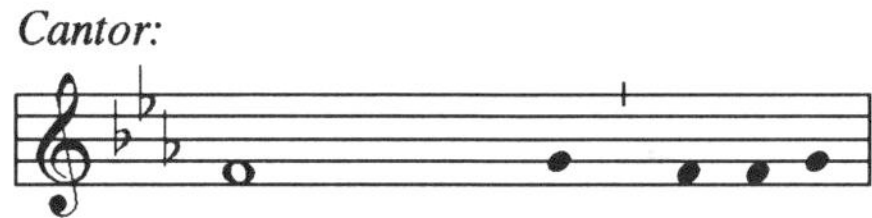

That we be drawn to God's **heart** ... **we** implore,
That we be drawn to God's **knowledge** ... **we** implore,
That we be drawn to God's **light** ... **we** implore,
That we be drawn to God's **presence** ... **we** implore,
That we be drawn to God's **justice** ... **we** implore,
That we be drawn to God's **trust** ... **we** implore,
That we be drawn to God's **judgment** ... **we** implore,
That we be drawn to God's **Spirit** ... **we** implore,
That the faithful departed be drawn to God's **resting place** ... **we** implore,

Our Father ...

Prayer
O God,
you have formed us in the hidden womb of your creative power:
draw us out to be your holy people in the world now and always. **Amen.**

CONCLUSION

Blessing
May the God who formed us
keep us safe this night and bless us
in the name of the Father, and of the Son, and of the Holy Spirit. **Amen.**

Dismissal
Go and rest in the enveloping bosom of a loving God. **Thanks be to God.**

THURSDAY 2 Morning Praise

MORNING HYMN

PSALMODY

Psalm 80 *To the choirmaster. "On lilies." Testimony. Of Asaf. Psalm.*

Choir 1 Give ear, O Shepherd of Israel,
you who lead Joseph like a flock;
you who are enthroned on the cherubim,
shine forth.
Before Ephraim, Benjamin and Manasseh,
arouse your strength
and come to save us!

All Bring us back, O God,
and let your face shine that we may be saved.

Choir 2 O LORD God of hosts,
how long will you be angry
in spite of the prayer of your people?
You feed them with the bread of tears;

you give them tears to drink in triple measure.
You set us up as an object of contention for our neighbors,
and our enemies have reasons to laugh among themselves.

All Bring us back, O God of hosts,
and let your face shine that we may be saved.

Choir 1 You have plucked out a vine from Egypt.
You have expelled nations and planted it.
You have cleared the ground for it
so that it may take root
and fill the land.
The mountains are covered with its shade
and the highest cedars with its branches.
It sends its branches to the sea
and its shoots to the river.

Choir 2 Why did you break down its fences
so that those who pass by on the way can pluck it?
The boar from the forest devours it
and the animals of the fields eat it up.
Turn back, O God of hosts;
look down from heaven and see.
Look after this vine,
the stock your right hand has planted,
on account of the one you made strong for yourself.
Like filth, they burned it with fire;
let them perish by the rebuke of your face.

Choir 1 Let your hand be on the one at your right hand,
the one you made strong for yourself.
Then we will not depart from you.
Give us life, and in your name we shall pray.

All Bring us back, O LORD God of hosts,
and let your face shine that we may be saved.

Psalm 57 *To the choirmaster. "Do not destroy." Of David. Poem.*
When he flew from the presence of Saul in the cave.

Solo 1 Have pity on me, O God,
have pity on me; for in you
my soul has taken refuge.

In the shade of your wings I will take refuge
until destruction passes away.

Solo 2 I keep crying to God the Most High,
to God who acts in my favor.
May God send from heaven my salvation
and put to shame the one who entraps me.

Selah (pause).

Solo 1 May God send out steadfast love and truth.
I am in the midst of lions,
lying among people who are like burning flames,
their teeth like spears and arrows,
their tongues like sharp swords.

All Rise up, O God, above the heavens;
let your glory be over all the earth!

Solo 2 They have prepared a trap for my steps;
my soul is fearful.
In my presence they have dug a pit,
but then they fell into it.

Selah (pause).

Solo 1 My heart is firm, O God,
my heart is firm.
I will sing, I will play music.
Awake, my soul!
Awake, O harp and lyre!
I will awake the dawn.
I will praise you among peoples, my Lord,
I will play music for you among nations.
For your steadfast love reaches to the skies,
and to the firmaments, your truth.

All Rise up, O God, above the heavens;
let your glory be over all the earth!

Word of God

Benedictus
Blessed be the Lord God of **Israel**,
who visited and redeemed the **people**,
who raised up for us a **mighty** savior
from the house of **ser**vant David.

Just as the Lord spoke through the mouths of the holy prophets of **old**—
salvation comes out of the hands of our enemies and those who **hate** us,
that, with our ancestors, we might perform **works** of mercy,
remembering the holy covenant **sworn** to Abraham—

so does the Lord deliver us from the hands **of** our enemies,
that we might serve without fear before **the** Lord,
worshiping in **ho**liness
and in righteousness **all** our days.

And you also, child, will be called a prophet of God Most **High**:
for you will go before the Lord to prepare a **way**,
bringing people knowledge of salvation by for**giveness** of sins;
because of the deep and tender mercy **of** our God.

Whereby a light rising from on high will **vis**it us
to appear to those in darkness and in a shadow **of** death,
to guide our feet along a **straight**, sure path
into a **way** of peace.

INTERCESSIONS

Invocations

Cantor, then Assembly:

Cantor:

Bounteous **God**, shepherd of Israel ...
Bounteous **God**, pro**mise** of freedom ...
Bounteous **God**, favor for a **plen**tiful land ...
Bounteous **God**, strength **of** your people ...

Bounteous **God**, giver of life ...
Bounteous **God**, waker of the dawn ...
Bounteous **God**, fountain of truth ...
Bounteous **God**, source of all power ...
Bounteous **God**, presence of glory ...

Our Father ...

Prayer
Ever faithful God,
you are the creator of all goodness
and the shepherd of those who heed your call:
as you led your people from bondage to a land of plenty,
so be with us in our labors this day
and lead us to an abundance of joys.
We pray through Jesus Christ. **Amen.**

CONCLUSION

Blessing
May the God who enables us to labor fruitfully bless us
in the name of the Father, and of the Son, and of the Holy Spirit. **Amen.**

Dismissal
Go forth, guided by our shepherd God. **Thanks be to God.**

THURSDAY 2 Evening Prayer

EVENING HYMN

PSALMODY

Psalm 66 *To the choirmaster. A Song. Psalm.*

Choir 1 Sound the trumpet for God, all the earth!
Make music to the glory of God's name!
Give glory and praise!
Say to God:
"How awesome are your deeds!
At the magnitude of your power,

your enemies cringe before you.
Let all the earth worship you,
let them sing to you,
let them sing to your name."

Selah (pause).

Choir 2 Come and see the accomplishments
of God—
an awesome work
on behalf of mortals.
God turned the sea into dry land,
they crossed through the river on foot.
Therefore let us rejoice in God,
who rules over the world with power
and whose eyes watch over the nations.
Let not the stubborn rise up against God.

Selah (pause).

All All you nations, bless our God!
Let the sound of praise be heard
for the one who gives life to our souls,
and who kept our feet from stumbling.

Choir 1 For you have tested us, O God;
you have tried us like silver is tried.
You have caught us in a net.
You have put a burden on our backs.
You have let mortals enslave us.
We went through fire and water,
but you brought us out to a fertile land.

Solo 1 I shall go into your house with offerings.
I will fulfill my promises to you
which my lips uttered
and my mouth spoke when I was in distress.
I will bring you offerings of fatlings;
along with the smoke of rams
I will offer bulls and goats.

Selah (pause).

Solo 2 Come, listen, all those who revere God,
and I will tell
all that God did for my soul.
I have cried out with my mouth,
extolling God with my tongue.
If I had harbored emptiness in my heart,
the Lord would not have listened.
But truly God has listened,
listened to the voice of my prayer.

Solo 1 Blessed be God
who has not rejected my prayer,
nor taken steadfast love away from me.

Psalm 122 *Song of ascents (pilgrimages). Of David.*

Solo 1 I rejoiced when they said to me,
"We shall go to the house of the LORD."

Choir 1 Our feet are standing
at your gates, O Jerusalem.
Jerusalem, you are built like a city
well-bound together.
There the tribes went up,
the tribes of the LORD,
to give thanks to the name of the LORD,
keeping a precept for Israel.
For there the thrones for judgment were placed,
the thrones for the house of David.

Choir 2 Pray for the peace of Jerusalem:
"May those who love you live in peace.
May peace be within your walls
and tranquility within your palaces."

Solo 1 For the sake of my kindred
and my companions, let me speak:
"Peace be upon you."
For the sake of the house of the LORD our God,
I will seek your prosperity.

Word of God

Magnificat
My soul does magni**fy** the Lord!
I delight in **God** my savior
who looked kindly **on** lowliness.

Now all ages will **call** me blessed
for the Mighty One **did** great things.
Holy is **God's** name;
mercy is from age to age for **those** in awe!

The Lord's strong arm did **mighty** deeds:
confused the proud in **their** smug hearts;
toppled sovereigns **from** their thrones,
and exalted **hum**ble ones;
filled the hungering with **good** things,
and sent the rich **a**way empty.

The Lord helped servant **Is**rael
to re**mem**ber mercy,
as was spoken to Ab**ra**ham
and his descendants for**e**vermore!

INTERCESSIONS

Petitions

Cantor, then Assembly:

Cantor:

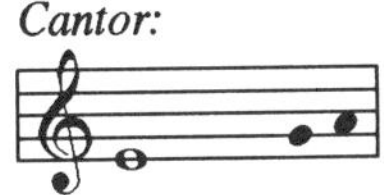

We give glory, praise, **and** thanks,
We rejoice in God's awe**some** works,
We fulfill our promise **of** love,
We revere God for great and won**drous** deeds,
We come before our God **in** awe,
We desire last**ing** peace,
We seek **pros**perity,
We hunger for stead**fast** love,
That those who have died today may live in eter**nal** life,

Our Father ...

Prayer
O good and gracious God,
you brought a vine out of Egypt
and planted it in a land flowing with milk and honey:
nurture us, your holy people,
and prepare us to enter into joy with you forever and ever. **Amen.**

CONCLUSION

Blessing
May our redeeming God bless us
in the name of the Father, and of the Son, and of the Holy Sirit. **Amen.**

Dismissal
Go to rest in the graciousness of our God. **Thanks be to God.**

FRIDAY 2 Morning Praise

MORNING HYMN

PSALMODY

Psalm 51 *To the choirmaster. Psalm of David. In the coming to him of Nathan the prophet, after David had been with Bathsheba.*

ANTIPHON

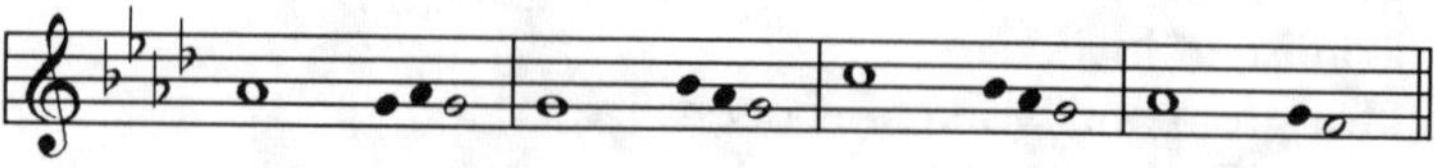

Be gracious to **me**, O God,
in your **stead**fast love.
According to the abundance **of** your mercy
blot out my **trans**gressions. ANTIPHON

Cleanse me completely **from** my guilt
and purify me **from** my sin.
For my transgressions I do **rec**ognize,
and my sin stands always **be**fore me.

Against you alone **have** I sinned,
and what is evil in your eyes **I** have done.
Thus you may be declared just in your ways,
  and pure **in** your judgments.
Indeed, I was born guilty,
  already a sinner when my mother **con**ceived me. ANTIPHON

Surely in truth **you** delight,
and deep within my self you will **teach** me wisdom.
Cleanse me from my sin with hyssop and I **will** be pure,
wash me and I shall be brighter **than** snow.

Let me hear glad**ness** and joy,
let the bones you **broke** exult.
Turn your face **from** my sins
and blot out all my iniq**ui**ties. ANTIPHON

Create in me a pure **heart**, O God,
and renew within me **a** firm spirit.
Do not dismiss me **from** your presence,
and do not take away from me your ho**ly** spirit.

Give me back the joy of **your** salvation,
and let a willing spirit lie **o**ver me.
I will teach transgress**ors** your ways,
and sinners will turn back **to** you. ANTIPHON

Deliver me from bloodshed, O God,
  God of **my** salvation,
and my tongue will **sing** your justice.
O Lord, o**pen** my lips,
and my mouth will tell **your** praise.

For you take no pleasure in **sac**rifice,
and you would not accept an offering were **I** to give it.
The perfect sacrifice for God is a **brok**en spirit.
A broken and humble heart,
  O God, you will not **des**pise. ANTIPHON

In your kindness bring prosperi**ty** to Zion;
rebuild the walls of Je**ru**salem.
Then you can delight in sacrifices of justice,
  burnt and complete **of**ferings;
then bulls can be offered on **your** altars. ANTIPHON

Psalm Prayer
Merciful God,
your steadfast love sustains us even in our transgressions:
wash us brighter than snow
and restore us to your favor now and forever. **Amen.**

Word of God

Benedictus
Blessed be the Lord God of **Israel**,
who visited and redeemed the **people**,
who raised up for us a **mighty** savior
from the house of **ser**vant David.

Just as the Lord spoke through the mouths of the holy prophets of **old**—
salvation comes out of the hands of our enemies and those who **hate** us,
that, with our ancestors, we might perform **works** of mercy,
remembering the holy covenant **sworn** to Abraham—

so does the Lord deliver us from the hands **of** our enemies,
that we might serve without fear before **the** Lord,
worshiping in **ho**liness
and in righteousness **all** our days.

And you also, child, will be called a prophet of God Most **High**:
for you will go before the Lord to prepare a **way**,
bringing people knowledge of salvation by for**giveness** of sins;
because of the deep and tender mercy **of** our God.

Whereby a light rising from on high will **vis**it us
to appear to those in darkness and in a shadow **of** death,
to guide our feet along a **straight**, sure path
into a **way** of peace.

INTERCESSIONS

Invocations

Cantor, then Assembly in canon:

1.
2.
KH
Hear our prayer, O God.
one or two voices
Hear, O God.

Cantor:

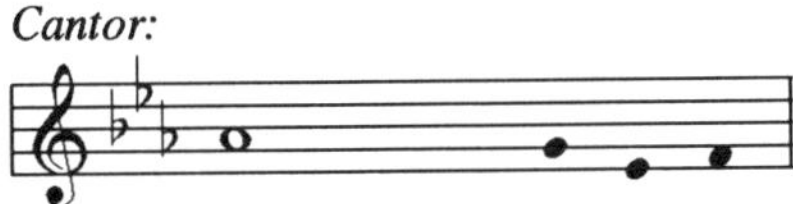

Jesus our Savior, **source** of mercy ...
Jesus our Savior, **source** of forgiveness ...
Jesus our Savior, **source** of compassion ...
Jesus our Savior, **source** of healing ...
Jesus our Savior, **source** of strength ...
Jesus our Savior, **source** of courage ...
Jesus our Savior, **source** of light ...
Jesus our Savior, **source** of life ...
Jesus our Savior, **source** of unity ...
Jesus our Savior, **source** of peace ...

Our Father ...

Prayer
Loving-kind God,
you show us mercy and compassion, truth and wisdom:
teach us always to do your holy will.
May our Friday penance restore to us a clean heart
that we may only hunger for you.
We pray through Jesus Christ our Savior. **Amen.**

CONCLUSION

Blessing
May God, the source of all mercy, bless us now and always
in the name of the Father, and of the Son, and of the Holy Spirit. **Amen.**

Dismissal
Go forth, and remain steadfast in our merciful God. **Thanks be to God.**

FRIDAY 2 Evening Prayer

EVENING HYMN

PSALMODY

Psalm 130 *Song of ascents (pilgrimages).*

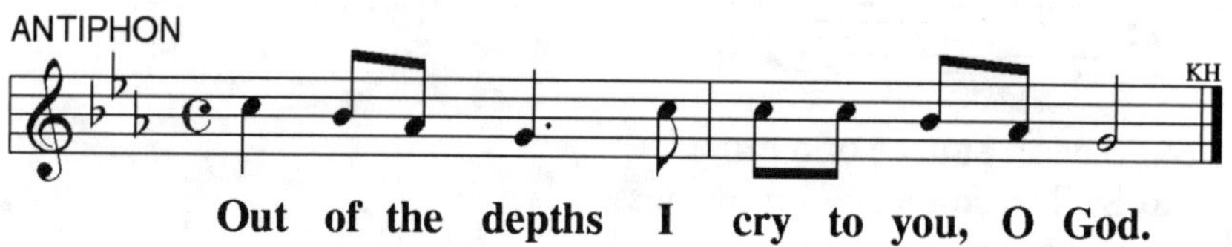
ANTIPHON
KH
Out of the depths I cry to you, O God.

Out of the depths, I cry to **you**, O LORD.
Lord, listen to **my** voice;
let your ears **be** attentive
to the voice of my sup**pli**cations. ANTIPHON

If you, O LORD, were to keep ini**quities** in mind,
Lord, who **could** stand?
But with you **is** forgiveness,
and for that you are **re**vered. ANTIPHON

I wait for the LORD;
  my soul waits, and for God's **word** I hope.
My soul waits for **the** Lord
more than watchers **of** the morning
watch for **the** dawn. ANTIPHON

Let Israel hope **in** the LORD,
for steadfast love is found with the LORD
  and abundance of **re**demption.
It is the LORD who shall redeem **Is**rael
from all iniq**ui**ties. ANTIPHON

Psalm Prayer
Attentive God,
you hear our voice with unfailing kindness:
forgive us our wanderings from the path
of your redeeming love now and always. **Amen.**

Psalm 138 *Of David.*

ANTIPHON
KH
I give you thanks, O God; with my
whole heart I sing your praise.

I give you thanks with **all** my heart;
instead of other gods, I **sing** to you.
I bow down toward the **ho**ly sanctuary,
and I give thanks to your name
  on account of your steadfast love **and** your truth.

For you have ex**alted** your promise
even a**bove** your name.
On the day I cried, you **ans**wered me;
you renewed cour**age** within me. ANTIPHON

Let all the rulers of the earth give thanks to you, O LORD,
  for they have heard the **words of** your mouth.
Let them sing about the ways of the LORD,
  for great is the **glory of** the LORD.
Although exalted,
  the LORD looks up**on** the lowly,
but recognizes the proud only **from** a distance. ANTIPHON

When I walk in the midst of distress,
you revive me against the **anger of** my enemies.
You stretch out your hand,
and your **right** hand saves me;
the LORD will do every**thing** for me.
O LORD, your steadfast love is forever.
Do not forsake the work **of** your hands. ANTIPHON

Psalm Prayer
Exalted God,
your name is above all others:
hear the thanksgiving prayer of your humble people
and increase our strength of soul
that we may preserve our life forever and ever. **Amen.**

Word of God

Magnificat
My soul does magni**fy** the Lord!
I delight in **God** my savior
who looked kindly **on** lowliness.

Now all ages will **call** me blessed
for the Mighty One **did** great things.
Holy is **God's** name;
mercy is from age to age for **those** in awe!

The Lord's strong arm did **mighty** deeds:
confused the proud in **their** smug hearts;
toppled sovereigns **from** their thrones,
and exalted **hum**ble ones;
filled the hungering with **good** things,
and sent the rich **a**way empty.

The Lord helped servant **Is**rael
to re**mem**ber mercy,
as was spoken to Ab**ra**ham
and his descendants for**ev**ermore!

INTERCESSIONS

Petitions

Cantor, then Assembly in canon:

1.
2.
KH
Hear our prayer, O God.
one or two voices
Hear, O God.

Cantor:

For **help** ...
For for**giv**eness ...
For **pa**tience ...
For **hope** ...
For re**demp**tion ...
For **mer**cy ...
For **strength** ...
For **cour**age ...
For de**li**verance ...
For sal**va**tion ...
For **thank**fulness ...
For the faithful de**part**ed ...

Our Father ...

Prayer
Merciful God,
you are full of steadfast love
and ever faithful to your word of truth:
preserve us against all dangers
as we seek rest in you forever and ever. **Amen.**

CONCLUSION

Blessing
May the God of the Cross,
who conquered death and promised life,
grant us strength and conviction and bless us
in the name of the Father, and of the Son, and of the Holy Spirit. **Amen.**

Dismissal
Go to rest confidently in our saving God. **Thanks be to God.**

SATURDAY 2 Morning Praise

MORNING HYMN

PSALMODY

Psalm 65 *To the choirmaster. Psalm of David. Psalm.*

ANTIPHON
KH
You ans- wer us, O God, with awe- some deeds.

To you praise is due,
  O God **in** Zion,
and for you promises will be **ful**filled.
O you who listen to prayer,
  to you all flesh **shall** come.
When our transgressions—our deeds of iniquity—overcome us,
  you **for**give them. ANTIPHON

Blessed is the one you elect and **bring** near;
that one shall dwell in **your** courts.
Let us be filled with the goodness of **your** house,
the holiness of **your** temple.

With awesome deeds you answer us **in** justice,
O God of our **sal**vation,
protector of all the ends of **the** earth
and of the dis**tant** seas. ANTIPHON

Girded with might,
  you establish mountains **in** strength.
You still the roaring of the seas—
  the roaring of their waves—
  and the clamor **of** nations.
Because of **your** signs,
the inhabitants of the ends of the earth will stand **in** awe. ANTIPHON

You cause the breaking of morning and of evening
  to burst **with** joy.
You visit the earth and give it water;
  abundantly, you **en**rich it:
the river of God
  is replete **with** water.
You provide people with grain,
  for you designed **it** so.

Its furrows you water **a**bundantly,
and you make **them** smooth.
You soften it **with** showers,
and you bless **its** sprout. ANTIPHON

You crown the year with your bounty,
  and fertility springs in the wake of **your** chariot.
The pastures of the wilderness drip with water,
  and the hills are girded **with** joy.
Meadows are clothed with flocks,
  and valleys are covered **with** grain.
They shout, even more, **they** sing. ANTIPHON

Psalm Prayer
O God of creation and salvation,
you provide us with all good things
and sustain us by your care:
receive our morning prayer
for all praise is your due forever and ever. **Amen.**

Psalm 96

ANTIPHON
KH
Sing a new song, all the earth;
sing a new song all the earth.

Sing to the LORD a **new** song.
Sing to the LORD, all **the** earth.
Sing to **the** LORD,
bless **God's** name. ANTIPHON

From day to day proclaim the good news of sal**vation**.
Recount among the nations God's glory,
  God's marvels among **all** peoples.
For great is the LORD, highly to **be** praised
and revered above **all** gods.

For all the gods of the nations are as **nothing**,
but the LORD made **the** heavens.
Honor and splendor stand be**fore** God,
might and glory fill **the** temple. ANTIPHON

Give to the LORD, O families of **peoples**.
Give to the LORD glory **and** might.
Give to **the** LORD
the glory of **God's** name. ANTIPHON

Bring an offering and come into the **courts**.
Worship the LORD with ho**ly** splendor.
Dance in the sac**red** presence,
all **the** earth.

Say among the nations: "The LORD **reigns.**"
Surely God formed the universe
  so that it would **not** falter.
God **will** judge
the peoples **in** equity. ANTIPHON

Let the heavens re**joice**
and the earth **exult.**
Let the sea and its full**ness** roar.
Let the fields and all within them **be** glad. ANTIPHON

Then all the trees of the forest will shout with **joy**
in the presence of the LORD **who** comes.
For God comes to judge the earth,
  to judge the universe **with** justice
and with fidelity, **the** peoples. ANTIPHON

Psalm Prayer
O glorious and ever living God,
you are worthy of all praise:
we exalt you for your wondrous deeds.
Draw us into your presence
so that we may offer you
a fitting sacrifice of praise now and always. **Amen.**

Word of God

Benedictus
Blessed be the Lord God of **Israel,**
who visited and redeemed the **people,**
who raised up for us a **mighty** savior
from the house of **ser**vant David.

Just as the Lord spoke through the mouths of the holy prophets of **old**—
salvation comes out of the hands of our enemies and those who **hate** us,
that, with our ancestors, we might perform **works** of mercy,
remembering the holy covenant **sworn** to Abraham—

so does the Lord deliver us from the hands **of** our enemies,
that we might serve without fear before **the** Lord,
worshiping in **ho**liness
and in righteousness **all** our days.

And you also, child, will be called a prophet of God Most **High**:
for you will go before the Lord to prepare a **way**,
bringing people knowledge of salvation by for**giveness** of sins;
because of the deep and tender mercy **of** our God.

Whereby a light rising from on high will **visit** us
to appear to those in darkness and in a shadow **of** death,
to guide our feet along a **straight**, sure path
into a **way** of peace.

INTERCESSIONS

Invocations

Cantor, then Assembly:

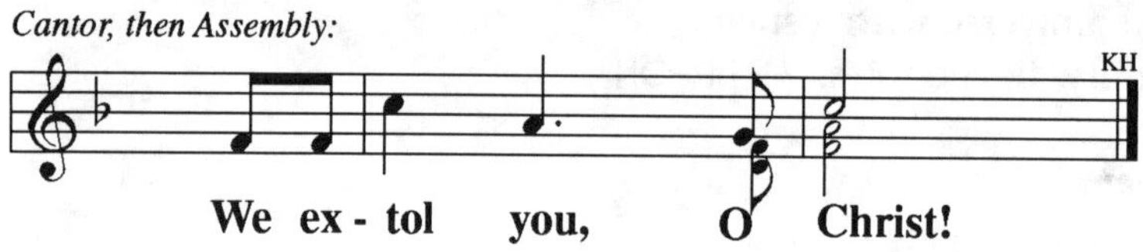

Cantor:

O living **Sav**ior, you **con**quer death,
O living **Sav**ior, you restore **us** to life,
O living **Sav**ior, you receive our **prom**ises,
O living **Sav**ior, you forgive **our** transgressions,
O living **Sav**ior, you favor us **with** prosperity,
O living **Sav**ior, you fill **us** with awe,
O living **Sav**ior, you call us **to** your presence,
O living **Sav**ior, you judge **us** with equity,
O living **Sav**ior, you bless us **with** your coming,

Our Father ...

Prayer
O redeeming God,
you shine the light of the risen Son upon us:
may that brightness guide us on our way today
as we look to the resurrection of your Son, Jesus Christ. **Amen.**

CONCLUSION

Blessing

Bow your heads and pray that almighty God bless us.

O God most holy: make your face shine on us today. **Amen.**

O Son most compassionate: look upon us with mercy. **Amen.**

O Spirit most loving: give us peace. **Amen.**

And may God bless us
in the name of the Father, and of the Son, and of the Holy Spirit. **Amen.**

Sign of Peace/Dismissal

Let us look upon the radiant face of others and offer a sign of peace.

SATURDAY 2 Evening Prayer

LIGHT SERVICE

Proclamation of the Light

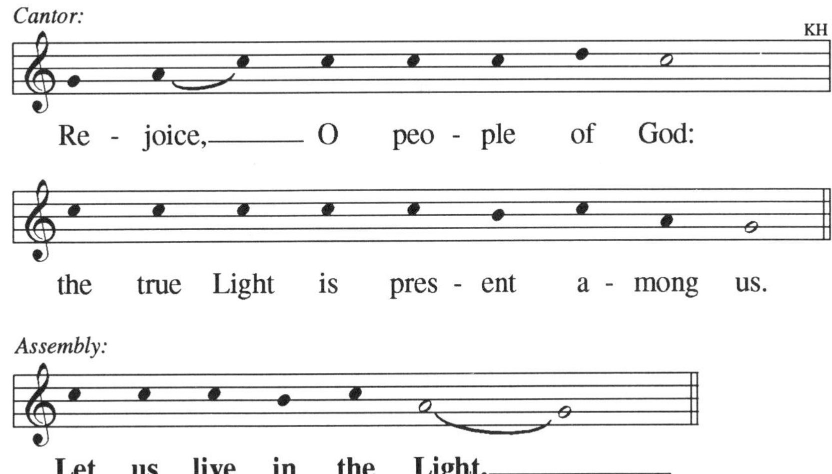
Cantor:
KH
Re - joice, O peo - ple of God:
the true Light is pres - ent a - mong us.
Assembly:
Let us live in the Light.

Evening Hymn

Thanksgiving for the Light

Cantor:
KH
We praise and thank you, O won-drous Cre - a - tor.

Your pow - er lifts the great light in the heav - ens.
Your glo - ry shines forth in the ris - en Son.
Your maj - es - ty lies o - ver all of cre - a - tion.
Your splen - dor clothes us with dig - ni - ty
and hon - or. Your good - ness o - ver-comes an - y
weak - ness. Your boun-ty sat - is - fies all hun - ger.
Your grace pro - claims our des - ti - ny.
Re - joice, O ho - ly peo - ple, in this great Light:
it is our sure sal - va - tion and glo - rious free - dom.
As our week-ly cel - e - bra - tion of res - ur - rec - tion draws near,

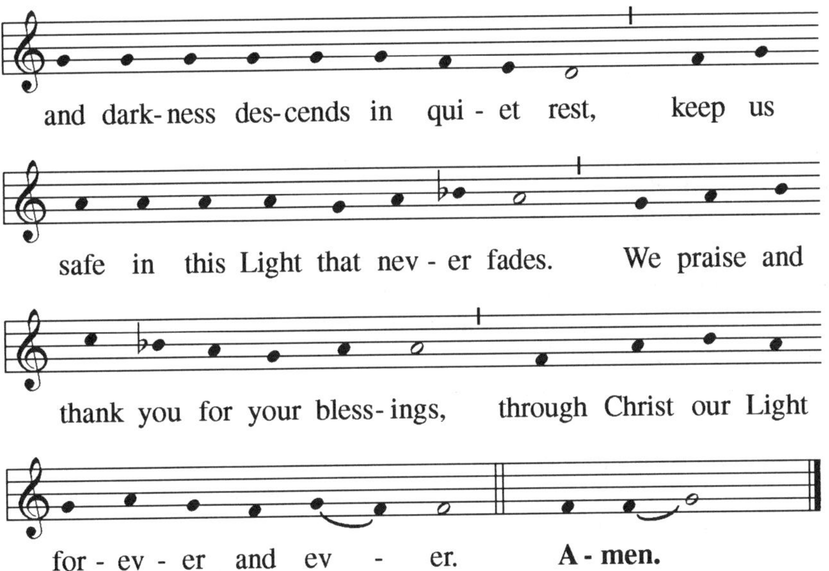
and dark- ness des- cends in qui - et rest, keep us
safe in this Light that nev - er fades. We praise and
thank you for your bless- ings, through Christ our Light
for - ev - er and ev - er. A - men.

PSALMODY

Psalm 141 *Psalm of David.*

ANTIPHON
KH
Let my prayer rise like in - cense.

O LORD, I cry **to** you:
"Hasten to me,
  listen to my voice
  when I cry **to** you."
Let my prayer rise
  like incense in **your** presence,
the lifting up of my hands
  like an evening **off**ering. ANTIPHON

Set, O LORD,
  a guard over **my** mouth,
keep the door of **my** lips.
Do not incline my heart to any evil,
  to performing wicked deeds
  with those who work **in**iquity;
let me not partake **in** their feasting. ANTIPHON

When a just person strikes me, it is **a** favor;
and when I am corrected, it is like anoin**ting** oil.
May my head never **re**fuse it,
while my prayer stands firm against **e**vil doings.

Let wicked judges be smashed against **the** rock,
and they will understand that my words **were** measured.
Like plowed and broken furrows on **the** land,
their bones are shattered at the **mouth** of Sheol. ANTIPHON

But my eyes look to you,
  O LORD, **my** Lord.
In you I take refuge;
  do not pour out **my** life.
Keep me from the snare they have prepared for me
  and from the traps of those who cre**ate** emptiness.
Let the wicked fall into their nets
  while I a**lone** escape. ANTIPHON

Psalm Prayer
O merciful God,
you hear the voice of those who call to you:
as our evening prayer rises on incense,
so may our gaze turn toward you forever and ever. **Amen.**

Psalm 30 *Psalm of David. Song for the dedication of the temple.*

ANTIPHON

KH
I will ex- alt you, God: you have set me free.

I will ex**alt** you, O LORD,
for you have **set** me free
and have not allowed my enemies to re**joice** over me. ANTIPHON

O LORD my God,
  I have cried to you and **you** have healed me.
O LORD, you have brought my soul
  up from Sheol.
You have restored me to life,
  preventing me from going **down** the Pit. ANTIPHON

Sing to the LORD, O **faith**ful ones;
celebrate a memorial **to** God's holiness.
For we stand only an instant in God's anger,
  but a whole lifetime in **God's** delight.

In the evening come tears,
  but in the morning come **shouts** of joy.
So I said in my tranquility,
  "I will not **falter** forever."
O LORD, in your delight
  you have established might **as** my mountain.

When you hid your face,
  I was **ter**rified.
To you, O **LORD**, I cry
and to you, O Lord, I raise my **sup**plication.

What profit is there in my blood,
  in my going down **to** the Pit?
Does dust give you thanks,
  and **tell** your truth?
Listen, O LORD, and have mercy;
  O LORD, be a **help** to me. ANTIPHON

You have changed my **mourning** to dancing;
you have **loosened** my sackcloth
and girded **me** with joy.

So I **sing** your glory;
I **am** not silent.
O LORD my God,
  I will give thanks to **you** forever. ANTIPHON

Psalm Prayer
Glorious God of the day,
you overcome darkness and restore us to life:
draw us to your loving presence,
heal us of all alienation,
and hear our evening prayer of thanksgiving
for we extol and give thanks to you always and everywhere. **Amen.**

Word of God

Magnificat
My soul does magni**fy** the Lord!
I delight in **God** my savior
who looked kindly **on** lowliness.

Now all ages will **call** me blessed
for the Mighty One **did** great things.
Holy is **God's** name;
mercy is from age to age for **those** in awe!

The Lord's strong arm did **migh**ty deeds:
confused the proud in **their** smug hearts;
toppled sovereigns **from** their thrones,
and exalted **hum**ble ones;
filled the hungering with **good** things,
and sent the rich **a**way empty.

The Lord helped servant **Is**rael
to re**mem**ber mercy,
as was spoken to Ab**ra**ham
and his descendants for**ev**ermore!

INTERCESSIONS

Petitions

Cantor, then Assembly:
Cantor:
KH
Come quick - ly, O my God!

Cantor:

To **guard** us,
To **strengthen** us,
To de**fend** us,
To de**liv**er us,
To **keep** us,
To **heal** us,
To re**store** us,
To de**light** us,
To en**rich** us,
To **bless** us,

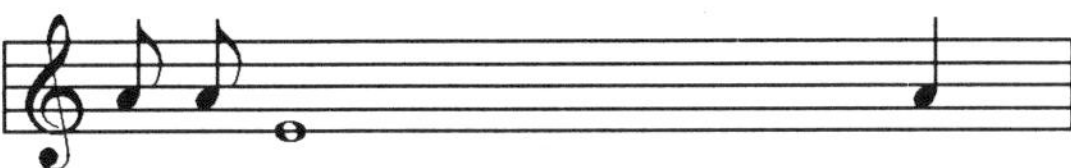

To re**ceive** those who have died this **day**,

Our Father ...

Prayer
Ever protector God and giver of life,
you sent your only Son
to gather your wandering children back
into your loving arms:
restore us to your holy courts
that we may praise you forever and ever. **Amen.**

CONCLUSION

Blessing
Bow your heads and pray that God bless us.
May God our creator nourish us as we await the fullness of resurrection. **Amen.**
May Jesus our brother lead us gently on the way. **Amen.**
May God the Spirit breathe within us while we wait with longing and patient endurance for the coming of our God. **Amen.**
And may God bless us
in the name of the Father, and of the Son, and of the Holy Spirit. **Amen.**

Sign of Peace/Dismissal
Let us offer one another a sign of the peace of Christ among us.

SUNDAY 2 Morning Praise

MORNING HYMN

PSALMODY

Psalm 95

ANTIPHON
KH
Let us shout with joy to our God!

Come! Let us shout with joy **for** the LORD;
let us make noise for the rock of our **sal**vation.
Let us come into God's presence in **thanks**giving;
with songs, let us **cry** out. ANTIPHON

For the LORD is a great God
  and a great Sovereign a**bove** all gods,
in whose hands are hidden the secrets of the earth
  and the treasures of **the** mountains.
The sea belongs to God,
  the one **who** made it,
and whose hands, too, shaped the **dry** land. ANTIPHON

Come! Let us bow **and** kneel down,
let us kneel down in the presence of the LORD our maker,
  who is **our** God;
we are **the** people,
the pasture, and **the** flock. ANTIPHON

Today, may you listen to the **voice** of God:
"Harden not your hearts as **at** Meribah,
as on the day at Massah in the desert
  where your ancestors test**ed** me.
They tried me even though they had seen **my** works.

Forty years I was disgusted by that **gen**eration,
and I said: 'They are a people of twisted hearts,
they did not recognize **my** ways.'
I swore indeed in **my** anger:
'They will not enter into my rest**ing**-place.'" ANTIPHON

Psalm Prayer
God of salvation,
you are our strength and sanctuary:
we bow down before your awe-inspiring majesty and creating power.
Draw your people to yourself
through your risen Son Jesus Christ. **Amen.**

Psalm 150

ANTIPHON

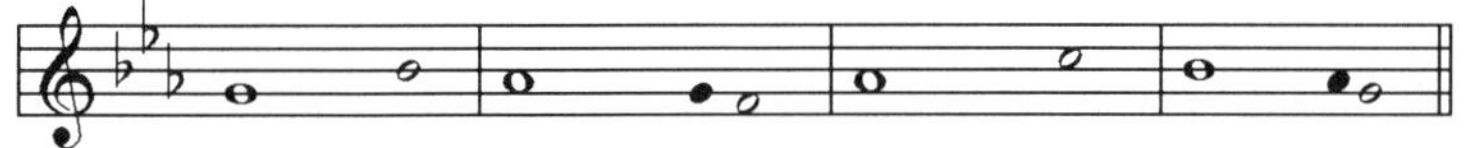

Praise God for **ho**liness;
praise God for the firmament **of** might.

Praise God for the mighty **deeds**;
praise God for unlimit**ed** greatness. ANTIPHON

Praise God with blast of **trumpet**;
praise God with lyre **and** harp.

Praise God with cymbal and **dance**;
praise God with strings **and** pipes. ANTIPHON

Praise God with resounding **drums**;
praise God with clamor**ous** drums.

Let all living **creatures**
praise **the** LORD. ANTIPHON

Psalm Prayer
O glorious God,
you are worthy of all praise:
may our whole being declare your marvels
and all creation sound a song of worship now and forever. **Amen.**

Word of God

Benedictus
Blessed be the Lord God of **Israel**,
who visited and redeemed the **people**,
who raised up for us a **mighty** savior
from the house of **ser**vant David.

Just as the Lord spoke through the mouths of the holy prophets of **old**—
salvation comes out of the hands of our enemies and those who **hate** us,
that, with our ancestors, we might perform **works** of mercy,
remembering the holy covenant **sworn** to Abraham—

so does the Lord deliver us from the hands **of** our enemies,
that we might serve without fear before **the** Lord,
worshiping in **ho**liness
and in righteousness **all** our days.

And you also, child, will be called a prophet of God Most **High**:
for you will go before the Lord to prepare a **way**,
bringing people knowledge of salvation by for**giveness** of sins;
because of the deep and tender mercy **of** our God.

Whereby a light rising from on high will **visit** us
to appear to those in darkness and in a shadow **of** death,
to guide our feet along a **straight**, sure path
into a **way** of peace.

INTERCESSIONS

Invocations

Cantor, then Assembly:

Cantor:

O risen Christ, **splen**did radiance **of** our God,
O risen Christ, **living** icon of **lov**ing covenant,
O risen Christ, **stead**fast rock of **our** salvation,
O risen Christ, **bril**liant joy of **a** new day,
O risen Christ, **satis**fying refreshment **for** the weary,
O risen Christ, **un**ending celebration of **res**urrection,
O risen Christ, **true** promise of ever**last**ing life,
O risen Christ, **stead**fast hope **in** the Spirit,

Our Father ...

Prayer
God of the universe,
you create all things good and keep them in existence:
we stand before you in the radiant light of Jesus' resurrection.
Receive our morning prayer of praise
as a fitting reflection of our covenant with you.
Draw us to your presence
so that we might offer you praise and thanksgiving by our lives
now and always.
We pray through Jesus the risen Christ. **Amen.**

CONCLUSION

Blessing
Let us bow before our ever-creating God and ask for a blessing.
May the God of dawn bless us with risen life. **Amen.**
May the Son of justice bless us with unwavering courage. **Amen.**
May the Spirit of goodness bless us with glad thankfulness. **Amen.**
And may God bless us
in the name of the Father, and of the Son, and of the Holy Spirit. **Amen.**

Sign of Peace/Dismissal
Let us offer one another a sign of the presence
of our creative, redeeming, and loving God among us.

SUNDAY 2 Evening Prayer

LIGHT SERVICE

Proclamation of the Light

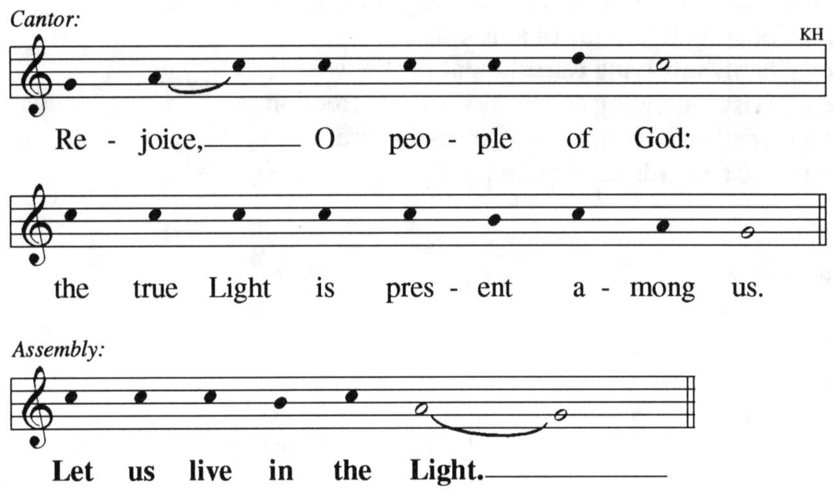
Cantor:
KH
Re - joice, O peo - ple of God:
the true Light is pres - ent a - mong us.
Assembly:
Let us live in the Light.

Evening Hymn

Thanksgiving for the Light

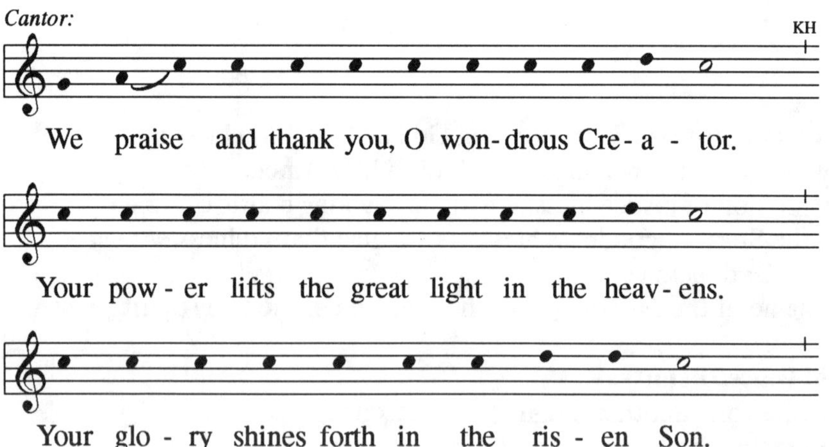
Cantor:
KH
We praise and thank you, O won-drous Cre - a - tor.
Your pow - er lifts the great light in the heav - ens.
Your glo - ry shines forth in the ris - en Son.

Your maj - es - ty lies o - ver all of cre - a - tion.
Your splen - dor clothes us with dig - ni - ty
and hon - or. Your good - ness o - ver-comes an - y
weak - ness. Your boun-ty sat - is - fies all hun - ger.
Your grace pro - claims our des - ti - ny.
Re - joice, O ho - ly peo - ple, in this great Light:
it is our sure sal - va - tion and glo - rious free - dom.
As our week-ly cel - e - bra - tion of res - ur - rec - tion draws to a
close, and dark-ness des-cends in qui - et rest, keep us
safe in this Light that nev - er fades. We praise and

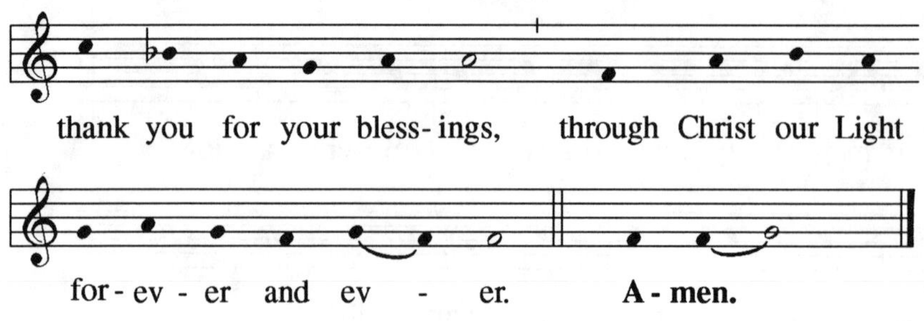
thank you for your bless-ings, through Christ our Light
for-ev-er and ev - er. A-men.

PSALMODY

Psalm 141 *Psalm of David.*

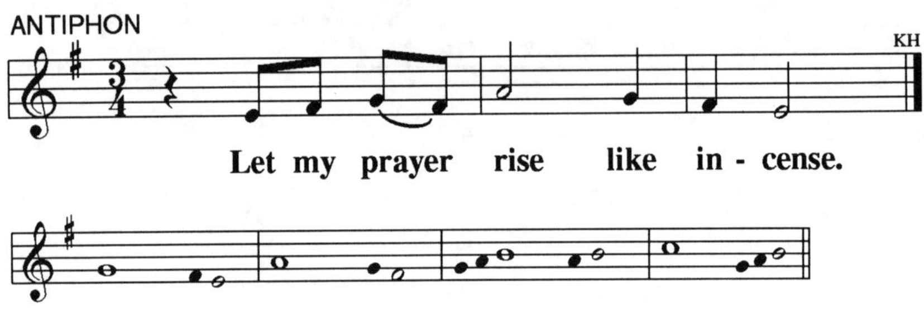
ANTIPHON
KH
Let my prayer rise like in-cense.

O LORD, I cry **to** you:
"Hasten to me,
  listen to my voice
  when I cry **to** you."
Let my prayer rise
  like incense in **your** presence,
the lifting up of my hands
  like an evening **of**fering. ANTIPHON

Set, O LORD,
  a guard over **my** mouth,
keep the door of **my** lips.
Do not incline my heart to any evil,
  to performing wicked deeds
  with those who work **ini**quity;
let me not partake **in** their feasting. ANTIPHON

When a just person strikes me, it is **a** favor;
and when I am corrected, it is like anoin**ting** oil.
May my head never **re**fuse it,
while my prayer stands firm against **e**vil doings.

Let wicked judges be smashed against **the** rock,
and they will understand that my words **were** measured.
Like plowed and broken furrows on **the** land,
their bones are shattered at the **mouth** of Sheol. ANTIPHON

But my eyes look to you,
  O LORD, **my** Lord.
In you I take refuge;
  do not pour out **my** life.
Keep me from the snare they have prepared for me
  and from the traps of those who cre**ate** emptiness.
Let the wicked fall into their nets
  while I a**lone** escape. ANTIPHON

Psalm Prayer
O merciful God,
you hear the voice of those who call to you
with faith and love:
as our evening prayer rises to you on incense,
so may our gaze turn toward you now and always. **Amen.**

Psalm 67 *To the choirmaster. With stringed instruments. Psalm. Song.*

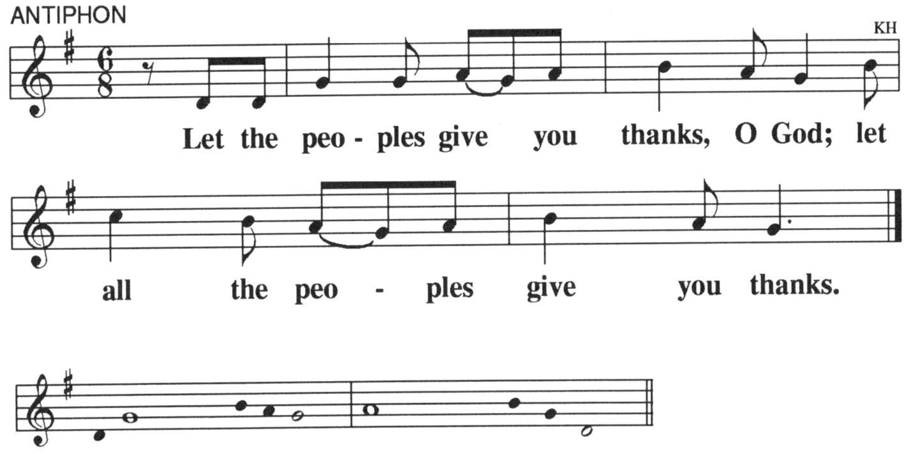
ANTIPHON
KH
Let the peo - ples give you thanks, O God; let
all the peo - ples give you thanks.

May God have mercy on us and **bless** us.
May God's face **shine** among us.

For your way is known **over** the earth,
and your salvation is known a**mong** all nations. ANTIPHON

May the nations rejoice and **shout** with joy,
for you judge the peoples rightly
  and the nations on the **earth** you guide. ANTIPHON

The earth has **given** its fruit.
May God, our God, **bless** us.

May God **bless** us,
and let all ends of the **earth** show reverence. ANTIPHON

Psalm Prayer
O gracious and powerful God,
you have blessed us with abundant gifts:
may all nations give thanks
and praise to your name forever and ever. **Amen.**

Word of God

Magnificat
My soul does magni**fy** the Lord!
I delight in **God** my savior
who looked kindly **on** lowliness.

Now all ages will **call** me blessed
for the Mighty One **did** great things.
Holy is **God's** name;
mercy is from age to age for **those** in awe!

The Lord's strong arm did **migh**ty deeds:
confused the proud in **their** smug hearts;
toppled sovereigns **from** their thrones,
and exalted **hum**ble ones;
filled the hungering with **good** things,
and sent the rich **a**way empty.

The Lord helped servant **Is**rael
to re**mem**ber mercy,
as was spoken to Ab**ra**ham
and his descendants for**e**vermore!

INTERCESSIONS

Petitions

Cantor, then Assembly:

Cantor:

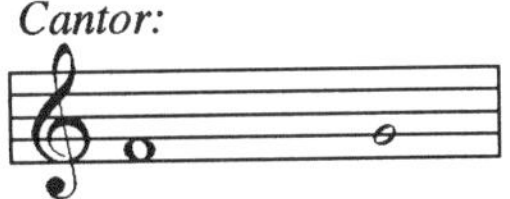

For the **Church** ...
For all **nations** ...
For civil **leaders** ...
For **cities** ...
For **farmlands** ...
For natural **resources** ...
For **children** ...
For **youth** ...
For the **oppressed** ...
For all those who died this **day** ...

Our Father ...

Prayer

O God,
you make us glad with the joy of your risen Son:
as we draw to a close our weekly celebration of redemption,
regard not our fickle ways and
guard us in the days to come
for we long to be in your sanctuary forever and ever. **Amen.**

CONCLUSION

Blessing

Let us bow before our redeeming God and ask for a blessing.
May the God who creates bless us with renewed strength. **Amen.**
May the God who saves bless us with fearless accountability. **Amen.**
May the God who anoints bless us with lasting courage. **Amen.**
And may God bless us
in the name of the Father, and of the Son, and of the Holy Spirit. **Amen.**

Sign of Peace/Dismissal

Let us strengthen one another with peace.

Advent
Christmas
Epiphany

MONDAY-TUESDAY-WEDNESDAY-THURSDAY
Morning Praise

ADVENT MORNING HYMN

PSALMODY

Psalm 143 *Psalm of David.*

Solo 1 O LORD, hear my prayer;
in your faithfulness give ear to my supplications.
Answer me in your justice.

All Do not enter into judgment against your servant,
for no living creature is just before you.

Solo 1 For the enemy has pursued me,
crushed my life to the ground,
and made me sit in darkness with those long dead.
My spirit languishes within me;
within me my heart is devastated.

Solo 2 I remember the days of the past;
I ponder over all your deeds.
I meditate upon the work of your hands.
I stretch out my hands to you--
to you my soul is like parched land.

Selah (pause).

Solo 1 Quickly answer me, O LORD,
for my spirit fails.
Do not hide your face from me
or I resemble those who go down the Pit.
Let me hear in the morning of your steadfast love,
for in you I put my trust.

Solo 2 Let me know the way I should go,
for to you I lift up my soul.
Deliver me from my enemies, O LORD,
for in you I take refuge.

Solo 1 Teach me to do your will,
for you are my God.
Let your good spirit guide me
in the land of integrity.

Solo 2 For the sake of your name, O LORD, give me life.
In your justice, bring me out of distress.
In your steadfast love, cut off my enemies
and destroy all my adversaries,
for I am your servant.

Psalm 110 *Of David. Psalm.*

Solo 1 Thus says the LORD to my lord:
"Sit on my right
until I place your enemies
as a footstool for your feet."

Choir 1 Let the LORD send from Zion
the scepter of your strength.
Rule in the midst of your enemies.

Choir 2 Your people bring free offerings
on the day of your might
in holy splendor.
From the womb of dawn,
a dew of rejuvenation comes to you.

Solo 1 The LORD has promised
and will not repent:
"According to my word,
you are a priest forever, my king of justice."

Choir 1 The Lord is at your right,
who has smashed rulers on the day of wrath.
The Lord judges against the nations,
piling them with corpses.

Choir 2 The Lord has smashed heads
all over the land.
From a torrent the Lord drinks on the way,
and rises up in triumph.

Word of God

Benedictus
Blessed be the Lord God of **Israel**,
who visited and redeemed the **people**,
who raised up for us a **mighty** savior
from the house of **ser**vant David.

Just as the Lord spoke through the mouths of the holy prophets of **old**—
salvation comes out of the hands of our enemies and those who **hate** us,
that, with our ancestors, we might perform **works** of mercy,
remembering the holy covenant **sworn** to Abraham—

so does the Lord deliver us from the hands **of** our enemies,
that we might serve without fear before **the** Lord,
worshiping in **ho**liness
and in righteousness **all** our days.

And you also, child, will be called a prophet of God Most **High**:
for you will go before the Lord to prepare a **way**,
bringing people knowledge of salvation by for**giveness** of sins;
because of the deep and tender mercy **of** our God.

Whereby a light rising from on high will **vis**it us
to appear to those in darkness and in a shadow **of** death,
to guide our feet along a **straight**, sure path
into a **way** of peace.

INTERCESSIONS

Invocations

Cantor, then Assembly:

Cantor: KH
Come in glo - ry, Christ!

Cantor:
Assembly:
To res-cue your peo-ple,
Assembly:
To sanc - ti - fy your Church,
To lead us in - to light,
Assembly:
To free us from guilt,
To ren-der your judg-ment,
To show us your jus - tice,
To teach us your will,
Assembly:
To re - veal your love,
To bring peace to na-tions,
To de - stroy all ev - il,
Assembly:
To es-tab-lish your vic-t'ry,
To raise up your peo-ple,

Our Father ...

Prayer

Good and glorious God,
you come to judge the nations
and bring us to peace:
open us to your faithful presence
and teach us to do your justice

as we await that day
when we may sit at your right hand.
We pray through Jesus Christ your victorious Son. **Amen.**

CONCLUSION

Blessing
May the God who comes in an abundance of ways bless us
in the name of the Father, and of the Son, and of the Holy Spirit. **Amen.**

Dismissal
Go forth and be surprised by God's glorious comings. **Thanks be to God.**

ADVENT Weeks 1 & 2
MONDAY-TUESDAY-WEDNESDAY-THURSDAY
Evening Prayer

ADVENT EVENING HYMN

PSALMODY

Psalm 36 *To the choirmaster. In honor of David, the servant of the Lord.*

Solo 1 The deceitful words of the wicked
enter my heart.
No fear of God
confronts their eyes;
in their own eyes they are flattered
when they admit their guilt and hate.
The words of their mouths speak emptiness and deceit;
they have ceased to discern how to do good.
Even when resting they contemplate emptiness;
they stand on a way that is not good
and do not despise evil.

All O LORD, in heaven is your steadfast love;
your truth rises to the firmament.

Choir 1 Your justice is like the highest mountains,
your judgment is like a great abyss.
Humankind and beast, you save, O LORD.

All How precious is your steadfast love, O God!

Choir 2 Humankind takes refuge
in the shade of your wings.
They are gratified with oil in your house,
and you inebriate them with the torrent of your delights.

All For with you is the source of life;
in your light, we see light.

Solo 1 Extend your steadfast love to those who know you,
and your justice to upright hearts.
Let not the foot of the arrogant touch me,
nor the hand of the wicked lead me astray.
The makers of emptiness fell,
they stumbled and could not rise.

Psalm 131 *Song of ascents (pilgrimages). Of David.*

Solo 1 O LORD, my heart has not boasted
and my eyes have not pretended.
Nor have I engaged in things too great
and too wondrous for me.

Solo 2 Have I not calmed
and quieted my soul?
Like a weaned child against a mother,
like a weaned child within me, so is my soul.

All Put your hope, O Israel, in the LORD,
from now and forever.

Word of God

Magnificat
My soul does magni**fy** the Lord!
I delight in **God** my savior
who looked kindly **on** lowliness.

Now all ages will **call** me blessed
for the Mighty One **did** great things.
Holy is **God's** name;
mercy is from age to age for **those** in awe!

The Lord's strong arm did **might**y deeds:
confused the proud in **their** smug hearts;
toppled sovereigns **from** their thrones,
and exalted **hum**ble ones;
filled the hungering with **good** things,
and sent the rich **a**way empty.

The Lord helped servant **Is**rael
to re**mem**ber mercy,
as was spoken to Ab**ra**ham
and his descendants for**ev**ermore!

INTERCESSIONS

Petitions

Cantor, then Assembly:

Cantor:

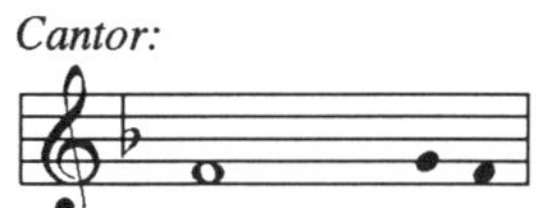

That we may **not** fear ...
That we may not be **emp**ty ...
That we may not do **e**vil ...
That we may not spurn **jus**tice ...
That we may not dwell in **dark**ness ...
That we may **see** light ...
That we may engage in **God's** things ...
That we may find calm and **qui**et ...
That we **may** hope ...
That those who have died may enjoy fullness of life for**ev**er ...

Our Father ...

Prayer
O God who is now and is to come,
you are ever present to us:
receive our evening prayer
by the kind judgment of your steadfast love.
Shelter us this night from all harm
and grant us rest now and always. **Amen.**

CONCLUSION

Blessing
May the Spirit hold us
against God's bosom of love and bless us
in the name of the Father, and of the Son, and of the Holy Spirit. **Amen.**

Dismissal
Go with quieted soul to rest in the hope of God. **Thanks be to God.**

ADVENT Weeks 1 & 2
FRIDAY Morning Praise

ADVENT MORNING HYMN

PSALMODY

Psalm 51 *To the choirmaster. Psalm of David. In the coming to him of Nathan the prophet, after David had been with Bathsheba.*

ANTIPHON

Be gracious to **me**, O God,
in your **stead**fast love.
According to the abundance **of** your mercy
blot out my **trans**gressions. ANTIPHON

Cleanse me completely **from** my guilt
and purify me **from** my sin.
For my transgressions I do **rec**ognize,
and my sin stands always **be**fore me.

Against you alone **have** I sinned,
and what is evil in your eyes **I** have done.
Thus you may be declared just in your ways,
  and pure **in** your judgments.
Indeed, I was born guilty,
  already a sinner when my mother **con**ceived me. ANTIPHON

Surely in truth **you** delight,
and deep within my self you will **teach** me wisdom.
Cleanse me from my sin with hyssop and I **will** be pure,
wash me and I shall be brighter **than** snow.

Let me hear glad**ness** and joy,
let the bones you **broke** exult.
Turn your face **from** my sins
and blot out all my iniq**ui**ties. ANTIPHON

Create in me a pure **heart**, O God,
and renew within me **a** firm spirit.
Do not dismiss me **from** your presence,
and do not take away from me your ho**ly** spirit.

Give me back the joy of **your** salvation,
and let a willing spirit lie **o**ver me.
I will teach transgres**sors** your ways,
and sinners will turn back **to** you. ANTIPHON

Deliver me from bloodshed, O God,
  God of **my** salvation,
and my tongue will **sing** your justice.
O Lord, o**pen** my lips,
and my mouth will tell **your** praise.

For you take no pleasure in **sac**rifice,
and you would not accept an offering were **I** to give it.
The perfect sacrifice for God is a **brok**en spirit.
A broken and humble heart,
  O God, you will not **de**spise. ANTIPHON

In your kindness bring prosperi**ty** to Zion;
rebuild the walls of Je**ru**salem.
Then you can delight in sacrifices of justice,
  burnt and complete **of**ferings;
then bulls can be offered on **your** altars. ANTIPHON

Psalm Prayer
O God,
you desire sacrifice from those who turn to you:
bring us prosperity as we delight in anticipating
the coming of your Son, Jesus Christ. **Amen.**

Word of God

Benedictus
Blessed be the Lord God of **Israel**,
who visited and redeemed the **people**,
who raised up for us a **mighty** savior
from the house of **ser**vant David.

Just as the Lord spoke through the mouths of the holy prophets of **old**—
salvation comes out of the hands of our enemies and those who **hate** us,
that, with our ancestors, we might perform **works** of mercy,
remembering the holy covenant **sworn** to Abraham—

so does the Lord deliver us from the hands **of** our enemies,
that we might serve without fear before **the** Lord,
worshiping in **ho**liness
and in righteousness **all** our days.

And you also, child, will be called a prophet of God Most **High**:
for you will go before the Lord to prepare a **way**,
bringing people knowledge of salvation by for**giveness** of sins;
because of the deep and tender mercy **of** our God.

Whereby a light rising from on high will **vis**it us
to appear to those in darkness and in a shadow **of** death,
to guide our feet along a **straight**, sure path
into a **way** of peace.

INTERCESSIONS

Invocations

Cantor, then Assembly:

KH
Come quick- ly, O God of glo - ry!

Cantor:

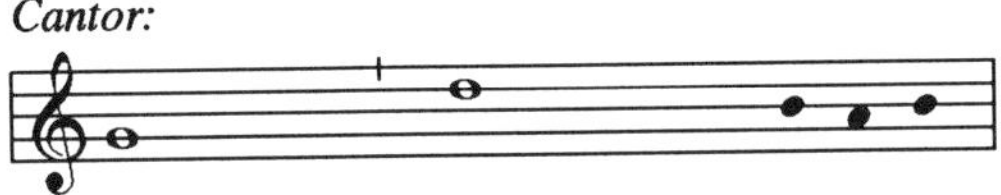

Jesus our Savior, be gra**cious** to us,
Jesus our Savior, blot out **our** transgressions,
Jesus our Savior, cleanse and puri**fy** us,
Jesus our Savior, bestow mer**cy** and truth,
Jesus our Savior, awaken our de**light** in you,
Jesus our Savior, teach **us** your wisdom,
Jesus our Savior, create in us **a** pure heart,
Jesus our Savior, renew your spir**it** within us,
Jesus our Savior, grant **us** salvation,
Jesus our Savior, draw us to **tell** your praise,

Our Father ...

Prayer
O saving God,
you visit your people to bring redemption
by your wondrous mercy:
extend to us this day your guiding hand
so that we may serve you faithfully.
We pray through Jesus Christ our Savior. **Amen.**

CONCLUSION

Blessing
May God, source of mercy and promise of redemption,
bless us now and always
in the name of the Father, and of the Son, and of the Holy Spirit. **Amen.**

Dismissal
Go forth to prepare for the coming of our God. **Thanks be to God.**

ADVENT Weeks 1 & 2
FRIDAY Evening Prayer

ADVENT EVENING HYMN

PSALMODY

Psalm 43

ANTIPHON

Judge **me**, O God,
and plead my trial
  against a nation **un**faithful.
From people of deceit **and** iniquity,
deli**ver** me. ANTIPHON

Since you are the God who **is** my fortress,
Why did you **re**ject me?
Why should I **wander** in darkness,
hard pressed by the en**e**my? ANTIPHON

Send your light **and** your truth;
they **will** guide me.
They will lead me to your **ho**ly mountain
and to **your** tents. ANTIPHON

So I will come to the **altar** of God,
to God who makes me rejoice **and** dance;
with harp **I** will praise
God **my** God. ANTIPHON

Why are you cast down my soul
  and dis**turbed** within me?
Put your hope **in** God—
my salvation **and** my God—
whom I will praise **a**gain. ANTIPHON

Psalm Prayer
O God,
you wil return to judge the world in righteousness:
send your light and truth
that we may come before you
fitting to live with you forever and ever. **Amen.**

Psalm 63 *Psalm of David. While he was in the desert of Judah.*

ANTIPHON

KH
O God, I seek you, my soul thirsts for you.

omit last time

O God, you are my God, **I** seek you;
my **soul** thirsts **for** you.
My flesh longs for you
  in a dry and **wast**ed land,
deprived **of** water. ANTIPHON

So in the sanctuary I have contemplated you
  to see your might and your **glo**ry.
Because your **stead**fast love is better than life,
  my lips will **praise** you.
So I will bless you **all** my life;
in your name I will raise **my** hands.

As with milk and rich food,
  my soul **is** filled;
my **mouth** gives praise with joy**ful** lips.
I remember you up**on** my bed,
pondering you throughout **the** night.

For you were a help **for** me;
in the **shade** of your wings I **keep** singing.
My soul **clings** to you;
your right hand **up**holds me. ANTIPHON

But let those who seek my des**truc**tion
be **cast** into the depths of **the** earth.
Let them be given over to the power **of** the sword;
let them become a prey **for** jackals. ANTIPHON

Then the king shall rejoice **in** God.
All **those** who swear by God will **be** praised,
for the mouths of liars will **be** shut. ANTIPHON

Psalm Prayer
O God of strength and glory,
you are the only One we seek:
keep us in the shade of your wings
that we may be ready to meet you
when you come now and always. **Amen.**

Word of God

Magnificat
My soul does magni**fy** the Lord!
I delight in **God** my savior
who looked kindly **on** lowliness.

Now all ages will **call** me blessed
for the Mighty One **did** great things.
Holy is **God's** name;
mercy is from age to age for **those** in awe!

The Lord's strong arm did **mighty** deeds:
confused the proud in **their** smug hearts;
toppled sovereigns **from** their thrones,
and exalted **hum**ble ones;
filled the hungering with **good** things,
and sent the rich **a**way empty.

The Lord helped servant **Is**rael
to re**mem**ber mercy,

as was spoken to Ab**ra**ham
and his descendants for**ev**ermore!

INTERCESSIONS

Petitions

Cantor, then Assembly:

Cantor:

From **ter**rible **judg**ments ...
From un**faith**ful **na**tions ...
From de**ceit** and ini**q**uity ...
From re**jec**tion and **dark**ness ...
From **dry** and wasted **lands** ...
From des**truc**tion and **lies** ...
To re**ceive** the faithful de**part**ed ...

Our Father ...

Prayer
God of power and might,
you judge all peoples in righteousness:
we raise our hands to you
in confident response to your faithfulness to us.
Grant us mercy and forgiveness
as we prepare for the coming of your Son in glory.
We pray through Jesus Christ. **Amen.**

CONCLUSION

Blessing
May the gracious God keep us and bless us
in the name of the Father, and of the Son, and of the Holy Spirit. **Amen.**

Dismissal
Rest in the peace of God as we await the glorious coming of our Savior Jesus Christ. **Thanks be to God.**

ADVENT Weeks 1 & 2
SATURDAY & SUNDAY Morning Praise

ADVENT MORNING HYMN

PSALMODY

Psalm 67 *To the choirmaster. With stringed instruments. Psalm. Song.*

ANTIPHON
KH
Let the peo - ples give you thanks, O God; let
all the peo - ples give you thanks.

May God have mercy on us and **bless** us.
May God's face **shine** among us.

For your way is known **over** the earth,
and your salvation is known a**mong** all nations. ANTIPHON

May the nations rejoice and **shout** with joy,
for you judge the peoples rightly
  and the nations on the **earth** you guide. ANTIPHON

The earth has **given** its fruit.
May God, our God, **bless** us.

May God **bless** us,
and let all ends of the **earth** show reverence. ANTIPHON

Psalm Prayer

O God,
you judge the nations rightly:
be with your people this day.
Bless us with guidance and fruitfulness
as we eagerly await the return of Jesus Christ. **Amen.**

Psalm 149

ANTIPHON
KH
Let us re- joice in God, our Sav - ior!

sing with first and final antiphon
Al - le- lu - ia! Al - le - lu - ia!

Sing a new song to the LORD,
  God's praise in the assembly of the **faith**ful.
Let Israel rejoice in its Creator,
  the children of Zion exult in **their** Sovereign.
Let them praise God's name with **danc**ing;
with drums and harp, let them play music **for** God. ANTIPHON

For the LORD takes delight in the people,
  adorning the poor with sal**va**tion.
Let the faithful exult **with** glory,
let them ring out joy on their **couch**es,
and cry out the great deeds of God from **their** throats. ANTIPHON

With two-edged swords in their hands,
  let them do vengeance against peoples
  and rebuke **na**tions;
let them tie their rulers with fetters
  and their nobles with chains **of** bronze,
in order to accomplish judgment against them as **writ**ten.
This is honor for all **the** faithful. ANTIPHON

Psalm Prayer
O God,
you are worthy of all praise:
we join the heavenly choir
and sing out your glory and splendor.
May we live our day in your presence
now and always through the risen Christ. **Amen.**

Word of God

Benedictus

Blessed be the Lord God of **Israel**,
who visited and redeemed the **people**,
who raised up for us a **mighty** savior
from the house of **ser**vant David.

Just as the Lord spoke through the mouths of the holy prophets of **old**—
salvation comes out of the hands of our enemies and those who **hate** us,
that, with our ancestors, we might perform **works** of mercy,
remembering the holy covenant **sworn** to Abraham—

so does the Lord deliver us from the hands **of** our enemies,
that we might serve without fear before **the** Lord,
worshiping in **ho**liness
and in righteousness **all** our days.

And you also, child, will be called a prophet of God Most **High**:
for you will go before the Lord to prepare a **way**,
bringing people knowledge of salvation by for**giveness** of sins;
because of the deep and tender mercy **of** our God.

Whereby a light rising from on high will **vis**it us
to appear to those in darkness and in a shadow **of** death,
to guide our feet along a **straight**, sure path
into a **way** of peace.

INTERCESSIONS

Invocations

Cantor, then Assembly:

Cantor:

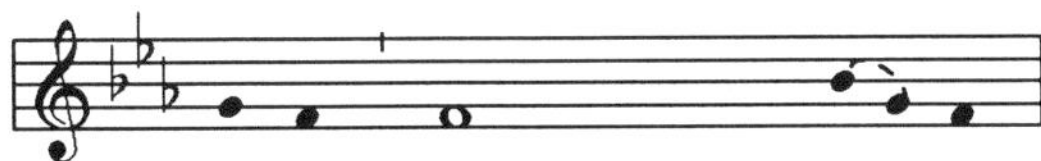

O Jesus **Christ**, have **mercy** on us ...
O Jesus **Christ**, **bless** us ...
O Jesus **Christ**, let your face **shine** on us ...
O Jesus **Christ**, make your salv**a**tion known ...
O Jesus **Christ**, judge the **na**tions rightly ...
O Jesus **Christ**, **reward** our labors ...
O Jesus **Christ**, take delight **in** your people ...
O Jesus **Christ**, continue **your** great deeds ...

Our Father ...

Prayer
Glorious God,
you bring us life and promise us the reward of glory
by the death and resurrection of your victorious Son:
be with us this day
as we celebrate your loving mercy.
We pray through Jesus Christ. **Amen.**

CONCLUSION

Blessing
May the God of glory envelop us with light and bless us
in the name of the Father, and of the Son, and of the Holy Spirit. **Amen.**

Dismissal
Go forth to live with the expectation of glory. **Thanks be to God.**

ADVENT Weeks 1 & 2
SATURDAY & SUNDAY Evening Prayer

LIGHT SERVICE

Proclamation of the Light

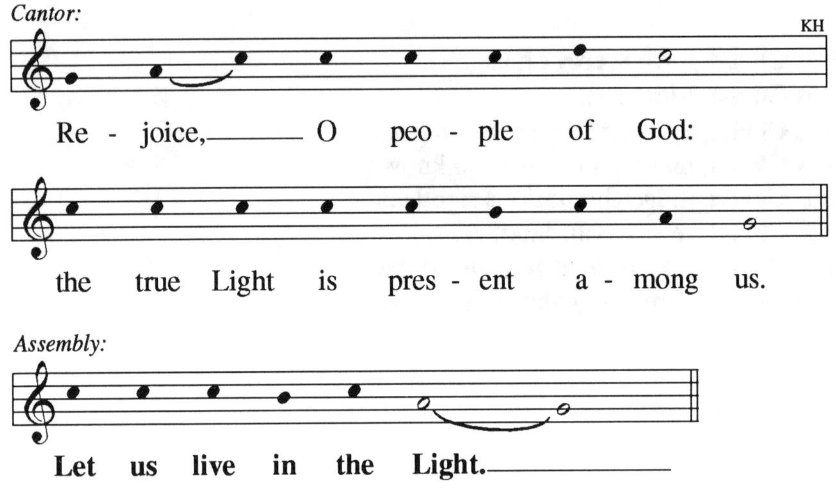

Advent Evening Hymn

Thanksgiving for the Light

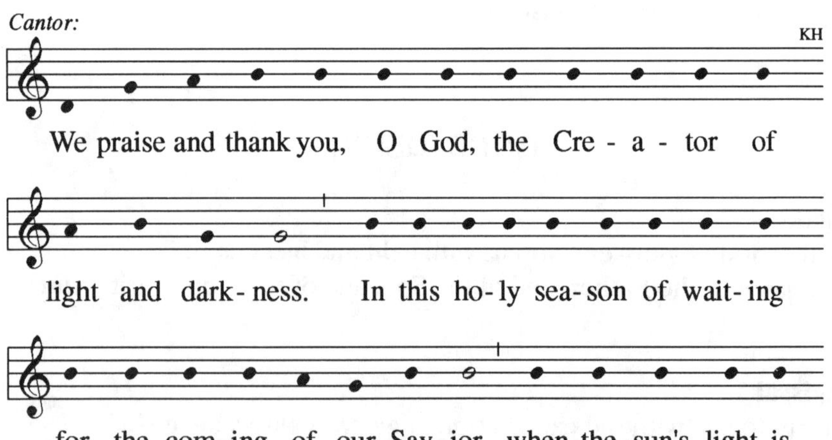

Cantor:
KH
We praise and thank you, O God, the Cre - a - tor of
light and dark- ness. In this ho- ly sea- son of wait- ing
for the com- ing of our Sav- ior, when the sun's light is

dim-in-ished by the grow-ing dark-ness of night, you re-veal
to us the e-ter-nal Light of your great splen-dor.
Through the pro-phets of old you call us to your cov-e-
nant of love. Now through the Spir-it you heal our
blind-ness and un-cov-er for us the glo-ry of your
pres-ence. Grant us a peace-ful night free from sin.
Free us to sing your praise and thanks-giv-ing, and keep us
ev-er in Christ. Through whom we of-fer you hon-or
and bless-ing in the u-ni-ty of the Ho-ly
Spir-it, now and al-ways and for ev-er

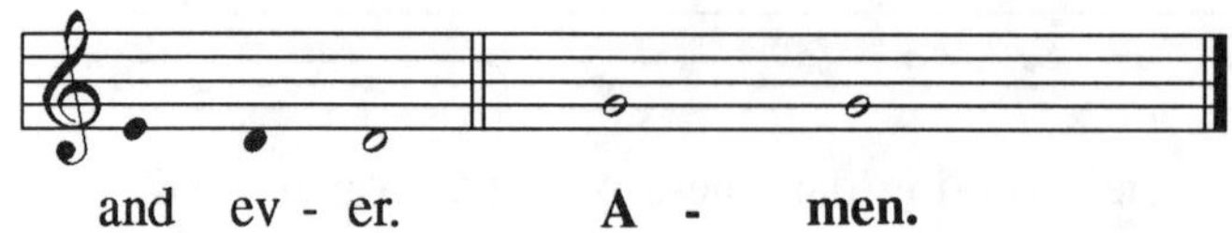
and ev - er. A - men.

PSALMODY

Psalm 141 *Psalm of David.*

ANTIPHON
KH
Let my prayer rise like in - cense.

O LORD, I cry **to** you:
"Hasten to me,
  listen to my voice
  when I cry **to** you."
Let my prayer rise
  like incense in **your** presence,
the lifting up of my hands
  like an evening **o**ffering. ANTIPHON

Set, O LORD,
  a guard over **my** mouth,
keep the door of **my** lips.
Do not incline my heart to any evil,
  to performing wicked deeds
  with those who work **ini**quity;
let me not partake **in** their feasting. ANTIPHON

When a just person strikes me, it is **a** favor;
and when I am corrected, it is like anoin**ting** oil.
May my head never **re**fuse it,
while my prayer stands firm against **e**vil doings.

Let wicked judges be smashed against **the** rock,
and they will understand that my words **were** measured.
Like plowed and broken furrows on **the** land,
their bones are shattered at the **mouth** of Sheol. ANTIPHON

But my eyes look to you,
  O LORD, **my** Lord.
In you I take refuge;
  do not pour out **my** life.
Keep me from the snare they have prepared for me
  and from the traps of those who cre**ate** emptiness.
Let the wicked fall into their nets
  while I a**lone** escape. ANTIPHON

Psalm Prayer

O God,
you come in glory and might:
we raise our evening prayer to you.
Hasten to us
that we may find refuge in you now and always. **Amen.**

Psalm 95

ANTIPHON

Come! Let us shout with joy **for** the LORD;
let us make noise for the rock of our **sal**vation.
Let us come into God's presence in **thanks**giving;
with songs, let us **cry** out. ANTIPHON

For the LORD is a great God
  and a great Sovereign a**bove** all gods,
in whose hands are hidden the secrets of the earth
  and the treasures of **the** mountains.
The sea belongs to God,

the one **who** made it,
and whose hands, too, shaped the **dry** land. ANTIPHON

Come! Let us bow **and** kneel down,
let us kneel down in the presence of the LORD our maker,
who is **our** God;
we are **the** people,
the pasture, and **the** flock. ANTIPHON

Today, may you listen to the **voice** of God:
"Harden not your hearts as **at** Meribah,
as on the day at Massah in the desert
where your ancestors test**ed** me.
They tried me even though they had seen **my** works.

Forty years I was disgusted by that **gen**eration,
and I said: 'They are a people of twisted hearts,
they did not recognize **my** ways.'
I swore indeed in **my** anger:
'They will not enter into my rest**ing**-place.'" ANTIPHON

Psalm Prayer
O God,
you speak to us and bring us joy by your presence:
draw us to yourself
that we may come to rest in you
through Jesus Christ. **Amen.**

Word of God

Magnificat

My soul does magni**fy** the Lord!
I delight in **God** my savior
who looked kindly **on** lowliness.

Now all ages will **call** me blessed
for the Mighty One **did** great things.
Holy is **God's** name;
mercy is from age to age for **those** in awe!

The Lord's strong arm did **might**y deeds:
confused the proud in **their** smug hearts;
toppled sovereigns **from** their thrones,
and exalted **hum**ble ones;
filled the hungering with **good** things,
and sent the rich **a**way empty.

The Lord helped servant **Is**rael
to re**mem**ber mercy,
as was spoken to Ab**ra**ham
and his descendants for**ev**ermore!

INTERCESSIONS

Petitions

Cantor, then Assembly:

Cantor:

With **haste**,
For **mercy**,
With **confidence**,
For **refuge**,
With **shouts**,
For for**giveness**,
With thanks**giving**,
For a resting place for the de**part**ed,

Our Father ...

Prayer
God of death and resurrection,
you promise us salvation by your great deeds:
we place ourselves before you
and plead for the steadfastness of your presence.
May our celebration bring confidence in your abiding love.
We pray through Jesus Christ. **Amen.**

CONCLUSION

Blessing
May the God of death and resurrection
bless us with a night of rest that we may rise refreshed
in the name of the Father, and of the Son, and of the Holy Spirit. **Amen.**

Dismissal
Go to rest this night, poised for God's coming. **Thanks be to God.**

ADVENT Weeks 3 & 4
MONDAY-TUESDAY-WEDNESDAY-THURSDAY
Morning Praise

ADVENT MORNING HYMN

PSALMODY

Psalm 130 *Song of ascents (pilgrimages).*

Solo 1 Out of the depths, I cry to you, O LORD.
Lord, listen to my voice;
let your ears be attentive
to the voice of my supplications.

Solo 2 If you, O LORD, were to keep iniquities in mind,
Lord, who could stand?
But with you is forgiveness,
and for that you are revered.

Solo 1 I wait for the LORD;
my soul waits,
and for God's word I hope.
My soul waits for the Lord
more than watchers of the morning
watch for the dawn.

All Let Israel hope in the LORD,
for steadfast love is found with the LORD
and abundance of redemption.

It is the LORD who shall redeem Israel
from all iniquities.

Psalm 5 *To the choirmaster. For the flutes. Psalm of David.*

Solo 1 Give ear to my words, O LORD,
perceive my groaning.
Be attentive to the sound of my cry,
my Sovereign and my God,
for to you I pray.
O LORD, in the morning
hear my voice.
In the morning I prepare for you
and I keep watching.

Choir 1 For you are not a God delighting in wickedness,
nor does evil daunt you.
Mockers cannot stand
before your eyes.
You hate all makers of emptiness,
and you will destroy speakers of deceit.
People of bloodshed and fraud,
the LORD abhors.

Solo 1 But I, in the abundance of your steadfast love,
shall come to your house.
With awe I shall prostrate myself in your holy temple.
O LORD, guide me in your justice
because of my adversaries;
straighten your way before me.

Choir 2 Nothing right comes from their mouths:
their insides are rotted,
their throats are open tombs,
their tongues are forked.
Prove them wrong, O God;
let them fall by their own counsels.
For their many transgressions,
drive them away
since they have rebelled against you.

All All who take refuge in you shall rejoice;
forever they will shout for joy.

You will lay protection over them
and all those who love your name
will exult in you.
For you bless the righteous, O LORD;
as with a shield of delight you will crown them.

Word of God

Benedictus

Blessed be the Lord God of **Israel**,
who visited and redeemed the **people**,
who raised up for us a **mighty** savior
from the house of **ser**vant David.

Just as the Lord spoke through the mouths of the holy prophets of **old**—
salvation comes out of the hands of our enemies and those who **hate** us,
that, with our ancestors, we might perform **works** of mercy,
remembering the holy covenant **sworn** to Abraham—

so does the Lord deliver us from the hands **of** our enemies,
that we might serve without fear before **the** Lord,
worshiping in **ho**liness
and in righteousness **all** our days.

And you also, child, will be called a prophet of God Most **High**:
for you will go before the Lord to prepare a **way**,
bringing people knowledge of salvation by for**giveness** of sins;
because of the deep and tender mercy **of** our God.

Whereby a light rising from on high will **vis**it us
to appear to those in darkness and in a shadow **of** death,
to guide our feet along a **straight**, sure path
into a **way** of peace.

INTERCESSIONS

Invocations

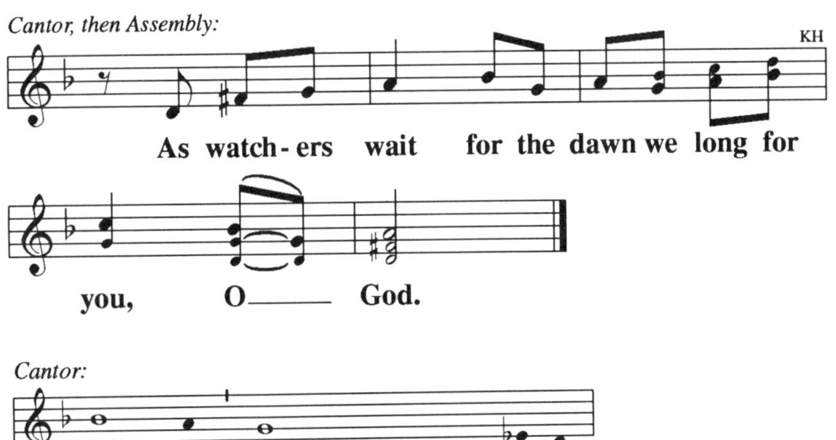
Cantor, then Assembly:
KH
As watch-ers wait for the dawn we long for
you, O___ God.
Cantor:

Incarnate Word of **God**, draw us into the depths **of** love ...
Incarnate Word of **God**, fill us with the hope **of re**demption ...
Incarnate Word of **God**, prepare us for your fullness **of** presence ...
Incarnate Word of **God**, cover us with **pro**tection ...
Incarnate Word of **God**, awe us by the justice of **your** mercy ...
Incarnate Word of **God**, bless us with a song of **de**light ...
Incarnate Word of **God**, shield us with the light of a **new** dawn ...

Our Father ...

Prayer
God of light and love beyond compare,
you prepare us to embrace your Word
in the quiet of a new dawn:
though we long to dwell with you forever,
be with us now
as we meet the challenges of living our day
according to your ways.
We pray through Jesus Christ. **Amen.**

CONCLUSION

Blessing
May almighty God accompany us
as we keep watch for the One who makes straight
God's way before us and may God bless us
in the name of the Father, and of the Son, and of the Holy Spirit. **Amen.**

Dismissal
Go forth and be faithful to the Word that dwells within us. **Thanks be to God.**

ADVENT Weeks 3 & 4
MONDAY-TUESDAY-WEDNESDAY-THURSDAY
Evening Prayer

ADVENT EVENING HYMN

PSALMODY

Psalm 123 *Song of ascents (pilgrimages).*

Solo 1 To you I lift up my eyes,
who dwell in heaven.

Choir 1 Behold, like the eyes of servants
look to the hand of their master,
like the eyes of a maid
look to the hand of her mistress,
so our eyes are lifted to the LORD our God
until mercy is bestowed upon us.

Choir 2 Have mercy on us, O LORD,
have mercy on us,
for we have been overwhelmed by contempt.
Our soul has been utterly filled
with the mockery of the indifferent
and the contempt of the arrogant.

Psalm 30 *Psalm of David. Song for the dedication of the temple.*

Solo 1 I will exalt you, O LORD,
for you have set me free
and have not allowed my enemies to rejoice over me.

Solo 2 O LORD my God,
I have cried to you
and you have healed me.

O LORD, you have brought my soul
up from Sheol.
You have restored me to life,
preventing me from going down the Pit.

All Sing to the LORD, O faithful ones;
celebrate a memorial to God's holiness.
For we stand only an instant in God's anger,
but a whole lifetime in God's delight.
In the evening come tears,
but in the morning come shouts of joy.

Solo 1 So I said in my tranquility,
"I will not falter forever."
O LORD, in your delight
you have established might as my mountain.

Solo 2 When you hid your face,
I was terrified.
To you, O LORD, I cry
and to you, O Lord, I raise my supplication.
What profit is there in my blood,
in my going down to the Pit?
Does dust give you thanks,
and tell your truth?
Listen, O LORD, and have mercy;
O LORD, be a help to me.

Solo 1 You have changed my mourning to dancing;
you have loosened my sackcloth
and girded me with joy.
So I sing your glory;
I am not silent.
O LORD my God,
I will give thanks to you forever.

Word of God

Magnificat

My soul does magni**fy** the Lord!
I delight in **God** my savior
who looked kindly **on** lowliness.

Now all ages will **call** me blessed
for the Mighty One **did** great things.
Holy is **God's** name;
mercy is from age to age for **those** in awe!

The Lord's strong arm did **mighty** deeds:
confused the proud in **their** smug hearts;
toppled sovereigns **from** their thrones,
and exalted **hum**ble ones;
filled the hungering with **good** things,
and sent the rich **a**way empty.

The Lord helped servant **Is**rael
to re**mem**ber mercy,
as was spoken to Ab**ra**ham
and his descendants for**ev**ermore!

INTERCESSIONS

Petitions

Cantor, then Assembly:

KH
We lift our eyes to the near-ness of our God.

Cantor:

To receive mercy in spite of our trans**gres**sions ...
To be cured of all **e**vil ...
To be restored to **life** ...
To be helped and **com**forted ...
To be loosened from **bond**age ...
To dance with our Re**deem**er ...
To delight in tran**quil**ity ...
To sing with **glo**ry ...
To give thanks for**ev**er ...
To ask release for the faithful de**part**ed ...

Our Father ...

Prayer
Exalted and ever faithful God,
the nearness of your coming
offers hope in the darkness of night:
give us courage to never lose sight of your merciful presence
and draw us to rest in you now and always. **Amen.**

CONCLUSION

Blessing
May the nearness of the Incarnate Word encourage us
and may God bless us
in the name of the Father, and of the Son, and of the Holy Spirit. **Amen.**

Dismissal
Go and rest confidently in the coming of our God. **Thanks be to God.**

ADVENT Weeks 3 & 4
FRIDAY Morning Praise

ADVENT MORNING HYMN

PSALMODY

Psalm 51 *To the choirmaster. Psalm of David. In the coming to him of Nathan the prophet, after David had been with Bathsheba.*

ANTIPHON
KH
Cre- ate in me a pure heart, O God.

Be gracious to **me**, O God,
in your **stead**fast love.
According to the abundance **of** your mercy
blot out my **trans**gressions. ANTIPHON

Cleanse me completely **from** my guilt
and purify me **from** my sin.
For my transgressions I do **rec**ognize,
and my sin stands always **be**fore me.

Against you alone **have** I sinned,
and what is evil in your eyes **I** have done.
Thus you may be declared just in your ways,
  and pure **in** your judgments.
Indeed, I was born guilty,
  already a sinner when my mother **con**ceived me. ANTIPHON

Surely in truth **you** delight,
and deep within my self you will **teach** me wisdom.
Cleanse me from my sin with hyssop and I **will** be pure,
wash me and I shall be brighter **than** snow.

Let me hear glad**ness** and joy,
let the bones you **broke** exult.
Turn your face **from** my sins
and blot out all my iniq**ui**ties. ANTIPHON

Create in me a pure **heart**, O God,
and renew within me **a** firm spirit.
Do not dismiss me **from** your presence,
and do not take away from me your ho**ly** spirit.

Give me back the joy of **your** salvation,
and let a willing spirit lie **o**ver me.
I will teach transgres**sors** your ways,
and sinners will turn back **to** you. ANTIPHON

Deliver me from bloodshed, O God,
  God of **my** salvation,
and my tongue will **sing** your justice.
O Lord, **o**pen my lips,
and my mouth will tell **your** praise.

For you take no pleasure in **sac**rifice,
and you would not accept an offering were **I** to give it.
The perfect sacrifice for God is a **brok**en spirit.
A broken and humble heart,
  O God, you will not **de**spise. ANTIPHON

In your kindness bring prosper**ity** to Zion;
rebuild the walls of Je**ru**salem.
Then you can delight in sacrifices of justice,
  burnt and complete **of**ferings;
then bulls can be offered on **your** altars. ANTIPHON

Psalm Prayer
O God,
you desire sacrifice from those who turn to you:
bring us prosperity as we delight in anticipating
the coming of your Son, Jesus Christ. **Amen.**

Word of God

Benedictus

Blessed be the Lord God of **Israel**,
who visited and redeemed the **people**,
who raised up for us a **mighty** savior
from the house of **ser**vant David.

Just as the Lord spoke through the mouths of the holy prophets of **old**—
salvation comes out of the hands of our enemies and those who **hate** us,
that, with our ancestors, we might perform **works** of mercy,
remembering the holy covenant **sworn** to Abraham—

so does the Lord deliver us from the hands **of** our enemies,
that we might serve without fear before **the** Lord,
worshiping in **ho**liness
and in righteousness **all** our days.

And you also, child, will be called a prophet of God Most **High**:
for you will go before the Lord to prepare a **way**,
bringing people knowledge of salvation by for**giveness** of sins;
because of the deep and tender mercy **of** our God.

Whereby a light rising from on high will **vis**it us
to appear to those in darkness and in a shadow **of** death,
to guide our feet along a **straight**, sure path
into a **way** of peace.

INTERCESSIONS

Invocations

Cantor, then Assembly:

KH
Come quick- ly, O God our Sav - ior!

Cantor:

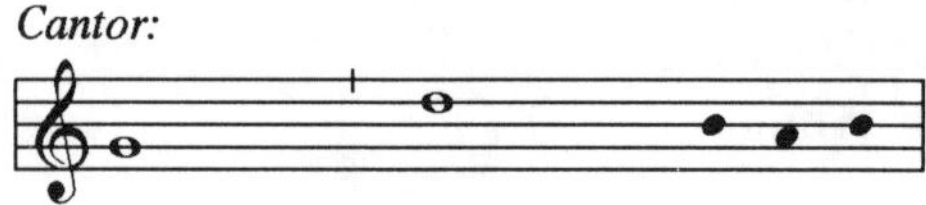

Jesus our Savior, be gr**acious** to us,
Jesus our Savior, blot out **our** transgressions,
Jesus our Savior, cleanse and puri**fy** us,
Jesus our Savior, bestow mer**cy** and truth,
Jesus our Savior, awaken our de**light** in you,
Jesus our Savior, teach **us** your wisdom,
Jesus our Savior, create in us **a** pure heart,
Jesus our Savior, renew your spir**it** within us,
Jesus our Savior, grant **us** salvation,
Jesus our Savior, draw us to **tell** your praise,

Our Father ...

Prayer
O saving God,
in your wondrous mercy you made your living Word flesh—
like us in all but sin—in order to win for us redemption:
extend to us this day your guiding hand
so that we may serve you faithfully.
We pray through Jesus Christ our Savior. **Amen.**

CONCLUSION

Blessing
May God, the source of mercy and promise of redemption,
bless us now and always
in the name of the Father, and of the Son, and of the Holy Spirit. **Amen.**

Dismissal
Go forth, and look for the coming of our God. **Thanks be to God.**

ADVENT Weeks 3 & 4
FRIDAY Evening Prayer

ADVENT EVENING HYMN

PSALMODY

Psalm 43

ANTIPHON
KH
Put your hope in God, our sal - va - tion.

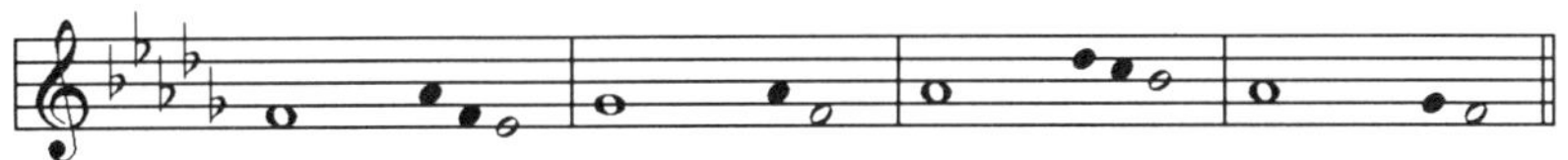

Judge **me**, O God,
and plead my trial
  against a nation **un**faithful.
From people of deceit **and** iniquity,
deliv**er** me. ANTIPHON

Since you are the God who **is** my fortress,
Why did you **re**ject me?
Why should I **wander** in darkness,
hard pressed by the enemy? ANTIPHON

Send your light **and** your truth;
they **will** guide me.
They will lead me to your **ho**ly mountain
and to **your** tents. ANTIPHON

So I will come to the **altar** of God,
to God who makes me rejoice **and** dance;
with harp **I** will praise
God **my** God. ANTIPHON

Why are you cast down my soul
  and dis**turbed** within me?
Put your hope **in** God—
my salvation **and** my God—
whom I will praise **a**gain. ANTIPHON

Psalm Prayer
O God,
you will return to judge the world in righteousness:
send your light and truth
that we may come before you
fitting to live with you forever and ever. **Amen.**

Psalm 63 *Psalm of David. While he was in the desert of Judah.*

ANTIPHON

KH
O God, I seek you, my soul thirsts for you.

omit last time

O God, you are my God, **I** seek you;
my **soul** thirsts **for** you.
My flesh longs for you
  in a dry and **wast**ed land,
deprived **of** water. ANTIPHON

So in the sanctuary I have contemplated you
  to see your might and your **glo**ry.
Because your **stead**fast love is better than life,
  my lips will **praise** you.
So I will bless you **all** my life;
in your name I will raise **my** hands.

As with milk and rich food,
  my soul **is** filled;
my **mouth** gives praise with joy**ful** lips.
I remember you up**on** my bed,
pondering you throughout **the** night.

For you were a help **for** me;
in the **shade** of your wings I **keep** singing.
My soul **clings** to you;
your right hand **up**holds me. ANTIPHON

But let those who seek my de**struc**tion
be **cast** into the depths of **the** earth.
Let them be given over to the power **of** the sword;
let them become a prey **for** jackals. ANTIPHON

Then the king shall rejoice **in** God.
All **those** who swear by God will **be** praised,
for the mouths of liars will **be** shut. ANTIPHON

Psalm Prayer
O God of strength and glory,
you are the only One we seek:
keep us in the shade of your wings
that we may be ready to meet you
when you come now and always. **Amen.**

Word of God

Magnificat

My soul does magni**fy** the Lord!
I delight in **God** my savior
who looked kindly **on** lowliness.

Now all ages will **call** me blessed
for the Mighty One **did** great things.
Holy is **God's** name;
mercy is from age to age for **those** in awe!

The Lord's strong arm did **migh**ty deeds:
confused the proud in **their** smug hearts;
toppled sovereigns **from** their thrones,
and exalted **hum**ble ones;
filled the hungering with **good** things,
and sent the rich **a**way empty.

The Lord helped servant **Is**rael
to re**mem**ber mercy,
as was spoken to Ab**ra**ham
and his descendants fore**ver**more!

INTERCESSIONS

Petitions

Cantor, then Assembly:

Cantor:

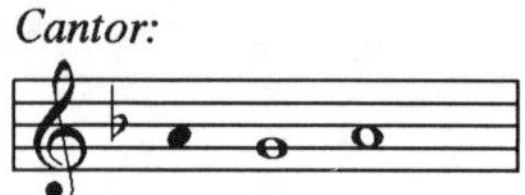

From **ter**rible **judg**ments ...
From un**faith**ful **na**tions ...
From de**ceit** and iniquity ...
From re**jec**tion and **dark**ness ...
From **dry** and wasted **lands** ...
From des**truc**tion and **lies** ...
To re**ceive** the faithful de**part**ed ...

Our Father ...

Prayer
God of those who grow weary of waiting,
you are faithful and merciful:
we give you thanks for protecting us in the shade of your wings
and for preserving us for life everlasting. **Amen.**

CONCLUSION

Blessing
May the God whose Word is made flesh and dwells within us bless us
in the name of the Father, and of the Son, and of the Holy Spirit. **Amen.**

Dismissal
Rest in God, confident that the Word is near. **Thanks be to God.**

ADVENT Weeks 3 & 4
SATURDAY & SUNDAY Morning Praise

ADVENT MORNING HYMN

PSALMODY

Psalm 67 *To the choirmaster. With stringed instruments. Psalm. Song.*

ANTIPHON
KH
Let the peo - ples give you thanks, O God; let
all the peo - ples give you thanks.

May God have mercy on us and **bless** us.
May God's face **shine** among us.

For your way is known **over** the earth,
and your salvation is known a**mong** all nations. ANTIPHON

May the nations rejoice and **shout** with joy,
for you judge the peoples rightly
  and the nations on the **earth** you guide. ANTIPHON

The earth has **given** its fruit.
May God, our God, **bless** us.

May God **bless** us,
and let all ends of the **earth** show reverence. ANTIPHON

Psalm Prayer

O God,
you judge the nations rightly:
be with your people this day.
Bless us with guidance and fruitfulness
as we eagerly await the coming of Jesus Christ. **Amen.**

Psalm 149

ANTIPHON
KH
Let us re-joice in God, our Sav - ior!

sing with first and final antiphon
Al - le-lu - ia! Al - le - lu - ia!

Sing a new song to the Lord,
  God's praise in the assembly of the **faith**ful.
Let Israel rejoice in its Creator,
  the children of Zion exult in **their** Sovereign.
Let them praise God's name with **danc**ing;
with drums and harp, let them play music **for** God. ANTIPHON

For the Lord takes delight in the people,
  adorning the poor with sal**va**tion.
Let the faithful exult **with** glory,
let them ring out joy on their **couch**es,
and cry out the great deeds of God from **their** throats. ANTIPHON

With two-edged swords in their hands,
  let them do vengeance against peoples
  and rebuke **na**tions;
let them tie their rulers with fetters
  and their nobles with chains **of** bronze,
in order to accomplish judgment against them as **writ**ten.
This is honor for all **the** faithful. ANTIPHON

Psalm Prayer
O God,
you are worthy of all praise:
we join the heavenly choir
and sing out your glory and splendor.
May we live our day in your presence
now and always through the risen Christ. **Amen**

Word of God

Benedictus

Blessed be the Lord God of **Israel**,
who visited and redeemed the **people**,
who raised up for us a **mighty** savior
from the house of **servant** David.

Just as the Lord spoke through the mouths of the holy prophets of **old**—
salvation comes out of the hands of our enemies and those who **hate** us,
that, with our ancestors, we might perform **works** of mercy,
remembering the holy covenant **sworn** to Abraham—

so does the Lord deliver us from the hands **of** our enemies,
that we might serve without fear before **the** Lord,
worshiping in **ho**liness
and in righteousness **all** our days.

And you also, child, will be called a prophet of God Most **High**:
for you will go before the Lord to prepare a **way**,
bringing people knowledge of salvation by for**giveness** of sins;
because of the deep and tender mercy **of** our God.

Whereby a light rising from on high will **vis**it us
to appear to those in darkness and in a shadow **of** death,
to guide our feet along a **straight**, sure path
into a **way** of peace.

INTERCESSIONS

Invocations

Cantor, then Assembly:

KH
As we wait for your com - ing.

Cantor:

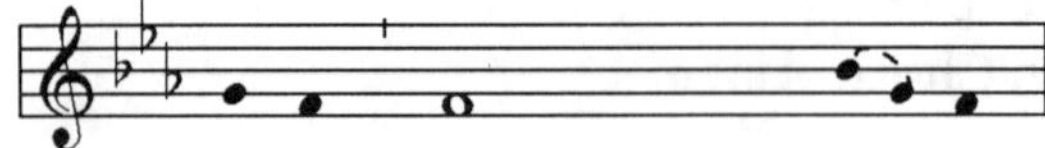

O Jesus **Christ**, have **mercy** on us ...
O Jesus **Christ**, **bless** us ...
O Jesus **Christ**, let your face **shine** on us ...
O Jesus **Christ**, may your sal**vation** be known ...
O Jesus **Christ**, judge the **na**tions rightly ...
O Jesus **Christ**, **reward** our labors ...
O Jesus **Christ**, take delight **in** your people ...
O Jesus **Christ**, continue **your** great deeds ...

Our Father ...

Prayer
Glorious God,
you bring us life and promise us the reward of glory
by the death and resurrection of your victorious Son:
be with us this day
as we celebrate your loving mercy.
We pray through Jesus Christ. **Amen.**

CONCLUSION

Blessing
May the God of glory envelop us with light and bless us
in the name of the Father, and of the Son, and of the Holy Spirit. **Amen.**

Dismissal
Go forth to live with the expectation of glory. **Thanks be to God.**

ADVENT Weeks 1 & 2
SATURDAY & SUNDAY Evening Prayer

LIGHT SERVICE

Proclamation of the Light

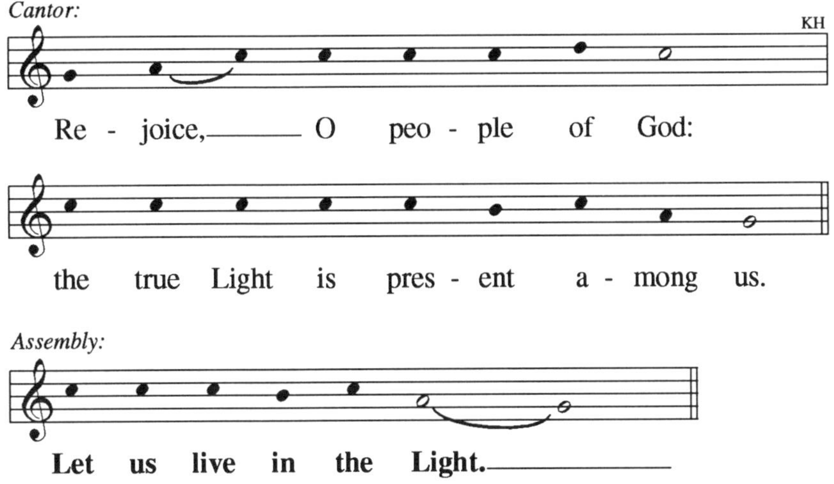

Advent Evening Hymn

Thanksgiving for the Light

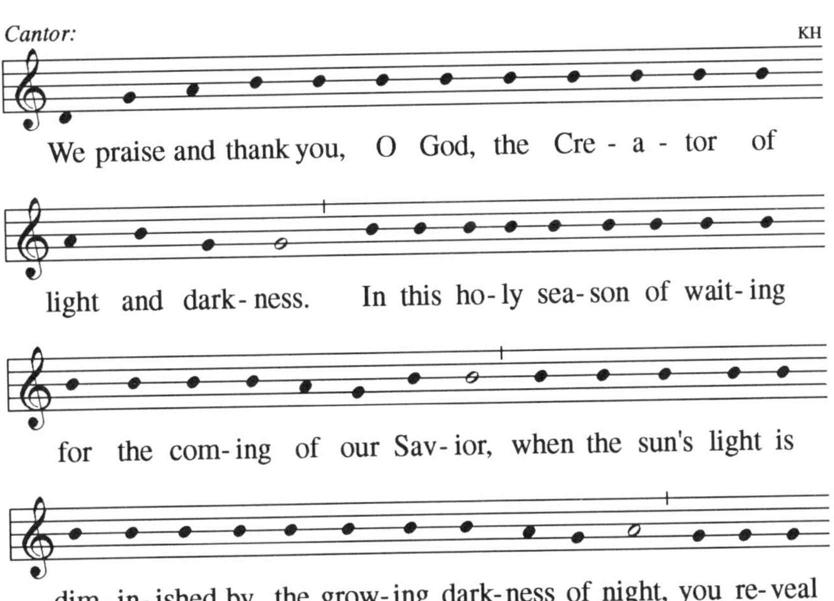

Cantor:
KH
We praise and thank you, O God, the Cre - a - tor of
light and dark- ness. In this ho- ly sea- son of wait- ing
for the com- ing of our Sav- ior, when the sun's light is
dim- in- ished by the grow- ing dark- ness of night, you re- veal

to us the e - ter- nal Light of your great splen - dor.
Through the proph-ets of old you call us to your cov-e-
nant of love. Now through the Spir - it you heal our
blind-ness and un - cov - er for us the glo - ry of your
pres - ence. Grant us a peace- ful night free from sin.
Free us to sing your praise and thanks- giv - ing, and keep us
ev - er in Christ. Through whom we of- fer you hon- or
and bless-ing in the u - ni - ty of the Ho - ly
Spir - it, now and al - ways and for ev - er
and ev - er. A - men.

PSALMODY

Psalm 141 *Psalm of David.*

ANTIPHON

KH
Let my prayer rise like in - cense.

O LORD, I cry **to** you:
"Hasten to me,
listen to my voice
when I cry **to** you."
Let my prayer rise
like incense in **your** presence,
the lifting up of my hands
like an evening **of**fering. ANTIPHON

Set, O LORD,
a guard over **my** mouth,
keep the door of **my** lips.
Do not incline my heart to any evil,
to performing wicked deeds
with those who work **in**iquity;
let me not partake **in** their feasting. ANTIPHON

When a just person strikes me, it is **a** favor;
and when I am corrected, it is like anoin**ting** oil.
May my head never **re**fuse it,
while my prayer stands firm against **ev**il doings.

Let wicked judges be smashed against **the** rock,
and they will understand that my words **were** measured.
Like plowed and broken furrows on **the** land,
their bones are shattered at the **mouth** of Sheol. ANTIPHON

But my eyes look to you,
O LORD, **my** Lord.

In you I take refuge;
  do not pour out **my** life.
Keep me from the snare they have prepared for me
  and from the traps of those who cre**ate** emptiness.
Let the wicked fall into their nets
  while I a**lone** escape. ANTIPHON

Psalm Prayer
O God,
you come in glory and might:
we raise our evening prayer to you.
Hasten to us
that we may find refuge in you now and always. **Amen.**

Psalm 95

ANTIPHON

Come! Let us shout with joy **for** the LORD;
let us make noise for the rock of our **sal**vation.
Let us come into God's presence in **thanks**giving;
with songs, let us **cry** out. ANTIPHON

For the LORD is a great God
  and a great Sovereign a**bove** all gods,
in whose hands are hidden the secrets of the earth
  and the treasures of **the** mountains.
The sea belongs to God,
  the one **who** made it,
and whose hands, too, shaped the **dry** land. ANTIPHON

Come! Let us bow **and** kneel down,
let us kneel down in the presence of the LORD our maker,
  who is **our** God;
we are **the** people,
the pasture, and **the** flock. ANTIPHON

Today, may you listen to the **voice** of God:
"Harden not your hearts as **at** Meribah,
as on the day at Massah in the desert
where your ancestors test**ed** me.
They tried me even though they had seen **my** works.

Forty years I was disgusted by that **gen**eration,
and I said: 'They are a people of twisted hearts,
they did not recognize **my** ways.'
I swore indeed in **my** anger:
'They will not enter into my rest**ing**-place.'" ANTIPHON

Psalm Prayer
O God,
you speak to us and bring us joy by your presence:
draw us to yourself
that we may come to rest in you
through Jesus Christ. **Amen.**

Word of God

Magnificat

My soul does magni**fy** the Lord!
I delight in **God** my savior
who looked kindly **on** lowliness.

Now all ages will **call** me blessed
for the Mighty One **did** great things.
Holy is **God's** name;
mercy is from age to age for **those** in awe!

The Lord's strong arm did **migh**ty deeds:
confused the proud in **their** smug hearts;
toppled sovereigns **from** their thrones,
and exalted **hum**ble ones;
filled the hungering with **good** things,
and sent the rich **a**way empty.

The Lord helped servant **Is**rael
to re**mem**ber mercy,
as was spoken to Abr**a**ham
and his descendants for**e**vermore!

INTERCESSIONS

Petitions

Cantor, then Assembly:

KH
We cry out for the com- ing of the Word.

Cantor:

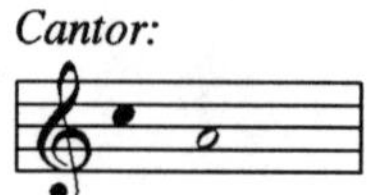

With **haste**,
For **mercy**,
With **confidence**,
For **refuge**,
With **shouts**,
For for**giveness**,
With thanks**giving**,
For a resting place for the de**part**ed,

Our Father ...

Prayer
O God,
you conquer darkness and preserve us for living in the Light:
may we rest in your mercy,
confident in your faithfulness that brings us life everlasting. **Amen.**

CONCLUSION

Blessing
May God keep us close and bless us
in the name of the Father, and of the Son, and of the Holy Spirit. **Amen.**

Dismissal
Go and rest in the confidence of the nearness of our God. **Thanks be to God.**

December 25
CHRISTMAS Morning Prayer

CHRISTMAS MORNING HYMN

PSALMODY

Psalm 2

ANTIPHON

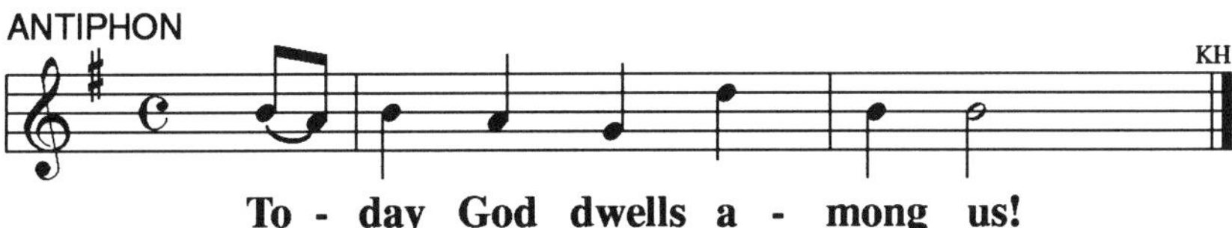

Why do people rage,
  and nations plot in **vain**?
The rulers of the earth have stood up,
  and nobles have gathered together
  against the LORD and against **the** Messiah:
"Let us cut **their** bonds
and cast their ties away **from** us." ANTIPHON

The one who dwells in heaven will laugh,
  the Lord will **mock** them.
Then God will speak to them in anger,
  and confound **them** in fury:
"But I have consecrated you **my** ruler
over Zion, my ho**ly** mountain." ANTIPHON

I will tell about the decree of the LORD
  who said to **me**
"You are my son, today I have be**got**ten you.
Ask from me

and I will give you people for your heritage,
and for your possession, the ends of **the** earth.
You will rule them with a scepter of bronze;
like a potter's vessel
you **will** break them." ANTIPHON

And now, O rulers, be **wise**;
accept this instruction, O you judges **of** the earth:
"Serve the LORD **with** reverence
and with trembling **exul**tation.

Pay tribute to the **son**,
lest God be angry
and you perish **on** the way.
For God's anger is quick **to** kindle."
Blessed are all those who take refuge **in** God! ANTIPHON

Psalm Prayer

Mighty God enthroned above,
you sent your only begotten Son to be Prince of Peace:
gather all your people to be your possession,
and grant us the heritage of life with you
now and always. **Amen.**

Psalm 27 *Of David.*

ANTIPHON
KH
The Son is our light and our sal - va - tion.

The LORD is my light and **my** salvation;
whom **shall** I fear?
The LORD is the stronghold **of** my life,
of whom shall I **be** afraid? ANTIPHON

When evildoers approached
  to devour me—
my adversaries and my enemies—
  they stum**bled** and fell.
If an army en**camps** against me,
my heart **shall** not fear.

If war rises against me,
  in **this** I trust:
One thing I ask from the LORD,
  this only **I** will seek,
to dwell in the house of the LORD
  all the days **of** my life,
to contemplate the favor of the LORD
  and to meditate **in** God's sanctuary. ANTIPHON

For **God** will hide me
in a shelter in the **day** of evil.
God will hide me in a **se**cret chamber.
Upon a rock God will **lift** me up. ANTIPHON

And now my head will be lifted above
  my enemies **who** surround me.
And I will offer sacrifices **in** God's chamber,
sacrifices with wild **ju**bilation.
I will sing and play music **for** the LORD. ANTIPHON

Listen to my voice, O LORD, **when** I cry.
Have pity on me and **ans**wer me.
About you my heart has said:
  "**Seek** God's face."
Your face, O LORD, **I** shall seek. ANTIPHON

Do not hide your face from me;
  do not send your servant **back** in anger.
You are my help;
  do not let me go, do not abandon me,
  O God of **my** salvation.
Even if my father and my mother a**ban**don me,
the LORD **will** receive me. ANTIPHON

Teach me your **way**, O LORD,
and lead me on an upright path

because **of** my enemies.
Do not give me over to their wiles,
for false witnesses have ris**en** against me,
breathing out **vi**olence. ANTIPHON

If only I could be proved right
by seeing the goodness **of** the LORD
in the land **of** the living.
Hope **in** the LORD!
Let your heart be strong and firm,
and hope **in** the LORD. ANTIPHON

Psalm Prayer

O God of light and salvation,
you sent your glory among all peoples
as the stronghold of our lives:
during this festival honoring the Word made flesh,
may we be led along the path of righteousness
that we may enjoy your goodness all the days of our lives. **Amen.**

Word of God

Benedictus

Blessed be the Lord God of **Israel**,
who visited and redeemed the **people**,
who raised up for us a **mighty** savior
from the house of **ser**vant David.

Just as the Lord spoke through the mouths of the holy prophets of **old**—
salvation comes out of the hands of our enemies and those who **hate** us,
that, with our ancestors, we might perform **works** of mercy,
remembering the holy covenant **sworn** to Abraham—

so does the Lord deliver us from the hands **of** our enemies,
that we might serve without fear before **the** Lord,
worshiping in **ho**liness
and in righteousness **all** our days.

And you also, child, will be called a prophet of God Most **High**:
for you will go before the Lord to prepare a **way**,

bringing people knowledge of salvation by for**giveness** of sins;
because of the deep and tender mercy **of** our God.

Whereby a light rising from on high will **visit** us
to appear to those in darkness and in a shadow **of** death,
to guide our feet along a **straight**, sure path
into a **way** of peace.

INTERCESSIONS

Invocations

Cantor, then Assembly:

Cantor:

Incarnate Word, a**noint**ed One,
Incarnate Word, only be**got**ten Son,
Incarnate Word, born in humble sim**pli**city,
Incarnate Word, promise **of** the nations,
Incarnate Word, possession **of** the righteous,
Incarnate Word, refuge **for** the weak,
Incarnate Word, light **for** the wayward,
Incarnate Word, salvation **for** the upright,
Incarnate Word, stronghold for **the** afflicted,
Incarnate Word, joy **of** the angels,
Incarnate Word, glory over **all** the earth,
Incarnate Word, music for **the** glad heart,
Incarnate Word, **face** of God,
Incarnate Word, hope **of** the world,

Our Father ...

Prayer
Mighty God of promise,
you sent your only begotten Son to be our Savior:
hear our litany of praise.
Be with us as we celebrate this wondrous festival

honoring Jesus your Son and our brother,
through whom we pray now and always. **Amen.**

CONCLUSION

Blessing

Bow your heads and pray that God bless us.
May the creator God embrace us as daughters and sons. **Amen.**
May the Incarnate Word lead us along a blameless path. **Amen.**
May the glorious Spirit guide us to peace. **Amen.**
And may God bless us
in the name of the Father, and of the Son, and of the Holy Spirit. **Amen.**

Sign of Peace/Dismissal

Let us offer one another the peace and joy of this holy festival.

CHRISTMAS Evening Prayer

LIGHT SERVICE

Proclamation of the Light

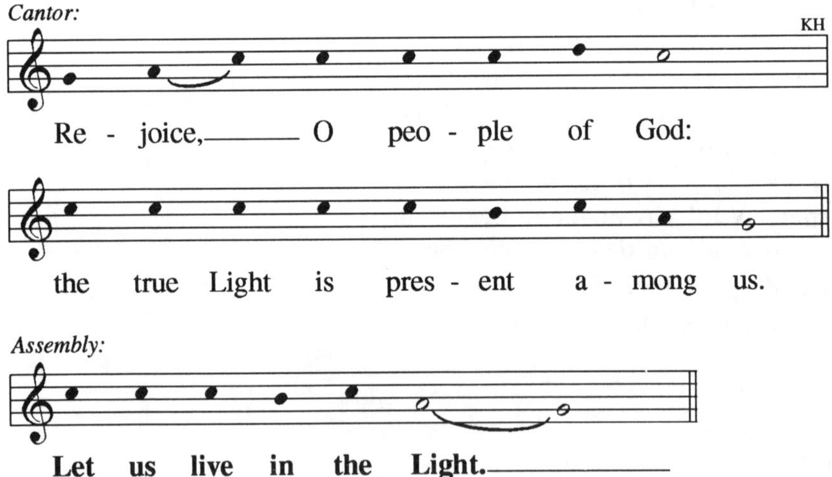
Cantor:
KH
Re - joice, O peo - ple of God:
the true Light is pres - ent a - mong us.
Assembly:
Let us live in the Light.

Festal Evening Hymn

Thanksgiving for the Light

Cantor:
KH
We praise and thank you, O God, the Cre - a - tor of
light and dark-ness. On this ho - ly Fes - ti - val when we
cel - e - brate the hu - man birth of your Son, you re - new
your prom - ise to re - veal a - mong us the splen - did light of
your glo - ry made vis - i - ble in the In - car - nate Word
Je - sus Christ. Through the proph-ets of old you call us
to your cov - e - nant of love. Now through the Spir - it you
o - pen our eyes to the peace of Christ's pres - ence.
So with the ho - ly an - gels on high we sing out:

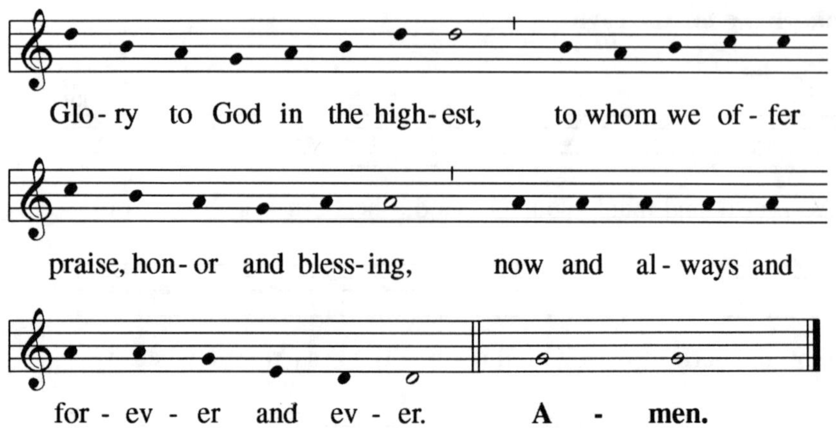
Glo - ry to God in the high - est, to whom we of - fer
praise, hon - or and bless - ing, now and al - ways and
for - ev - er and ev - er. A - men.

PSALMODY

Psalm 113

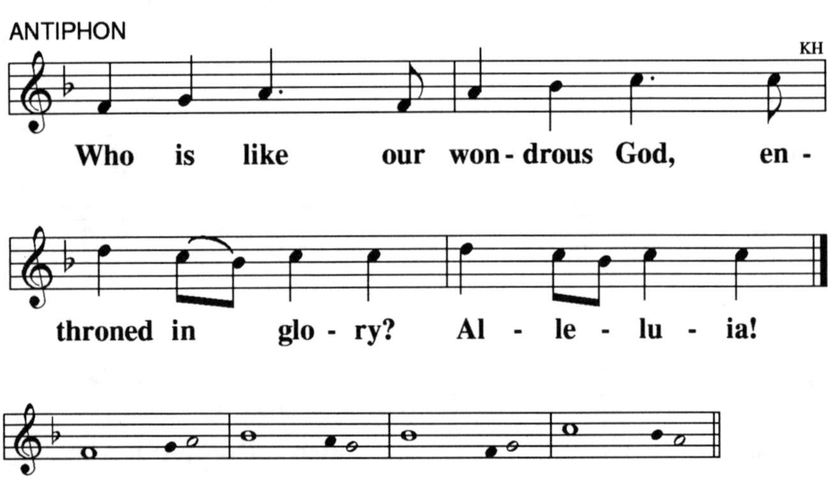
ANTIPHON
KH
Who is like our won - drous God, en -
throned in glo - ry? Al - le - lu - ia!

Give praise, servants of **the** LORD;
praise the name of **the** LORD.
Let the name of the LORD **be** blessed
from now on and **for**ever.

From the rising of the sun to **its** setting,
let the name of the LORD **be** praised.
The LORD is exalted above **all** nations;
God's glory is greater than **the** heavens. ANTIPHON

Who looks down to watch over
  the skies and **the** earth?
Who raises the weak from dust
  and the poor **from** ashes,
to return them to the company of nobles,
  the nobles of **the** people?
Who brings home the sterile woman,
  now a rejoicing mother of many children? ANTIPHON

Psalm Prayer
O wondrous God,
your glory is greater than all the heavens
and your Light shines brighter than even the sun:
we offer you our evening prayer
to celebrate the birth of your Son, the Incarnate Word
who lives with you and the Holy Spirit, one God forever and ever. **Amen.**

Psalm 67 *To the choirmaster. With stringed instruments. Psalm. Song.*

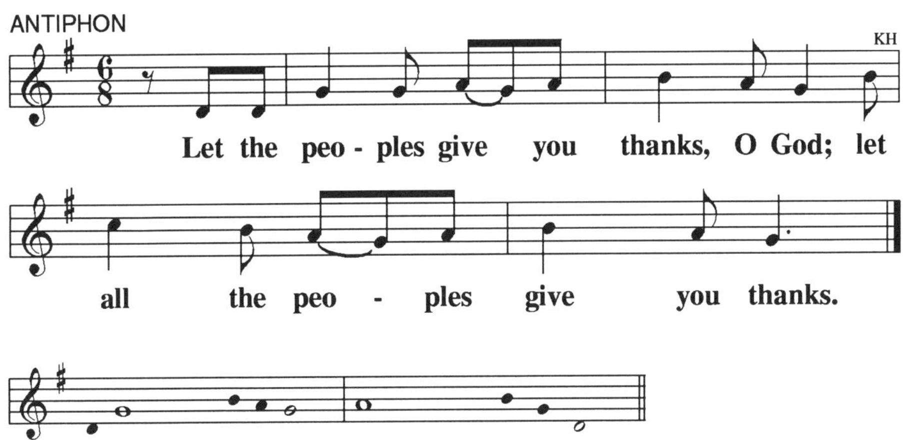
ANTIPHON
KH
Let the peo - ples give you thanks, O God; let
all the peo - ples give you thanks.

May God have mercy on us and **bless** us.
May God's face **shine** among us.

For your way is known **over** the earth,
and your salvation is known a**mong** all nations. ANTIPHON

May the nations rejoice and **shout** with joy,
for you judge the peoples rightly
  and the nations on the **earth** you guide. ANTIPHON

The earth has **given** its fruit.
May God, our God, **bless** us.

May God **bless** us,
and let all ends of the **earth** show reverence. ANTIPHON

Psalm Prayer
Merciful God,
your face shines among us
and brings us salvation:
receive our prayer of thanks
that we may reverence you
and your Incarnate Word made flesh,
with the Holy Spirit, one God,
forever and ever. **Amen.**

Word of God

Magnificat

My soul does magni**fy** the Lord!
I delight in **God** my savior
who looked kindly **on** lowliness.

Now all ages will **call** me blessed
for the Mighty One **did** great things.
Holy is **God's** name;
mercy is from age to age for **those** in awe!

The Lord's strong arm did **might**y deeds:
confused the proud in **their** smug hearts;
toppled sovereigns **from** their thrones,
and exalted **hum**ble ones;
filled the hungering with **good** things,
and sent the rich **a**way empty.

The Lord helped servant **Is**rael
to re**mem**ber mercy,
as was spoken to Ab**ra**ham
and his descendants for**e**vermore!

INTERCESSIONS

Petitions

Cantor, then Assembly:

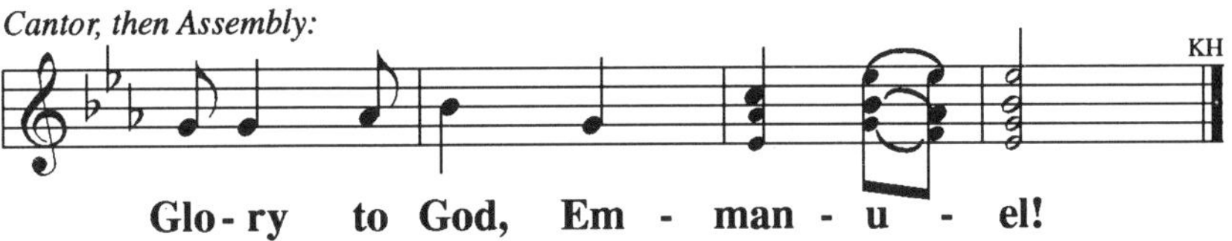

Cantor:

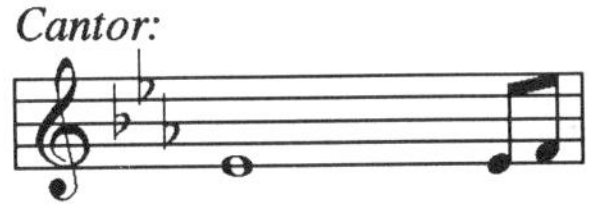

Let us praise **and** give
Let us adore **and** give
Let us revere **and** give
Let us honor **and** give
Let us rejoice **and** give
Let us pray for mercy **and** give
Let us pray for salvation **and** give
Let us pray for guidance **and** give
Let us pray for fruitfulness **and** give
Let us pray for the faithful departed **and** give

Our Father

Prayer
O God of darkness and light,
on this night when all the angels sing your praise,
we join with them to honor you with our gladsome song:
fill us with hope
as we celebrate your presence among us
through Jesus Christ the Incarnate Word,
with the Holy Spirit, one God, forever and ever. **Amen.**

CONCLUSION

Blessing
Bow your heads and ask for God's blessing.
May the gracious God who orders all things clothe us in splendid Light. **Amen.**
May the Son who dwells among us safeguard our life. **Amen.**
May the Holy Spirit who protects from all harm favor us with peace. **Amen.**

And may our wondrous God bless us
in the name of the Father, and of the Son, and of the Holy Spirit. **Amen.**

Sign of Peace/Dismissal
With the joyful spirit of this holy festival,
let us turn to each other and offer a sign of peace.

December 26
Feast of ST. STEPHEN, First Martyr
Morning Praise

FESTAL MORNING HYMN

PSALMODY

Psalm 8 *To the choirmaster. On the gittith. Of David.*

All O LORD our Lord,
how magnificent is your name
over all the earth!

Choir 1 You set your glory above the skies.
From the mouths of babes and infants,
you have established strength against your adversaries
to still the enemy and avenger.

Solo 1 If I look at your skies,
the work of your fingers,
the moon and stars that you have set in place,
What are mortals that you remember them?
And human beings that you care for them?

Choir 2 But you have made them slightly less than a god,
and with glory and radiance you crown them.
You made them rule over the work of your hands.
You have placed everything under their feet—
sheep and cattle, all together,
and even the beasts from the fields,
the birds of heaven

and the fish from the sea,
all that crosses along the paths of the seas.

All O LORD our Lord,
how magnificent is your name
over all the earth!

Psalm 3 *Psalm of David. In his flight from Absalom his son.*

Solo 1 O LORD, how many are my adversaries!
Many are rising against me;
many are saying to my soul:
"There is no salvation
for you in God."

Selah (pause).

Solo 2 But you, O LORD,
are a shield over me,
my glory and the one lifting my head.
With my voice to the LORD I will cry,
and God will answer me from the holy mountain.

Selah (pause).

Solo 1 I lie down and sleep;
I wake up
for the LORD sustains me.
I shall not fear the multitudes of people
positioning themselves
around and against me.

Solo 2 Arise, O LORD;
save me, my God,
for you strike all my enemies on the cheek
and you shatter the teeth of the wicked.

All From the LORD, salvation!
Upon your people, blessing!

Selah (pause).

Word of God

Benedictus

Blessed be the Lord God of **Israel**,
who visited and redeemed the **people**,
who raised up for us a **might**y savior
from the house of **ser**vant David.

Just as the Lord spoke through the mouths of the holy prophets of **old**—
salvation comes out of the hands of our enemies and those who **hate** us,
that, with our ancestors, we might perform **works** of mercy,
remembering the holy covenant **sworn** to Abraham—

so does the Lord deliver us from the hands **of** our enemies,
that we might serve without fear before **the** Lord,
worshiping in **ho**liness
and in righteousness **all** our days.

And you also, child, will be called a prophet of God Most **High**:
for you will go before the Lord to prepare a **way**,
bringing people knowledge of salvation by for**giveness** of sins;
because of the deep and tender mercy **of** our God.

Whereby a light rising from on high will **vis**it us
to appear to those in darkness and in a shadow **of** death,
to guide our feet along a **straight**, sure path
into a **way** of peace.

INTERCESSIONS

Invocations

Cantor, then Assembly:

Cantor:

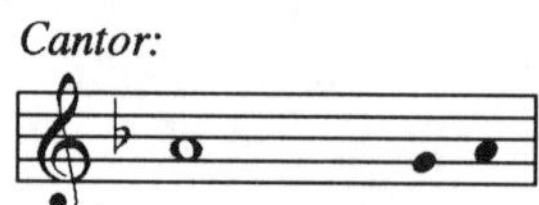

O risen Christ, you are **our** glory ...
O risen Christ, you are **our** strength ...
O risen Christ, you are our **sal**vation ...

O risen Christ, you are **our** shield ...
O risen Christ, you are **our** blessing ...
O risen Christ, you made us in **your** image ...
O risen Christ, you made us with a crown **of** radiance ...
O risen Christ, you made us fearless of **our** adversaries ...
O risen Christ, you made us witness to **your** name ...

Our Father ...

Prayer
O mighty God,
you opened the heavens and allowed Stephen to see your glory:
as he was given strength even to the point of death
so that he might witness to your steadfast love,
so too stengthen us to live faithfully in Jesus' name
now and always. **Amen.**

CONCLUSION

Blessing
May our steadfast God bless us
in the name of the Father, and of the Son, and of the Holy Spirit. **Amen.**

Dismissal
Go forth and witness to God's steadfast love. **Thanks be to God.**

December 26
Feast of ST. STEPHEN, First Martyr
Evening Prayer

FESTAL EVENING HYMN

PSALMODY

Psalm 16 *A poem. Of David.*

Solo 1 Keep me, O God,
for I take refuge in you.
I say to the LORD:

"You are my Lord,
my happiness is only in you."

All As for idols in the land,
they are mighty only for those who delight in them.
People multiply these idols
after which they hurry.

Solo 2 But I will not offer them sacrifices of blood,
nor will I raise their names to my lips.
O LORD, my given portion and my cup,
you support my destiny
which has fallen for me in pleasant places,
nothing but a goodly heritage.

Solo 1 I bless the LORD who gives me counsel.
Even at night my heart instructs me.
I keep the LORD always before me.
Because God is at my right hand,
I shall not be moved.

Solo 2 Hence my heart rejoices
and my soul exults.
Even my body rests secure
because you do not abandon me to Sheol.
You do not allow your faithful
to experience the Pit.
You teach me the path of life.

All In your presence there is fullness of joy;
in your right hand, pleasures for eternity.

Psalm 86 *A prayer of David.*

Solo 1 Turn your ear, O LORD,
and answer me,
for I am poor and needy.
Keep my soul
for I am faithful.
Save your servant who trusts in you;
you are my God.
Have pity on me, O Lord,
for I cry to you all day long.

Bring joy to the soul of your servant,
as I lift up my soul to you, O Lord.

All For you are good, O Lord, and forgiving,
abounding in steadfast love for all those who cry to you.

Solo 1 Give ear, O LORD, to my prayer;
be attentive to the voice of my supplications.
I cry to you in the day of my distress,
and you answer me.
There is no one like you, O Lord, among the gods,
and there is nothing like your achievements.
All the nations that you have made
will come and worship in your presence, O Lord,
and give glory to your name.

All For you are great and work wonders;
you alone are God.

Solo 1 Teach me, O LORD, your ways,
and I shall walk in your truth.
Gather together my heart for the reverence of your name;
I will thank you, O Lord my God, with all my heart.
Let me give glory to your name forever.
For your steadfast love for me is great:
you have delivered my soul from the depths of Sheol.
O God, the arrogant have risen up against me,
and a council of violent people have sought my life,
for they have not kept you in mind.

All But you, O Lord, are a merciful and gracious God,
slow to anger and rich in steadfast love and truth.

Solo 1 Turn to me and be gracious to me;
give your strength to your servant.
Bring salvation to the offspring of your servant.
Make me a sign of goodness,
that those who hate me shall see and be put to shame.
Because you are the LORD,
you help me and comfort me.

Word of God

Magnificat

My soul does magni**fy** the Lord!
I delight in **God** my savior
who looked kindly **on** lowliness.

Now all ages will **call** me blessed
for the Mighty One **did** great things.
Holy is **God's** name;
mercy is from age to age for **those** in awe!

The Lord's strong arm did **mighty** deeds:
confused the proud in **their** smug hearts;
toppled sovereigns **from** their thrones,
and exalted **hum**ble ones;
filled the hungering with **good** things,
and sent the rich **a**way empty.

The Lord helped servant **Is**rael
to re**mem**ber mercy,
as was spoken to Ab**ra**ham
and his descendants for**e**vermore!

INTERCESSIONS

Petitions

Cantor, then Assembly:

Cantor:

For those who **seek** refuge ...
For those who inher**it** goodness ...
For those who bless **the** wise ...
For those who rest **se**cure ...
For those who re**main** faithful ...
For those who teach the path of right**eous**ness ...
For those who trust in gra**cious**ness ...
For those who for**give** others ...

For those who re**vere** truth ...
For those who comfort the sick **and** dying ...
For those who mourn the faithful **de**parted ...

Our Father ...

Prayer
O gracious God,
you receive the souls of the just who cry out to you:
we celebrate Stephen's martyrdom
even as we celebrate the birth of our crucified Savior among us.
Grant us steadfast faith,
that we may persevere in spreading the Good News
of your Son Jesus Christ, the Incarnate Word now and always. **Amen.**

CONCLUSION

Blessing
May the God who grants everlasting life bless us
in the name of the Father, and of the Son, and of the Holy Spirit. **Amen.**

Dismissal
Go and be refreshed by rest in God. **Thanks be to God.**

December 27
Feast of JOHN, Apostle and Evangelist
Morning Praise

FESTAL MORNING HYMN

PSALMODY

Psalm 8 *To the choirmaster. On the gittith. Of David.*

All O LORD our Lord,
how magnificent is your name
over all the earth!

Choir 1 You set your glory above the skies.
From the mouths of babes and infants,

you have established strength against your adversaries
to still the enemy and avenger.

Solo 1 If I look at your skies,
the work of your fingers,
the moon and stars that you have set in place,
What are mortals that you remember them?
And human beings that you care for them?

Choir 2 But you have made them slightly less than a god,
and with glory and radiance you crown them.
You made them rule over the work of your hands.
You have placed everything under their feet—
sheep and cattle, all together,
and even the beasts from the fields,
the birds of heaven
and the fish from the sea,
all that crosses along the paths of the seas.

All O LORD our Lord,
how magnificent is your name
over all the earth!

Psalm 3 *Psalm of David. In his flight from Absalom his son.*

Solo 1 O LORD, how many are my adversaries!
Many are rising against me;
many are saying to my soul:
"There is no salvation
for you in God."

Selah (pause).

Solo 2 But you, O LORD,
are a shield over me,
my glory and the one lifting my head.
With my voice to the LORD I will cry,
and God will answer me from the holy mountain.

Selah (pause).

Solo 1 I lie down and sleep;
I wake up

for the LORD sustains me.
I shall not fear the multitudes of people
positioning themselves
around and against me.

Solo 2 Arise, O LORD;
save me, my God,
for you strike all my enemies on the cheek
and you shatter the teeth of the wicked.

All From the LORD, salvation!
Upon your people, blessing!

Selah (pause).

Word of God

Benedictus

Blessed be the Lord God of **Israel**,
who visited and redeemed the **people**,
who raised up for us a **mighty** savior
from the house of **ser**vant David.

Just as the Lord spoke through the mouths of the holy prophets of **old**—
salvation comes out of the hands of our enemies and those who **hate** us,
that, with our ancestors, we might perform **works** of mercy,
remembering the holy covenant **sworn** to Abraham—

so does the Lord deliver us from the hands **of** our enemies,
that we might serve without fear before **the** Lord,
worshiping in **ho**liness
and in righteousness **all** our days.

And you also, child, will be called a prophet of God Most **High**:
for you will go before the Lord to prepare a **way**,
bringing people knowledge of salvation by for**giveness** of sins;
because of the deep and tender mercy **of** our God.

Whereby a light rising from on high will **vi**sit us
to appear to those in darkness and in a shadow **of** death,
to guide our feet along a **straight**, sure path
into a **way** of peace.

INTERCESSIONS

Invocations

Cantor, then Assembly:

Cantor:

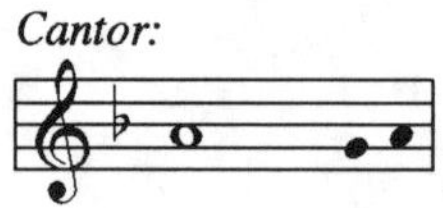

Word made flesh, you are **our** glory ...
Word made flesh, you are **our** strength ...
Word made flesh, you are our **sal**vation ...
Word made flesh, you are **our** shield ...
Word made flesh, you are **our** blessing ...
Word made flesh, you made us in **your** image ...
Word made flesh, you made us with a crown **of** radiance ...
Word made flesh, you made us fearless of **our** adversaries ...
Word made flesh, you made us witnesses to **your** name ...

Our Father ...

Prayer
O mighty God,
you endowed the beloved apostle John
with depth of insight and power of wisdom:
help us to remain faithful witnesses to
the Good News of your Son Jesus Christ forever and ever. **Amen.**

CONCLUSION

Blessing
May our gracious God bless us
in the name of the Father, and of the Son, and of the Holy Spirit. **Amen.**

Dismissal
Go forth and witness to God's grace and truth. **Thanks be to God.**

Feast of JOHN, Apostle and Evangelist
Evening Prayer

FESTAL EVENING HYMN

PSALMODY

Psalm 16 *A poem. Of David.*

Solo 1 Keep me, O God,
for I take refuge in you.
I say to the LORD:
"You are my Lord,
my happiness is only in you."

All As for idols in the land,
they are mighty only for those who delight in them.
People multiply these idols
after which they hurry.

Solo 2 But I will not offer them sacrifices of blood,
nor will I raise their names to my lips.
O LORD, my given portion and my cup,
you support my destiny
which has fallen for me in pleasant places,
nothing but a goodly heritage.

Solo 1 I bless the LORD who gives me counsel.
Even at night my heart instructs me.
I keep the LORD always before me.
Because God is at my right hand,
I shall not be moved.

Solo 2 Hence my heart rejoices
and my soul exults.
Even my body rests secure
because you do not abandon me to Sheol.
You do not allow your faithful
to experience the Pit.
You teach me the path of life.

All In your presence there is fullness of joy;
in your right hand, pleasures for eternity.

Psalm 86 *A prayer of David.*

Solo 1 Turn your ear, O LORD,
and answer me,
for I am poor and needy.
Keep my soul
for I am faithful.
Save your servant who trusts in you;
you are my God.
Have pity on me, O Lord,
for I cry to you all day long.
Bring joy to the soul of your servant,
as I lift up my soul to you, O Lord.

All For you are good, O Lord, and forgiving,
abounding in steadfast love for all those who cry to you.

Solo 1 Give ear, O LORD, to my prayer;
be attentive to the voice of my supplications.
I cry to you in the day of my distress,
and you answer me.
There is no one like you, O Lord, among the gods,
and there is nothing like your achievements.
All the nations that you have made
will come and worship in your presence, O Lord,
and give glory to your name.

All For you are great and work wonders;
you alone are God.

Solo 1 Teach me, O LORD, your ways,
and I shall walk in your truth.
Gather together my heart for the reverence of your name;
I will thank you, O Lord my God, with all my heart.
Let me give glory to your name forever.
For your steadfast love for me is great:
you have delivered my soul from the depths of Sheol.
O God, the arrogant have risen up against me,
and a council of violent people have sought my life,
for they have not kept you in mind.

All But you, O Lord, are a merciful and gracious God,
slow to anger and rich in steadfast love and truth.

Solo 1 Turn to me and be gracious to me;
give your strength to your servant.
Bring salvation to the offspring of your servant.
Make me a sign of goodness,
that those who hate me shall see and be put to shame.
Because you are the LORD,
you help me and comfort me.

Word of God

Magnificat
My soul does magni**fy** the Lord!
I delight in **God** my savior
who looked kindly **on** lowliness.

Now all ages will **call** me blessed
for the Mighty One **did** great things.
Holy is **God's** name;
mercy is from age to age for **those** in awe!

The Lord's strong arm did **migh**ty deeds:
confused the proud in **their** smug hearts;
toppled sovereigns **from** their thrones,
and exalted **hum**ble ones;
filled the hungering with **good** things,
and sent the rich **a**way empty.

The Lord helped servant **Is**rael
to re**mem**ber mercy,
as was spoken to Ab**ra**ham
and his descendants for**e**vermore!

INTERCESSIONS

Petitions

Cantor, then Assembly:

Cantor:

For those who **seek** refuge ...
For those who inher**it** goodness ...
For those who bless **the** wise ...
For those who rest **se**cure ...
For those who remain faithful to the **Good** News ...
For those who teach the path of right**eous**ness ...
For those who trust in gra**cious**ness ...
For those who for**give** others ...
For those who re**vere** truth ...
For those who abide in **God's** love ...
For those who are children of **the** Light ...
For those who are signs **of** love ...
For those who comfort the sick **and** dying ...
For those who mourn the faithful **de**parted ...

Our Father ...

Prayer
Gracious God,
your Son Jesus called John to be his beloved apostle:
may we always abide in your great love.
Grant us steadfast faith,
that we may persevere in spreading the Good News
of your Son Jesus Christ, the Incarnate Word now and always. **Amen.**

CONCLUSION

Blessing
May the God who grants everlasting life bless us
in the name of the Father, and of the Son, and of the Holy Spirit. **Amen.**

Dismissal
Go and be refreshed by rest in God. **Thanks be to God.**

December 28
Feast of HOLY INNOCENTS, Martyrs
Morning Praise

FESTAL MORNING HYMN

PSALMODY

Psalm 8 *To the choirmaster. On the gittith. Of David.*

All O LORD our Lord,
how magnificent is your name
over all the earth!

Choir 1 You set your glory above the skies.
From the mouths of babes and infants,
you have established strength against your adversaries
to still the enemy and avenger.

Solo 1 If I look at your skies,
the work of your fingers,
the moon and stars that you have set in place,
What are mortals that you remember them?
And human beings that you care for them?

Choir 2 But you have made them slightly less than a god,
and with glory and radiance you crown them.
You made them rule over the work of your hands.
You have placed everything under their feet—
sheep and cattle, all together,
and even the beasts from the fields,
the birds of heaven
and the fish from the sea,
all that crosses along the paths of the seas.

All O LORD our Lord,
how magnificent is your name
over all the earth!

Psalm 3 *Psalm of David. In his flight from Absalom his son.*

Solo 1 O LORD, how many are my adversaries!
Many are rising against me;
many are saying to my soul:
"There is no salvation
for you in God."

Selah (pause).

Solo 2 But you, O LORD,
are a shield over me,
my glory and the one lifting my head.
With my voice to the LORD I will cry,
and God will answer me from the holy mountain.

Selah (pause).

Solo 1 I lie down and sleep;
I wake up
for the LORD sustains me.
I shall not fear the multitudes of people
positioning themselves
around and against me.

Solo 2 Arise, O LORD;
save me, my God,
for you strike all my enemies on the cheek
and you shatter the teeth of the wicked.

All From the LORD, salvation!
Upon your people, blessing!

Selah (pause).

Word of God

Benedictus

Blessed be the Lord God of **Israel**,
who visited and redeemed the **people**,
who raised up for us a **might**y savior
from the house of **ser**vant David.

Just as the Lord spoke through the mouths of the holy prophets of **old**—
salvation comes out of the hands of our enemies and those who **hate** us,
that, with our ancestors, we might perform **works** of mercy,
remembering the holy covenant **sworn** to Abraham—

so does the Lord deliver us from the hands **of** our enemies,
that we might serve without fear before **the** Lord,
worshiping in **ho**liness
and in righteousness **all** our days.

And you also, child, will be called a prophet of God Most **High**:
for you will go before the Lord to prepare a **way**,
bringing people knowledge of salvation by for**giveness** of sins;
because of the deep and tender mercy **of** our God.

Whereby a light rising from on high will **vis**it us
to appear to those in darkness and in a shadow **of** death,
to guide our feet along a **straight**, sure path
into a **way** of peace.

INTERCESSIONS

Invocations

Cantor, then Assembly:

Cantor:

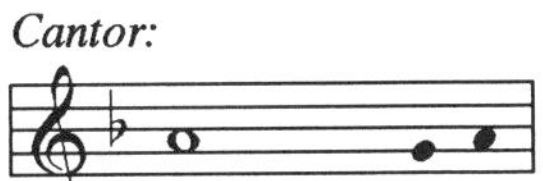

O risen Christ, you are **our** glory ...
O risen Christ, you are **our** strength ...
O risen Christ, you are our **sal**vation ...
O risen Christ, you are **our** shield ...
O risen Christ, you are **our** blessing ...
O risen Christ, you are our star rising in **the** east ...
O risen Christ, you made us in **your** image ...
O risen Christ, you made us innocent **as** children ...
O risen Christ, you made us with a crown **of** radiance ...
O risen Christ, you made us fearless of **our** adversaries ...
O risen Christ, you made us witnesses to **your** name ...

Our Father ...

Prayer
O mighty God,
your innocent children died
and you crowned them with eternal life:
as Joseph was faithful to your message
to take Mary and Jesus to safety,
stengthen us to live faithfully in Jesus' name forever and ever. **Amen.**

CONCLUSION

Blessing
May our steadfast God bless us
in the name of the Father, and of the Son, and of the Holy Spirit. **Amen.**

Dismissal
Go forth and witness to God's steadfast love. **Thanks be to God.**

Feast of HOLY INNOCENTS, Martyrs
Evening Prayer

FESTAL EVENING HYMN

PSALMODY

Psalm 16 *A poem. Of David.*

Solo 1 Keep me, O God,
for I take refuge in you.
I say to the LORD:
"You are my Lord,
my happiness is only in you."

All As for idols in the land,
they are mighty only for those who delight in them.
People multiply these idols
after which they hurry.

Solo 2 But I will not offer them sacrifices of blood,
nor will I raise their names to my lips.
O LORD, my given portion and my cup,
you support my destiny
which has fallen for me in pleasant places,
nothing but a goodly heritage.

Solo 1 I bless the LORD who gives me counsel.
Even at night my heart instructs me.
I keep the LORD always before me.
Because God is at my right hand,
I shall not be moved.

Solo 2 Hence my heart rejoices
and my soul exults.
Even my body rests secure
because you do not abandon me to Sheol.
You do not allow your faithful
to experience the Pit.
You teach me the path of life.

All In your presence there is fullness of joy;
in your right hand, pleasures for eternity.

Psalm 86 *A prayer of David.*

Solo 1 Turn your ear, O LORD,
and answer me,
for I am poor and needy.
Keep my soul
for I am faithful.
Save your servant who trusts in you;
you are my God.
Have pity on me, O Lord,
for I cry to you all day long.
Bring joy to the soul of your servant,
as I lift up my soul to you, O Lord.

All For you are good, O Lord, and forgiving,
abounding in steadfast love for all those who cry to you.

Solo 1 Give ear, O LORD, to my prayer;
be attentive to the voice of my supplications.

I cry to you in the day of my distress,
and you answer me.
There is no one like you, O Lord, among the gods,
and there is nothing like your achievements.
All the nations that you have made
will come and worship in your presence, O Lord,
and give glory to your name.

All For you are great and work wonders;
you alone are God.

Solo 1 Teach me, O LORD, your ways,
and I shall walk in your truth.
Gather together my heart for the reverence of your name;
I will thank you, O Lord my God, with all my heart.
Let me give glory to your name forever.
For your steadfast love for me is great:
you have delivered my soul from the depths of Sheol.
O God, the arrogant have risen up against me,
and a council of violent people have sought my life,
for they have not kept you in mind.

All But you, O Lord, are a merciful and gracious God,
slow to anger and rich in steadfast love and truth.

Solo 1 Turn to me and be gracious to me;
give your strength to your servant.
Bring salvation to the offspring of your servant.
Make me a sign of goodness,
that those who hate me shall see and be put to shame.
Because you are the LORD,
you help me and comfort me.

Word of God

Magnificat

My soul does magni**fy** the Lord!
I delight in **God** my savior
who looked kindly **on** lowliness.

Now all ages will **call** me blessed
for the Mighty One **did** great things.

Holy is **God's** name;
mercy is from age to age for **those** in awe!

The Lord's strong arm did **mighty** deeds:
confused the proud in **their** smug hearts;
toppled sovereigns **from** their thrones,
and exalted **hum**ble ones;
filled the hungering with **good** things,
and sent the rich **a**way empty.

The Lord helped servant **Is**rael
to re**mem**ber mercy,
as was spoken to Ab**ra**ham
and his descendants for**e**vermore!

INTERCESSIONS

Petitions

Cantor, then Assembly:

Cantor:

For those who **seek** refuge ...
For those who inher**it** goodness ...
For those who **bless** the wise ...
For those who rest **se**cure ...
For those who re**main** faithful ...
For those who teach the path of right**eous**ness ...
For those who trust in gra**cious**ness ...
For those who for**give** others ...
For those who re**vere** truth ...
For those who comfort the sick **and** dying ...
For those who mourn the faithful **de**parted ...

Our Father ...

Prayer
O gracious God,
you receive the souls of the innocent who cry out to you:
we celebrate the martyrdom of children
even as we celebrate the birth of our crucified Savior among us.
Grant us steadfast faith,
that we may persevere in spreading the Good News
of your Son Jesus Christ, the Incarnate Word now and always. **Amen.**

CONCLUSION

Blessing
May the God who grants everlasting life bless us
in the name of the Father, and of the Son, and of the Holy Spirit. **Amen.**

Dismissal
Go and be refreshed by rest in God. **Thanks be to God.**

On other days in the octave of Christmas,
pray as on CHRISTMAS DAY, p. 193.

Sunday within the Octave of Christmas or December 30

Feast of the HOLY FAMILY
Morning Prayer

FESTAL MORNING HYMN

PSALMODY

Psalm 96

ANTIPHON
KH
Sing a new song, all the earth;
sing a new song all the earth.

Sing to the LORD a **new** song.
Sing to the LORD, all **the** earth.
Sing to **the** LORD,
bless **God's** name. ANTIPHON

From day to day proclaim the good news of sal**vation**.
Recount among the nations God's glory,
  God's marvels among **all** peoples.
For great is the LORD, highly to **be** praised
and revered above **all** gods.

For all the gods of the nations are as **nothing**,
but the LORD made **the** heavens.
Honor and splendor stand be**fore** God,
might and glory fill **the** temple. ANTIPHON

Give to the LORD, O families of **peoples**.
Give to the LORD glory **and** might.
Give to **the** LORD
the glory of **God's** name. ANTIPHON

Bring an offering and come into the **courts**.
Worship the LORD with ho**ly** splendor.
Dance in the sac**red** presence,
all **the** earth.

Say among the nations: "The LORD **reigns**."
Surely God formed the universe
  so that it would **not** falter.

God **will** judge
the peoples **in** equity. ANTIPHON

Let the heavens re**joice**
and the earth **exult**.
Let the sea and its full**ness** roar.
Let the fields and all within them **be** glad. ANTIPHON

Then all the trees of the forest will shout with **joy**
in the presence of the LORD **who** comes.
For God comes to judge the earth,
  to judge the universe **with** justice
and with fidelity, **the** peoples. ANTIPHON

Psalm Prayer
Mighty God enthroned above,
you sent your only begotten Son to be Prince of Peace:
protect all families that they may reflect unity in the Holy Spirit,
now and always. **Amen.**

Psalm 27 *Of David.*

ANTIPHON

KH
The Son is our light and our sal - va - tion.

The LORD is my light and **my** salvation;
whom **shall** I fear?
The LORD is the stronghold **of** my life,
of whom shall I **be** afraid? ANTIPHON

When evildoers approached
  to devour me—
my adversaries and my enemies—
  they stum**bled** and fell.
If an army en**camps** against me,
my heart **shall** not fear.

If war rises against me,
  in **this** I trust:
One thing I ask from the LORD,
  this only **I** will seek,
to dwell in the house of the LORD
  all the days **of** my life,
to contemplate the favor of the LORD
  and to meditate **in** God's sanctuary. ANTIPHON

For **God** will hide me
in a shelter in the **day** of evil.
God will hide me in a **se**cret chamber.
Upon a rock God will **lift** me up. ANTIPHON

And now my head will be lifted above
  my enemies **who** surround me.
And I will offer sacrifices **in** God's chamber,
sacrifices with wild **ju**bilation.
I will sing and play music **for** the LORD. ANTIPHON

Listen to my voice, O LORD, **when** I cry.
Have pity on me and **an**swer me.
About you my heart has said:
  "**Seek** God's face."
Your face, O LORD, **I** shall seek. ANTIPHON

Do not hide your face from me;
  do not send your servant **back** in anger.
You are my help;
  do not let me go, do not abandon me,
  O God of **my** salvation.
Even if my father and my mother a**ban**don me,
the LORD **will** receive me. ANTIPHON

Teach me your **way**, O LORD,
and lead me on an upright path
  because **of** my enemies.
Do not give me over to their wiles,
  for false witnesses have ris**en** against me,
breathing out **vi**olence. ANTIPHON

If only I could be proved right
  by seeing the goodness **of** the LORD

in the land **of** the living.
Hope **in** the LORD!
Let your heart be strong and firm,
 and hope **in** the LORD. ANTIPHON

Psalm Prayer
O God of light and salvation,
you sent your glory among all peoples
as the stronghold of our lives:
during this celebration of the Holy Family,
may all families be led along the path of righteousness
and enjoy your goodness all the days of their lives. **Amen.**

Word of God

Benedictus

Blessed be the Lord God of **Israel**,
who visited and redeemed the **people**,
who raised up for us a **might**y savior
from the house of **ser**vant David.

Just as the Lord spoke through the mouths of the holy prophets of **old**—
salvation comes out of the hands of our enemies and those who **hate** us,
that, with our ancestors, we might perform **works** of mercy,
remembering the holy covenant **sworn** to Abraham—

so does the Lord deliver us from the hands **of** our enemies,
that we might serve without fear before **the** Lord,
worshiping in **ho**liness
and in righteousness **all** our days.

And you also, child, will be called a prophet of God Most **High**:
for you will go before the Lord to prepare a **way**,
bringing people knowledge of salvation by for**giveness** of sins;
because of the deep and tender mercy **of** our God.

Whereby a light rising from on high will **vis**it us
to appear to those in darkness and in a shadow **of** death,
to guide our feet along a **straight**, sure path
into a **way** of peace.

INTERCESSIONS

Invocations

Cantor, then Assembly:

Cantor:

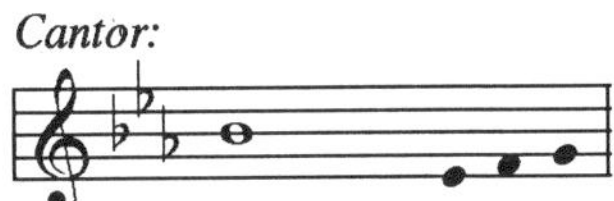

Incarnate Word, a**noint**ed One,
Incarnate Word, only be**got**ten Son,
Incarnate Word, born in humble sim**pli**city,
Incarnate Word, promise **of** the nations,
Incarnate Word, possession **of** the righteous,
Incarnate Word, refuge **for** the weak,
Incarnate Word, light **for** the wayward,
Incarnate Word, salvation **for** the upright,
Incarnate Word, stronghold **for** the afflicted,
Incarnate Word, joy **of** the angels,
Incarnate Word, glory over **all** the earth,
Incarnate Word, music for **the** glad heart,
Incarnate Word, **face** of God,
Incarnate Word, obedient Son of **Mary** and Joseph,
Incarnate Word, **hope** for families,

Our Father ...

Prayer
Mighty God of promise,
you sent your only begotten Son to be our Savior:
hear our litany of praise.
Be with us as we celebrate this festival
honoring the Holy Family
now and always. **Amen.**

CONCLUSION

Blessing
Bow your heads and pray that God bless us.
May the creator God embrace us as daughters and sons. **Amen.**

May the Incarnate Word lead us along a blameless path. **Amen.**
May the glorious Spirit guide us to peace. **Amen.**
And may God bless us
in the name of the Father, and of the Son, and of the Holy Spirit. **Amen.**

Sign of Peace/Dismissal
Let us offer one another the peace and joy of this holy festival.

Feast of the HOLY FAMILY
Evening Prayer

LIGHT SERVICE

Proclamation of the Light

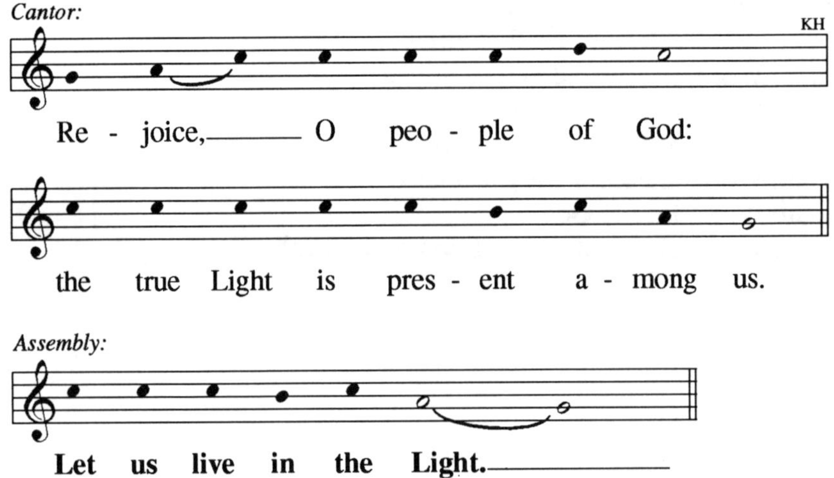
Cantor:
KH
Re - joice, O peo - ple of God:
the true Light is pres - ent a - mong us.
Assembly:
Let us live in the Light.

Festal Evening Hymn

Thanksgiving for the Light

Cantor:
KH
We praise and thank you, O God, the Cre - a - tor of

light and dark - ness. In this ho - ly sea - son when
the time of dark-ness is long-est, you re - new
your prom - ise to re - veal a - mong us the splen-did
light of your glo - ry, the In - car - nate Word made
vis - i - ble to us in Je - sus Christ, your Son.
Through the proph-ets of old you call us to your
cov - e - nant of love. Now through the Spir - it you
o - pen our eyes to the peace of Christ's pres-ence.
So with the ho - ly an - gels on high we sing out:
Glo - ry to God in the high-est, to whom we of - fer

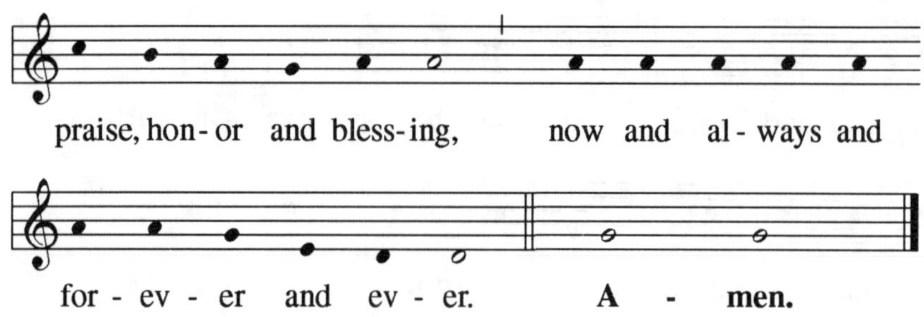
praise, hon- or and bless- ing, now and al - ways and
for - ev - er and ev - er. A - men.

PSALMODY

Psalm 113

ANTIPHON

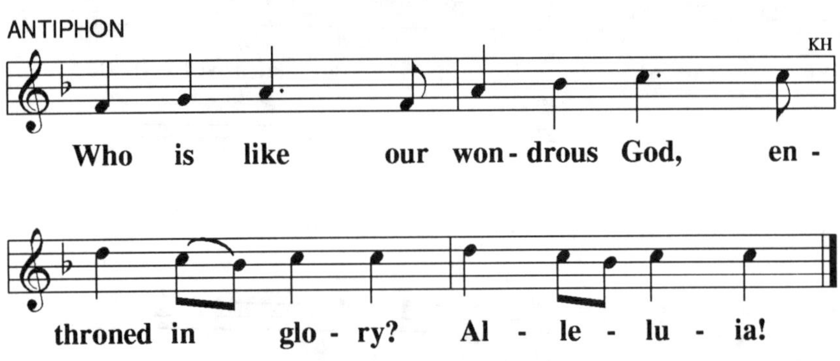
KH
Who is like our won - drous God, en -
throned in glo - ry? Al - le - lu - ia!

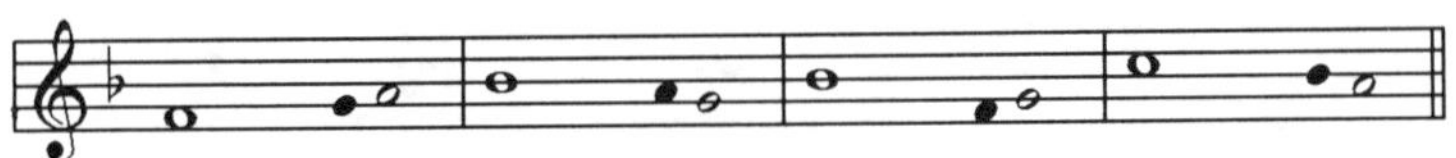

Give praise, servants of **the** LORD;
praise the name of **the** LORD.
Let the name of the LORD **be** blessed
from now on and **for**ever.

From the rising of the sun to **its** setting,
let the name of the LORD **be** praised.
The LORD is exalted above **all** nations;
God's glory is greater than **the** heavens. ANTIPHON

Who looks down to watch over
  the skies and **the** earth?
Who raises the weak from dust
  and the poor **from** ashes,

to return them to the company of nobles,
  the nobles of **the** people?
Who brings home the sterile woman,
  now a rejoicing mother of many children? ANTIPHON

Psalm Prayer
O wondrous God,
your glory is greater than all the heavens
and your light shines brighter than even the sun:
we offer you our evening prayer
to celebrate the birth of your Son, the Incarnate Word
who lives with you and the Holy Spirit forever and ever. **Amen.**

Psalm 67 *To the choirmaster. With stringed instruments. Psalm. Song.*

ANTIPHON
KH
Let the peo - ples give you thanks, O God; let
all the peo - ples give you thanks.

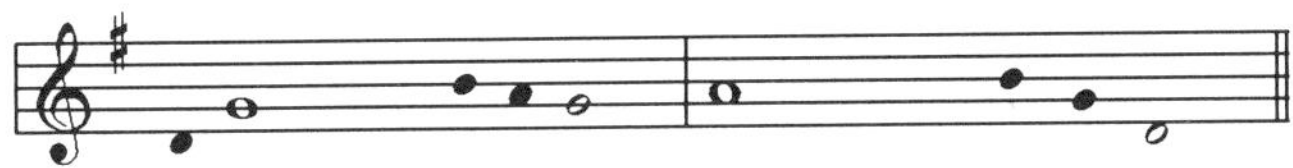

May God have mercy on us and **bless** us.
May God's face **shine** among us.

For your way is known **over** the earth,
and your salvation is known a**mong** all nations. ANTIPHON

May the nations rejoice and **shout** with joy,
for you judge the peoples rightly
  and the nations on the **earth** you guide. ANTIPHON

The earth has **given** its fruit.
May God, our God, **bless** us.

May God **bless** us,
and let all ends of the **earth** show reverence. ANTIPHON

Psalm Prayer
Merciful God,
your face shines among us
and brings us salvation:
receive our prayer of thanks
that we may reverence you
and your Incarnate Word made flesh,
with the Holy Spirit, one God,
forever and ever. **Amen.**

Word of God

Magnificat
My soul does magni**fy** the Lord!
I delight in **God** my savior
who looked kindly **on** lowliness.

Now all ages will **call** me blessed
for the Mighty One **did** great things.
Holy is **God's** name;
mercy is from age to age for **those** in awe!

The Lord's strong arm did **mighty** deeds:
confused the proud in **their** smug hearts;
toppled sovereigns **from** their thrones,
and exalted **hum**ble ones;
filled the hungering with **good** things,
and sent the rich **a**way empty.

The Lord helped servant **Is**rael
to re**mem**ber mercy,
as was spoken to Ab**ra**ham
and his descendants for**e**vermore!

INTERCESSIONS

Petitions

Cantor, then Assembly:

Cantor:

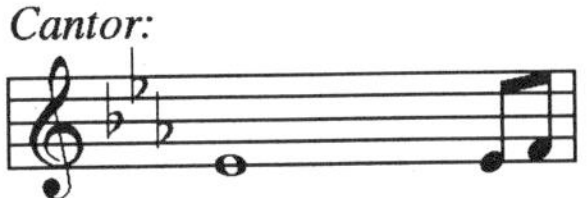

Let us praise **and** give
Let us adore **and** give
Let us revere **and** give
Let us honor **and** give
Let us rejoice **and** give
Let us pray for mercy **and** give
Let us pray for salvation **and** give
Let us pray for guidance **and** give
Let us pray for fruitfulness **and** give
Let us pray for unity **and** give
Let us pray for the faithful departed **and** give

Our Father

Prayer
O triune God,
in your wisdom you gave us the Holy Family
to be a model of your perfect harmony and love:
fill us with hope
as we celebrate your presence among us
through the Son Jesus Christ,
with the Holy Spirit, one God, forever and ever. **Amen.**

CONCLUSION

Blessing
Bow your heads and ask for God's blessing.
May the gracious God who orders all things clothe us in splendid light. **Amen.**
May the obedient Son who dwells among us safeguard our life. **Amen.**
May the holy Spirit who protects from all harm favor us with peace. **Amen.**
And may our wondrous God bless us
in the name of the Father, and of the Son, and of the Holy Spirit. **Amen.**

Sign of Peace/Dismissal
With the joyful spirit of this festival honoring the Holy Family, let us turn to each other and offer a sign of peace.

January 1
Solemnity of MARY, MOTHER OF GOD
Morning Praise

FESTAL MORNING HYMN

PSALMODY

Psalm 113

ANTIPHON

KH
Who is like our won - drous God, en -

throned in glo - ry? Al - le - lu - ia!

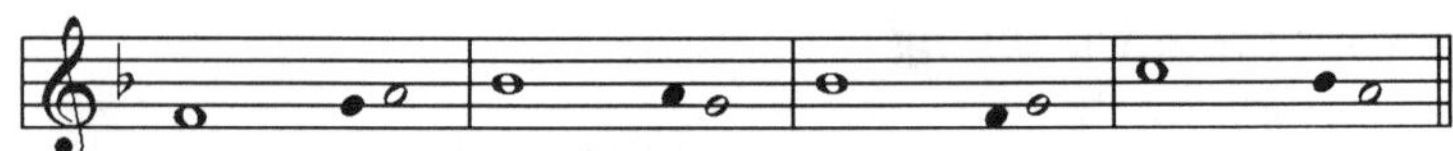

Give praise, servants of **the** LORD;
praise the name of **the** LORD.
Let the name of the LORD **be** blessed
from now on and **for**ever.

From the rising of the sun to **its** setting,
let the name of the LORD **be** praised.
The LORD is exalted above **all** nations;
God's glory is greater than **the** heavens. ANTIPHON

Who looks down to watch over
 the skies and **the** earth?

Who raises the weak from dust
 and the poor **from** ashes,
to return them to the company of nobles,
 the nobles of **the** people?
Who brings home the sterile woman,
 now a rejoicing mother of many children? ANTIPHON

Psalm Prayer
O mighty God,
you raised up Mary to be the mother
of your divine Son:
may you be praised
for lifting up the lowly and
for bringing hope to the downtrodden.
We pray through your Son Jesus Christ. **Amen.**

Psalm 149

ANTIPHON
KH
Let us re- joice in God, our Sav - ior!

sing with first and final antiphon
Al - le- lu - ia! Al - le - lu - ia!

Sing a new song to the LORD,
 God's praise in the assembly of the **faith**ful.
Let Israel rejoice in its Creator,
 the children of Zion exult in **their** Sovereign.
Let them praise God's name with **danc**ing;
with drums and harp, let them play music **for** God. ANTIPHON

For the LORD takes delight in the people,
 adorning the poor with sal**va**tion.
Let the faithful exult **with** glory,

let them ring out joy on their **couch**es,
and cry out the great deeds of God from **their** throats. ANTIPHON

With two-edged swords in their hands,
  let them do vengeance against peoples
  and rebuke **na**tions;
let them tie their rulers with fetters
  and their nobles with chains **of** bronze,
in order to accomplish judgment against them as **writ**ten.
This is honor for all **the** faithful. ANTIPHON

Psalm Prayer
O Creator Most Holy,
you delight in saving your people:
may you judge the nations favorably
as you honored Mary with
unspotted holiness and righteousness.
We pray through your Son Jesus Christ. **Amen.**

Word of God

Benedictus

Blessed be the Lord God of **Israel**,
who visited and redeemed the **people**,
who raised up for us a **mighty** savior
from the house of **ser**vant David.

Just as the Lord spoke through the mouths of the holy prophets of **old**—
salvation comes out of the hands of our enemies and those who **hate** us,
that, with our ancestors, we might perform **works** of mercy,
remembering the holy covenant **sworn** to Abraham—

so does the Lord deliver us from the hands **of** our enemies,
that we might serve without fear before **the** Lord,
worshiping in **ho**liness
and in righteousness **all** our days.

And you also, child, will be called a prophet of God Most **High**:
for you will go before the Lord to prepare a **way**,
bringing people knowledge of salvation by for**giveness** of sins;
because of the deep and tender mercy **of** our God.

Whereby a light rising from on high will **visit** us
to appear to those in darkness and in a shadow **of** death,
to guide our feet along a **straight**, sure path
into a **way** of peace.

INTERCESSIONS

Invocations

Cantor, then Assembly:

Cantor:

O saving **Son**, worthy **of** all praise,
O saving **Son**, exalted a**bove** all nations,
O saving **Son**, glorified **in** the heavens,
O saving **Son**, en**throned** with splendor,
O saving **Son**, delight **of** the people,
O saving **Son**, bearer **of** great joy,
O saving **Son**, fountain of **right**eous judgment,
O saving **Son**, honor for **all** the faithful,
O saving **Son**, obedient to your **Moth**er Mary,

Our Father ...

Prayer
O good and gracious God,
your choosing Mary to be the mother of your Son
brings salvation to all the world:
may we, too, hear your call and
answer with willing hearts and faithful service.
We pray through the intercession of Mary our Mother
and Jesus her Son. **Amen.**

CONCLUSION

Blessing
Bow your heads and pray for God's blessing.

May the God who calls strengthen us. **Amen.**
May the Son who saves redeem us. **Amen.**
May the Spirit who loves guide us. **Amen.**
And may God bless us
in the name of the Father, and of the Son, and of the Holy Spirit. **Amen.**

Sign of Peace/Dismissal
Let us offer one another a sign of peace,
sending each other forth with the protection of Mary our Mother.

Solemnity of MARY, MOTHER OF GOD
Evening Prayer

LIGHT SERVICE

Proclamation of the Light

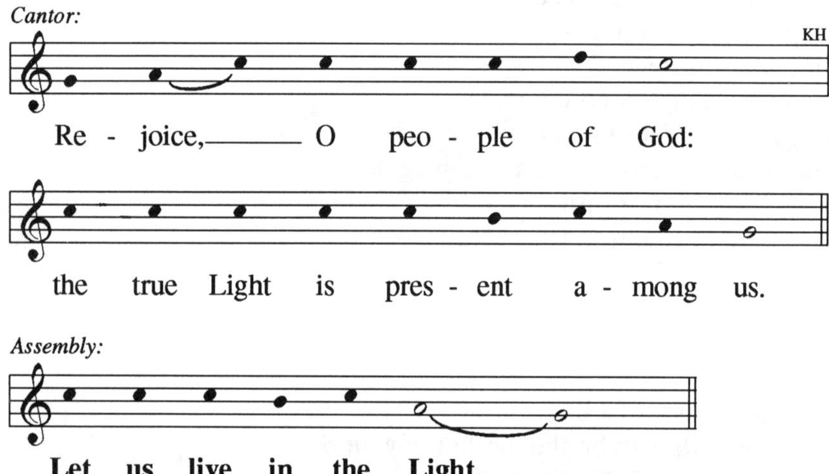
Cantor:
KH
Re - joice, O peo - ple of God:
the true Light is pres - ent a - mong us.
Assembly:
Let us live in the Light.

Evening Hymn

Thanksgiving for the Light

Cantor:
KH
We praise and thank you, O God, the Cre - a - tor of

light and dark - ness. In this ho - ly sea - son when
the time of dark-ness is long-est, you re - new
your prom - ise to re - veal a - mong us the splen-did
light of your glo - ry, the In - car - nate Word made
vis - i - ble to us in Je - sus Christ, your Son,
by the pow - er of the Ho - ly Spir - it o - ver -
shad-ow - ing Ma - ry, his moth - er and ours.
Through the proph-ets of old you call us to your
cov - e - nant of peace. Now through the Spir - it you
o - pen our eyes to the peace of Christ's pres-ence.

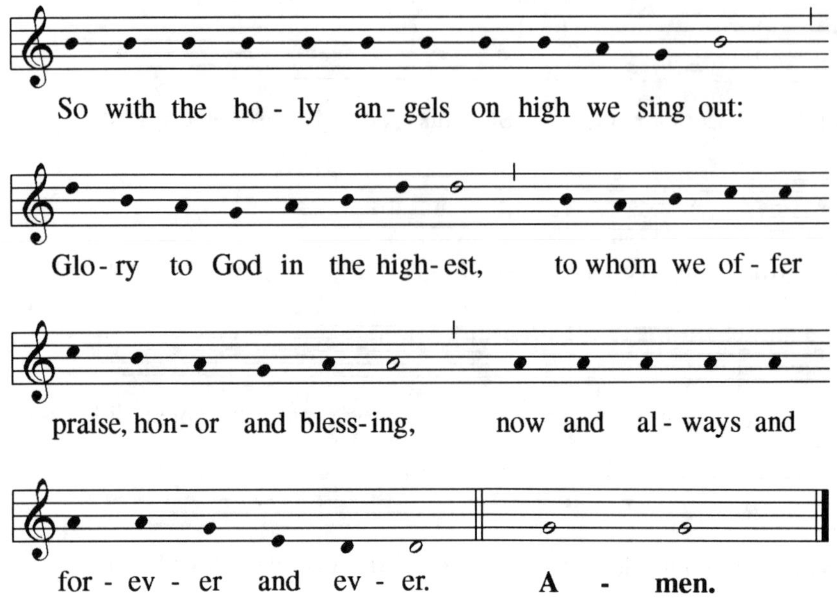
So with the ho - ly an - gels on high we sing out:
Glo - ry to God in the high - est, to whom we of - fer
praise, hon - or and bless - ing, now and al - ways and
for - ev - er and ev - er. A - men.

PSALMODY

Psalm 141 *Psalm of David.*

ANTIPHON
KH
Let my prayer rise like in - cense.

O LORD, I cry **to** you:
"Hasten to me,
listen to my voice
when I cry **to** you."
Let my prayer rise
like incense in **your** presence,
the lifting up of my hands
like an evening **of**fering. ANTIPHON

Set, O LORD,
a guard over **my** mouth,

keep the door of **my** lips.
Do not incline my heart to any evil,
to performing wicked deeds
with those who work **in**iquity;
let me not partake **in** their feasting. ANTIPHON

When a just person strikes me, it is **a** favor;
and when I am corrected, it is like anoin**ting** oil.
May my head never **re**fuse it,
while my prayer stands firm against **e**vil doings.

Let wicked judges be smashed against **the** rock,
and they will understand that my words **were** measured.
Like plowed and broken furrows on **the** land,
their bones are shattered at the **mouth** of Sheol. ANTIPHON

But my eyes look to you,
O LORD, **my** Lord.
In you I take refuge;
do not pour out **my** life.
Keep me from the snare they have prepared for me
and from the traps of those who cre**ate** emptiness.
Let the wicked fall into their nets
while I a**lone** escape. ANTIPHON

Psalm Prayer
O merciful God,
you hear the voice of those who call to you
with faith and love:
as our evening prayer rises to you on incense,
so may our gaze turn toward you now and always. **Amen.**

Psalm 110 *Of David. Psalm.*

ANTIPHON
KH
Pour forth your strength up - on us.

Thus says the LORD **to** my lord:
"Sit on my right
  until I place your enemies
  as a footstool for **your** feet."
Let the LORD send from Zion
  the scepter of **your** strength.
Rule in the midst of **your** enemies. ANTIPHON

Your people bring free **o**fferings
on the day of your might
  in hol**y** splendor.
From the womb **of** dawn,
a dew of rejuvenation comes **to** you. ANTIPHON

The LORD has promised
  and will **not** repent:
"According to my word,
  you are a priest forever, my king **of** justice."
The Lord is at **your** right,
who has smashed rulers on the day **of** wrath.

The Lord judges a**gainst** the nations,
piling them **with** corpses.
The Lord has smashed heads
  all over **the** land.
From a torrent the Lord drinks on the way,
  and rises up **in** triumph. ANTIPHON

Psalm Prayer
O mighty God,
as your Son came forth from the womb of Mary,
so did life come to us from the womb of dawn:
sustain us by your holy splendor
that we may one day be with you forever and ever. **Amen.**

Word of God

Magnificat

My soul does magni**fy** the Lord!
I delight in **God** my savior
who looked kindly **on** lowliness.

Now all ages will **call** me blessed
for the Mighty One **did** great things.
Holy is **God's** name;
mercy is from age to age for **those** in awe!

The Lord's strong arm did **migh**ty deeds:
confused the proud in **their** smug hearts;
toppled sovereigns **from** their thrones,
and exalted **hum**ble ones;
filled the hungering with **good** things,
and sent the rich **a**way empty.

The Lord helped servant **Is**rael
to re**mem**ber mercy,
as was spoken to Ab**ra**ham
and his descendants for**e**vermore!

INTERCESSIONS

Petitions

Cantor, then Assembly:

Cantor:

That God may listen **to** our voices ...
That God may guard **our** words and ways ...
That God may protect us **from** all evil ...
That God may rule **o**ver our lives ...
That God may judge **us** with mercy ...
That God may favor **us** with honor ...
That God may grant the dead life **ev**erlasting ...

Our Father ...

Prayer
O wondrous God,
you entrusted Mary with the life of your divine Son:
bless us now with a good life
that we may raise grateful hearts
to honor you now and always. **Amen.**

CONCLUSION

Blessing
Bow your heads and pray for God's blessing.
May the Creator God sustain our lives. **Amen.**
May the Divine Son ask his Mother to intercede for us. **Amen.**
May the Loving Spirit overshadow us with grace and peace. **Amen.**
And may God bless us
in the name of the Father, and of the Son, and of the Holy Spirit. **Amen.**

Sign of Peace/Dismissal
Let us offer each other a sign of peace,
to go forth to rest under Mother Mary's watchful eye.

Sunday between January 2 & 8
Solemnity of the EPIPHANY
Morning Praise

FESTAL MORNING HYMN

PSALMODY

Psalm 8 *To the choirmaster. On the gittith. Of David.*

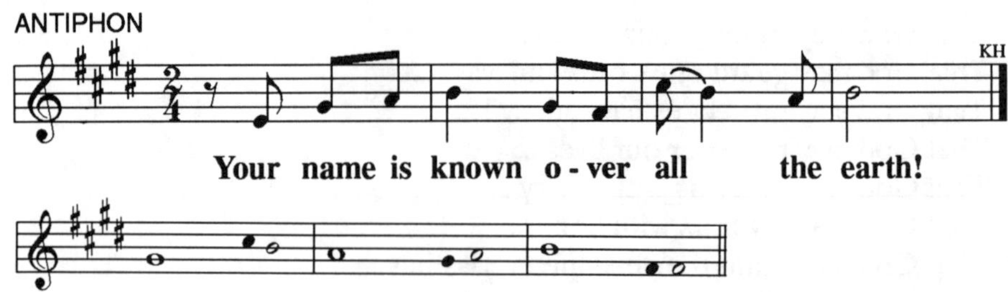
ANTIPHON
KH
Your name is known o - ver all the earth!

O LORD **our** Lord,
how magnificent is **your** name
over all **the** earth! ANTIPHON

You set your glory above **the** skies.
From the mouths of babes **and** infants,
you have established strength against your adversaries
to still the enemy and **a**venger. ANTIPHON

If I look at your skies,
the work of **your** fingers,
the moon and stars that you have set **in** place,
What are mortals that you remember them?
And human beings that you care **for** them? ANTIPHON

But you have made them slightly less than **a** god,
and with glory and radiance **you** crown them.
You made them rule over the work of **your** hands.

You have placed everything under **their** feet—
sheep and cattle, all together,
and even the beasts from **the** fields,
the birds of heaven
and the fish from the sea,
all that crosses along the paths of **the** seas. ANTIPHON

O LORD **our** Lord,
how magnificent is **your** name
over all **the** earth! ANTIPHON

Psalm Prayer
Magnificent God,
your name is known over all the earth:
may you always reveal your glory and radiance to us
as we labor to spread the Good News
of your Son Jesus Christ. **Amen.**

Psalm 66 *To the choirmaster. A Song. Psalm.*

ANTIPHON
KH
Sound the trum - pet for God!

omit first and last strophe

Sound the trumpet for God, all **the** earth!
Make music to the glory **of** God's name!
Give **glory** and praise! ANTIPHON

Say to God:
  "How awesome are **your** deeds!
At the magnitude of your power,
  your enemies **cringe** before you.
Let all the earth **wor**ship you,
let them sing to you,
  let them sing to **your** name." ANTIPHON

Come and see the accomplishments **of** God—
an awesome work
  on be**half** of mortals.
God turned the sea **into** dry land,
they crossed through the river **on** foot.

Therefore let us rejoice **in** God,
who rules over the **world** with power
and whose eyes watch **over** the nations.
Let not the stubborn rise up a**gainst** God. ANTIPHON

All you nations, bless **our** God!
Let the sound of **praise** be heard
for the one who gives **life to** our souls,
and who kept our feet **from** stumbling. ANTIPHON

For you have tested us, O God;
  you have tried us like silver **is** tried.
You have caught us **in** a net.
You have put a burden on our backs;
  you have let **mortals** enslave us.
We went through fire and water,
  but you brought us out to a fer**tile** land. ANTIPHON

I shall go into your house **with** offerings.
I will fulfill my promises to you
  which my lips uttered
  and my mouth spoke when I was **in** distress.
I will bring you **offerings** of fatlings;
along with the smoke of rams
  I will offer bulls **and** goats. ANTIPHON

Come, listen, all those who re**vere** God,
and I will tell
  all that God did for **my** soul.
I have cried out **with** my mouth,
extolling God with **my** tongue.

If I had harbored emptiness in **my** heart,
the Lord would **not** have listened.
But truly **God** has listened,
listened to the voice of **my** prayer. ANTIPHON

Blessed **be** God
who has not re**jected** my prayer,
nor taken steadfast love away **from** me. ANTIPHON

Psalm Prayer
Glorious God,
your deeds are awesome and
your power is great:
may we always sing your praises
as your presence is manifested
among all the nations.
We pray through Jesus Christ. **Amen.**

Word of God

Benedictus

Blessed be the Lord God of **Israel**,
who visited and redeemed the **people**,
who raised up for us a **mighty** savior
from the house of **ser**vant David.

Just as the Lord spoke through the mouths of the holy prophets of **old**—
salvation comes out of the hands of our enemies and those who **hate** us,

that, with our ancestors, we might perform **works** of mercy,
remembering the holy covenant **sworn** to Abraham—

so does the Lord deliver us from the hands **of** our enemies,
that we might serve without fear before **the** Lord,
worshiping in **ho**liness
and in righteousness **all** our days.

And you also, child, will be called a prophet of God Most **High**:
for you will go before the Lord to prepare a **way**,
bringing people knowledge of salvation by for**giveness** of sins;
because of the deep and tender mercy **of** our God.

Whereby a light rising from on high will **vis**it us
to appear to those in darkness and in a shadow **of** death,
to guide our feet along a **straight**, sure path
into a **way** of peace.

INTERCESSIONS

Invocations

Cantor, then Assembly:

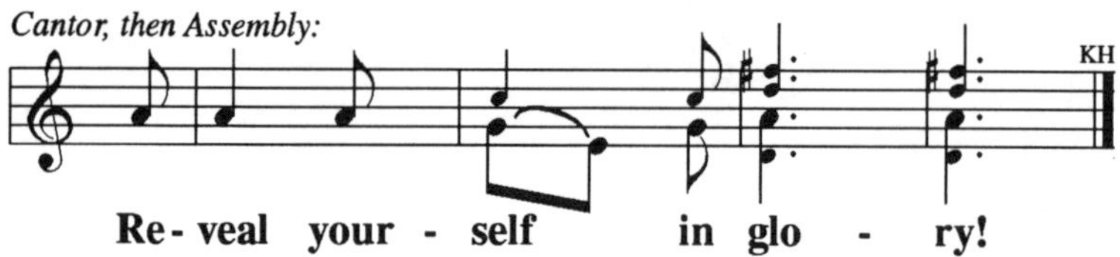

KH
Re- veal your - self in glo - ry!

Cantor:

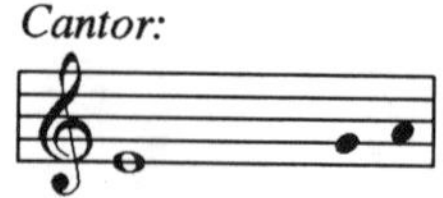

O Jesus Christ, your name is worthy of **all** praise,
O Jesus Christ, your radiance is over all **the** earth,
O Jesus Christ, your rule extends to **all** nations,
O Jesus Christ, your deeds bring us **sal**vation,
O Jesus Christ, your power be**gets** life,
O Jesus Christ, your heart listens to **our** prayer,
O Jesus Christ, your love is steadfast **and** faithful,

Our Father ...

Prayer
O God,
you manifest yourself to the nations in glory:
receive our morning prayer of praise
and help us to honor you now and always. **Amen.**

CONCLUSION

Blessing
Bow your heads and pray for God's blessing.
May God continue awesome deeds on our behalf. **Amen.**
May Jesus Christ reveal the power of his Good News. **Amen.**
May their Spirit give us wisdom and courage. **Amen.**
And may God bless us
in the name of the Father, and of the Son, and of the Holy Spirit. **Amen.**

Sign of Peace/Dismissal
Let us exchange a sign of peace as we go forth to bask in the radiance of Christ.

Solemnity of the EPIPHANY Evening Prayer

LIGHT SERVICE

Proclamation of the Light

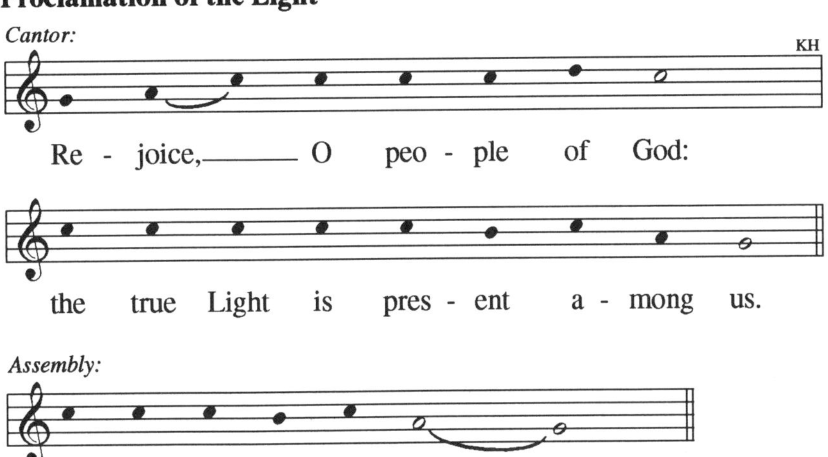
Cantor:
KH
Re - joice, O peo - ple of God:
the true Light is pres - ent a - mong us.
Assembly:
Let us live in the Light.

Festal Evening Hymn

Thanksgiving for the Light

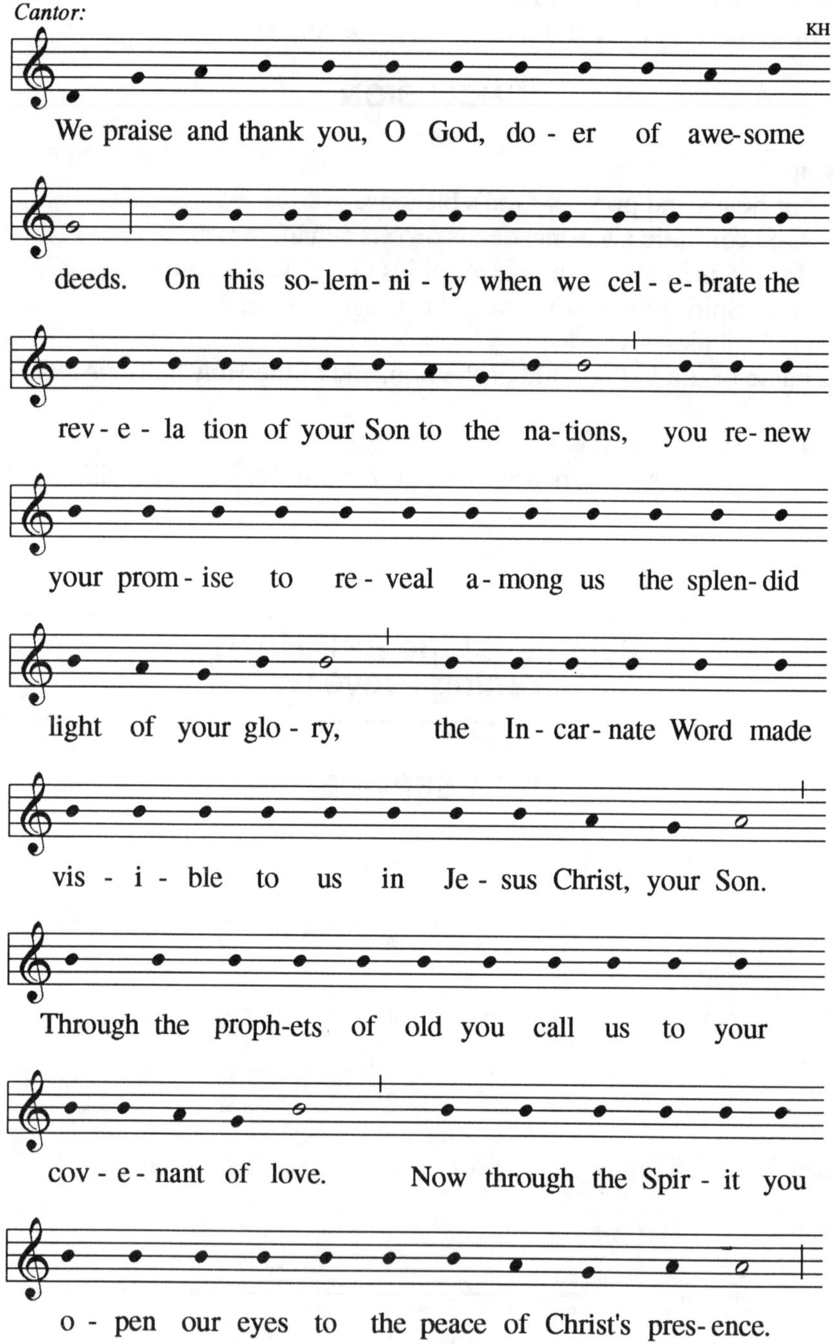
Cantor:
KH
We praise and thank you, O God, do - er of awe-some
deeds. On this so-lem-ni - ty when we cel - e- brate the
rev - e - la tion of your Son to the na-tions, you re-new
your prom - ise to re - veal a-mong us the splen-did
light of your glo - ry, the In - car- nate Word made
vis - i - ble to us in Je - sus Christ, your Son.
Through the proph-ets of old you call us to your
cov - e - nant of love. Now through the Spir - it you
o - pen our eyes to the peace of Christ's pres-ence.

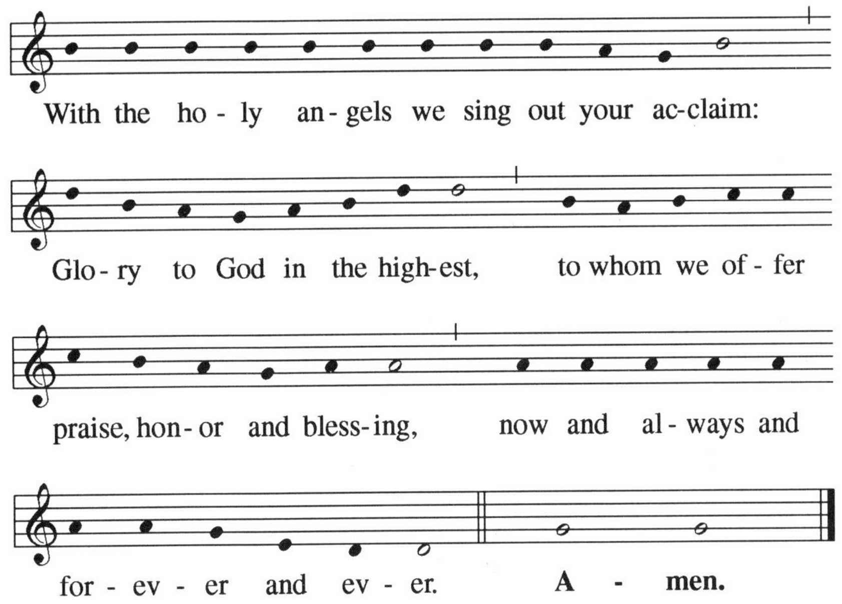

With the ho - ly an - gels we sing out your ac-claim:
Glo - ry to God in the high-est, to whom we of - fer
praise, hon - or and bless - ing, now and al - ways and
for - ev - er and ev - er. A - men.

PSALMODY

Psalm 141 *Psalm of David.*

ANTIPHON

O LORD, I cry **to** you:
"Hasten to me,
  listen to my voice
  when I cry **to** you."
Let my prayer rise
  like incense in **your** presence,
the lifting up of my hands
  like an evening **of**fering. ANTIPHON

Set, O LORD,
  a guard over **my** mouth,
keep the door of **my** lips.
Do not incline my heart to any evil,
  to performing wicked deeds
  with those who work **ini**quity;
let me not partake **in** their feasting. ANTIPHON

When a just person strikes me, it is **a** favor;
and when I am corrected, it is like anoin**ting** oil.
May my head never **re**fuse it,
while my prayer stands firm against **e**vil doings.

Let wicked judges be smashed against **the** rock,
and they will understand that my words **were** measured.
Like plowed and broken furrows on **the** land,
their bones are shattered at the **mouth** of Sheol. ANTIPHON

But my eyes look to you,
  O LORD, **my** Lord.
In you I take refuge;
  do not pour out **my** life.
Keep me from the snare they have prepared for me
  and from the traps of those who cre**ate** emptiness.
Let the wicked fall into their nets
  while I a**lone** escape. ANTIPHON

Psalm Prayer
O merciful God,
you hear the voice of those who call to you
with faith and love:
as our evening prayer rises to you on incense,
so may our gaze recognize the manifestation of your presence
now and always. **Amen.**

Psalm 111

ANTIPHON

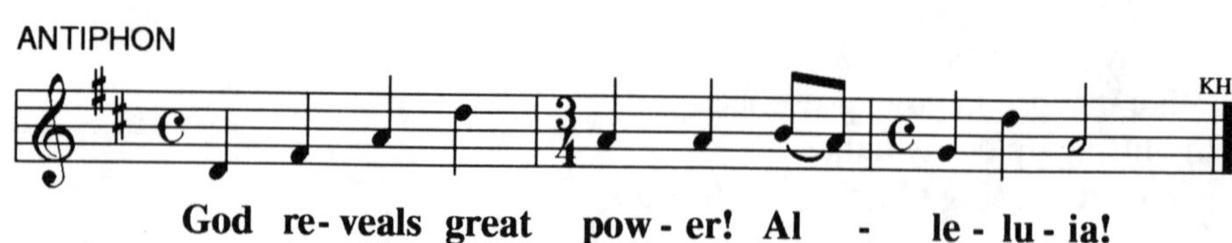

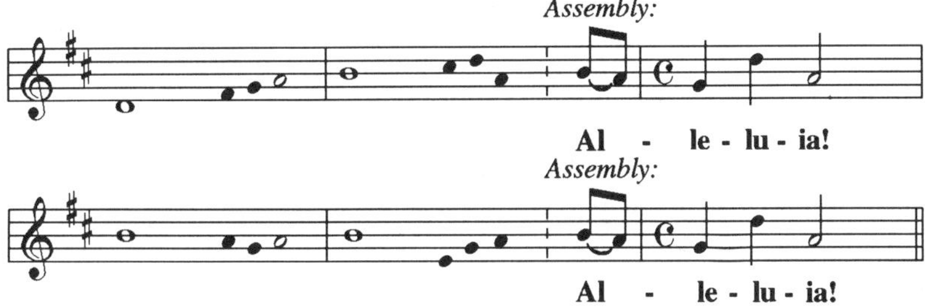
Assembly:
Al - le - lu - ia!
Assembly:
Al - le - lu - ia!

I will give thanks to the LORD with **all** my heart
in the council of the righteous and **the** assembly.
Great are the deeds **of** the LORD,
pondered by all who de**light** in them. ANTIPHON

God's work is majes**ty** and splendor,
and justice **stands** forever.
A memorial God has made **of** these wonders;
gracious and merciful **is** the LORD. ANTIPHON

God has given food to those **who** show reverence,
remembering the cove**nant** forever.
God has revealed to the people the power **of** these deeds
in giving them the nations **for** their heritage. ANTIPHON

The deeds of God's hands are **truth** and justice;
the precepts of God **all** are trustworthy.
They are established forev**er** and ever,
wrought in truth and eq**uity**. ANTIPHON

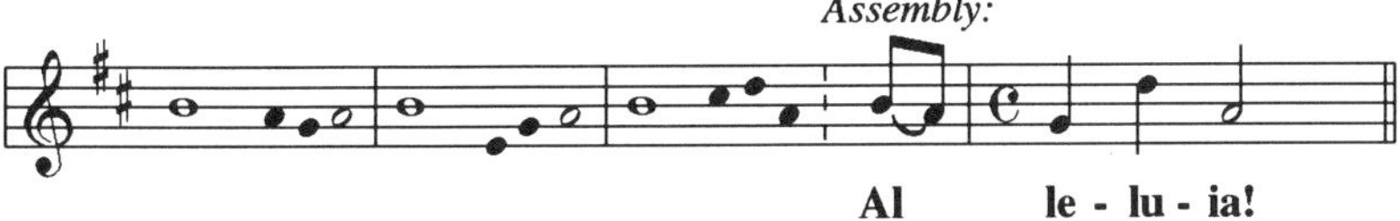
Assembly:
Al le - lu - ia!

God has sent deliverance **to** the people,
appointing the cove**nant** forever;
holy and to be revered **is** God's name.

The beginning of wisdom is reverence **for** the LORD,
and its practice brings about clear **un**derstanding.
The praise of God **stands** forever! ANTIPHON

Psalm Prayer
God of majesty and splendor,
your wonders fill all the earth:
look kindly on us your faithful servants,
so that we may see your glory now and forever. **Amen.**

Word of God

Magnificat

My soul does magni**fy** the Lord!
I delight in **God** my savior
who looked kindly **on** lowliness.

Now all ages will **call** me blessed
for the Mighty One **did** great things.
Holy is **God's** name;
mercy is from age to age for **those** in awe!

The Lord's strong arm did **mighty** deeds:
confused the proud in **their** smug hearts;
toppled sovereigns **from** their thrones,
and exalted **hum**ble ones;
filled the hungering with **good** things,
and sent the rich **a**way empty.

The Lord helped servant **Is**rael
to re**mem**ber mercy,
as was spoken to Ab**ra**ham
and his descendants for**e**vermore!

INTERCESSIONS

Petitions

Cantor, then Assembly:

Cantor:

For listening to **our** cries ...
For offering refuge **and** solace ...
For keeping us **from** harm ...
For giving us an abundance **of** riches ...
For remembering the covenant ...
For revealing majesty **and** power ...

For establishing truth **and** justice ...
For initiating a reign **of** peace ...
For delivering the faithful **de**parted ...

Our Father ...

Prayer
God of the nations,
you manifest your presence for the good of all:
hear our prayer of gratitude
that we may always be open to your overtures of love.
We pray through Jesus Christ. **Amen.**

CONCLUSION

Blessing
Bow your heads and pray for God's blessing.
May God manifest awesome deeds. **Amen.**
May Christ manifest gracious mercy. **Amen.**
May the Spirit manifest steadfast love. **Amen.**
And may God bless us
in the name of the Father, and of the Son, and of the Holy Spirit. **Amen.**

Dismissal
Exchange a sign of peace as you go forth to rest in God's revealed presence.

Sunday after the Epiphany

Feast of the BAPTISM OF THE LORD Morning Praise

FESTAL MORNING HYMN

PSALMODY

Psalm 2
ANTIPHON

Why do people rage,
  and nations plot in **vain**?
The rulers of the earth have stood up,
  and nobles have gathered together
  against the LORD and against **the** Messiah:
"Let us cut **their** bonds
and cast their ties away **from** us." ANTIPHON

The one who dwells in heaven will laugh,
  the Lord will **mock** them.
Then God will speak to them in anger,
  and confound **them** in fury:
"But I have consecrated you **my** ruler
over Zion, my ho**ly** mountain." ANTIPHON

I will tell about the decree of the LORD
  who said to **me**
"You are my son, today I have be**got**ten you.
Ask from me
  and I will give you people for your heritage,
  and for your possession, the ends of **the** earth.
You will rule them with a scepter of bronze;
  like a potter's vessel
  you **will** break them." ANTIPHON

And now, O rulers, be **wise**;
accept this instruction, O you judges **of** the earth:
"Serve the LORD **with** reverence
and with trembling ex**ul**tation.

Pay tribute to the **son**,
lest God be angry
  and you perish **on** the way.
For God's anger is quick **to** kindle."
Blessed are all those who take refuge **in** God! ANTIPHON

Psalm Prayer
Loving God,
you announced pleasure in your beloved Son:

be pleased with our efforts to serve you
as sons and daughters now and always. **Amen.**

Psalm 65 *To the choirmaster. Psalm of David. Psalm.*

ANTIPHON

KH
You ans- wer us, O God, with awe- some deeds.

To you praise is due,
  O God **in** Zion,
and for you promises will be **ful**filled.
O you who listen to prayer,
  to you all flesh **shall** come.
When our transgressions—our deeds of iniquity—overcome us,
  you **for**give them. ANTIPHON

Blessed is the one you elect and **bring** near;
that one shall dwell in **your** courts.
Let us be filled with the goodness of **your** house,
the holiness of **your** temple.

With awesome deeds you answer us **in** justice,
O God of our **sal**vation,
protector of all the ends of **the** earth
and of the dis**tant** seas. ANTIPHON

Girded with might,
  you establish mountains **in** strength.
You still the roaring of the seas—
  the roaring of their waves—
  and the clamor **of** nations.
Because of **your** signs,
the inhabitants of the ends of the earth will stand **in** awe. ANTIPHON

You cause the breaking of morning and of evening
  to burst **with** joy.
You visit the earth and give it water;
  abundantly, you **en**rich it:

the river of God
  is replete **with** water.
You provide people with grain,
  for you designed **it** so.

Its furrows you water **a**bundantly,
and you make **them** smooth.
You soften it **with** showers,
and you bless **its** sprout. ANTIPHON

You crown the year with your bounty,
  and fertility springs in the wake of **your** chariot.
The pastures of the wilderness drip with water,
  and the hills are girded **with** joy.
Meadows are clothed with flocks,
  and valleys are covered **with** grain.
They shout, even more, **they** sing. ANTIPHON

Psalm Prayer
Blessed God,
you chose your Son Jesus Christ to be first among the elect:
fill us with your goodness
that we may offer you fitting praise now and always. **Amen.**

Word of God

Benedictus

Blessed be the Lord God of **Israel**,
who visited and redeemed the **people**,
who raised up for us a **mighty** savior
from the house of **ser**vant David.

Just as the Lord spoke through the mouths of the holy prophets of **old**—
salvation comes out of the hands of our enemies and those who **hate** us,
that, with our ancestors, we might perform **works** of mercy,
remembering the holy covenant **sworn** to Abraham—

so does the Lord deliver us from the hands **of** our enemies,
that we might serve without fear before **the** Lord,
worshiping in **ho**liness
and in righteousness **all** our days.

And you also, child, will be called a prophet of God Most **High**:
for you will go before the Lord to prepare a **way**,
bringing people knowledge of salvation by for**giveness** of sins;
because of the deep and tender mercy **of** our God.

Whereby a light rising from on high will **vis**it us
to appear to those in darkness and in a shadow **of** death,
to guide our feet along a **straight**, sure path
into a **way** of peace.

INTERCESSIONS

Invocations

Cantor, then Assembly:

Cantor:

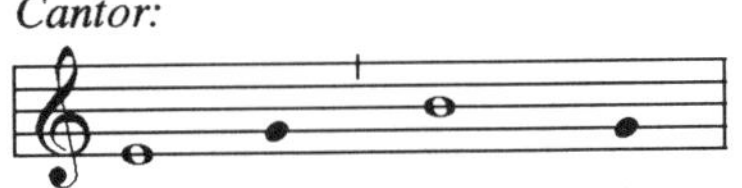

Beloved **Son**, you are our herit**age** ...
Beloved **Son**, you are our wise **judge** ...
Beloved **Son**, you are the e**lect** ...
Beloved **Son**, you are the just **one** ...
Beloved **Son**, you are our **strength** ...
Beloved **Son**, you are the joy of our sal**vation** ...
Beloved **Son**, you are the delight of our **baptism** ...
Beloved **Son**, you are the name we **bear** ...

Our Father ...

Prayer
Gracious God,
you sent your Spirit to rest on your beloved Son
when he was baptized in the Jordan:
pour forth that same Spirit on us through Jesus Christ. **Amen.**

CONCLUSION

Blessing
Bow your heads and pray for God's blessing.

May God smile upon us. **Amen.**
May the Son draw us near. **Amen.**
May the Spirit rest on us. **Amen.**
And may God bless us
in the name of the Father, and of the Son, and of the Holy Spirit. **Amen.**

Sign of Peace/Dismissal
Exchange a sign of peace as you go forth to live as God's elect.

Feast of the BAPTISM OF THE LORD
Evening Prayer

LIGHT SERVICE

Proclamation of the Light

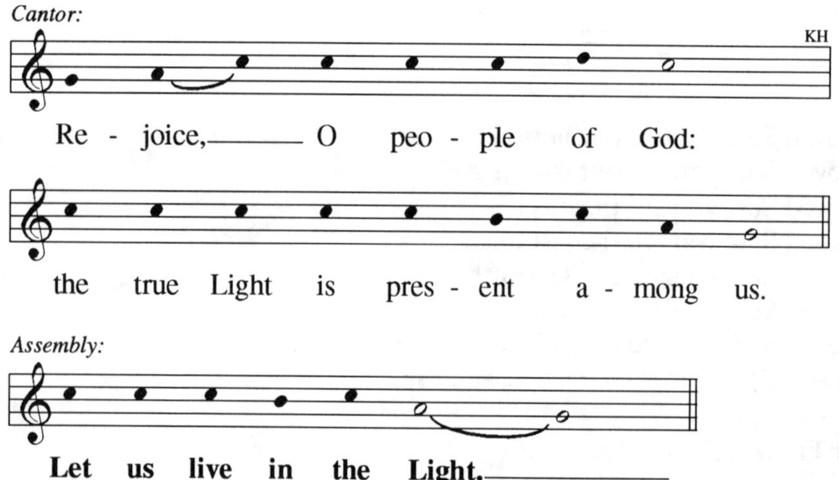
Cantor:
KH
Re - joice, O peo - ple of God:
the true Light is pres - ent a - mong us.
Assembly:
Let us live in the Light.

Festal Evening Hymn

Thanksgiving for the Light

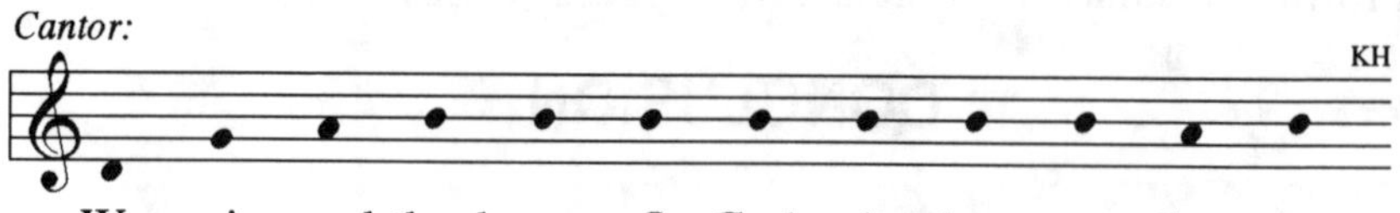
Cantor:
KH
We praise and thank you, O God, who chose your Son for

fav - or. On this ho - ly fes - ti - val when we
re - mem - ber Je - sus' bap - tism, you re - new
your prom - ise to re - veal a - mong us the splen- did
light of your glo - ry, the In - car - nate Word made
vis - i - ble to us in Je - sus Christ, your Son.
Through the proph-ets of old you call us to your
cov - e - nant of love. Now through the Spir - it you
o - pen our eyes to the peace of Christ's pres- ence.
With the ho - ly an - gels we sing out your ac-claim:
Glo - ry to God in the high-est, to whom we of - fer

praise, hon- or and bless- ing, now and al - ways and
for - ev - er and ev - er. A - men.

PSALMODY

Psalm 110 *Of David. Psalm.*

ANTIPHON

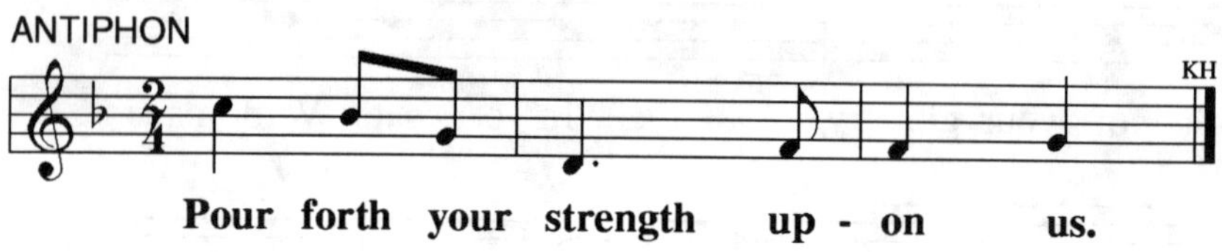
KH
Pour forth your strength up - on us.

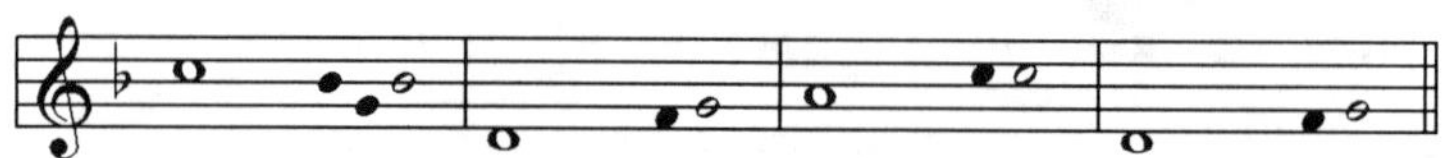

Thus says the LORD **to** my lord:
"Sit on my right
  until I place your enemies
  as a footstool for **your** feet."
Let the LORD send from Zion
  the scepter of **your** strength.
Rule in the midst of **your** enemies. ANTIPHON

Your people bring free **of**ferings
on the day of your might
  in ho**ly** splendor.
From the womb **of** dawn,
a dew of rejuvenation comes **to** you. ANTIPHON

The LORD has promised
  and will **not** repent:
"According to my word,
  you are a priest forever, my king **of** justice."
The Lord is at **your** right,
who has smashed rulers on the day **of** wrath.

The Lord judges **against** the nations,
piling them **with** corpses.
The Lord has smashed heads
  all over **the** land.
From a torrent the Lord drinks on the way,
  and rises up **in** triumph. ANTIPHON

Psalm Prayer
God of promise,
you fulfilled the expectation of the nations
by sending your Spirit upon your beloved Son:
rise up in triumph that we might enjoy life everlasting. **Amen.**

Psalm 9 *To the choirmaster. Muth lebben. Psalm of David.*

ANTIPHON

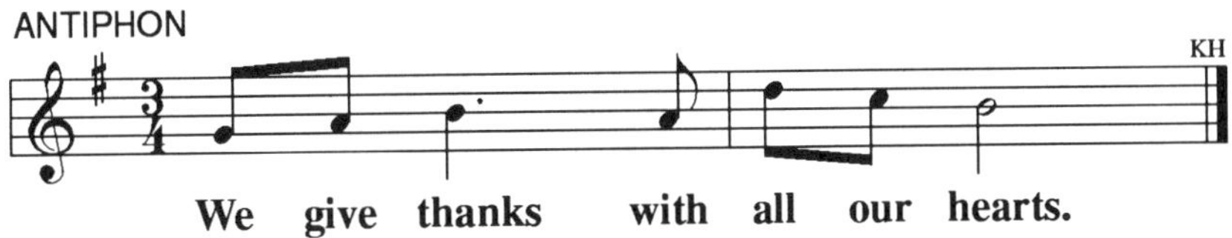

KH
We give thanks with all our hearts.

I will give thanks, O LORD, with **all** my heart.
I will tell of all your won**der**ful deeds.
I will rejoice, I will ex**ult** in you,
and I will play music for your name, **O** Most High. ANTIPHON

When my enemies turned back
  they stumbled and per**ished** before you,
for you had taken up my case **and** my judgment.
You sat **on** the throne
as the one who judg**es** with justice.

You re**buked** nations;
you destroyed the wicked,
  erasing their names
  forev**er** and ever.
The enemy has vanished
  in ruins **for** eternity.
You destroyed cities—
  even their memo**ry** has perished. ANTIPHON

But the LORD remains en**throned** forever,
making firm the **throne** of judgment.
God judges the **world** in justice
and the peoples in eq**ui**ty. ANTIPHON

The LORD will be
  a refuge **for** the poor,
a refuge in times **of** distress.
Those who know your name
  will **trust** in you,
for you do not abandon those who seek **you**, O LORD. ANTIPHON

Psalm Prayer
O Most High God,
you exalted your Son
when he was baptized by John in the Jordan:
raise us up to give thanks to you now and always. **Amen.**

Word of God

Magnificat

My soul does magni**fy** the Lord!
I delight in **God** my savior
who looked kindly **on** lowliness.

Now all ages will **call** me blessed
for the Mighty One **did** great things.
Holy is **God's** name;
mercy is from age to age for **those** in awe!

The Lord's strong arm did **migh**ty deeds:
confused the proud in **their** smug hearts;
toppled sovereigns **from** their thrones,
and exalted **hum**ble ones;
filled the hungering with **good** things,
and sent the rich **a**way empty.

The Lord helped servant **Is**rael
to re**mem**ber mercy,
as was spoken to Ab**ra**ham
and his descendants for**e**vermore!

INTERCESSIONS

Cantor, then Assembly:
KH
We ex - ult in our God.

Cantor:

For overcoming **all** enemies,
For accepting our **free** offerings,
For promising **sal**vation,
For judg**ing** justly,
For rising up **in** triumph,
For doing won**der**ful deeds,
For remaining stead**fast** in love,
For send**ing** the Spirit,
For abandoning not those **who** have died,

Our Father ...

Prayer
God of salvation,
you called John to baptize your beloved Son
and ushered in a new era of salvation:
save us, your holy people.
Give us strength to live our own baptism
as befitting your sons and daughters.
We pray through Jesus Christ. **Amen.**

CONCLUSION

Blessing
Bow your heads and pray for God's blessing.
May God receive us. **Amen.**
May the Son call us. **Amen.**
May the Spirit enliven us. **Amen.**
And may God bless us,
in the name of the Father, and of the Son, and of the Holy Spirit. **Amen.**

Sign of Peace/Dismissal
Exchange a sign of peace as we go to rest, faithful to our own baptismal commitment.

CG

Lent
Triduum
Easter

ASH WEDNESDAY Morning Praise

LENTEN MORNING HYMN

PSALMODY

From WEDNESDAY 2 Morning Praise, p. 94.

INTERCESSIONS

Invocations

Cantor, then Assembly:

KH
Je - sus Christ, our Good News and Sav - ior.

Cantor:

Hear **our** prayer ...
Remain faithful **to** us ...
Hide not your face **from** us ...
Teach us **your** ways ...
Lead us to act **just**ly ...
Draw us **to** prayer ...
Guide us in **fast**ing ...
Prompt us to alms**giv**ing ...
Deliver us from **e**vil ...
Judge us **kind**ly ...
Raise us to **new** life ...

Our Father ...

Prayer
O God of salvation,
you are quick with your mercy
and steadfast with your love:
as we begin Lent help us to
pray with ardor,
fast with a hunger for you,
and be generous with those in need.
May our Lenten practices turn us from evil
and instill in us a love for righteousness.
We pray through Jesus Christ
our Savior and brother. **Amen.**

CONCLUSION

Blessing
May God strengthen our desire for conversion and bless us
in the name of the Father, and of the Son, and of the Holy Spirit. **Amen.**

Dismissal
Go forth to begin Lent with a resolve for conversion. **Thanks be to God.**

ASH WEDNESDAY Evening Prayer

LENTEN EVENING HYMN

PSALMODY

From WEDNESDAY 2 Evening Prayer, p. 98.

INTERCESSIONS

Petitions

Cantor, then Assembly:

Cantor:

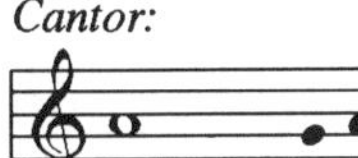

That we hide nothing **from** God ...
That we seek **God's** face ...
That we be open to God's **com**passion ...
That we accept **God's** ways ...
That we loathe injustice and **in**equity ...
That we heed God's right**eous** judgments ...
That we be firm in our Lenten works **of** penance ...
That those who have died may enjoy God's steadfast love **for**ever ...

Our Father ...

Prayer
Merciful God,
you are just in your judgments but
rich in kindness:
grant us strength of resolve and
an openness to overcome our weaknesses.
We ask this through Christ our Savior. **Amen.**

CONCLUSION

Blessing
May the God of mercy bless us
in the name of the Father, and of the Son, and of the Holy Spirit. **Amen.**

Dismissal
Go to rest in the mercy of God. **Thanks be to God.**

THURSDAY after Ash Wednesday
Morning Praise

LENTEN MORNING HYMN

PSALMODY

From THURSDAY 2 Morning Praise, p. 102.

INTERCESSIONS

Invocations

Cantor, then Assembly:

Cantor:

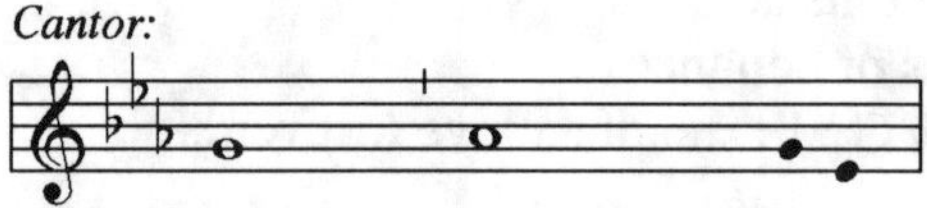

Shepherd of Israel, lead us **to** you ...
Shepherd of Israel, save us **from** harm ...
Shepherd of Israel, bring us back **from** straying ...
Shepherd of Israel, give **us** life ...
Shepherd of Israel, have pity **on** us ...
Shepherd of Israel, act in **our** favor ...
Shepherd of Israel, send **sal**vation ...
Shepherd of Israel, put sinners **to** shame ...
Shepherd of Israel, ease our **fearful**ness ...
Shepherd of Israel, make firm our lag**ging** spirits ...

Our Father ...

Prayer
O Shepherd of Israel,
you are ever faithful and merciful:
open our hearts to repent of our sins
and lead us to praise you now and always. **Amen.**

CONCLUSION

Blessing
May the God who watches over us bless us
in the name of the Father, and of the Son, and of the Holy Spirit. **Amen.**

Dismissal
Go forth to do Lenten penance, guided by our Shepherd God. **Thanks be to God.**

THURSDAY after Ash Wednesday Evening Prayer

LENTEN EVENING HYMN

PSALMODY

From THURSDAY 2 Evening Prayer, p. 106.

INTERCESSIONS

Petitions

Cantor, then Assembly:

Cantor:

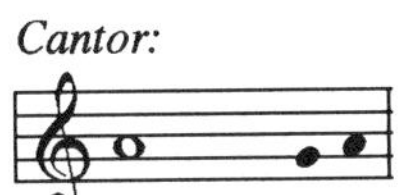

To recognize God's awe**some** deeds ...
To surrender ourselves to **God's** power ...
To follow **God's** call ...
To listen to **God's** voice ...
To keep **God's** precepts ...
To promote peace a**mong** peoples ...
To approach God **in** worship ...
To seek prosperity **for** all ...
To commend the faithful departed to **God's** love ...

Our Father ...

Prayer
God of great deeds,
you show us favor by your mercy:
may our Lenten promises
strengthen our commitment to you and
bring us to give you thanks now and always. **Amen.**

CONCLUSION

Blessing
May our redeeming God bless us
in the name of the Father, and of the Son, and of the Holy Spirit. **Amen.**

Dismissal
Go and rest in God's care. **Thanks be to God.**

FRIDAY after Ash Wednesday
Morning Praise

LENTEN MORNING HYMN

PSALMODY

From FRIDAY 2 Morning Praise, p. 110.

INTERCESSIONS

Invocations

Cantor, then Assembly:

Cantor:

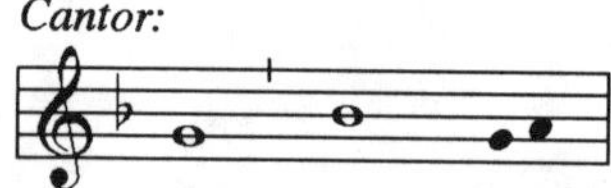

Compassionate Savior, cleanse us of **our** guilt ...
Compassionate Savior, help us to recognize **our** weaknesses ...
Compassionate Savior, grant us delight **in** truth ...
Compassionate Savior, teach **us** wisdom ...
Compassionate Savior, give us **pure** hearts ...
Compassionate Savior, deliver us **from** evil ...
Compassionate Savior, rebuild our fail**ing** spirits ...
Compassionate Savior, save us from discour**age**ment ...

Our Father ...

Prayer
Loving-kind God,
you show us mercy and compassion, truth and wisdom:
teach us always to do your holy will.
May our Lenten penance restore to us a clean heart
that we may only hunger for you.
We pray through our Savior Jesus Christ. **Amen.**

CONCLUSION

Blessing
May God, the source of mercy, bless us
in the name of the Father, and of the Son, and of the Holy Spirit. **Amen.**

Dismissal
Go forth to live God's will. **Thanks be to God.**

FRIDAY after Ash Wednesday Evening Prayer

LENTEN EVENING HYMN

PSALMODY

From FRIDAY 2 Evening Prayer, p. 114.

INTERCESSIONS

Petitions

Cantor, then Assembly:

Cantor:

For for**giveness** ...
For **patience** ...

For **hope** ...
For **endurance** ...
For **salvation** ...
For **courage** ...
For **mercy** ...
For **strength** ...
For those who have **died** ...

Our Father ...

Prayer
Merciful God,
your Son endured death on a cross
that we might gain salvation:
hear our prayer and
give us strength of resolve
to do your holy will now and always. **Amen.**

CONCLUSION

Blessing
May the God of the Cross,
who conquered death and promised life,
grant us strength and conviction and bless us
in the name of the Father, and of the Son, and of the Holy Spirit. **Amen.**

Dismissal
Go and rest in our Savior's goodness and mercy. **Thanks be to God.**

SATURDAY after Ash Wednesday Morning Praise

LENTEN MORNING HYMN

PSALMODY

From SATURDAY 2 Morning Praise, p. 118.

INTERCESSIONS

Invocations

Cantor, then Assembly:

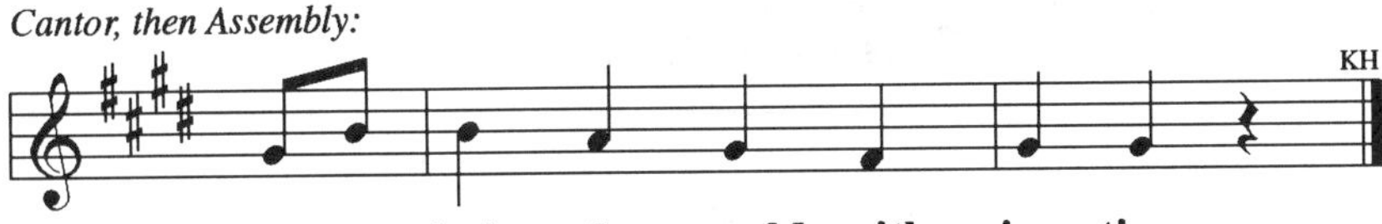
KH
For you judge the world with jus - tice.

Cantor:

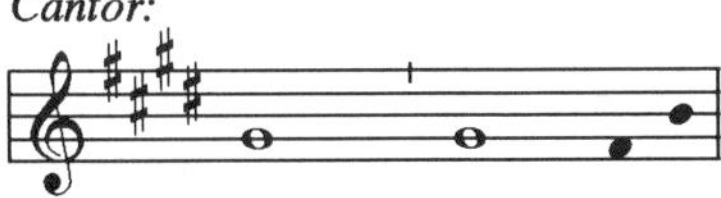

O Jesus Christ, to you praise **is** due ...
O Jesus Christ, to you everyone **shall** come ...
O Jesus Christ, to you all praise **is** raised ...
O Jesus Christ, from you blessings **pour** forth ...
O Jesus Christ, from you holiness **a**bounds ...
O Jesus Christ, from you abundance covers **the** earth ...
O Jesus Christ, with you days burst **with** joy ...
O Jesus Christ, with you honor and splendor stand be**fore** God ...
O Jesus Christ, with you God's reign **is** manifest ...

Our Father ...

Prayer
O redeeming God,
you shine the Light of your risen Son upon us:
may that brightness guide us through darkness
as we look to the unfailing Light
of the resurrection of Jesus Christ. **Amen.**

CONCLUSION

Blessing
Bow your heads and pray for God's blessing.
O God of redemption: make your face shine on us. **Amen.**
O Son of compassion: look upon us with mercy. **Amen.**
O Spirit of love: give us strength. **Amen.**
And may God bless us
in the name of the Father, and of the Son, and of the Holy Spirit. **Amen.**

Sign of Peace/Dismissal
Let us reach out with compassion and offer a sign of peace to others.

SATURDAY after Ash Wednesday Evening Prayer

LIGHT SERVICE

Proclamation of the Light

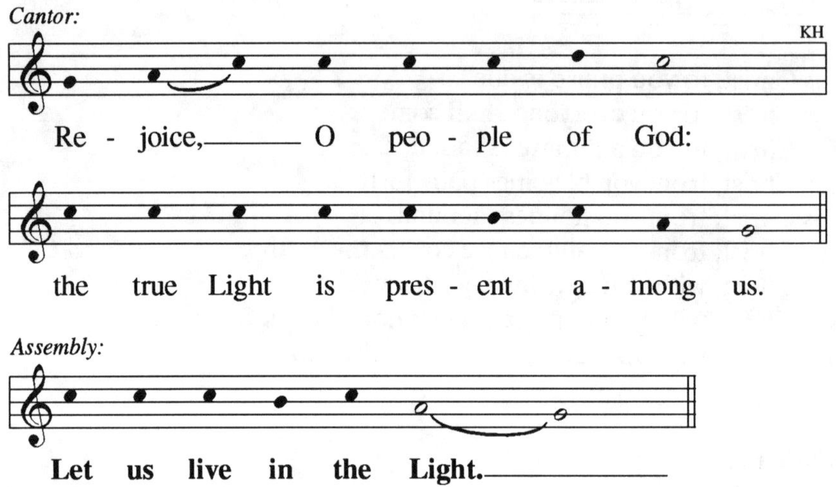
Cantor:
KH
Re - joice, O peo - ple of God:
the true Light is pres - ent a - mong us.
Assembly:
Let us live in the Light.

Lenten Evening Hymn

Thanksgiving for the Light

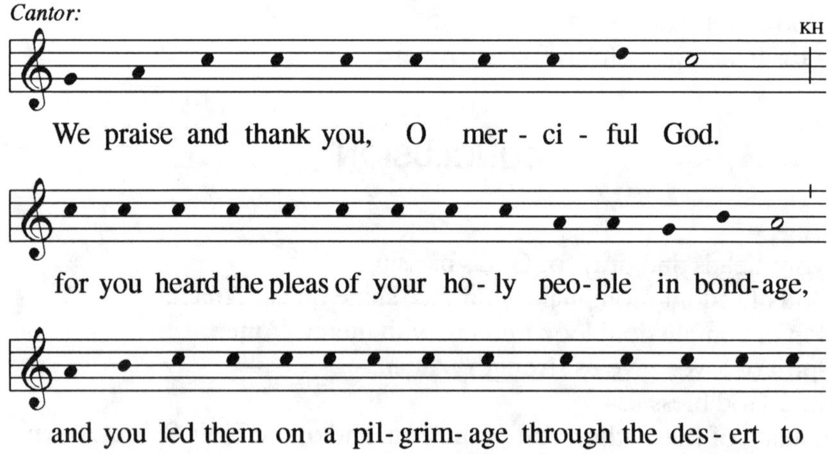
Cantor:
KH
We praise and thank you, O mer - ci - ful God.
for you heard the pleas of your ho - ly peo - ple in bond - age,
and you led them on a pil - grim - age through the des - ert to

a land of free-dom. In these for - ty days you lead us
on a pil - grim - age of re - pent - ance, that through
our sur - ren - der to pen - ance and prayer, we might learn
once more to be your faith - ful peo - ple. Light
our hearts with the fire of your love; o - pen
our eyes to the ten - der - ness of your care; free our
hands to lead oth - ers to the sure - ness of your
for - give - ness. Be with us in these days that
we may ov - er come what - ev - er binds us.
Set us free to live in the glo - rious light of

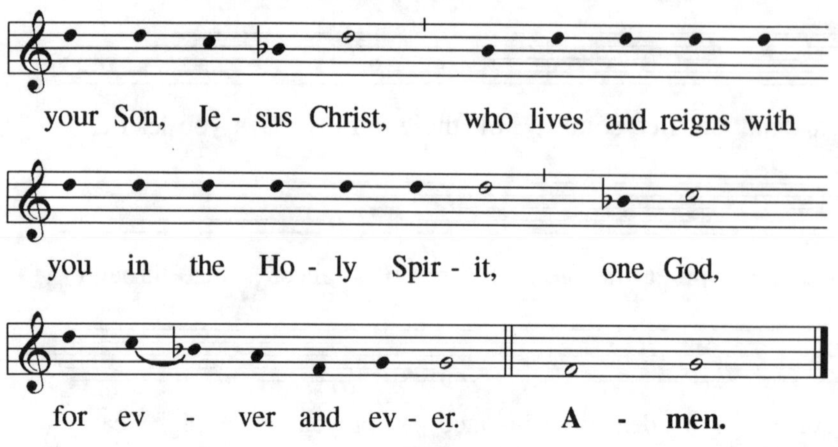
your Son, Je - sus Christ, who lives and reigns with
you in the Ho - ly Spir - it, one God,
for ev - ver and ev - er. A - men.

PSALMODY

From SATURDAY 2 Evening Prayer, p. 123.

INTERCESSIONS

Petitions

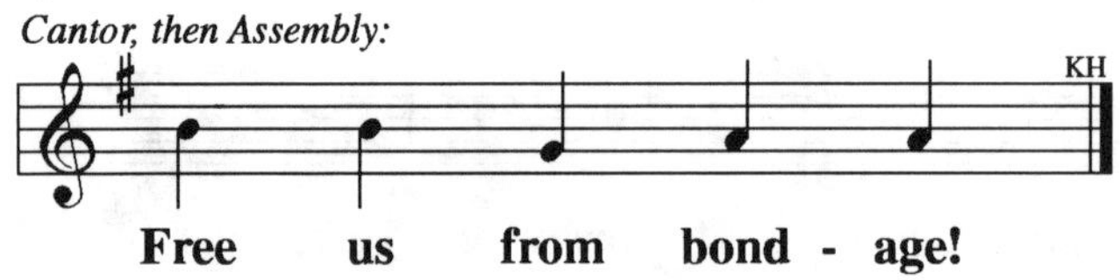
Cantor, then Assembly:
KH
Free us from bond - age!

Cantor:

That we may lift our prayer **to** God ... **and** cry out,
That we may do works **of** mercy ... **and** cry out,
That we may look only **to** God ... **and** cry out,
That we may take refuge **in** God ... **and** cry out,
That we may escape **all** harm ... **and** cry out,
That we may rejoice in be**ing** healed ... **and** cry out,
That we may be restored **to** life ... **and** cry out,
That we may remember **God's** holiness ... **and** cry out,
That we may stand in **God's** delight ... **and** cry out,
That we may give thanks **forever** ... **and** cry out,
That the faithful departed may have life ever**las**ting ... **and** cry out,

Our Father ...

Prayer
God who liberates,
you free us from all that binds us to slavery:
strengthen our Lenten resolve
that we may one day enjoy life with you forever. **Amen.**

CONCLUSION

Blessing
Bow your heads and pray for God's blessing.
May God who leads from bondage free us from all evil. **Amen.**
May Jesus who died for us teach us the Good News of salvation. **Amen.**
May the Spirit who baptized us give us new life. **Amen.**
And may God bless us
in the name of the Father, and of the Son, and of the Holy Spirit. **Amen.**

Sign of Peace/Dismissal
Give one another a sign of peace as brothers and sisters in Christ.

LENT Weeks 1, 3, & 5
SUNDAY Morning Praise

LENTEN MORNING HYMN

PSALMODY

Psalm 63 *Psalm of David. While he was in the desert of Judah.*

ANTIPHON
KH
In your name I will raise my hands.

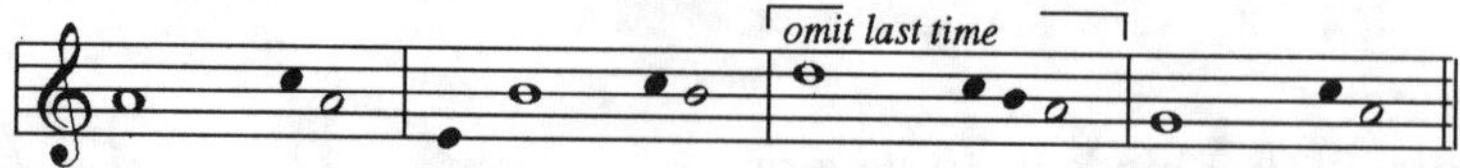

O God, you are my God, **I** seek you;
my **soul** thirsts **for** you.
My flesh longs for you
in a dry and **wast**ed land,
deprived **of** water. ANTIPHON

So in the sanctuary I have contemplated you
to see your might and your **glo**ry.
Because your **stead**fast love is better than life,
my lips will **praise** you.
So I will bless you **all** my life;
in your name I will raise **my** hands.

As with milk and rich food,
my soul **is** filled;
my **mouth** gives praise with joy**ful** lips.
I remember you up**on** my bed,
pondering you throughout **the** night.

For you were a help **for** me;
in the **shade** of your wings I **keep** singing.
My soul **clings** to you;
your right hand **up**holds me. ANTIPHON

But let those who seek my de**struc**tion
be **cast** into the depths of **the** earth.
Let them be given over to the power **of** the sword;
let them become a prey **for** jackals. ANTIPHON

Then the king shall rejoice **in** God.
All **those** who swear by God will **be** praised,
for the mouths of liars will **be** shut. ANTIPHON

Psalm Prayer
O God whom we seek,
your steadfast love is better than life:
keep us in the shade of your wings
as we celebrate the resurrection
of your Son and our Savior Jesus Christ. **Amen.**

Psalm 66 *To the choirmaster. A Song. Psalm.*

ANTIPHON

Tru - ly God has lis- tened to the voice of my prayer.

Sound the trumpet for God, all **the** earth!
Make music to the glory **of** God's name!
Give **glory** and praise! ANTIPHON

Say to God:
"How awesome are **your** deeds!
At the magnitude of your power,
your enemies **cringe** before you.
Let all the earth **wor**ship you,
let them sing to you,
let them sing to **your** name." ANTIPHON

Come and see the accomplishments **of** God—
an awesome work
on be**half** of mortals.
God turned the sea **into** dry land,
they crossed through the river **on** foot.

Therefore let us rejoice **in** God,
who rules over the **world** with power
and whose eyes watch **over** the nations.
Let not the stubborn rise up a**gainst** God. ANTIPHON

All you nations, bless **our** God!
Let the sound of **praise** be heard
for the one who gives **life to** our souls,
and who kept our feet **from** stumbling. ANTIPHON

For you have tested us, O God;
you have tried us like silver **is** tried.
You have caught us **in** a net.
You have put a burden on our backs;
you have let **mortals** enslave us.

We went through fire and water,
but you brought us out to a fer**tile** land. ANTIPHON

I shall go into your house **with** offerings.
I will fulfill my promises to you
which my lips uttered
and my mouth spoke when I was **in** distress.
I will bring you **offerings** of fatlings;
along with the smoke of rams
I will offer bulls **and** goats. ANTIPHON

Come, listen, all those who re**vere** God,
and I will tell
all that God did for **my** soul.
I have cried out **with** my mouth,
extolling God with **my** tongue.

If I had harbored emptiness in **my** heart,
the Lord would **not** have listened.
But truly **God** has listened,
listened to the voice of **my** prayer. ANTIPHON

Blessed **be** God
who has not re**jected** my prayer,
nor taken steadfast love away **from** me. ANTIPHON

Psalm Prayer
O great God,
your deeds are mighty and fruitful:
as you led your people of old from bondage to freedom,
so lead us during this Lenten season
to everlasting freedom with you
through your Son, Jesus our Savior. **Amen.**

Word of God

Benedictus
Blessed be the Lord God of **Israel**,
who visited and redeemed the **people**,
who raised up for us a **mighty** savior
from the house of **ser**vant David.

Just as the Lord spoke through the mouths of the holy prophets of **old**—
salvation comes out of the hands of our enemies and those who **hate** us,
that, with our ancestors, we might perform **works** of mercy,
remembering the holy covenant **sworn** to Abraham—

so does the Lord deliver us from the hands **of** our enemies,
that we might serve without fear before **the** Lord,
worshiping in **ho**liness
and in righteousness **all** our days.

And you also, child, will be called a prophet of God Most **High**:
for you will go before the Lord to prepare a **way**,
bringing people knowledge of salvation by for**giveness** of sins;
because of the deep and tender mercy **of** our God.

Whereby a light rising from on high will **vis**it us
to appear to those in darkness and in a shadow **of** death,
to guide our feet along a **straight**, sure path
into a **way** of peace.

INTERCESSIONS

Invocations

Cantor, then Assembly:

KH
We will cel - e- brate you for - ev - er!

Cantor:

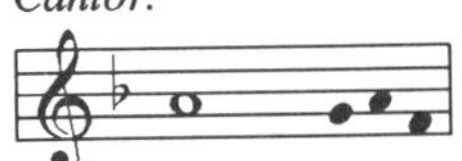

For your unfail**ing** presence,
For your works of **cre**ation,
For your voice **of** solace,
For your endur**ing** patience,
For your **great** holiness,
For your **mighty** deeds,
For your care **and** nurture,
For your offer of **sal**vation,
For your sus**tain**ing life,
For your calling those **to** be baptized,

Our Father ...

Prayer
God of the universe,
each week you give us a special day
to remember your Son's resurrection:
renew within us a zest for life
that we may live with you forever and ever. **Amen.**

CONCLUSION

Blessing
Bow your heads and ask for God's blessing.
May the God of dawn bless us with new life. **Amen.**
May the Son of salvation bless us with renewed fervor. **Amen.**
May the Spirit of peace bless us with consolation. **Amen.**
And may God bless us
in the name of the Father, and of the Son, and of the Holy Spirit. **Amen.**

Sign of Peace/Dismissal
Let us offer one another a sign of the peace of Christ.

LENT Weeks 1, 3, & 5
SUNDAY Evening Prayer

LIGHT SERVICE

Proclamation of the Light

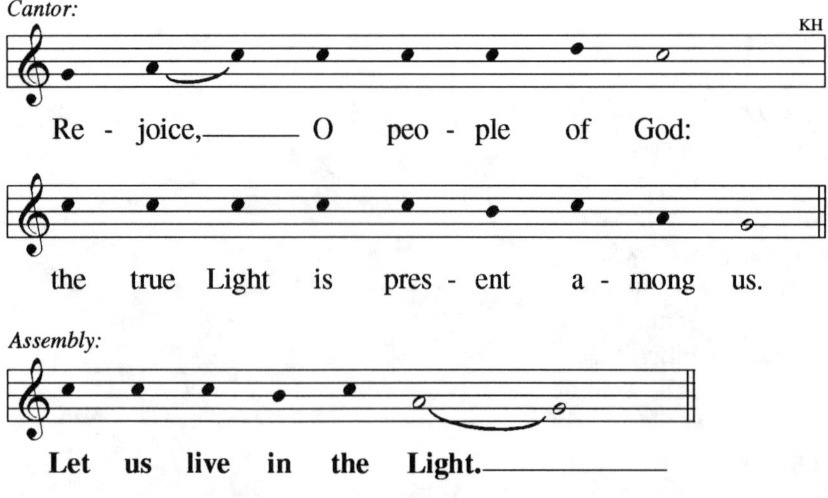
Cantor:
KH
Re - joice, O peo - ple of God:
the true Light is pres - ent a - mong us.
Assembly:
Let us live in the Light.

Lenten Evening Hymn

Thanksgiving for the Light

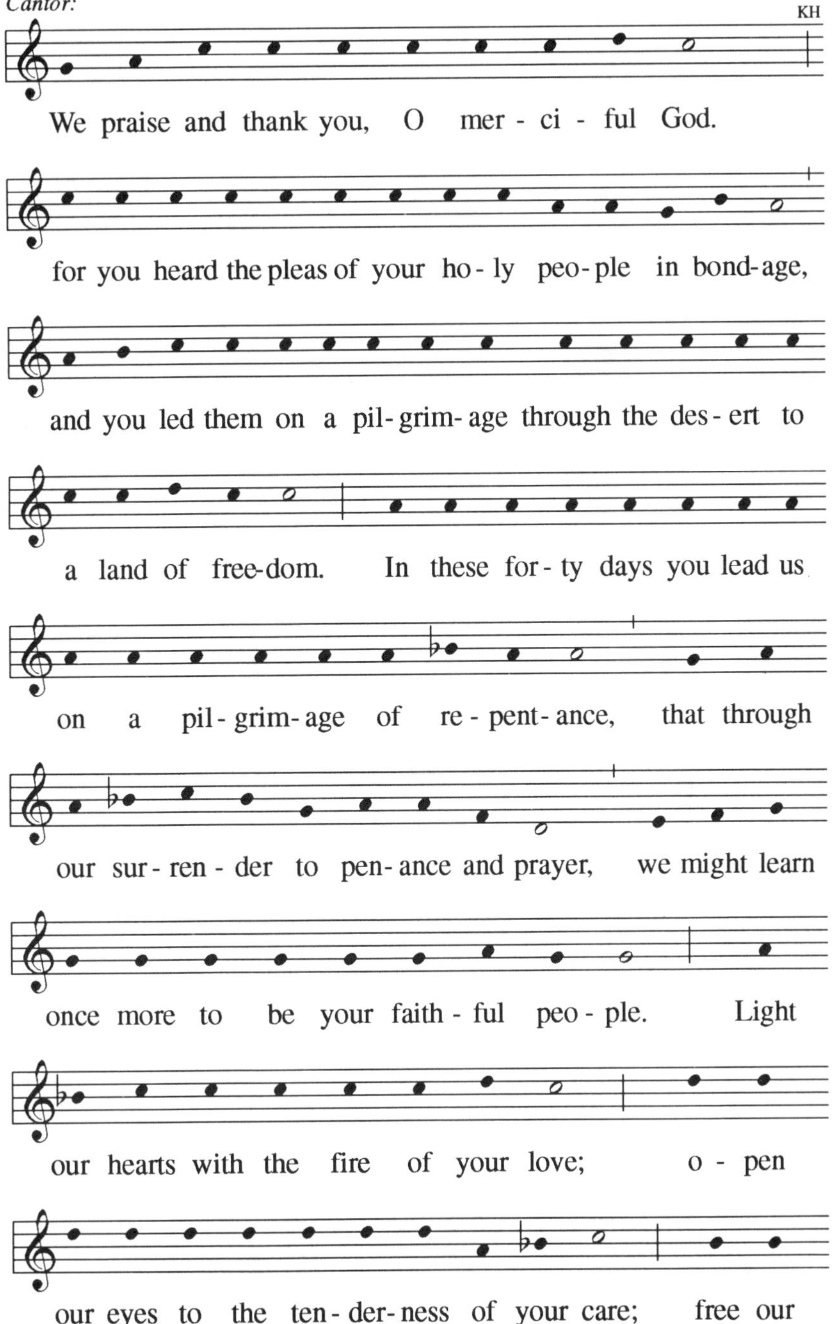
Cantor:
KH
We praise and thank you, O mer - ci - ful God.
for you heard the pleas of your ho - ly peo - ple in bond - age,
and you led them on a pil - grim - age through the des - ert to
a land of free - dom. In these for - ty days you lead us
on a pil - grim - age of re - pent - ance, that through
our sur - ren - der to pen - ance and prayer, we might learn
once more to be your faith - ful peo - ple. Light
our hearts with the fire of your love; o - pen
our eyes to the ten - der - ness of your care; free our

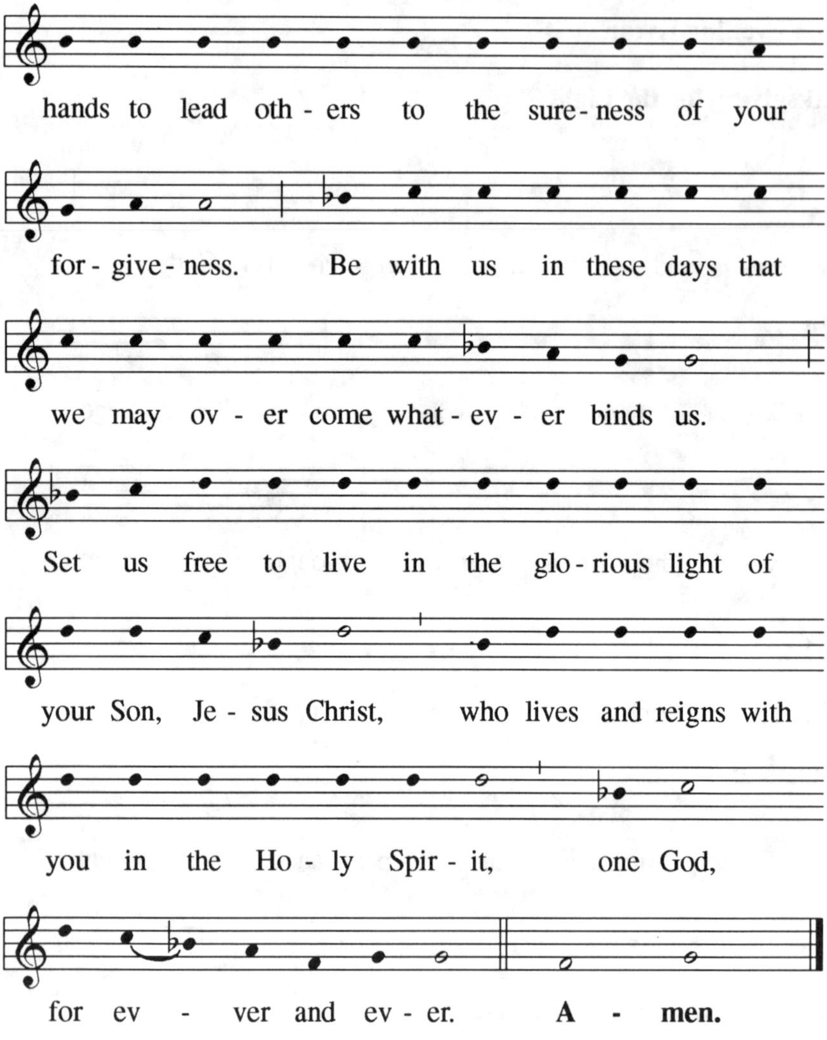

hands to lead oth - ers to the sure - ness of your
for - give - ness. Be with us in these days that
we may ov - er come what - ev - er binds us.
Set us free to live in the glo - rious light of
your Son, Je - sus Christ, who lives and reigns with
you in the Ho - ly Spir - it, one God,
for ev - ver and ev - er. A - men.

PSALMODY

Psalm 141 *Psalm of David.*

ANTIPHON

KH
Lis- ten to our cries for mer - cy.

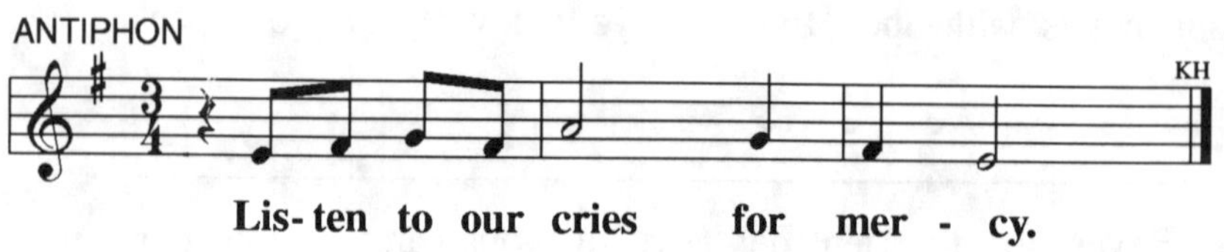

O LORD, I cry **to** you:
"Hasten to me,
  listen to my voice
  when I cry **to** you."
Let my prayer rise
  like incense in **your** presence,
the lifting up of my hands
  like an evening **of**fering. ANTIPHON

Set, O LORD,
  a guard over **my** mouth,
keep the door of **my** lips.
Do not incline my heart to any evil,
  to performing wicked deeds
  with those who work **in**iquity;
let me not partake **in** their feasting. ANTIPHON

When a just person strikes me, it is **a** favor;
and when I am corrected, it is like anoin**ting** oil.
May my head never **re**fuse it,
while my prayer stands firm against **ev**il doings.

Let wicked judges be smashed against **the** rock,
and they will understand that my words **were** measured.
Like plowed and broken furrows on **the** land,
their bones are shattered at the **mouth** of Sheol. ANTIPHON

But my eyes look to you,
  O LORD, **my** Lord.
In you I take refuge;
  do not pour out **my** life.
Keep me from the snare they have prepared for me
  and from the traps of those who cre**ate** emptiness.
Let the wicked fall into their nets
  while I a**lone** escape. ANTIPHON

Psalm Prayer
O merciful God,
you hear the voice of those who call to you

with faith and love:
hear our cry during this Lenten season
that we may gaze only on you now and always. **Amen.**

Psalm 110 *Of David. Psalm.*

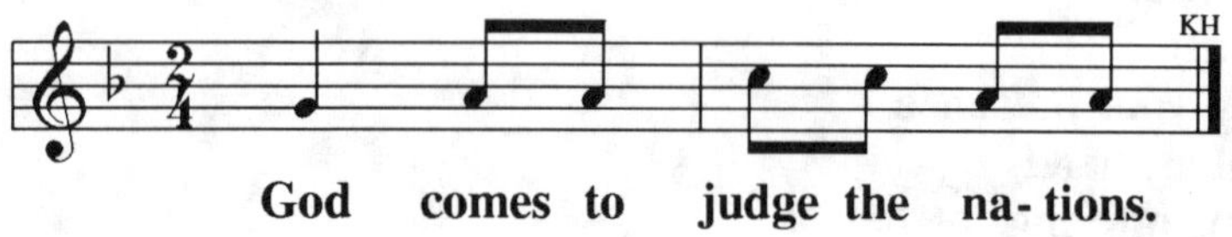

Thus says the LORD **to** my lord:
"Sit on my right
until I place your enemies
as a footstool for **your** feet."
Let the LORD send from Zion
the scepter of **your** strength.
Rule in the midst of **your** enemies. ANTIPHON

Your people bring free **of**ferings
on the day of your might
in ho**ly** splendor.
From the womb **of** dawn,
a dew of rejuvenation comes **to** you. ANTIPHON

The LORD has promised
and will **not** repent:
"According to my word,
you are a priest forever, my king **of** justice."
The Lord is at **your** right,
who has smashed rulers on the day **of** wrath.

The Lord judges a**gainst** the nations,
piling them **with** corpses.
The Lord has smashed heads
all over **the** land.
From a torrent the Lord drinks on the way,
and rises up **in** triumph. ANTIPHON

Psalm Prayer
O merciful God,
you judge with justice and compassion:
hear our evening prayer
that we may be faithful to you now and always. **Amen.**

Word of God

Magnificat
My soul does magni**fy** the Lord!
I delight in **God** my savior
who looked kindly **on** lowliness.

Now all ages will **call** me blessed
for the Mighty One **did** great things.
Holy is **God's** name;
mercy is from age to age for **those** in awe!

The Lord's strong arm did **migh**ty deeds:
confused the proud in **their** smug hearts;
toppled sovereigns **from** their thrones,
and exalted **hum**ble ones;
filled the hungering with **good** things,
and sent the rich **a**way empty.

The Lord helped servant **Is**rael
to re**mem**ber mercy,
as was spoken to Ab**ra**ham
and his descendants for**e**vermore!

INTERCESSIONS

Petitions

Cantor, then Assembly:
KH
Have mer - cy on us and bless us.

Cantor:

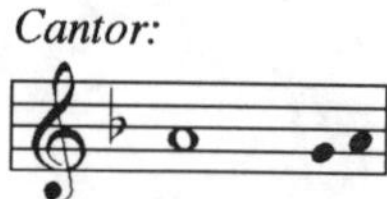

We **cry** out ...
We lift our hands in **thanks**giving ...
We renew our efforts **to do** good ...
We stand firm a**gainst** evil ...
We pour out our lives **for** others ...
We make known **God's** ways ...
We open ourselves to **sal**vation ...
We rejoice for God's **just** judgments ...
We seek guidance on nations **and** peoples ...
We beg for rejuvenation ...
We cry out for **the** dead ...

Our Father ...

Prayer
O God,
you renew us by our celebration
of the resurrection of your Son:
grant us fresh strength to meet the challenges
of this new week, that we may come to you
faithfully now and always. **Amen.**

CONCLUSION

Blessing
Bow your heads and pray for God's blessing.
May the Creator bless us with faith made sure. **Amen.**
May the Son bless us with hope made visible. **Amen.**
May the Spirit bless us with Love made flesh. **Amen.**
And may God bless us
in the name of the Father, and of the Son, and of the Holy Spirit. **Amen.**

Sign of Peace/Dismissal
Exchange with one another a sign of our renewal in the peace of Christ.

LENT Weeks 1, 3, & 5
MONDAY Morning Praise

LENTEN MORNING HYMN

PSALMODY

From MONDAY 1 Morning Praise, p. 21.

INTERCESSIONS

Invocations

Cantor, then Assembly:

Cantor:

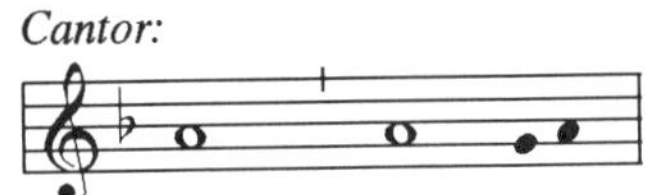

O saving Christ, you bless us **with** strength ...
O saving Christ, you lead us on **our** pilgrimage ...
O saving Christ, you cover us **with** blessings ...
O saving Christ, you hear **our** prayer ...
O saving Christ, you shield us **from** evil ...
O saving Christ, you perceive **our** groaning ...
O saving Christ, you guide us by **your** justice ...
O saving Christ, you straighten our paths **be**fore us ...
O saving Christ, you protect those who love **your** name ...
O saving Christ, you crown the righteous with **de**light ...

Our Father ...

Prayer
Gracious God,
you have been present to us
in the abundance of your mercy:
accompany us on our Lenten journey,
that we may one day rest with you forever and ever. **Amen.**

CONCLUSION

Blessing
May almighty God protect us from straying and bless us
in the name of the Father, and of the Son, and of the Holy Spirit. **Amen.**

Dismissal
Go forth and live your day with discipline. **Thanks be to God.**

LENT Weeks 1, 3, & 5
MONDAY Evening Prayer

LENTEN EVENING HYMN

PSALMODY

From MONDAY 1 Evening Prayer, p. 25.

INTERCESSIONS

Petitions

Cantor, then Assembly:

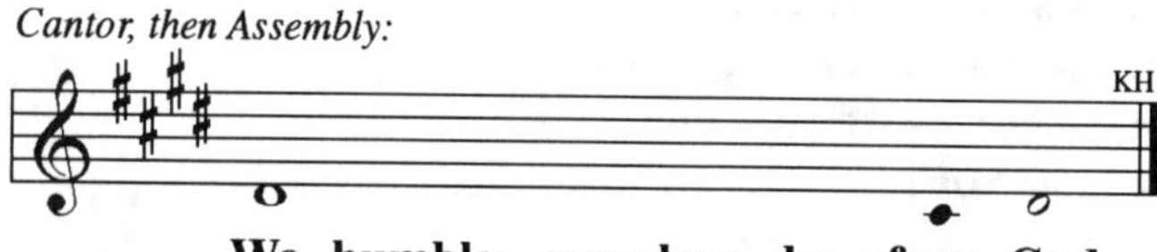

Cantor:

That we **not** boast ...
That we be **not** smug ...
That we not **pre**tend ...
That we be not **pre**tentious ...
That we not **des**pair ...
That we be not **un**quiet ...
That we **not** waver ...
That we be not **un**faithful ...
That we **not** grumble ...
That we be **not** joyless ...
That we not **con**demn ...
That we be **not** empty ...
That we **not** sin ...
That we be **not** self-righteous ...
That the departed be not **for**gotten ...

Our Father ...

Prayer
O God our rock,
you give strength to those in need:
grant us rest this night that we may wake refreshed and
ready to struggle against all iniquity.
We pray through Jesus Christ. **Amen.**

CONCLUSION

Blessing
May God protect us and bless us
in the name of the Father, and of the Son, and of the Holy Spirit. **Amen.**

Dismissal
Go and rest with confidence in the strength of God. **Thanks be to God.**

LENT Weeks 1, 3, & 5
TUESDAY Morning Praise

LENTEN MORNING HYMN

PSALMODY

From TUESDAY 1 Morning Praise, p. 29 (omit Psalm 113 Alleluias).

INTERCESSIONS

Invocations

Cantor, then Assembly:
KH
We trust in your mer - cy.

Cantor:

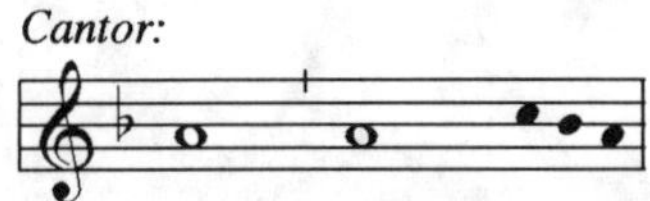

O shielding Savior, you watch **o**ver us ...
O shielding Savior, you **raise** the weak ...
O shielding Savior, you pro**tect** the poor ...
O shielding Savior, you overcome **ad**versaries ...
O shielding Savior, you lift **up** our spirits ...
O shielding Savior, you sus**tain** our efforts ...
O shielding Savior, you bring blessings up**on** your people ...

Our Father ...

Prayer
O God who guards and protects,
you watch over your holy people with care and compassion:
be with us today as a shield that surrounds us,
and help us to trust in your mercy now and always. **Amen.**

CONCLUSION

Blessing
May our caring God protect us and bless us
in the name of the Father, and of the Son, and of the Holy Spirit. **Amen.**

Dismissal
Go forth to trust God in all you do. **Thanks be to God.**

LENT Weeks 1, 3, & 5
TUESDAY Evening Prayer

LENTEN EVENING HYMN

PSALMODY

From TUESDAY 1 Evening Prayer, p. 32.

INTERCESSIONS

Petitions

Cantor, then Assembly:

Cantor:

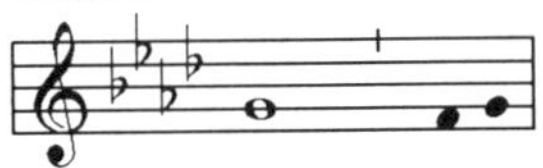

That we refuse to sin with our tongues ... **we** plead,
That we recognize our frailty ... **we** plead,
That we hope only in God ... **we** plead,
That we scorn the foolhardy ... **we** plead,
That we remain always faithful ... **we** plead,
That we abound in God's steadfast love ... **we** plead,
That we learn to walk in truth ... **we** plead,
That we be a sign of God's goodness ... **we** plead,
That the faithful departed be comforted always ... **we** plead,

Our Father ...

Prayer
Loving God,
your faithful presence has guarded us against frailty and weakness:
at the end of this day fill us with confidence in you
so that we may rest peacefully with you now and forever. **Amen.**

CONCLUSION

Blessing
May our loving God guard us against transgressions and bless us
in the name of the Father, and of the Son, and of the Holy Spirit. **Amen.**

Dismissal
Go and rest peacefully under the watchful shadow of God. **Thanks be to God.**

LENT Weeks 1, 3, & 5
WEDNESDAY Morning Praise

LENTEN MORNING HYMN

PSALMODY

From WEDNESDAY 1 Morning Praise, p. 36.

INTERCESSIONS

Invocations

Cantor, then Assembly:

Cantor:

O gentle Savior, you still the enemy **with**in us ... **so** we cry,
O gentle Savior, you rule over us **with** care ... **so** we cry,
O gentle Savior, you desire our **re**pentance ... **so** we cry,
O gentle Savior, you refresh those who cling **to** you ... **so** we cry,
O gentle Savior, you teach us submission to **your** will ... **so** we cry,
O gentle Savior, you bring comfort to **the** fearful ... **so** we cry,
O gentle Savior, you favor us with strength and **en**durance ... **so** we cry,

Our Father ...

Prayer
O loving-kind God,
you are gentle and full of compassion,
our refuge and our strength:
help us to recognize your righteous wrath
and to turn from anything that leads us away from you.
We pray through Jesus Christ. **Amen.**

CONCLUSION

Blessing
May our loving-kind God bless us
in the name of the Father, and of the Son, and of the Holy Spirit. **Amen.**

Dismissal
Go forth to live in the refuge of God. **Thanks be to God.**

LENT Weeks 1, 3, & 5
WEDNESDAY Evening Prayer

LENTEN EVENING HYMN

PSALMODY

From WEDNESDAY 1 Evening Prayer, p. 40.

INTERCESSIONS

Petitions

Cantor, then Assembly:

Cantor:

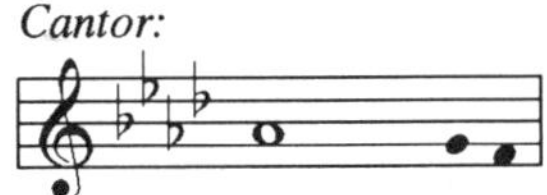

That we admit **any** guilt ...
That we curb **any** hatred ...
That we refrain from **any** falsehood ...
That we resist **empti**ness ...
That we discern how **to do** good ...
That we **despise** evil ...
That we put off **arro**gance ...
That we avoid disdain **and** scorn ...
That we give thanks for the faithfulness of those **de**parted ...

Our Father ...

Prayer
O God of our salvation,
your steadfast love and fidelity
encourage us to turn toward you:

help us to overcome our weaknesses
that we may rest confidently in you now and always. **Amen.**

CONCLUSION

Blessing
May God strengthen us against all evil and bless us
in the name of the Father, and of the Son, and of the Holy Spirit. **Amen.**

Dismissal
Go and rest in truth and fidelity. **Thanks be to God.**

LENT Weeks 1, 3, & 5
THURSDAY Morning Praise

LENTEN MORNING HYMN

PSALMODY

From THURSDAY 1 Morning Praise, p. 44.

INTERCESSIONS

Invocations

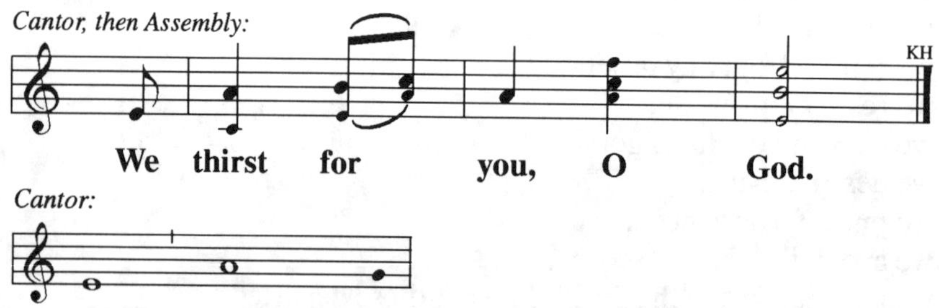
Cantor, then Assembly:
KH
We thirst for you, O God.
Cantor:

O loving Savior, we seek **you** ...
O loving Savior, we long for **you** ...
O loving Savior, we contemplate **you** ...
O loving Savior, we praise **you** ...
O loving Savior, we bless **you** ...
O loving Savior, we remember **you** ...
O loving Savior, we cling to **you** ...

O loving Savior, we rejoice in **you** ...
O loving Savior, we return to **you** ...

Our Father ...

Prayer
O God of our salvation,
you saved your people of old:
save us now from alienation from you
so that we may praise you now and always. **Amen.**

CONCLUSION

Blessing
My God preserve us from all evil and bless us
in the name of the Father, and of the Son, and of the Holy Spirit. **Amen.**

Dismissal
Go forth to live in God's abundant mercy. **Thanks be to God.**

LENT Weeks 1, 3, & 5
THURSDAY Evening Prayer

LENTEN EVENING HYMN

PSALMODY

From THURSDAY 1 Evening Prayer, p. 47.

INTERCESSIONS

Petitions

Cantor, then Assembly:

Cantor:

That God may cher**ish** us ...
That God may withhold justi**fied** wrath ...
That God may put away displeasure **with** us ...
That God may suppress right**eous** anger ...
That God may revive us so we may **re**joice ...
That God may speak words of truth **and** justice ...
That God may grant prosperity **and** peace ...
That God may judge with **eq**uity ...
That God may extoll those who have died **this** day ...

Our Father ...

Prayer
Forgiving and forbearing God,
you cherish the people who turn back to you:
help us to live more perfectly
the Good News of your Son, Jesus Christ. **Amen.**

CONCLUSION

Blessing
May the God of mercy bless us
in the name of the Father, and of the Son, and of the Holy Spirit. **Amen.**

Dismissal
Go and rest in the abundance of God. **Thanks be to God.**

LENT Weeks 1, 3, & 5
FRIDAY Morning Praise

LENTEN MORNING HYMN

PSALMODY

From FRIDAY 1 Morning Praise, p. 50.

INTERCESSIONS

Invocations

Cantor, then Assembly:

Cantor:

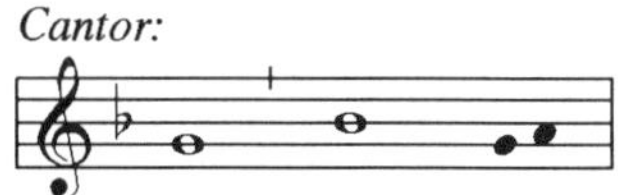

Compassionate Savior, cleanse us of **our** guilt ...
Compassionate Savior, help us to recognize **our** weaknesses ...
Compassionate Savior, grant us delight **in** truth ...
Compassionate Savior, teach **us** wisdom ...
Compassionate Savior, give us **pure** hearts ...
Compassionate Savior, deliver us **from** evil ...
Compassionate Savior, rebuild our fail**ing** spirits ...
Compassionate Savior, save us from discour**age**ment ...

Our Father ...

Prayer
Loving-kind God,
you show us mercy and compassion, truth and wisdom:
teach us always to do your holy will.
May our Lenten penance restore to us a clean heart
that we may only hunger for you.
We pray through our Savior Jesus Christ. **Amen.**

CONCLUSION

Blessing
May God, the source of mercy, bless us
in the name of the Father, and of the Son, and of the Holy Spirit. **Amen.**

Dismissal
Go forth to live God's will. **Thanks be to God.**

LENTEN EVENING HYMN

PSALMODY

From FRIDAY 1 Evening Prayer, p. 54.

INTERCESSIONS

Petitions

Cantor, then Assembly:

May God hear our cries.

Cantor:

For for**giveness** ...
For **patience** ...
For **hope** ...
For en**durance** ...
For sal**vation** ...
For **courage** ...
For **mercy** ...
For **strength** ...
For those who have **died** ...

Our Father ...

Prayer
Merciful God,
your Son endured death on a cross
that we might gain salvation:
hear our prayer and
give us strength of resolve
to do your holy will now and always. **Amen.**

CONCLUSION

Blessing
May the God of the Cross,
who conquered death and promised life,

grant us strength and conviction and bless us
in the name of the Father, and of the Son, and of the Holy Spirit. **Amen.**

Dismissal
Go and rest in our Savior's goodness and mercy. **Thanks be to God.**

LENT Weeks 1, 3, & 5
SATURDAY Morning Praise

LENTEN MORNING HYMN

PSALMODY

From SATURDAY 1 Morning Praise, p. 58.

INTERCESSIONS

Invocations

Cantor, then Assembly:

KH
For you judge the world with jus - tice.

Cantor:

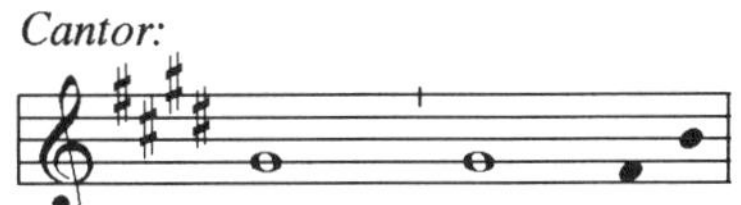

O Jesus Christ, to you praise **is** due ...
O Jesus Christ, to you everyone **shall** come ...
O Jesus Christ, to you all praise **is** raised ...
O Jesus Christ, from you blessings **pour** forth ...
O Jesus Christ, from you holiness **a**bounds ...
O Jesus Christ, from you abundance covers **the** earth ...
O Jesus Christ, with you days burst **with** joy ...
O Jesus Christ, with you honor and splendor stand be**fore** God ...
O Jesus Christ, with you God's reign **is** manifest ...

Our Father ...

Prayer
O redeeming God,
you shine the Light of your risen Son upon us:
may that brightness guide us through darkness
as we look to the unfailing Light
of the resurrection of Jesus Christ. **Amen.**

CONCLUSION

Blessing
Bow your heads and pray for God's blessing.
O God of redemption: make your face shine on us. **Amen.**
O Son of compassion: look upon us with mercy. **Amen.**
O Spirit of love: give us strength. **Amen.**
And may God bless us
in the name of the Father, and of the Son, and of the Holy Spirit. **Amen.**

Sign of Peace/Dismissal
Let us reach out with compassion and offer a sign of peace to others.

LENT Weeks 1, 3, & 5
SATURDAY Evening Prayer

LIGHT SERVICE

Proclamation of the Light

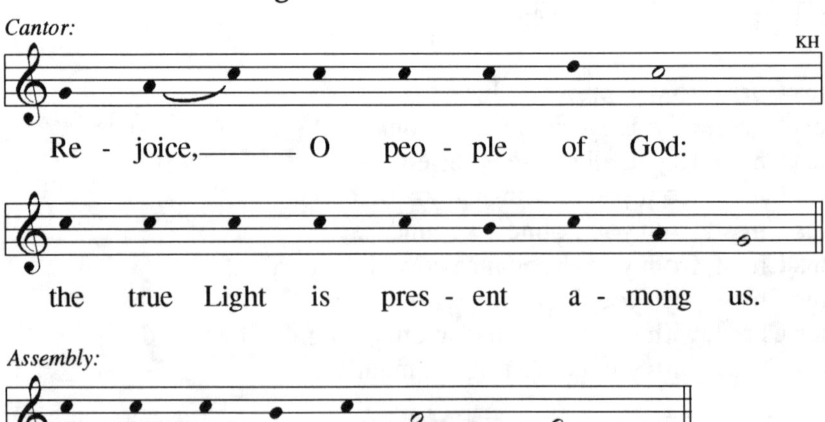
Cantor:
KH
Re - joice, O peo - ple of God:
the true Light is pres - ent a - mong us.
Assembly:
Let us live in the Light.

Lenten Evening Hymn

Thanksgiving for the Light

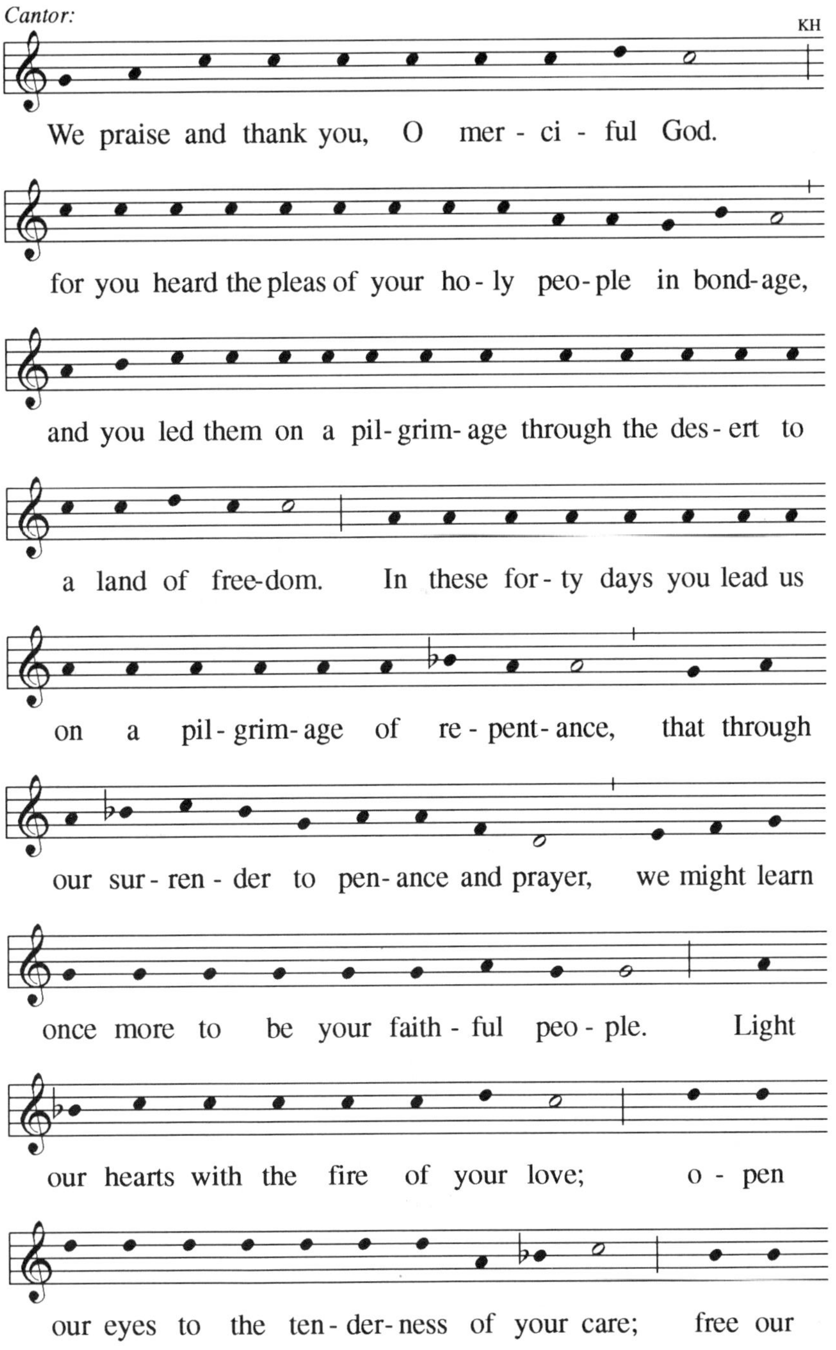
Cantor:
KH
We praise and thank you, O mer - ci - ful God.
for you heard the pleas of your ho - ly peo - ple in bond-age,
and you led them on a pil - grim - age through the des - ert to
a land of free-dom. In these for - ty days you lead us
on a pil - grim - age of re - pent - ance, that through
our sur - ren - der to pen - ance and prayer, we might learn
once more to be your faith - ful peo - ple. Light
our hearts with the fire of your love; o - pen
our eyes to the ten - der - ness of your care; free our

hands to lead oth - ers to the sure - ness of your
for - give - ness. Be with us in these days that
we may ov - er come what - ev - er binds us.
Set us free to live in the glo - rious light of
your Son, Je - sus Christ, who lives and reigns with
you in the Ho - ly Spir - it, one God,
for ev - ver and ev - er. A - men.

PSALMODY

From SATURDAY 1 Evening Prayer, p. 63.

INTERCESSIONS

Petitions

Cantor, then Assembly:

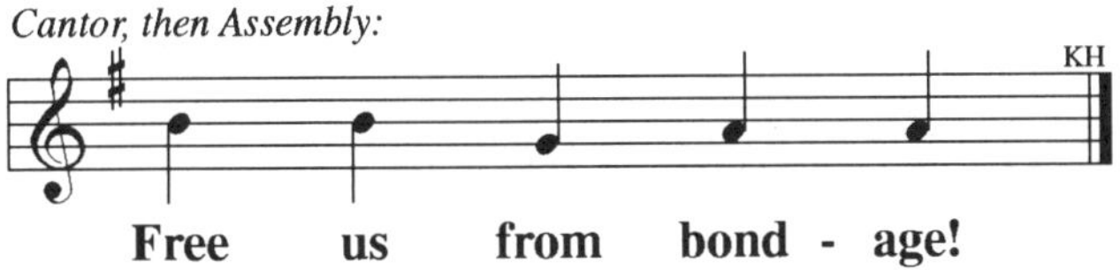

Cantor:

That we may lift our prayer **to** God ... **and** cry out,
That we may do works **of** mercy ... **and** cry out,
That we may look only **to** God ... **and** cry out,
That we may take refuge **in** God ... **and** cry out,
That we may escape **all** harm ... **and** cry out,
That we may rejoice in be**ing** healed ... **and** cry out,
That we may be restored **to** life ... **and** cry out,
That we may remember **God's** holiness ... **and** cry out,
That we may stand in **God's** delight ... **and** cry out,
That we may give thanks **for**ever ... **and** cry out,
That the faithful departed may have life ev**er**lasting ... **and** cry out,

Our Father ...

Prayer
God who liberates,
you free us from all that binds us to slavery:
strengthen our Lenten resolve
that we may one day enjoy life with you forever. **Amen.**

CONCLUSION

Blessing
Bow your heads and pray for God's blessing.
May God who leads from bondage free us from all evil. **Amen.**
May Jesus who died for us teach us the Good News of salvation. **Amen.**
May the Spirit who baptized us give us new life. **Amen.**
And may God bless us
in the name of the Father, and of the Son, and of the Holy Spirit. **Amen.**

Sign of Peace/Dismissal
Give one another a sign of peace as brothers and sisters in Christ.

LENT Week 2 & 4
SUNDAY Morning Praise

LENTEN MORNING HYMN

PSALMODY

Psalm 63 *Psalm of David. While he was in the desert of Judah.*

ANTIPHON
KH
In your name I will raise my hands.

omit last time

O God, you are my God, I seek you;
my **soul** thirsts **for** you.
My flesh longs for you
  in a dry and **wast**ed land,
deprived **of** water. ANTIPHON

So in the sanctuary I have contemplated you
  to see your might and your **glo**ry.
Because your **stead**fast love is better than life,
  my lips will **praise** you.
So I will bless you **all** my life;
in your name I will raise **my** hands.

As with milk and rich food,
  my soul **is** filled;
my **mouth** gives praise with joy**ful** lips.
I remember you up**on** my bed,
pondering you throughout **the** night.

For you were a help **for** me;
in the **shade** of your wings I **keep** singing.
My soul **clings** to you;
your right hand **up**holds me. ANTIPHON

But let those who seek my des**truc**tion
be **cast** into the depths of **the** earth.
Let them be given over to the power **of** the sword;
let them become a prey **for** jackals. ANTIPHON

Then the king shall rejoice **in** God.
All **those** who swear by God will **be** praised,
for the mouths of liars will **be** shut. ANTIPHON

Psalm Prayer
O God whom we seek,
your steadfast love is better than life:
keep us in the shade of your wings
as we celebrate the resurrection
of your Son and our Savior Jesus Christ. **Amen.**

Psalm 66 *To the choirmaster. A Song. Psalm.*

ANTIPHON

KH
Tru - ly God has lis- tened to the voice of my prayer.

omit first and last strophe

Sound the trumpet for God, all **the** earth!
Make music to the glory **of** God's name!
Give **glory** and praise! ANTIPHON

Say to God:
"How awesome are **your** deeds!
At the magnitude of your power,
your enemies **cringe** before you.
Let all the earth **wor**ship you,
let them sing to you,
let them sing to **your** name." ANTIPHON

Come and see the accomplishments **of** God—
an awesome work
on be**half** of mortals.
God turned the sea **into** dry land,
they crossed through the river **on** foot.

Therefore let us rejoice **in** God,
who rules over the **world** with power
and whose eyes watch **over** the nations.
Let not the stubborn rise up a**gainst** God. ANTIPHON

All you nations, bless **our** God!
Let the sound of **praise** be heard
for the one who gives **life to** our souls,
and who kept our feet **from** stumbling. ANTIPHON

For you have tested us, O God;
  you have tried us like silver **is** tried.
You have caught us **in** a net.
You have put a burden on our backs;
  you have let **mortals** enslave us.
We went through fire and water,
  but you brought us out to a fer**tile** land. ANTIPHON

I shall go into your house **with** offerings.
I will fulfill my promises to you
  which my lips uttered
  and my mouth spoke when I was **in** distress.
I will bring you **offerings** of fatlings;
along with the smoke of rams
  I will offer bulls **and** goats. ANTIPHON

Come, listen, all those who re**vere** God,
and I will tell
  all that God did for **my** soul.
I have cried out **with** my mouth,
extolling God with **my** tongue.

If I had harbored emptiness in **my** heart,
the Lord would **not** have listened.
But truly **God** has listened,
listened to the voice of **my** prayer. ANTIPHON

Blessed **be** God
who has not re**jected** my prayer,
nor taken steadfast love away **from** me. ANTIPHON

Psalm Prayer
O great God,

your deeds are mighty and fruitful:
as you led your people of old from bondage to freedom,
so lead us during this Lenten season
to everlasting freedom with you
through your Son, Jesus our Savior. **Amen.**

Word of God

Benedictus
Blessed be the Lord God of **Israel**,
who visited and redeemed the **people**,
who raised up for us a **mighty** savior
from the house of **ser**vant David.

Just as the Lord spoke through the mouths of the holy prophets of **old**—
salvation comes out of the hands of our enemies and those who **hate** us,
that, with our ancestors, we might perform **works** of mercy,
remembering the holy covenant **sworn** to Abraham—

so does the Lord deliver us from the hands **of** our enemies,
that we might serve without fear before **the** Lord,
worshiping in **ho**liness
and in righteousness **all** our days.

And you also, child, will be called a prophet of God Most **High**:
for you will go before the Lord to prepare a **way**,
bringing people knowledge of salvation by for**giveness** of sins;
because of the deep and tender mercy **of** our God.

Whereby a light rising from on high will **visit** us
to appear to those in darkness and in a shadow **of** death,
to guide our feet along a **straight**, sure path
into a **way** of peace.

INTERCESSIONS

Invocations

Cantor, then Assembly:
KH
We will cel - e - brate you for - ev - er!

Cantor:

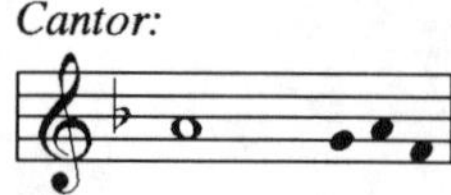

For your unfail**ing** presence,
For your works of **cre**ation,
For your voice **of** solace,
For your endur**ing** patience,
For your **great** holiness,
For your **might**y deeds,
For your care **and** nurture,
For your offer of **sal**vation,
For your sus**tain**ing life,
For your calling those who are **to** be baptized,

Our Father ...

Prayer
God of the universe,
each week you give us a special day
to remember your Son's resurrection:
draw those to be baptized this Easter to life and
renew within us a zest for life
that we may live with you forever and ever. **Amen.**

CONCLUSION

Blessing
Bow your heads and ask for God's blessing.
May the God of dawn bless us with new life. **Amen.**
May the Son of salvation bless us with renewed fervor. **Amen.**
May the Spirit of peace bless us with consolation. **Amen.**
And may God bless us
in the name of the Father, and of the Son, and of the Holy Spirit. **Amen.**

Sign of Peace/Dismissal
Let us offer one another a sign of the peace of Christ.

LENT Weeks 2 & 4
SUNDAY Evening Prayer

LIGHT SERVICE

Proclamation of the Light

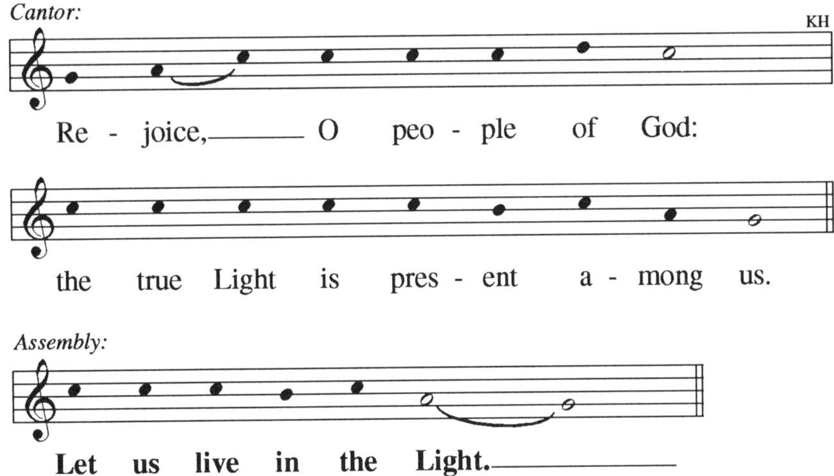
Cantor:
KH
Re - joice, O peo - ple of God:
the true Light is pres - ent a - mong us.
Assembly:
Let us live in the Light.

Lenten Evening Hymn

Thanksgiving for the Light

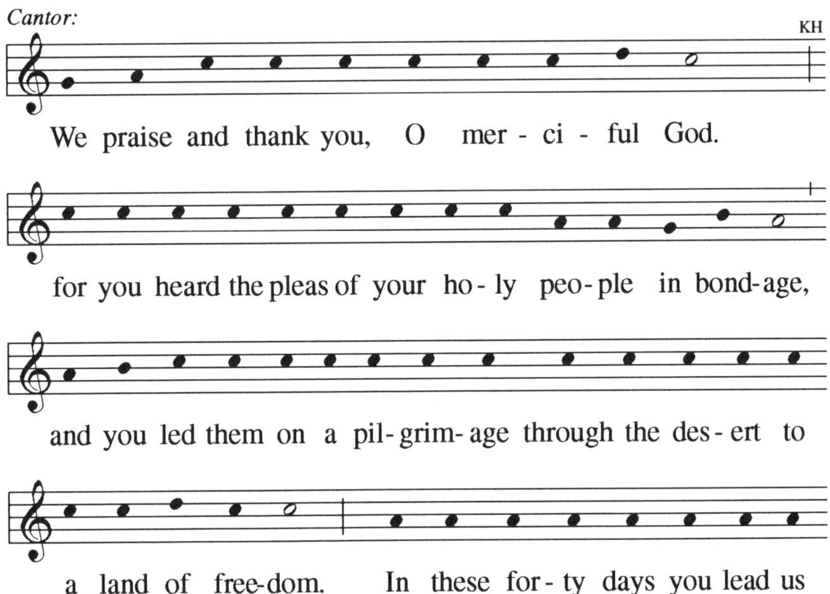
Cantor:
KH
We praise and thank you, O mer - ci - ful God.
for you heard the pleas of your ho - ly peo - ple in bond - age,
and you led them on a pil - grim - age through the des - ert to
a land of free - dom. In these for - ty days you lead us

on a pil-grim-age of re-pent-ance, that through
our sur-ren-der to pen-ance and prayer, we might learn
once more to be your faith-ful peo-ple. Light
our hearts with the fire of your love; o-pen
our eyes to the ten-der-ness of your care; free our
hands to lead oth-ers to the sure-ness of your
for-give-ness. Be with us in these days that
we may ov-er come what-ev-er binds us.
Set us free to live in the glo-rious light of
your Son, Je-sus Christ, who lives and reigns with

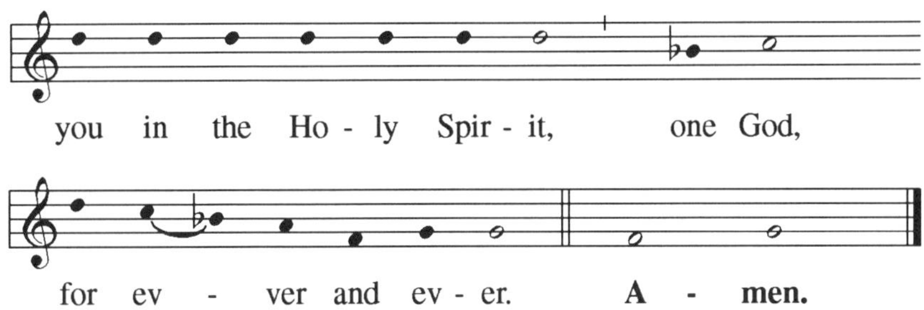

you in the Ho - ly Spir - it, one God,
for ev - ver and ev - er. A - men.

PSALMODY

Psalm 141 *Psalm of David.*

O LORD, I cry **to** you:
"Hasten to me,
  listen to my voice
  when I cry **to** you."
Let my prayer rise
  like incense in **your** presence,
the lifting up of my hands
  like an evening **of**fering. ANTIPHON

Set, O LORD,
  a guard over **my** mouth,
keep the door of **my** lips.
Do not incline my heart to any evil,
  to performing wicked deeds
  with those who work **in**iquity;
let me not partake **in** their feasting. ANTIPHON

When a just person strikes me, it is **a** favor;
and when I am corrected, it is like anoin**ting** oil.
May my head never **re**fuse it,
while my prayer stands firm against **e**vil doings.

Let wicked judges be smashed against **the** rock,
and they will understand that my words **were** measured.
Like plowed and broken furrows on **the** land,
their bones are shattered at the **mouth** of Sheol. ANTIPHON

But my eyes look to you,
O LORD, **my** Lord.
In you I take refuge;
do not pour out **my** life.
Keep me from the snare they have prepared for me
and from the traps of those who cre**ate** emptiness.
Let the wicked fall into their nets
while I a**lone** escape. ANTIPHON

Psalm Prayer
O merciful God,
you hear the voice of those who call to you
with faith and love:
hear our cry during this Lenten season
that we may gaze only on you now and always. **Amen.**

Psalm 110 *Of David. Psalm.*

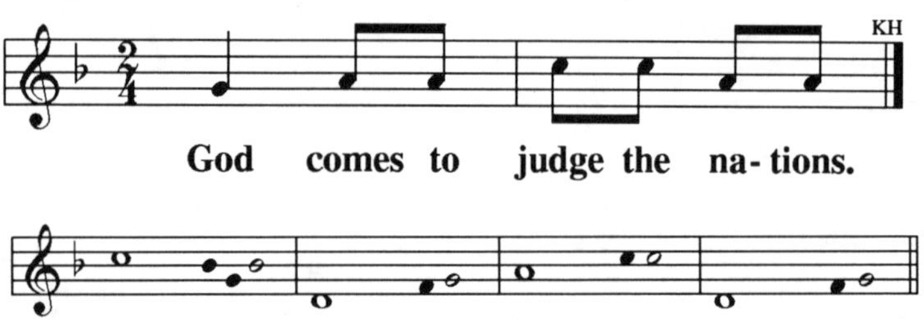

Thus says the LORD **to** my lord:
"Sit on my right
until I place your enemies
as a footstool for **your** feet."
Let the LORD send from Zion
the scepter of **your** strength.
Rule in the midst of **your** enemies. ANTIPHON

Your people bring free **of**ferings
on the day of your might
in ho**ly** splendor.

From the womb **of** dawn,
a dew of rejuvenation comes **to** you. ANTIPHON

The LORD has promised
  and will **not** repent:
"According to my word,
  you are a priest forever, my king **of** justice."
The Lord is at **your** right,
who has smashed rulers on the day **of** wrath.

The Lord judges a**gainst** the nations,
piling them **with** corpses.
The Lord has smashed heads
  all over **the** land.
From a torrent the Lord drinks on the way,
  and rises up **in** triumph. ANTIPHON

Psalm Prayer
O merciful God,
you judge with justice and compassion:
hear our evening prayer
that we may be faithful to you
now and always. **Amen.**

Word of God

Magnificat

My soul does magni**fy** the Lord!
I delight in **God** my savior
who looked kindly **on** lowliness.

Now all ages will **call** me blessed
for the Mighty One **did** great things.
Holy is **God's** name;
mercy is from age to age for **those** in awe!

The Lord's strong arm did **mighty** deeds:
confused the proud in **their** smug hearts;
toppled sovereigns **from** their thrones,
and exalted **hum**ble ones;
filled the hungering with **good** things,
and sent the rich **a**way empty.

The Lord helped servant **I**srael
to re**mem**ber mercy,
as was spoken to Ab**ra**ham
and his descendants for**e**vermore!

INTERCESSIONS

Petitions

Cantor, then Assembly:

KH
Have mer - cy on us and bless us.

Cantor:

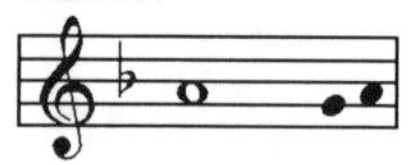

We **cry** out ...
We lift our hands in **thanks**giving ...
We renew our efforts **to do** good ...
We stand firm a**gainst** evil ...
We pour out our lives **for** others ...
We make known **God's** ways ...
We open ourselves to **sal**vation ...
We rejoice for God's **just** judgments ...
We seek guidance on nations **and** peoples ...
We beg for reju**ve**nation ...
We stand with those to **be** baptized ...
We cry out for **the** dead ...

Our Father ...

Prayer
O God,
you renew us by our celebration
of the resurrection of your Son:
grant us fresh strength to meet the challenges
of this new week, that we may come to you
faithfully now and always. **Amen.**

CONCLUSION

Blessing

Bow your heads and pray for God's blessing.
  May the Creator bless us with faith made sure. **Amen.**
  May the Son bless us with hope made visible. **Amen.**
  May the Spirit bless us with Love made flesh. **Amen.**
And may God bless us
in the name of the Father, and of the Son, and of the Holy Spirit. **Amen.**

Sign of Peace/Dismissal

Exchange with one another a sign of our renewal in the peace of Christ.

LENT Weeks 2 & 4

MONDAY Morning Praise

LENTEN MORNING HYMN

PSALMODY

From MONDAY 2 Morning Praise, p. 80.

INTERCESSIONS

Invocations

Cantor, then Assembly:

Cantor:

Jesus our Savior, when shall we see **your** face? ...
Jesus our Savior, why are our souls cast down **with**in us? ...
Jesus our Savior, how shall we praise you **for**ever? ...
Jesus our Savior, where can we **find** rest? ...
Jesus our Savior, who **shall** judge us? ...
Jesus our Savior, why should we wander **in** darkness? ...
Jesus our Savior, how can we put our hope **in** you? ...
Jesus our Savior, what gives us **re**freshment? ...

Our Father ...

Prayer
O God of our longing,
you wipe our tears gently with the caress of your love:
lift up our downcast spirits,
that we may renew our commitment
to love you above all now and always. **Amen.**

CONCLUSION

Blessing
May the God who answers all pleas bless us
in the name of the Father, and of the Son, and of the Holy Spirit. **Amen.**

Dismissal
Go forth with uplifted spirits to live in God. **Thanks be to God.**

LENT Weeks 2 & 4
MONDAY Evening Prayer

LENTEN EVENING HYMN

PSALMODY

From MONDAY 2 Evening Prayer, p. 84.

INTERCESSIONS

Petitions

Cantor, then Assembly:
KH
We lift up our eyes to God.

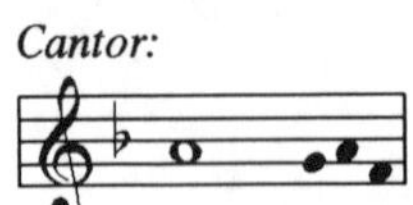
Cantor:

Turning to **God's** mercy ...
Scorning **the** wicked ...
Standing with **the** upright ...
Mindful of **the** covenant ...
Keeping **God's** precepts ...
Practicing **for**bearance ...
Embrac**ing** penitence ...
Rejoicing **in** faithfulness ...
Commending to God those who have **died** this day ...

Our Father ...

Prayer
O God who dwells in the heavens,
you deign to be present to us:
forgive us for the times we have strayed
and help us to be open to the salvation you offer
through your Son, Jesus Christ. **Amen.**

CONCLUSION

Blessing
May God keep us ever faithful and bless us
in the name of the Father, and of the Son, and of the Holy Spirit. **Amen.**

Dismissal
Go and rest in God's love. **Thanks be to God.**

LENT Weeks 2 & 4
TUESDAY Morning Praise

LENTEN MORNING HYMN

PSALMODY

From TUESDAY 2 Morning Praise, p. 87.

INTERCESSIONS

Invocations

Cantor, then Assembly:

Cantor:

Jesus, you are **our** light ...
Jesus, you are **our** salvation ...
Jesus, you are **our** life ...
Jesus, you are **our** help ...
Jesus, you are **our** teacher ...
Jesus, you are **our** goodness ...
Jesus, you are **our** comfort ...
Jesus, you are **our** peace ...

Our Father ...

Prayer
God in whom we trust,
you are faithful in word and deed:
fill us with the Light of your Son
that we may cling to your mercy now and always. **Amen.**

CONCLUSION

Blessing
May God, our stronghold and deliverer, bless us
in the name of the Father, and of the Son, and of the Holy Spirit. **Amen.**

Dismissal
Go forth to trust in God in all you do. **Thanks be to God.**

LENT Weeks 2 & 4
TUESDAY Evening Prayer

LENTEN EVENING HYMN

PSALMODY

From TUESDAY 2 Evening Prayer, p. 90.

INTERCESSIONS

Petitions

Cantor, then Assembly:

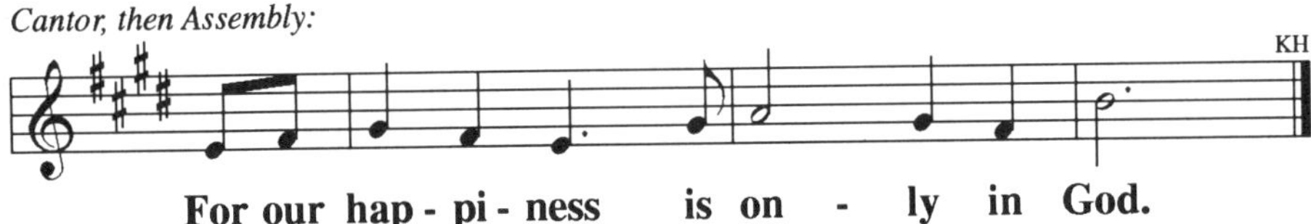

Cantor:

That we smash any idols in **our** lives ...
That we seek only God's good**ly** heritage ...
That we be unswerving on the path **of** life ...
That we rebound **from** stumbling ...
That we resolve to avoid **de**ceit ...
That we return to God the goodness we have **been** given ...
That we call on the name of **our** Savior ...
That we fulfill **our** promises ...
That we commend the faithful departed **to** God ...

Our Father ...

Prayer
O saving God,
you are our source of life and holiness,
mercy and compassion:
wipe away our sins
that we may pass from darkness
to live in the Light of your Son Jesus Christ now and always. **Amen.**

CONCLUSION

Blessing
May God protect us with saving presence and bless us
in the name of the Father, and of the Son, and of the Holy Spirit. **Amen.**

Dismissal
Go and rest in the refuge of God. **Thanks be to God.**

LENT Weeks 2 & 4
WEDNESDAY Morning Praise

LENTEN MORNING HYMN

PSALMODY

From WEDNESDAY 2 Morning Praise, p. 94.

INTERCESSIONS

Invocations

Cantor, then Assembly:

Je - sus Christ, our Good News and Sav - ior.

Cantor:

Hear **our** prayer ...
Remain faithful **to** us ...
Hide not your face **from** us ...
Teach us **your** ways ...
Lead us to act **just**ly ...
Draw us **to** prayer ...
Guide us in **fast**ing ...
Prompt us to alms**giv**ing ...
Deliver us from **e**vil ...
Judge us **kind**ly ...
Raise us to **new** life ...

Our Father ...

Prayer
O God of salvation,
you are quick with your mercy
and steadfast with your love:
as we observe Lent help us to
pray with ardor,

fast with a hunger for you,
and be generous with those in need.
May our Lenten practices turn us from evil
and instill in us a love for righteousness.
We pray through Jesus Christ our Savior and brother. **Amen.**

CONCLUSION

Blessing
May God strengthen our desire for conversion and bless us
in the name of the Father, and of the Son, and of the Holy Spirit. **Amen.**

Dismissal
Go forth to live Lent with a resolve for conversion. **Thanks be to God.**

LENT Weeks 2 & 4
WEDNESDAY Evening Prayer

LENTEN EVENING HYMN

PSALMODY

From WEDNESDAY 2 Evening Prayer, p. 98.

INTERCESSIONS

Petitions

Cantor, then Assembly:

Cantor:

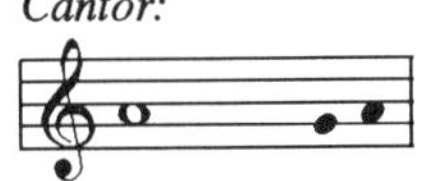

That we hide nothing **from** God ...
That we seek **God's** face ...
That we be open to God's **com**passion ...
That we accept **God's** ways ...

That we loathe injustice and **in**equity ...
That we heed God's right**eous** judgments ...
That we be firm in our Lenten works **of** penance ...
That those who have died may enjoy God's steadfast love **for**ever ...

Our Father ...

Prayer
Merciful God,
you are just in your judgments but
rich in kindness:
grant us strength of resolve and
an openness to overcome our weaknesses.
We ask this through Christ our Savior. **Amen.**

CONCLUSION

Blessing
May the God of mercy bless us
in the name of the Father, and of the Son, and of the Holy Spirit. **Amen.**

Dismissal
Go to rest in the mercy of God. **Thanks be to God.**

LENT Weeks 2 & 4
THURSDAY Morning Praise

LENTEN MORNING HYMN

PSALMODY

From THURSDAY 2 Morning Praise, p. 102.

INTERCESSIONS

Invocations

Cantor, then Assembly:

Cantor:

Shepherd of Israel, lead us **to** you ...
Shepherd of Israel, save us **from** harm ...
Shepherd of Israel, bring us back **from** straying ...
Shepherd of Israel, give **us** life ...
Shepherd of Israel, have pity **on** us ...
Shepherd of Israel, act in **our** favor ...
Shepherd of Israel, send **sal**vation ...
Shepherd of Israel, put sinners **to** shame ...
Shepherd of Israel, ease our **fearful**ness ...
Shepherd of Israel, make firm our lag**ging** spirits ...

Our Father ...

Prayer
O Shepherd of Israel,
you are ever faithful and merciful:
open our hearts to repent of our sins
and lead us to praise you now and always. **Amen.**

CONCLUSION

Blessing
May the God who watches over us bless us
in the name of the Father, and of the Son, and of the Holy Spirit. **Amen.**

Dismissal
Go forth to do Lenten penance, guided by our Shepherd God. **Thanks be to God.**

LENT Weeks 2 & 4
THURSDAY Evening Prayer

LENTEN EVENING HYMN

PSALMODY

From THURSDAY 2 Evening Prayer, p. 106.

INTERCESSIONS

Petitions

Cantor, then Assembly:

Cantor:

To recognize God's awe**some** deeds ...
To surrender ourselves to **God's** power ...
To follow **God's** call ...
To listen to **God's** voice ...
To keep **God's** precepts ...
To promote peace a**mong** peoples ...
To approach God **in** worship ...
To seek prosperity **for** all ...
To commend the faithful departed to **God's** love ...

Our Father ...

Prayer
God of great deeds,
you show us favor by your mercy:
may our Lenten promises
strengthen our commitment to you and
bring us to give you thanks now and always. **Amen.**

CONCLUSION

Blessing
May our redeeming God bless us
in the name of the Father, and of the Son, and of the Holy Spirit. **Amen.**

Dismissal
Go and rest in God's care. **Thanks be to God.**

LENT Weeks 2 & 4
FRIDAY Morning Praise

LENTEN MORNING HYMN

PSALMODY

From FRIDAY 2 Morning Praise, p. 110.

INTERCESSIONS

Invocations

Cantor, then Assembly:
KH
Blot out our trans- gres - sions.

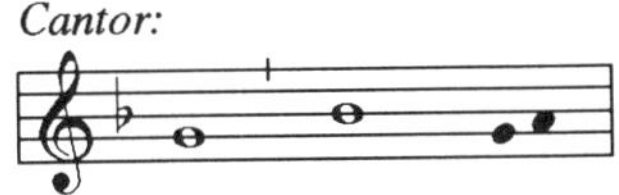
Cantor:

Compassionate Savior, cleanse us of **our** guilt ...
Compassionate Savior, help us to recognize **our** weaknesses ...
Compassionate Savior, grant us delight **in** truth ...
Compassionate Savior, teach **us** wisdom ...
Compassionate Savior, give us **pure** hearts ...
Compassionate Savior, deliver us **from** evil ...
Compassionate Savior, rebuild our fail**ing** spirits ...
Compassionate Savior, save us from discour**age**ment ...

Our Father ...

Prayer
Loving-kind God,
you show us mercy and compassion, truth and wisdom:
teach us always to do your holy will.
May our Lenten penance restore to us a clean heart
that we may only hunger for you.
We pray through our Savior Jesus Christ. **Amen.**

CONCLUSION

Blessing
May God, the source of mercy, bless us
in the name of the Father, and of the Son, and of the Holy Spirit. **Amen.**

Dismissal
Go forth to live God's will. **Thanks be to God.**

LENT Weeks 2 & 4
FRIDAY Evening Prayer

LENTEN EVENING HYMN

PSALMODY

From FRIDAY 2 Evening Prayer, p. 114.

INTERCESSIONS

Petitions

Cantor, then Assembly:
KH
May God hear our cries.

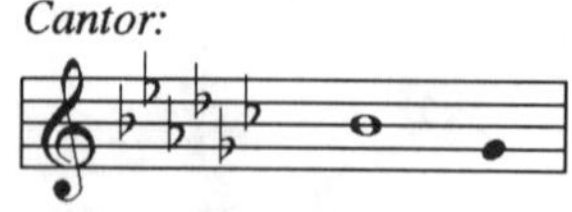
Cantor:

For for**giveness** ...
For **patience** ...

For **hope** ...
For end**urance** ...
For sal**vation** ...
For **courage** ...
For **mercy** ...
For **strength** ...
For those who have **died** ...

Our Father ...

Prayer
Merciful God,
your Son endured death on a cross
that we might gain salvation:
hear our prayer and
give us strength of resolve
to do your holy will now and always. **Amen.**

CONCLUSION

Blessing
May the God of the Cross,
who conquered death and promised life,
grant us strength and conviction and bless us
in the name of the Father, and of the Son, and of the Holy Spirit. **Amen.**

Dismissal
Go and rest in our Savior's goodness and mercy. **Thanks be to God.**

LENT Weeks 2 & 4
SATURDAY Morning Praise

LENTEN MORNING HYMN

PSALMODY

From SATURDAY 2 Morning Praise, p. 118.

INTERCESSIONS

Invocations

Cantor, then Assembly:

For you judge the world with jus - tice.

Cantor:

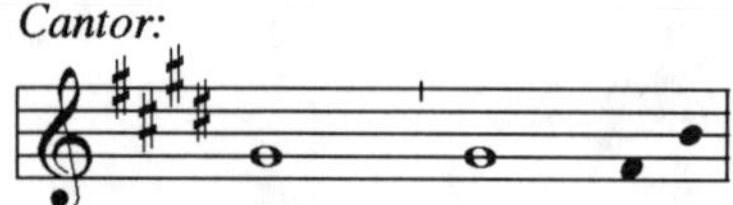

O Jesus Christ, to you praise **is** due ...
O Jesus Christ, to you everyone **shall** come ...
O Jesus Christ, to you all praise **is** raised ...
O Jesus Christ, from you blessings **pour** forth ...
O Jesus Christ, from you holiness **a**bounds ...
O Jesus Christ, from you abundance covers **the** earth ...
O Jesus Christ, with you days burst **with** joy ...
O Jesus Christ, with you honor and splendor stand be**fore** God ...
O Jesus Christ, with you God's reign **is** manifest ...

Our Father ...

Prayer
O redeeming God,
you shine the Light of your risen Son upon us:
may that brightness guide us through darkness
as we look to the unfailing Light
of the resurrection of Jesus Christ. **Amen.**

CONCLUSION

Blessing
Bow your heads and pray for God's blessing.
O God of redemption: make your face shine on us. **Amen.**
O Son of compassion: look upon us with mercy. **Amen.**
O Spirit of love: give us strength. **Amen.**
And may God bless us
in the name of the Father, and of the Son, and of the Holy Spirit. **Amen.**

Sign of Peace/Dismissal
Let us reach out with compassion and offer a sign of peace to others.

LENT Weeks 2 & 4
SATURDAY Evening Prayer

LIGHT SERVICE

Proclamation of the Light

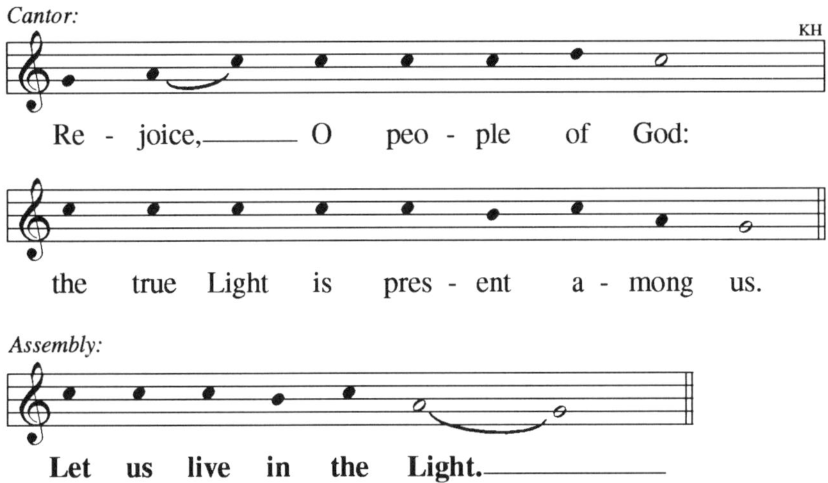
Cantor:
KH
Re - joice, O peo - ple of God:
the true Light is pres - ent a - mong us.
Assembly:
Let us live in the Light.

Lenten Evening Hymn

Thanksgiving for the Light

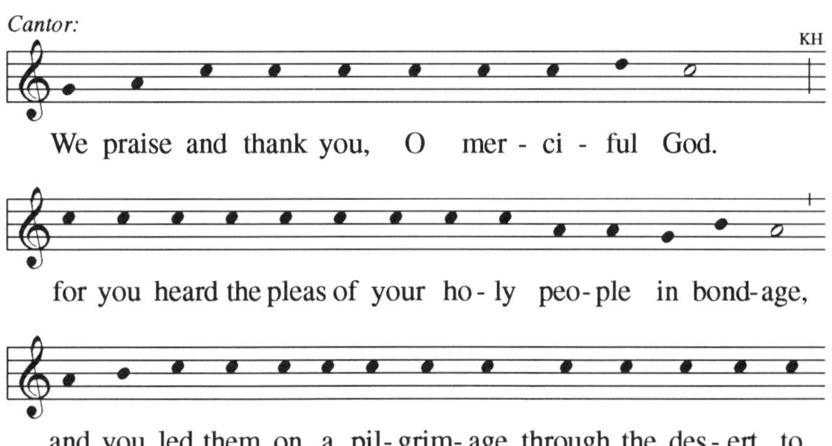
Cantor:
KH
We praise and thank you, O mer - ci - ful God.
for you heard the pleas of your ho - ly peo - ple in bond - age,
and you led them on a pil - grim - age through the des - ert to

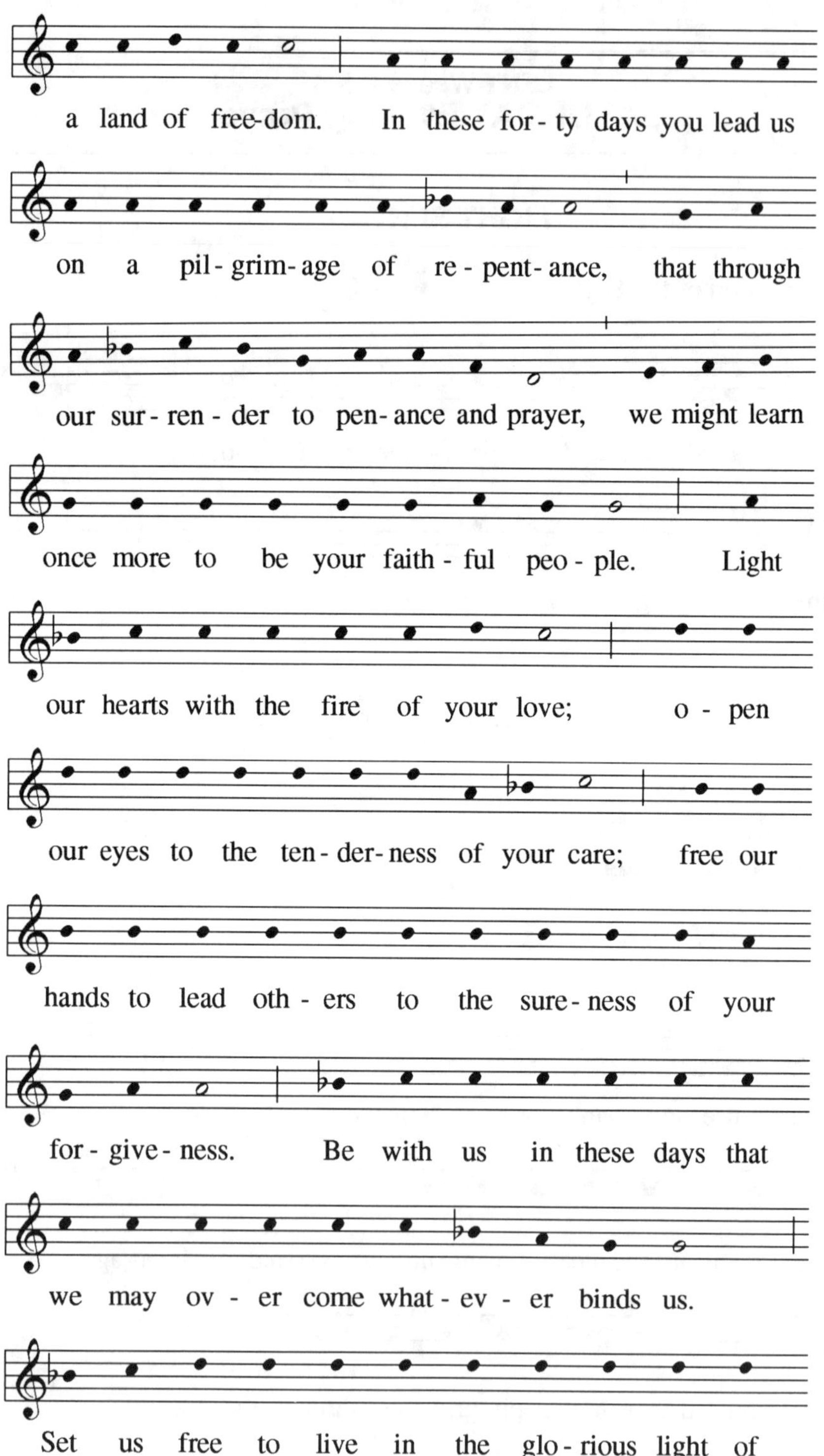
a land of free-dom. In these for-ty days you lead us
on a pil-grim-age of re-pent-ance, that through
our sur-ren-der to pen-ance and prayer, we might learn
once more to be your faith-ful peo-ple. Light
our hearts with the fire of your love; o-pen
our eyes to the ten-der-ness of your care; free our
hands to lead oth-ers to the sure-ness of your
for-give-ness. Be with us in these days that
we may ov-er come what-ev-er binds us.
Set us free to live in the glo-rious light of

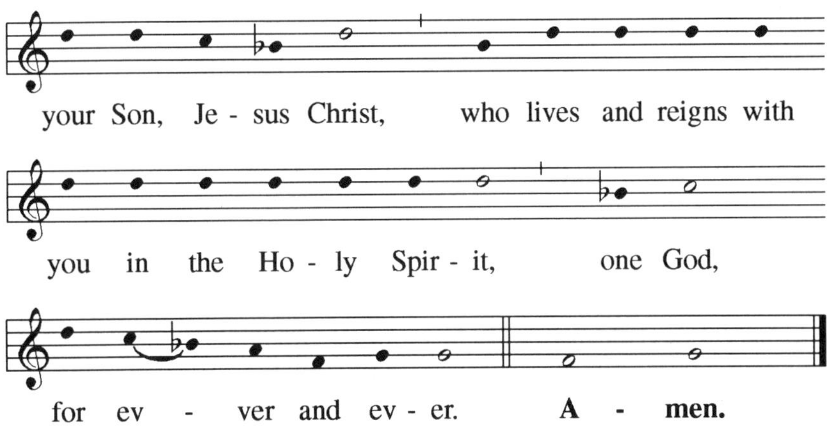
your Son, Je - sus Christ, who lives and reigns with
you in the Ho - ly Spir - it, one God,
for ev - ver and ev - er. A - men.

PSALMODY

From SATURDAY 2 Evening Prayer, p. 123.

INTERCESSIONS

Petitions

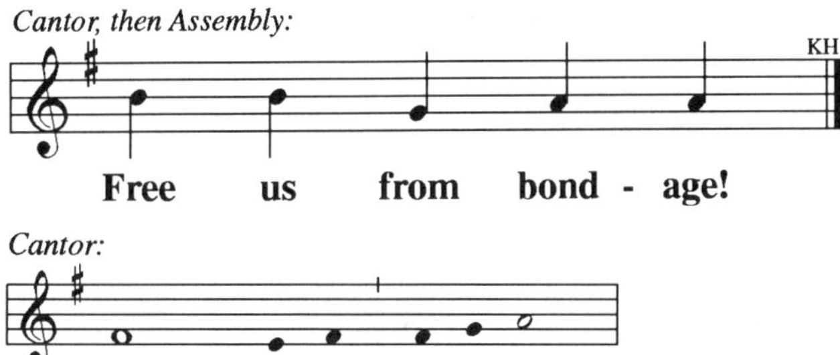
Cantor, then Assembly:
KH
Free us from bond - age!
Cantor:

That we may lift our prayer **to** God ... **and** cry out,
That we may do works **of** mercy ... **and** cry out,
That we may look only **to** God ... **and** cry out,
That we may take refuge **in** God ... **and** cry out,
That we may escape **all** harm ... **and** cry out,
That we may rejoice in be**ing** healed ... **and** cry out,
That we may be restored **to** life ... **and** cry out,
That we may remember **God's** holiness ... **and** cry out,
That we may stand in **God's** delight ... **and** cry out,
That we may give thanks **for**ever ... **and** cry out,
That the faithful departed may have life ever**l**asting ... **and** cry out,

Our Father ...

Prayer
God who liberates,
you free us from all that binds us to slavery:
strengthen our Lenten resolve
that we may one day enjoy life with you forever. **Amen.**

CONCLUSION

Blessing
Bow your heads and pray for God's blessing.
May God who leads from bondage free us from all evil. **Amen.**
May Jesus who died for us teach us the Good News of salvation. **Amen.**
May the Spirit who baptized us give us new life. **Amen.**
And may God bless us
in the name of the Father, and of the Son, and of the Holy Spirit. **Amen.**

Sign of Peace/Dismissal
Give one another a sign of peace as brothers and sisters in Christ.

PASSION (PALM) SUNDAY
Morning Praise

LENTEN MORNING HYMN

PSALMODY

Psalm 63 *Psalm of David. While he was in the desert of Judah.*

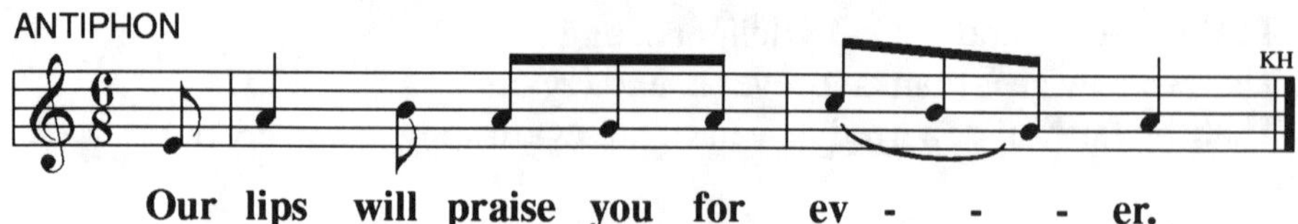
ANTIPHON
KH
Our lips will praise you for ev - - - - er.

O God, you are my God, **I** seek you;
my **soul** thirsts **for** you.
My flesh longs for you
  in a dry and **wast**ed land,
deprived **of** water. ANTIPHON

So in the sanctuary I have contemplated you
  to see your might and your **glo**ry.
Because your **stead**fast love is better than life,
  my lips will **praise** you.
So I will bless you **all** my life;
in your name I will raise **my** hands.

As with milk and rich food,
  my soul **is** filled;
my **mouth** gives praise with joy**ful** lips.
I remember you up**on** my bed,
pondering you throughout **the** night.

For you were a help **for** me;
in the **shade** of your wings I **keep** singing.
My soul **clings** to you;
your right hand **up**holds me. ANTIPHON

But let those who seek my de**struc**tion
be **cast** into the depths of **the** earth.
Let them be given over to the power **of** the sword;
let them become a prey **for** jackals. ANTIPHON

Then the king shall rejoice **in** God.
All **those** who swear by God will **be** praised,
for the mouths of liars will **be** shut. ANTIPHON

Psalm Prayer
O God whom we seek,
your steadfast love is better than life:
keep us in the shade of your wings
as we celebrate the triumph
of your Son and our Savior Jesus Christ. **Amen.**

Psalm 66 *To the choirmaster. A Song. Psalm.*

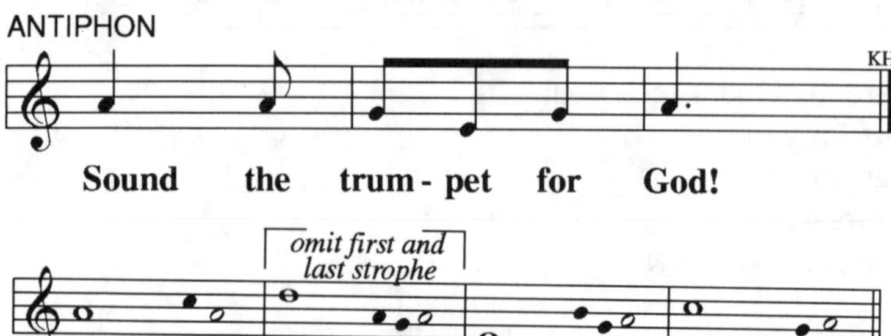
ANTIPHON
KH
Sound the trum - pet for God!
omit first and last strophe

Sound the trumpet for God, all **the** earth!
Make music to the glory **of** God's name!
Give **glory** and praise! ANTIPHON

Say to God:
"How awesome are **your** deeds!
At the magnitude of your power,
your enemies **cringe** before you.
Let all the earth **wor**ship you,
let them sing to you,
let them sing to **your** name." ANTIPHON

Come and see the accomplishments **of** God—
an awesome work
on be**half** of mortals.
God turned the sea **into** dry land,
they crossed through the river **on** foot.

Therefore let us rejoice **in** God,
who rules over the **world** with power
and whose eyes watch **over** the nations.
Let not the stubborn rise up a**gainst** God. ANTIPHON

All you nations, bless **our** God!
Let the sound of **praise** be heard
for the one who gives **life to** our souls,
and who kept our feet **from** stumbling. ANTIPHON

For you have tested us, O God;
you have tried us like silver **is** tried.
You have caught us **in** a net.
You have put a burden on our backs;
you have let **mortals** enslave us.

We went through fire and water,
  but you brought us out to a fer**tile** land. ANTIPHON

I shall go into your house **with** offerings.
I will fulfill my promises to you
  which my lips uttered
  and my mouth spoke when I was **in** distress.
I will bring you **offerings** of fatlings;
along with the smoke of rams
  I will offer bulls **and** goats. ANTIPHON

Come, listen, all those who re**vere** God,
and I will tell
  all that God did for **my** soul.
I have cried out **with** my mouth,
extolling God with **my** tongue.

If I had harbored emptiness in **my** heart,
the Lord would **not** have listened.
But truly **God** has listened,
listened to the voice of **my** prayer. ANTIPHON

Blessed **be** God
who has not re**jected** my prayer,
nor taken steadfast love away **from** me. ANTIPHON

Psalm Prayer
O great God,
your deeds are mighty and fruitful:
as you led your people of old from bondage to freedom,
so lead us during this Holy Week
to everlasting freedom with you
through your Son, Jesus our Savior. **Amen.**

Word of God

Benedictus
Blessed be the Lord God of **Israel**,
who visited and redeemed the **people**,
who raised up for us a **mighty** savior
from the house of **ser**vant David.

Just as the Lord spoke through the mouths of the holy prophets of **old**—
salvation comes out of the hands of our enemies and those who **hate** us,
that, with our ancestors, we might perform **works** of mercy,
remembering the holy covenant **sworn** to Abraham—

so does the Lord deliver us from the hands **of** our enemies,
that we might serve without fear before **the** Lord,
worshiping in **ho**liness
and in righteousness **all** our days.

And you also, child, will be called a prophet of God Most **High**:
for you will go before the Lord to prepare a **way**,
bringing people knowledge of salvation by for**giveness** of sins;
because of the deep and tender mercy **of** our God.

Whereby a light rising from on high will **vis**it us
to appear to those in darkness and in a shadow **of** death,
to guide our feet along a **straight**, sure path
into a **way** of peace.

INTERCESSIONS

Invocations

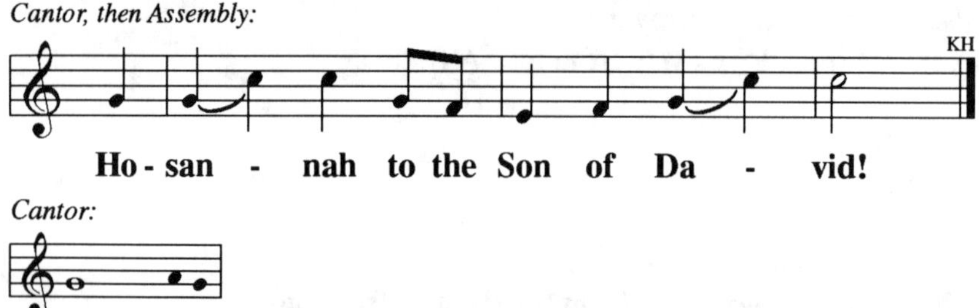
Cantor, then Assembly:
KH
Ho - san - nah to the Son of Da - vid!
Cantor:

For your unfailing **pres**ence,
For your works of re**demp**tion,
For your voice of **sol**ace,
For your enduring **pa**tience,
For your great **hol**iness,
For your **mighty** deeds,
For your care and **nur**ture,
For your offer of sal**va**tion,
For your sus**taining** life,

Our Father ...

Prayer
God of redemption,
you received the acclaims of your people seeking the Messiah:
save us and renew within us a zest for life
that we may live with you forever and ever. **Amen.**

CONCLUSION

Blessing
Bow your heads and ask for God's blessing.
May the God of dawn bless us with new life. **Amen.**
May the Son of salvation bless us with renewed fervor. **Amen.**
May the Spirit of peace bless us with joy. **Amen.**
And may God bless us
in the name of the Father, and of the Son, and of the Holy Spirit. **Amen.**

Sign of Peace/Dismissal
Let us offer one another a sign of the peace of the Messiah.

PASSION (PALM) SUNDAY
Evening Prayer

LIGHT SERVICE

Proclamation of the Light

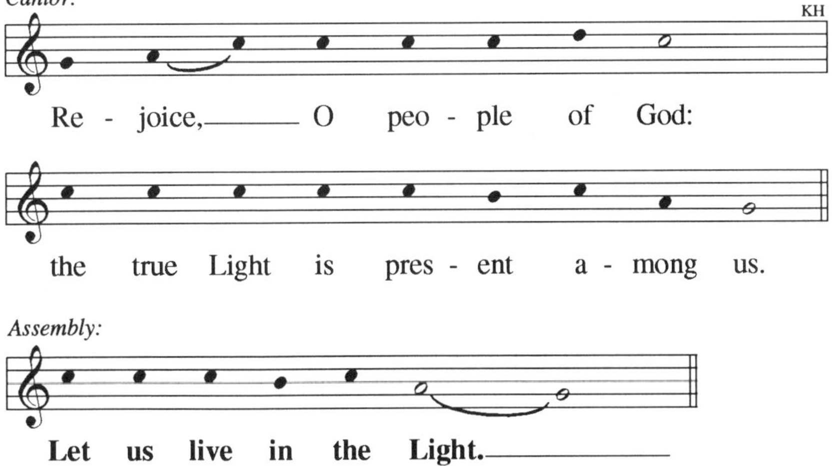

Cantor:
KH
Re - joice, O peo - ple of God:
the true Light is pres - ent a - mong us.
Assembly:
Let us live in the Light.

Lenten Evening Hymn

Thanksgiving for the Light

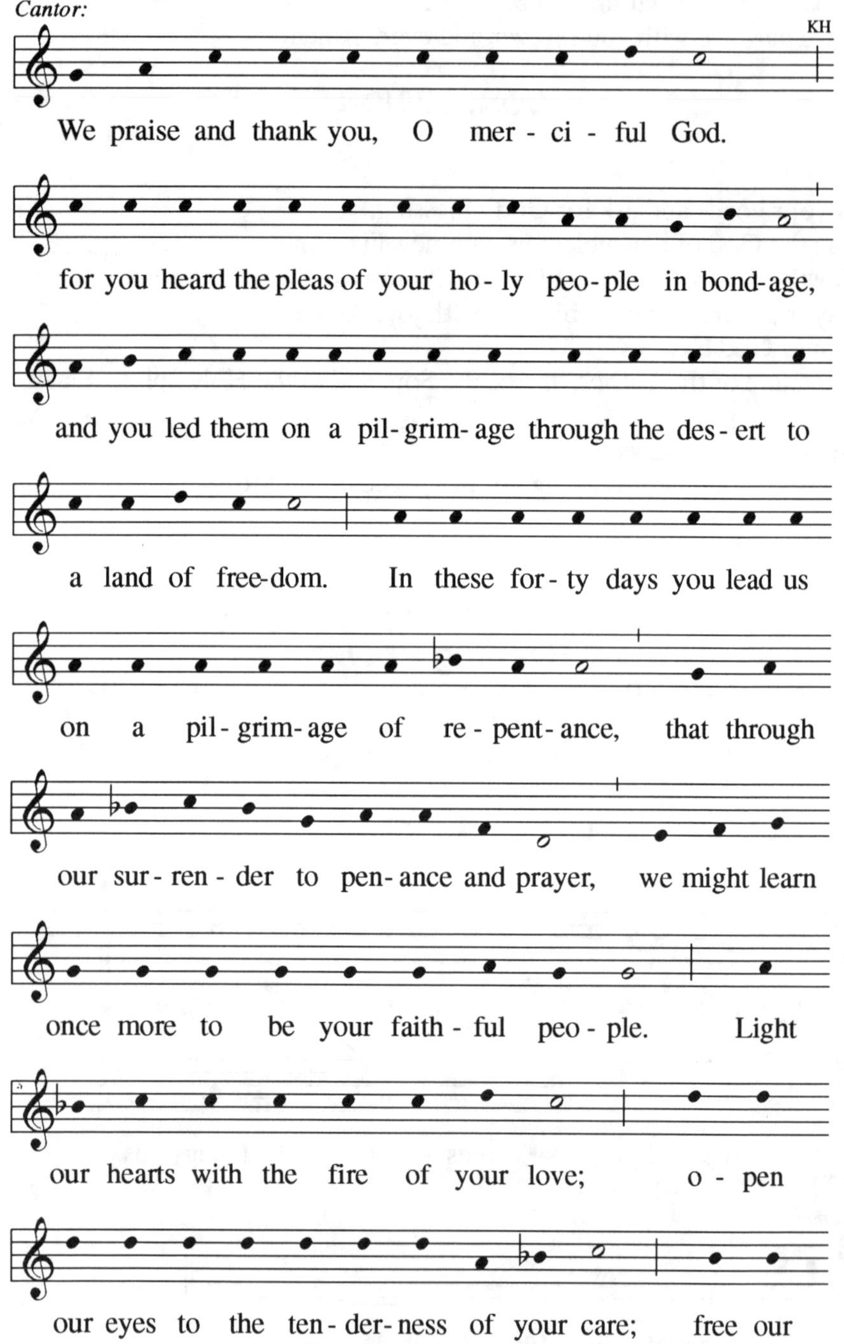
Cantor:
KH
We praise and thank you, O mer - ci - ful God.
for you heard the pleas of your ho - ly peo - ple in bond - age,
and you led them on a pil - grim - age through the des - ert to
a land of free - dom. In these for - ty days you lead us
on a pil - grim - age of re - pent - ance, that through
our sur - ren - der to pen - ance and prayer, we might learn
once more to be your faith - ful peo - ple. Light
our hearts with the fire of your love; o - pen
our eyes to the ten - der - ness of your care; free our

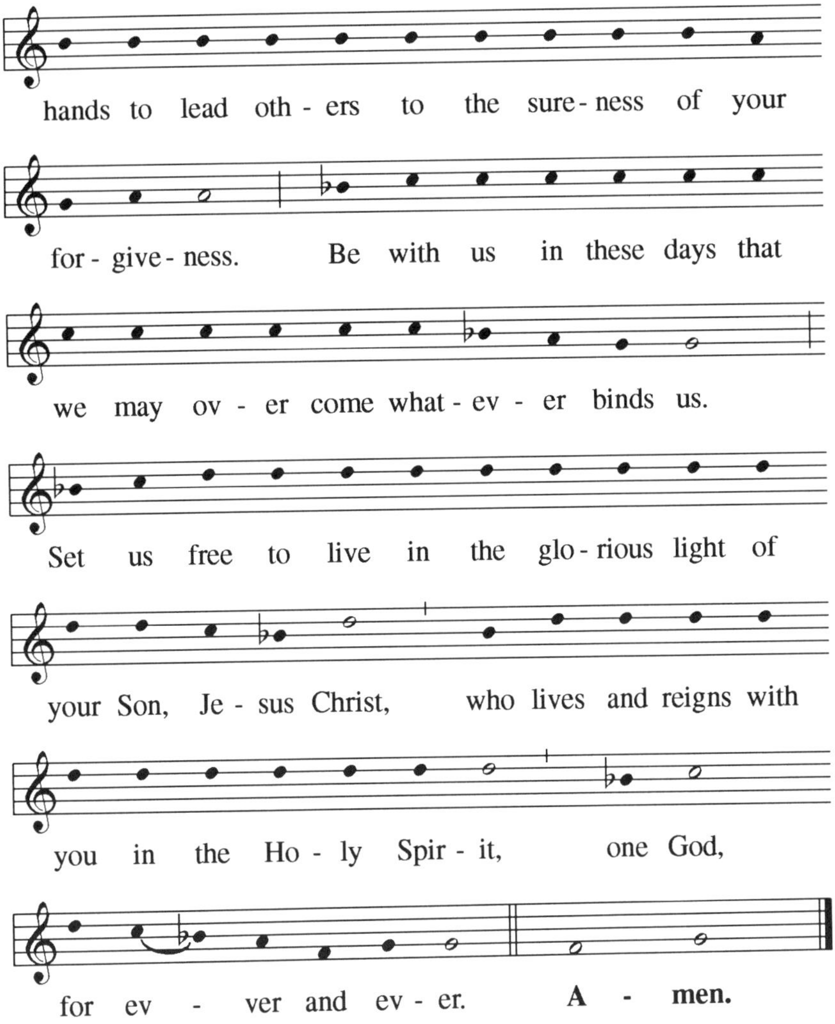

hands to lead oth - ers to the sure - ness of your
for - give - ness. Be with us in these days that
we may ov - er come what - ev - er binds us.
Set us free to live in the glo - rious light of
your Son, Je - sus Christ, who lives and reigns with
you in the Ho - ly Spir - it, one God,
for ev - ver and ev - er. A - men.

PSALMODY

Psalm 141 *Psalm of David.*

ANTIPHON

KH
Let my prayer rise like in - cense.

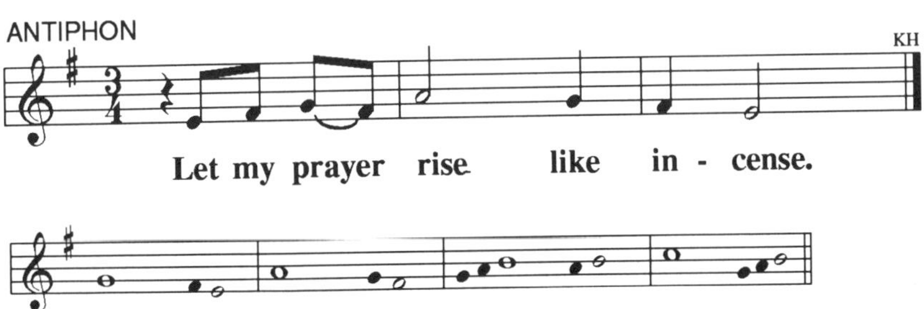

O LORD, I cry **to** you:
"Hasten to me,
  listen to my voice
  when I cry **to** you."
Let my prayer rise
  like incense in **your** presence,
the lifting up of my hands
  like an evening **of**fering. ANTIPHON

Set, O LORD,
  a guard over **my** mouth,
keep the door of **my** lips.
Do not incline my heart to any evil,
  to performing wicked deeds
  with those who work **ini**quity;
let me not partake **in** their feasting. ANTIPHON

When a just person strikes me, it is **a** favor;
and when I am corrected, it is like anoin**ting** oil.
May my head never **re**fuse it,
while my prayer stands firm against **e**vil doings.

Let wicked judges be smashed against **the** rock,
and they will understand that my words **were** measured.
Like plowed and broken furrows on **the** land,
their bones are shattered at the **mouth** of Sheol. ANTIPHON

But my eyes look to you,
  O LORD, **my** Lord.
In you I take refuge;
  do not pour out **my** life.
Keep me from the snare they have prepared for me
  and from the traps of those who cre**ate** emptiness.
Let the wicked fall into their nets
  while I a**lone** escape. ANTIPHON

Psalm Prayer
O merciful God,
you hear the voice of those who call to you
with faith and love:
hear our cry during this Lenten season
that we may gaze only on you now and always. **Amen.**

Psalm 110 *Of David. Psalm.*

ANTIPHON

Thus says the LORD **to** my lord:
"Sit on my right
until I place your enemies
as a footstool for **your** feet."
Let the LORD send from Zion
the scepter of **your** strength.
Rule in the midst of **your** enemies. ANTIPHON

Your people bring free **of**ferings
on the day of your might
in ho**ly** splendor.
From the womb **of** dawn,
a dew of rejuvenation comes **to** you. ANTIPHON

The LORD has promised
and will **not** repent:
"According to my word,
you are a priest forever, my king **of** justice."
The Lord is at **your** right,
who has smashed rulers on the day **of** wrath.

The Lord judges a**gainst** the nations,
piling them **with** corpses.
The Lord has smashed heads
all over **the** land.
From a torrent the Lord drinks on the way,
and rises up **in** triumph. ANTIPHON

Psalm Prayer
O merciful God,
you judge with justice and compassion:
hear our evening prayer

that we may be faithful to you
now and always. **Amen.**

Word of God

Magnificat
My soul does magni**fy** the Lord!
I delight in **God** my savior
who looked kindly **on** lowliness.

Now all ages will **call** me blessed
for the Mighty One **did** great things.
Holy is **God's** name;
mercy is from age to age for **those** in awe!

The Lord's strong arm did **mighty** deeds:
confused the proud in **their** smug hearts;
toppled sovereigns **from** their thrones,
and exalted **hum**ble ones;
filled the hungering with **good** things,
and sent the rich **a**way empty.

The Lord helped servant **Is**rael
to re**mem**ber mercy,
as was spoken to Ab**ra**ham
and his descendants for**e**vermore!

INTERCESSIONS

Petitions

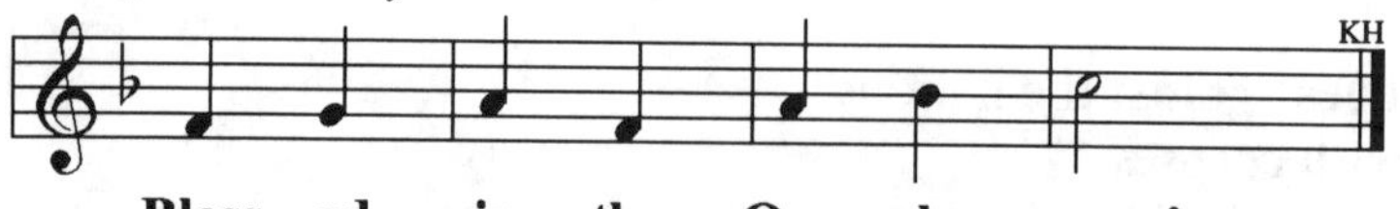

Bless - ed is the One who comes!

Cantor:

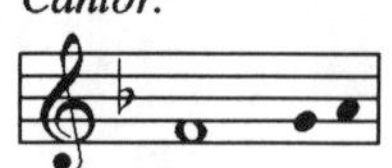

We **cry** out,
We lift our hands in **thanks**giving,
We renew our efforts **to do** good,
We stand firm a**gainst** evil,

We pour out our lives **for** others,
We make known **God's** ways,
We open ourselves to **sal**vation,
We rejoice for God's **just** judgments,
We seek guidance on nations **and** peoples,
We beg for rejuv**en**ation,
We cry out for **the** dead,

Our Father ...

Prayer
O God,
you renew us by our celebration
of the triumph of your messiah Son:
grant us fresh strength to meet the challenges
of this Holy Week, that we may come to you
faithfully now and always. **Amen.**

CONCLUSION

Blessing
Bow your heads and pray for God's blessing.
May the Creator bless us with faith made sure. **Amen.**
May the Son bless us with hope made visible. **Amen.**
May the Spirit bless us with Love made flesh. **Amen.**
And may God bless us
in the name of the Father, and of the Son, and of the Holy Spirit. **Amen.**

Sign of Peace/Dismissal
Send each other off, renewed in the peace of Christ.

MONDAY in HOLY WEEK
Morning Praise

LENTEN MORNING HYMN

PSALMODY

From MONDAY 2 Morning Praise, p. 80.

INTERCESSIONS

Invocations

Cantor, then Assembly:
KH
Our tears have been our food.

Cantor:

Jesus our Savior, when shall we see **your** face? ...
Jesus our Savior, why are our souls cast down **with**in us? ...
Jesus our Savior, how shall we praise you **for**ever? ...
Jesus our Savior, where can we **find** rest? ...
Jesus our Savior, who **shall** judge us? ...
Jesus our Savior, why should we wander **in** darkness? ...
Jesus our Savior, how can we put our hope **in** you? ...
Jesus our Savior, what gives us **re**freshment? ...

Our Father ...

Prayer
O God of our longing,
you wipe our tears gently with the caress of your love:
lift up our downcast spirits,
that during this Holy Week we may renew our commitment
to love you above all now and always. **Amen.**

CONCLUSION

Blessing
May the God who answers all prayers bless us
in the name of the Father, and of the Son, and of the Holy Spirit. **Amen.**

Dismissal
Go forth with uplifted spirits to live in God. **Thanks be to God.**

MONDAY in HOLY WEEK
Evening Prayer

LENTEN EVENING HYMN

PSALMODY

From MONDAY 2 Evening Prayer, p. 84.

INTERCESSIONS

Petitions

Cantor, then Assembly:

Cantor:

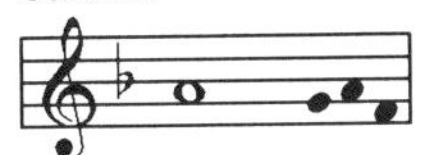

Turning to **God's** mercy ...
Scorning **the** wicked ...
Standing with **the** upright ...
Mindful of **the** covenant ...
Keeping **God's** precepts ...
Practicing **for**bearance ...
Embrac**ing** penitence ...
Rejoicing **in** faithfulness ...
Commending to God those who have **died** this day ...

Our Father ...

Prayer
O God who dwells in the heavens,
you deign to be present to us:
forgive us for the times we have strayed
and help us to be open to the salvation we celebrate this week
through your Son, Jesus Christ. **Amen.**

CONCLUSION

Blessing
May God keep us ever faithful and bless us
in the name of the Father, and of the Son, and of the Holy Spirit. **Amen.**

Dismissal
Go and rest in God's love. **Thanks be to God.**

TUESDAY in HOLY WEEK
Morning Praise

LENTEN MORNING HYMN

PSALMODY

From TUESDAY 2 Morning Praise, p. 87.

INTERCESSIONS

Invocations

Cantor, then Assembly:

Cantor:

Jesus, you are **our** light ...
Jesus, you are **our** salvation ...
Jesus, you are **our** life ...
Jesus, you are **our** help ...
Jesus, you are **our** teacher ...
Jesus, you are **our** goodness ...
Jesus, you are **our** comfort ...
Jesus, you are **our** peace ...

Our Father ...

Prayer
God in whom we trust,
you are faithful in word and deed:
fill us with the Light of your Son
that we may cling to your mercy now and always. **Amen.**

CONCLUSION

Blessing
May God, our stronghold and deliverer, bless us
in the name of the Father, and of the Son, and of the Holy Spirit. **Amen.**

Dismissal
Go forth to trust in God in all you do. **Thanks be to God.**

TUESDAY in HOLY WEEK
Evening Prayer

LENTEN EVENING HYMN

PSALMODY

From TUESDAY 2 Evening Prayer, p. 90.

INTERCESSIONS

Petitions

Cantor, then Assembly:

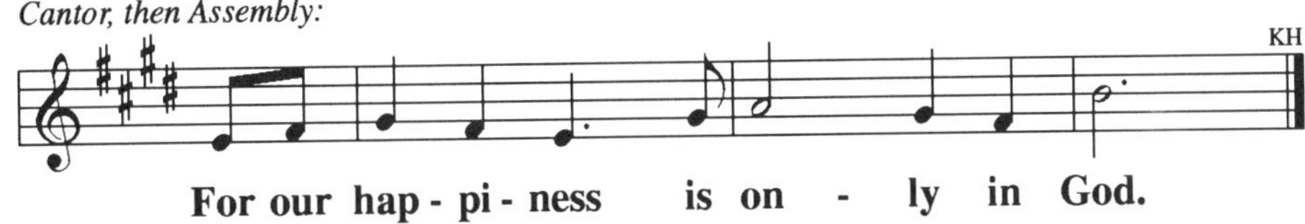

Cantor:

That we smash any idols in **our** lives ...
That we seek only God's good**ly** heritage ...
That we be unswerving on the path **of** life ...
That we rebound **from** stumbling ...

That we resolve to avoid **de**ceit ...
That we return to God the goodness we have **been** given ...
That we call on the name of **our** Savior ...
That we fulfill **our** promises ...
That we commend the faithful departed **to** God ...

Our Father ...

Prayer
O saving God,
you are our source of life and holiness,
mercy and compassion:
wipe away our sins
that we may pass from darkness
to live in the Light of your Son Jesus Christ now and always. **Amen.**

CONCLUSION

Blessing
May God protect us with saving presence and bless us
in the name of the Father, and of the Son, and of the Holy Spirit. **Amen.**

Dismissal
Go and rest in the refuge of God. **Thanks be to God.**

WEDNESDAY in HOLY WEEK
Morning Praise

LENTEN MORNING HYMN

PSALMODY

From WEDNESDAY 2 Morning Praise, p. 94.

INTERCESSIONS

Invocations

Cantor, then Assembly:

KH
Je - sus Christ, our Good News and Sav - ior.

Cantor:

Hear **our** prayer ...
Remain faithful **to** us ...
Hide not your face **from** us ...
Teach us **your** ways ...
Lead us to **act** justly ...
Draw us **to** prayer ...
Guide us **in** fasting ...
Prompt us **to** almsgiving ...
Deliver us **from** evil ...
Judge **us** kindly ...
Raise us to **new** life ...

Our Father ...

Prayer
O God of salvation,
you are quick with your mercy
and steadfast with your love:
as we draw Lent to a conclusion help us to
pray with ardor,
fast with a hunger for you,
and be generous with those in need.
We pray through Jesus Christ
our Savior and brother. **Amen.**

CONCLUSION

Blessing
May God strengthen our desire for conversion and bless us
in the name of the Father, and of the Son, and of the Holy Spirit. **Amen.**

Dismissal
Go forth to live with a resolve for conversion. **Thanks be to God.**

WEDNESDAY in HOLY WEEK
Evening Prayer

LENTEN EVENING HYMN

PSALMODY

From WEDNESDAY 2 Evening Prayer, p. 98.

INTERCESSIONS

Petitions

Cantor, then Assembly:
KH
Search us, and have mer - cy.

Cantor:

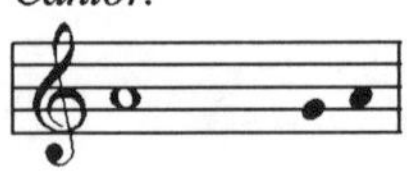

That we hide nothing **from** God ...
That we seek **God's** face ...
That we be open to God's **com**passion ...
That we accept **God's** ways ...
That we loathe injustice and **in**equity ...
That we heed God's right**eous** judgments ...
That we be firm in our Lenten works **of** penance ...
That those who have died may enjoy God's steadfast love **for**ever ...

Our Father ...

Prayer
Merciful God,
you are just in your judgments but
rich in kindness:
grant us strength of resolve and
an openness to overcome our weaknesses.
We ask this through Christ our Savior. **Amen.**

CONCLUSION

Blessing
May the God of mercy bless us
in the name of the Father, and of the Son, and of the Holy Spirit. **Amen.**

Dismissal
Go and rest in the mercy of God. **Thanks be to God.**

HOLY THURSDAY Morning Praise

MORNING HYMN

PSALMODY

From THURSDAY 2 Morning Praise, p. 102.

INTERCESSIONS

Invocations

Cantor, then Assembly:

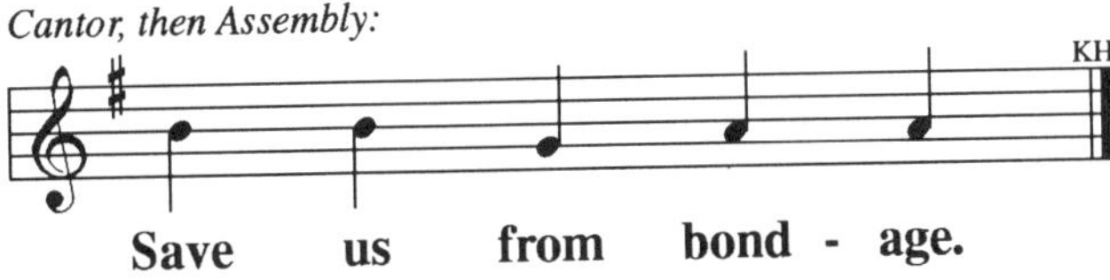

Cantor:

O loving Savior, you lead your rem**nant** flock,
O loving Savior, you save your cho**sen** people,
O loving Savior, you feed your wan**dering** followers,
O loving Savior, you plant seeds of **new** life,
O loving Savior, protect us in the shade of **your** wings,
O loving Savior, awaken our hunger **for** you,
O loving Savior, draw us to celebrate your stead**fast** love,
O loving Savior, free us to sing **your** praises,

Prayer
O mighty God,
you sent your only-begotten Son to free us from all bondage:
lead us to your holy presence
that we may be nourished by your abundance.
We pray through your Son, Jesus Christ. **Amen.**

CONCLUSION

Blessing
May the God who promises us all good things bless us
in the name of the Father, and of the Son, and of the Holy Spirit. **Amen.**

Dismissal
Go forth to live in the generous abundance of God. **Thanks be to God.**

HOLY THURSDAY Evening Prayer

(Evening Prayer is said only by those who do not celebrate the Evening Mass of the Lord's Supper.)

EVENING HYMN

PSALMODY

From THURSDAY 2 Evening Prayer, p. 106.

INTERCESSIONS

Petitions

Cantor, then Assembly:

Cantor:

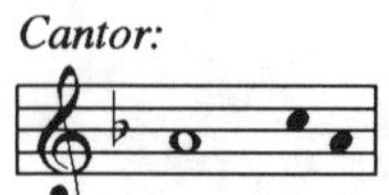

That we recognize **God's** glory,
That we embrace **the** covenant,
That we open ourselves to **God's** might,
That we bless God for our **a**bundance,
That we enter God's house in **thanks**giving,
That we fulfill our vows with **fi**delity,
That we listen to **God's** voice,
That we prosper **with** peace,

That we **seek** good,
That those who died today may enjoy the **messianic** banquet,

Our Father ...

Prayer
O good and gracious God,
you brought your people Israel from bondage to freedom:
bring us into the freedom of your presence
by our receiving the Bread of Life and the Cup of Salvation.
May we serve you in each other
and enjoy the reward of everlasting life
through Jesus Christ. **Amen.**

CONCLUSION

Blessing
May the God of freedom bless us
in the name of the Father, and of the Son, and of the Holy Spirit. **Amen.**

Dismissal
Go and rest in the freedom of the sons and daughters of God. **Thanks be to God.**

GOOD FRIDAY Morning Praise

MORNING HYMN

PSALMODY

From FRIDAY 2 Morning Praise, p. 110.

INTERCESSIONS

Invocations

Cantor, then Assembly:

Cantor:

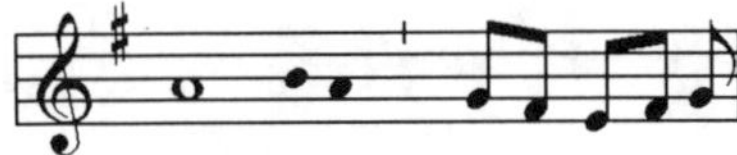

For for**give**ness ... **we** commend ourselves,
For purifi**ca**tion ... **we** commend ourselves,
For **judg**ment ... **we** commend ourselves,
For **wis**dom ... **we** commend ourselves,
For joy and **glad**ness ... **we** commend ourselves,
For a **pure** heart ... **we** commend ourselves,
For a firm **spir**it ... **we** commend ourselves,
For sal**va**tion ... **we** commend ourselves,
For de**liv**erance ... **we** commend ourselves,
For pros**per**ity ... **we** commend ourselves,

Our Father

Prayer
O savior God,
your Son was nailed to the cross
so that we might enjoy everlasting life with you:
may we see through the pain and suffering of our own lives
to the glory of salvation that your Son won for us.
We pray through Jesus Christ. **Amen.**

CONCLUSION

Blessing
May the God who humbled self to be nailed to a cross bless us
in the name of the Father, and of the Son, and of the Holy Spirit. **Amen.**

Dismissal
Go forth and live in the shadow of the Cross of Christ. **Thanks be to God.**

GOOD FRIDAY Evening Prayer

(Evening Prayer is said only by those who do not celebrate the Liturgy of the Lord's Passion.)

EVENING HYMN

PSALMODY

From FRIDAY 2 Evening Prayer, p. 114.

INTERCESSIONS

Petitions

Cantor, then Assembly:

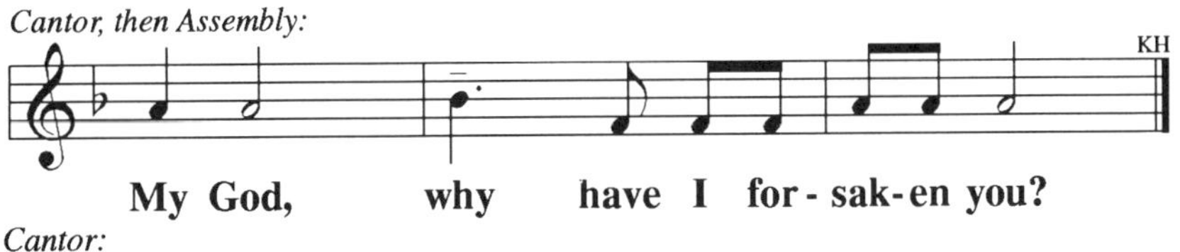

KH
My God, why have I for - sak - en you?

Cantor:

Who was **struck** ...
Who was in**sult**ed ...
Who was **spat** upon ...
Who was de**spised** ...
Who was re**jected** ...
Who was burdened with our in**firm**ities ...
Who was stricken with our dis**eases** ...
Who was **wounded** ...
Who was **crushed** ...
Who was **bruised** ...
Who was op**pressed** ...
Who was af**flicted** ...
Who was **silent** ...
Who was led to the **slaughter** ...
Who was cut **off** ...
Who was an **of**fering ...
Who emptied **self** ...
Who took the form of a **slave** ...
Who was born in human **like**ness ...

Who humbled **self** ...
Who was obedient unto **death** ...
Who was **stripped** ...
Who was **nailed** ...
Who died on a **cross** ...
Who for**gives** ...
Who bears our ini**q**uities ...
Who raises the dead to new **life** ...

Our Father

Prayer
O devoted Savior,
your bore our weakness
so that we might rise with lively strength:
receive this offering of our selves—
frail and imperfect though we be—
and restore us to the perfection of your image forever. **Amen.**

CONCLUSION

Blessing
May the God who selflessly loves bless us
in the name of the Father, and of the Son, and of the Holy Spirit. **Amen.**

Dismissal
Go and rest secure in the salvation of our faithful God. **Thanks be to God.**

HOLY SATURDAY Morning Praise

FESTAL MORNING HYMN

PSALMODY

From SATURDAY 2 Morning Praise, p. 118.

INTERCESSIONS

Invocations

Cantor, then Assembly:

Cantor:

O Savior laid **in** a tomb, to you praise **is** due ...
O Savior laid **in** a tomb, to you vows are **ful**filled ...
O Savior laid **in** a tomb, to you prayers **are** raised ...
O Savior laid **in** a tomb, to you shouts of joy **are** lifted ...
O Savior laid **in** a tomb, to you blessings **are** given ...
O Savior laid **in** a tomb, to you glory **be**longs ...
O Savior laid **in** a tomb, to you honor **a**rises ...
O Savior laid **in** a tomb, to you offering **is** made ...
O Savior laid **in** a tomb, to you worship **is** fitting ...

Our Father ...

Prayer
Almighty God,
your Son was laid in a tomb to await the power of your glory:
give us patient endurance during every day of our lives
so that we might share in that same glory.
We pray through Jesus Christ. **Amen.**

CONCLUSION

Blessing
May the God who promises life bless us
in the name of the Father, and of the Son, and of the Holy Spirit. **Amen.**

Dismissal
Go forth to await the glory of our God. **Thanks be to God.**

FESTAL EVENING HYMN

PSALMODY

From SATURDAY 2 Evening Prayer, p. 123.

INTERCESSIONS

Petitions

Cantor, then Assembly:
KH
Re - store us to new life!
Cantor:

That God may hear our prayer, **we** pray,
That God may guard our words, **we** pray,
That God may mend our wayward ways, **we** pray,
That God may draw us to refuge, **we** pray,
That God may delight in our conversions, **we** pray,
That God may receive our grateful hearts, **we** pray,
That God may raise the dead to new life, **we** pray,

Our Father ...

Prayer
O God who is above all and in all,
you promise life to those who turn to you:
as we await our celebration of the resurrection of Jesus,
may we rejoice in the fidelity of your presence.
We pray through Jesus Christ. **Amen.**

CONCLUSION

Blessing
May the God of life bless us
in the name of the Father, and of the Son, and of the Holy Spirit. **Amen.**

Dismissal
Go and rest in anticipation of Jesus' glorious resurrection. **Thanks be to God.**

SUNDAYS of EASTER Morning Praise

EASTER MORNING HYMN

PSALMODY

Psalm 95

ANTIPHON

Come! Let us shout with joy **for** the LORD;
let us make noise for the rock of our **sal**vation.
Let us come into God's presence in **thanks**giving;
with songs, let us **cry** out. ANTIPHON

For the LORD is a great God
  and a great Sovereign a**bove** all gods,
in whose hands are hidden the secrets of the earth
  and the treasures of **the** mountains.
The sea belongs to God,
  the one **who** made it,
and whose hands, too, shaped the **dry** land. ANTIPHON

Come! Let us bow **and** kneel down,
let us kneel down in the presence of the LORD our maker,
  who is **our** God;
we are **the** people,
the pasture, and **the** flock. ANTIPHON

Today, may you listen to the **voice** of God:
"Harden not your hearts as **at** Meribah,
as on the day at Massah in the desert
  where your ancestors test**ed** me.
They tried me even though they had seen **my** works.

Forty years I was disgusted by that **gen**eration,
and I said: 'They are a people of twisted hearts,
  they did not recognize **my** ways.'
I swore indeed in **my** anger:
'They will not enter into my rest**ing**-place.'" ANTIPHON

Psalm Prayer
Mighty God,
you raised your Son from death to life:
we bow before your majesty and great power.
Give us new life
through your risen Son, Jesus Christ. **Amen.**

Psalm 148

ANTIPHON
KH
Al - le - lu - ia, al - le - lu - ia, al - le - lu - ia!

Praise the LORD from the heavens:
  praise God in the **highest**,
praise God, O you messengers,
  praise God, O **you** hosts,
praise God, sun and moon,
  praise God, all shining **stars**
praise God, farthest heavens
  and waters from above **the** heavens. ANTIPHON

Let them praise the name of the **Lord**,
who commanded and they were **cre**ated,
who established them forever and **ever**,
fixing a limit that they can**not** cross. ANTIPHON

Praise the LORD from the earth:
sea monsters and all deep **waters**,
fire and hail,
snow and frost,
stormy winds fulfilling **God's** word,
mountains and all hills,
fruit trees and all **cedars**,
living creatures and all cattle,
reptiles and fly**ing** birds. ANTIPHON

Rulers of the earth and all nations,
nobles and all judges of the **earth**,
youthful men and women,
elderly and **young** people:
let them praise the LORD,
for God's name only is most **high**.
God's glory is above earth and heaven;
God will act mightily for **the** people. ANTIPHON

Praise from all the **faithful**,
from the children of Is**ra**el,
the people close to **God**!
Alle**lu**ia!

Psalm Prayer
O God,
you are worthy of all praise
from the heavens and all the earth:
hear our prayer of jubilation
that we may rejoice in your Son's risen presence
now and always. **Amen.**

Word of God

Benedictus
Blessed be the Lord God of **Israel**,
who visited and redeemed the **people**,
who raised up for us a **mighty** savior
from the house of **ser**vant David.

Just as the Lord spoke through the mouths of the holy prophets of **old**—
salvation comes out of the hands of our enemies and those who **hate** us,
that, with our ancestors, we might perform **works** of mercy,
remembering the holy covenant **sworn** to Abraham—

so does the Lord deliver us from the hands **of** our enemies,
that we might serve without fear before **the** Lord,
worshiping in **ho**liness
and in righteousness **all** our days.

And you also, child, will be called a prophet of God Most **High**:
for you will go before the Lord to prepare a **way**,
bringing people knowledge of salvation by for**giveness** of sins;
because of the deep and tender mercy **of** our God.

Whereby a light rising from on high will **visit** us
to appear to those in darkness and in a shadow **of** death,
to guide our feet along a **straight**, sure path
into a **way** of peace.

INTERCESSIONS

Invocations

Cantor, then Assembly:
KH
Al- le - lu - ia, Al - le - lu - ia!
Cantor:

O risen Savior, we sing to **you** with joy,
O risen Savior, we ac**claim** your greatness,
O risen Savior, we rejoice in your **res**urrection,
O risen Savior, we pro**claim** your glory,

O risen Savior, sun **and** moon praise you,
O risen Savior, the highest **hea**vens praise you,
O risen Savior, sea **crea**tures praise you,
O risen Savior, fire **and** hail praise you,
O risen Savior, snow **and** frost praise you,
O risen Savior, storm**y** winds praise you,
O risen Savior, mountains **and** hills praise you,
O risen Savior, fruit trees and all ev**er**greens praise you,
O risen Savior, animals and insects **and** birds praise you,
O risen Savior, all those in author**i**ty praise you,
O risen Savior, dreamers and **sag**es praise you,
O risen Savior, children **and** youth praise you,
O risen Savior, parents and grand**par**ents praise you,
O risen Savior, your holy ministers to the people **of** God praise you,
O risen Savior, your name is **a**bove all,
O risen Savior, your reign is estab**lished** forever,
O risen Savior, your salvation brings life **ev**erlasting,

Our Father ...

Prayer for Sundays of Easter Weeks 1, 2, & 3
O glorious God,
you raised your Son to new life and
established him at your right hand forever:
the whole world sings with joy.
The risen Jesus revealed his startling presence
by the simple human actions of
seeing and naming, touching, and feasting.
May we foster this risen life within ourselves
and one day stand in the company
of the angels and saints
victorious forever and ever. **Amen.**

Prayer for Sunday of Easter Week 4
O shepherd of Israel,
your Son is the loving shepherd of your new people:
keep us always in your love and care
that we may glorify you now and always. **Amen.**

Prayer for Sundays of Easter Weeks 5, 6, & 7
Loving Teacher,
you show love and concern for your disciples:
keep us in your care

as we labor to make known your Good News through the world.
We pray to God in the unity of the Holy Spirit,
one God, forever and ever. **Amen.**

CONCLUSION

Blessing
Bow your heads and pray that our glorious God bless us.
May the God who raised Jesus to resurrected life recreate us in that life. **Amen.**
May Jesus Christ touch us with his presence. **Amen.**
May the Spirit enliven us with joy and peace. **Amen.**
And may almighty God bless us
in the name of the Father, and of the Son, and of the Holy Spirit. **Amen.**

Sign of Peace/Dismissal
Let us offer one another a sign of the joy and peace of the resurrected Christ.

SUNDAYS of EASTER Evening Prayer

LIGHT SERVICE

Proclamation of the Light

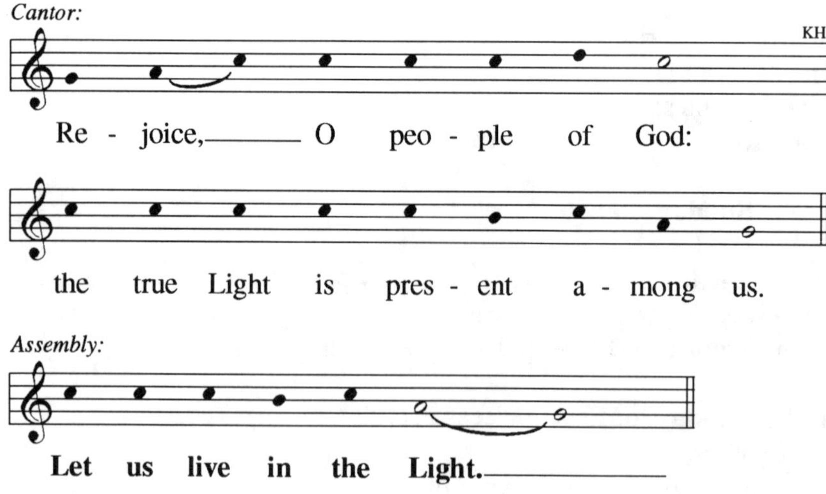
Cantor:
KH
Re - joice, O peo - ple of God:
the true Light is pres - ent a - mong us.
Assembly:
Let us live in the Light.

Easter Evening Hymn

Thanksgiving for the Light

Cantor:
KH
We praise and thank you, O glo - ri - ous God!
Your pow - er lifts the great light in the heav - ens.
Your glo - ry shines forth in the ris - en Son.
Your maj - es - ty lies o - ver all of cre - a - tion.
Your splen - dor clothes us with dig - ni - ty
and hon - or. Your good - ness o - ver-comes an - y
weak - ness. Your boun-ty sat - is - fies all hun - ger.
Your grace pro - claims our des - ti - ny.
Re - joice, O ho - ly peo - ple, in this great Light:

on this day Je - sus was raised from the dead, and now

lives for - ev - er at the right hand of the e - ter -

nal God. As our day draws to a close,

and dark-ness des-cends in qui - et rest, keep us

safe in this Light that nev - er fades. We praise and

thank you for your bless-ings, through the ris - en Christ our

Light for-ev - er and ev - er. **A - men.**

PSALMODY

Psalm 110 *Of David. Psalm.*

ANTIPHON

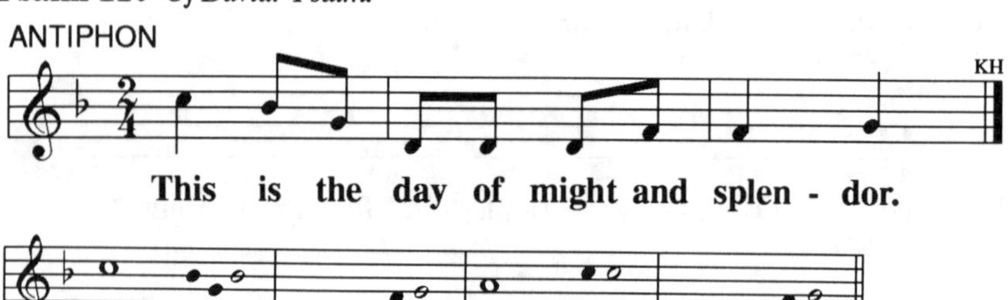

KH
This is the day of might and splen - dor.

Thus says the LORD **to** my lord:
"Sit on my right
  until I place your enemies
  as a footstool for **your** feet."
Let the LORD send from Zion
  the scepter of **your** strength.
Rule in the midst of **your** enemies. ANTIPHON

Your people bring free **of**ferings
on the day of your might
  in ho**ly** splendor.
From the womb **of** dawn,
a dew of rejuvenation comes **to** you. ANTIPHON

The LORD has promised
  and will **not** repent:
"According to my word,
  you are a priest forever, my king **of** justice."
The Lord is at **your** right,
who has smashed rulers on the day **of** wrath.

The Lord judges a**gainst** the nations,
piling them **with** corpses.
The Lord has smashed heads
  all over **the** land.
From a torrent the Lord drinks on the way,
  and rises up **in** triumph. ANTIPHON

Psalm Prayer
O mighty God,
you raised up your Son to sit at your right hand:
give us new life that we might
enjoy everlasting peace with you now and always. **Amen.**

Psalm 67 *To the choirmaster. With stringed instruments. Psalm. Song.*

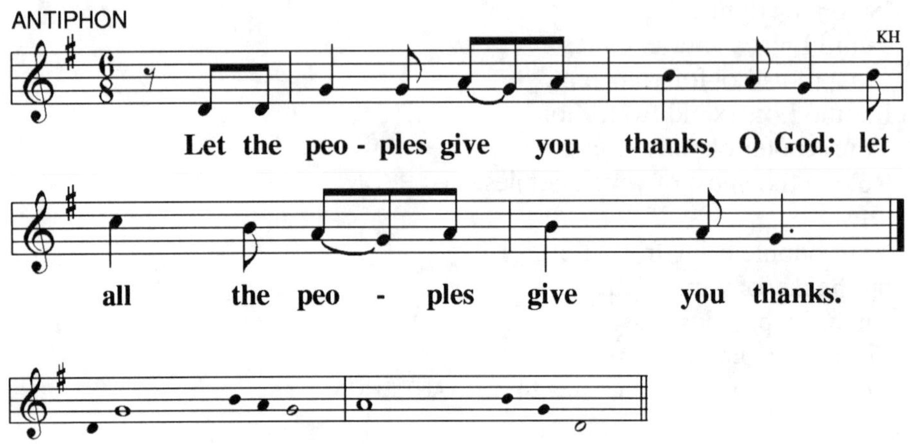
ANTIPHON
KH
Let the peo - ples give you thanks, O God; let
all the peo - ples give you thanks.

May God have mercy on us and **bless** us.
May God's face **shine** among us.

For your way is known **over** the earth,
and your salvation is known a**mong** all nations. ANTIPHON

May the nations rejoice and **shout** with joy,
for you judge the peoples rightly
  and the nations on the **earth** you guide. ANTIPHON

The earth has **given** its fruit.
May God, our God, **bless** us.

May God **bless** us,
and let all ends of the **earth** show reverence. ANTIPHON

Psalm Prayer
God of our salvation,
you are worthy of all thanks and praise:
receive our evening prayer
as a sign of our reverence for you now and always. **Amen.**

Word of God

Magnificat
My soul does magni**fy** the Lord!
I delight in **God** my savior
who looked kindly **on** lowliness.

Now all ages will **call** me blessed
for the Mighty One **did** great things.
Holy is **God's** name;
mercy is from age to age for **those** in awe!

The Lord's strong arm did **might**y deeds:
confused the proud in **their** smug hearts;
toppled sovereigns **from** their thrones,
and exalted **hum**ble ones;
filled the hungering with **good** things,
and sent the rich **a**way empty.

The Lord helped servant **Is**rael
to re**mem**ber mercy,
as was spoken to Ab**ra**ham
and his descendants for**ev**ermore!

INTERCESSIONS

Petitions

Cantor, then Assembly:

KH
Al - le - lu - ia, al - le - lu - ia, al - le - lu - ia!

Cantor:

God raises the Son **to** life!
God sets the Son as eternal **high** priest!
God has mercy **on** us!
God's face shines **on** us!
God's way is known over all **the** earth!
God's salvation dawns up**on** us!
God judges the peo**ples** rightly!
God guides the nations **on** earth!
God nourishes us abun**dant**ly!
God **made** us!
God calls us to glori**ous** presence!
God's steadfast love is **for**ever!
God's faithfulness is **en**during!

God's promises are **ful**filled!
God's life is up**on** us!
God raises all the dead to **new** life!

Our Father ...

Prayer
O glorious God,
you bring us joy and peace
by the resurrection of your Son:
may we continually open ourselves
to your overtures of love and mercy.
We pray through Jesus your risen Son. **Amen.**

CONCLUSION

Blessing
Bow your heads and pray that our glorious God bless us.
May the God who raised Jesus to new life recreate us in that life. **Amen.**
May Jesus Christ touch us with his presence. **Amen.**
May the Spirit enliven us with joy and peace. **Amen.**
And may almighty God bless us
in the name of the Father, and of the Son, and of the Holy Spirit. **Amen.**

Sign of Peace/Dismissal
Let us offer one another a sign of the joy and peace of the resurrected Christ.

MONDAYS of EASTER Morning Praise

EASTER MORNING HYMN

PSALMODY

Psalm 84 *To the choirmaster. On the gittith. By the Qorahites. Psalm.*

Solo 1 How lovable are your tents,
O LORD of hosts.
My soul longs—indeed faints—
for the courts of the LORD.
My heart and my flesh sing for joy

to the living God.
Even the sparrow finds a home
and the swallow a nest for herself
where she sets her young
next to your altars,
O LORD of hosts,
my Sovereign and my God.
Blessed are those who dwell in your house;
they will continue to praise you.

Selah (pause).

All Blessed is the one whose strength resides in you.
Those whose hearts are set on pilgrimage
make the valley of tears a place of fountains
as they travel through it.
Even the early rain covers it with blessings.
They walk with ever greater strength:
the God of gods will be seen in Zion.

Solo 1 O LORD God of hosts,
hear my prayer;
listen, O God of Jacob.

Selah (pause).

All See our shield, O God,
and consider the face of your Messiah.
For one day in your courts is better
than a thousand elsewhere.

Solo 1 I would rather stand at the threshold
of the house of my God,
than live in the tents of the wicked.
For the LORD is a sun and a shield;
God is grace and glory.
The LORD gives,
and does not refuse any good
to those who walk in integrity.

All O LORD of hosts,
blessed is the one
who trusts in you.

Psalm 5 *To the choirmaster. For the flutes. Psalm of David.*

Solo 1 Give ear to my words, O LORD,
perceive my groaning.
Be attentive to the sound of my cry,
my Sovereign and my God,
for to you I pray.
O LORD, in the morning
hear my voice.
In the morning I prepare for you
and I keep watching.

Choir 1 For you are not a God delighting in wickedness,
nor does evil daunt you.
Mockers cannot stand
before your eyes.
You hate all makers of emptiness,
and you will destroy speakers of deceit.
People of bloodshed and fraud,
the LORD abhors.

Solo 1 But I, in the abundance of your steadfast love,
shall come to your house.
With awe I shall prostrate myself in your holy temple.
O LORD, guide me in your justice
because of my adversaries;
straighten your way before me.

Choir 2 Nothing right comes from their mouths:
their insides are rotted,
their throats are open tombs,
their tongues are forked.
Prove them wrong, O God;
let them fall by their own counsels.
For their many transgressions,
drive them away
since they have rebelled against you.

All All who take refuge in you shall rejoice;
forever they will shout for joy.
You will lay protection over them
and all those who love your name
will exult in you.

For you bless the righteous, O LORD;
as with a shield of delight you will crown them.

Word of God

Benedictus
Blessed be the Lord God of **Israel**,
who visited and redeemed the **people**,
who raised up for us a **mighty** savior
from the house of **ser**vant David.

Just as the Lord spoke through the mouths of the holy prophets of **old**—
salvation comes out of the hands of our enemies and those who **hate** us,
that, with our ancestors, we might perform **works** of mercy,
remembering the holy covenant **sworn** to Abraham—

so does the Lord deliver us from the hands **of** our enemies,
that we might serve without fear before **the** Lord,
worshiping in **ho**liness
and in righteousness **all** our days.

And you also, child, will be called a prophet of God Most **High**:
for you will go before the Lord to prepare a **way**,
bringing people knowledge of salvation by for**giveness** of sins;
because of the deep and tender mercy **of** our God.

Whereby a light rising from on high will **visit** us
to appear to those in darkness and in a shadow **of** death,
to guide our feet along a **straight**, sure path
into a **way** of peace.

INTERCESSIONS

Invocations

Cantor, then Assembly:

You have ris - en as you said!

Cantor:

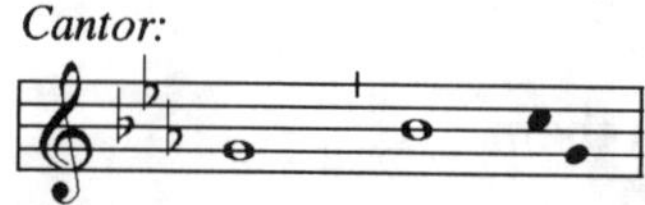

Risen Christ, **you** are **our** dwelling place,
Risen Christ, **you** are **our** joy,
Risen Christ, **you** are **our** strength,
Risen Christ, **you** are **our** justice,
Risen Christ, **you** are **our** refuge,
Risen Christ, **you** are **our** protection,
Risen Christ, **you** are **our** blessing,
Risen Christ, **you** are **our** life,

Our Father ...

Prayer
O ever-living God,
your presence is known to us
in the temple of your glory:
instill in us your life
that we may faithfully live your covenant.
We pray through Jesus Christ your risen Son. **Amen.**

CONCLUSION

Blessing
May the Risen Christ give us new life and bless us
in the name of the Father, and of the Son, and of the Holy Spirit. **Amen.**

Dismissal
Go forth to live in the shade of Christ's resurrection. **Thanks be to God.**

MONDAYS of EASTER Evening Prayer

EASTER EVENING HYMN

PSALMODY

Psalm 131 *Song of ascents (pilgrimages). Of David.*

Solo 1 O LORD, my heart has not boasted
and my eyes have not pretended.

Nor have I engaged in things too great
and too wondrous for me.

Solo 2 Have I not calmed
and quieted my soul?
Like a weaned child against a mother,
like a weaned child within me, so is my soul.

All Put your hope, O Israel, in the LORD,
from now and forever.

Psalm 92 *Psalm. Song for the day of the Sabbath.*

All It is good to give thanks to the LORD,
to sing to your name, O Most High;
to recount your steadfast love in the morning
and your faithfulness during the night,
with the lute, the lyre,
and the sound of the harp.

Solo 1 For you have given me joy, O LORD,
by your work;
about your handiwork, I will shout with joy.

All How great are your works, O LORD!
Your plans are very profound.
The foolish do not know them,
and the stupid do not understand.
In their blossoming, the wicked are like grass;
all makers of emptiness flourish
only to perish forever and ever.

Solo 2 But you, O LORD, are exalted forever.
Behold, your enemies, O LORD,
behold, your enemies will perish.
All makers of emptiness will be scattered.

Solo 1 But you have exalted my strength like that of the wild ox,
anointing me with fresh oil.
My eyes have beheld my enemies
and my ears have heard those who rise against me.

Solo 2 The righteous will flourish like a palm tree,
and rise like a cedar in Lebanon.
Planted in the house of the LORD,
in the courts of our God, they will flourish.
Even in old age they will give fruit—
they will be fresh and full of sap—
recounting that the LORD is upright.
God is my rock, in whom there is no iniquity.

Word of God

Magnificat
My soul does magni**fy** the Lord!
I delight in **God** my savior
who looked kindly **on** lowliness.

Now all ages will **call** me blessed
for the Mighty One **did** great things.
Holy is **God's** name;
mercy is from age to age for **those** in awe!

The Lord's strong arm did **mighty** deeds:
confused the proud in **their** smug hearts;
toppled sovereigns **from** their thrones,
and exalted **hum**ble ones;
filled the hungering with **good** things,
and sent the rich **a**way empty.

The Lord helped servant **Is**rael
to re**mem**ber mercy,
as was spoken to Ab**ra**ham
and his descendants for**e**vermore!

INTERCESSIONS

Petitions

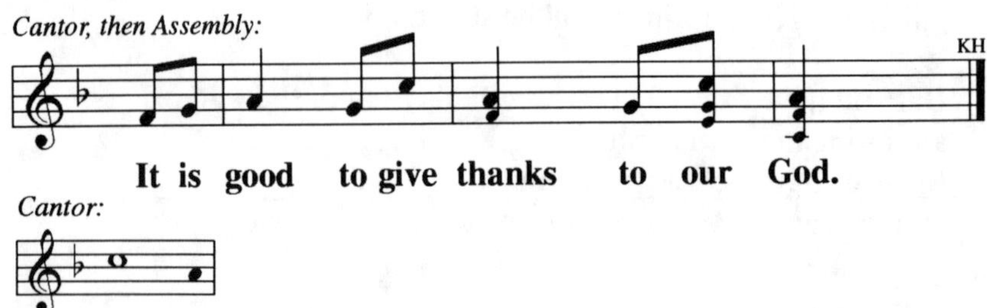
Cantor, then Assembly:
KH
It is good to give thanks to our God.
Cantor:

For wondrous **deeds** ...
For calm and **quiet** ...
For hope and **trust** ...
For steadfast **love** ...
For everlasting **faith**fulness ...
For exalted **strength** ...
For resurrected **life** ...
For promised **fruit**fulness ...
For life for the faithful de**part**ed ...

Our Father ...

Prayer
God Most High,
your great works bring salvation and peace:
be with us this night and refresh us
that we may continue our joy in the resurrection
of your Son and our brother, Jesus Christ. **Amen.**

CONCLUSION

Blessing
May God keep us safe and bless us
in the name of the Father, and of the Son, and of the Holy Spirit. **Amen.**

Dismissal
Go and rest in the peace of risen life. **Thanks be to God.**

TUESDAYS of EASTER Morning Praise

EASTER MORNING HYMN

PSALMODY

Psalm 113

All Alleluia!

Choir 1 Give praise, servants of the LORD;
praise the name of the LORD.

Let the name of the LORD be blessed
from now on and forever.
From the rising of the sun to its setting,
let the name of the LORD be praised.
The LORD is exalted above all nations;
God's glory is greater than the heavens.

All Who is like the LORD our God,
enthroned above?

Choir 2 Who looks down to watch over
the skies and the earth?
Who raises the weak from dust
and the poor from ashes,
to return them to the company of nobles,
the nobles of the people?
Who brings home the sterile woman,
now a rejoicing mother of many children?

All Alleluia!

Psalm 3 *Psalm of David. In his flight from Absalom his son.*

Solo 1 O LORD, how many are my adversaries!
Many are rising against me;
many are saying to my soul:
"There is no salvation
for you in God."

Selah (pause).

Solo 2 But you, O LORD,
are a shield over me,
my glory and the one lifting my head.
With my voice to the LORD I will cry,
and God will answer me from the holy mountain.

Selah (pause).

Solo 1 I lie down and sleep;
I wake up
for the LORD sustains me.
I shall not fear the multitudes of people

positioning themselves
around and against me.

Solo 2 Arise, O LORD;
save me, my God,
for you strike all my enemies on the cheek
and you shatter the teeth of the wicked.

All From the LORD, salvation!
Upon your people, blessing!

Selah (pause).

Word of God

Benedictus
Blessed be the Lord God of **Israel**,
who visited and redeemed the **people**,
who raised up for us a **mighty** savior
from the house of **ser**vant David.

Just as the Lord spoke through the mouths of the holy prophets of **old**—
salvation comes out of the hands of our enemies and those who **hate** us,
that, with our ancestors, we might perform **works** of mercy,
remembering the holy covenant **sworn** to Abraham—

so does the Lord deliver us from the hands **of** our enemies,
that we might serve without fear before **the** Lord,
worshiping in **ho**liness
and in righteousness **all** our days.

And you also, child, will be called a prophet of God Most **High**:
for you will go before the Lord to prepare a **way**,
bringing people knowledge of salvation by for**giveness** of sins;
because of the deep and tender mercy **of** our God.

Whereby a light rising from on high will **vis**it us
to appear to those in darkness and in a shadow **of** death,
to guide our feet along a **straight**, sure path
into a **way** of peace.

INTERCESSIONS

Invocations

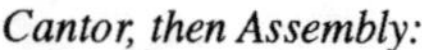
Cantor, then Assembly:

KH
Al- le - lu - ia, Al - le - lu - ia!

Cantor:

Risen Christ, your **name** is holy,
Risen Christ, you are raised **to** new life,
Risen Christ, you are exalted above **all** creation,
Risen Christ, your salvation shields **us** from harm,
Risen Christ, you sus**tain** our goodness,
Risen Christ, you bless **us** with peace,
Risen Christ, your pres**ence** brings life,

Our Father ...

Prayer
God of might and life,
you raised your Son to sit at your right hand:
give us that same life that we may
one day enjoy life with you forever and ever. **Amen.**

CONCLUSION

Blessing
May the God of life bless us
in the name of the Father, and of the Son, and of the Holy Spirit. **Amen.**

Dismissal
Go forth to live the Good News of the resurrection. **Thanks be to God.**

TUESDAYS of EASTER Evening Prayer

EASTER EVENING HYMN

PSALMODY

Psalm 16 *A poem. Of David.*

Solo 1 Keep me, O God,
for I take refuge in you.
I say to the LORD:
"You are my Lord,
my happiness is only in you."

All As for idols in the land,
they are mighty only for those who delight in them.
People multiply these idols
after which they hurry.

Solo 2 But I will not offer them sacrifices of blood,
nor will I raise their names to my lips.
O LORD, my given portion and my cup,
you support my destiny
which has fallen for me in pleasant places,
nothing but a goodly heritage.

Solo 1 I bless the LORD who gives me counsel.
Even at night my heart instructs me.
I keep the LORD always before me.
Because God is at my right hand,
I shall not be moved.

Solo 2 Hence my heart rejoices
and my soul exults.
Even my body rests secure
because you do not abandon me to Sheol.
You do not allow your faithful
to experience the Pit.
You teach me the path of life.

All In your presence there is fullness of joy;
in your right hand, pleasures for eternity.

Psalm 116

Solo 1 I love the LORD
who has heard
the voice of my supplications.

For God has turned an ear to me
as I cry all my days.

Solo 2 Deadly chains have fettered me,
and the anguish of Sheol has reached up to me.
Distress and terror, I have encountered;
but I have called on the name of the LORD.
How long, O LORD?
Deliver my soul.

All The LORD is gracious and just;
our God is merciful.

Solo 1 The LORD is the protector of the innocent;
I was poor and God brought salvation to me.
Return, O my soul, to your rest,
for the LORD has done good to you.

Solo 2 For you have delivered my soul from death,
my eye from tears
and my foot from stumbling,
that I may walk in the presence of the LORD
in the land of the living.

Solo 1 Yes, I was right in saying,
"I am greatly afflicted."
In my agitation, I have said,
"Every human being is a liar."

Solo 2 What shall I return to the LORD
for all the bounty in my favor?
I will lift up the cup of salvation
and I will call on the name of the LORD.
Indeed, I will fulfill my promises to the LORD
in the presence of all the people.

All Precious in the eyes of the LORD
is the death of the faithful ones.

Solo 1 How long, O LORD?
For I am your servant,
I am your servant, the offspring of your handmaid.
You have loosened my bonds.

Solo 2 To you I will offer a sacrifice of thanksgiving
and I will call on the name of the LORD.
Indeed, I will fulfill my promises to the LORD
in the presence of all the people,
in the courts of the house of the LORD,
in your midst, O Jerusalem.

All Alleluia!

Word of God

Magnificat
My soul does magni**fy** the Lord!
I delight in **God** my savior
who looked kindly **on** lowliness.

Now all ages will **call** me blessed
for the Mighty One **did** great things.
Holy is **God's** name;
mercy is from age to age for **those** in awe!

The Lord's strong arm did **mighty** deeds:
confused the proud in **their** smug hearts;
toppled sovereigns **from** their thrones,
and exalted **hum**ble ones;
filled the hungering with **good** things,
and sent the rich **a**way empty.

The Lord helped servant **Is**rael
to re**mem**ber mercy,
as was spoken to Abr**a**ham
and his descendants for**e**vermore!

INTERCESSIONS

Petitions

Cantor, then Assembly:

Cantor:

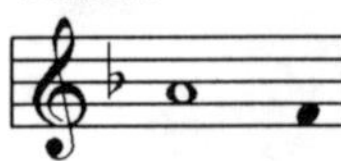

That our happiness be only in **God** ...
That our destiny be directed to **God** ...
That our counsel come only through **God** ...
That our security rest firmly in **God** ...
That our pleasures point us toward resur**rection** ...
That our deliverance be **sure** ...
That our protection be gracious and **just** ...
That our promises be ful**filled** ...
That our bonds be **loosened** ...
That the faithful departed receive everlasting **life** ...

Our Father ...

Prayer
God of holiness,
you showed pleasure in your Son
by raising him to new life:
show us favor now and always.
We pray through Jesus Christ. **Amen.**

CONCLUSION

Blessing
May the God who raised Jesus to life bless us
in the name of the Father, and of the Son, and of the Holy Spirit. **Amen.**

Dismissal
Go and rest in God's love. **Thanks be to God.**

WEDNESDAYS of EASTER Morning Praise

EASTER MORNING HYMN

PSALMODY

Psalm 8 *To the choirmaster. On the gittith. Of David.*

All O LORD our Lord,
how magnificent is your name
over all the earth!

Choir 1 You set your glory above the skies.
From the mouths of babes and infants,
you have established strength against your adversaries
to still the enemy and avenger.

Solo 1 If I look at your skies,
the work of your fingers,
the moon and stars that you have set in place,
What are mortals that you remember them?
And human beings that you care for them?

Choir 2 But you have made them slightly less than a god,
and with glory and radiance you crown them.
You made them rule over the work of your hands.
You have placed everything under their feet—
sheep and cattle, all together,
and even the beasts from the fields,
the birds of heaven
and the fish from the sea,
all that crosses along the paths of the seas.

All O LORD our Lord,
how magnificent is your name
over all the earth!

Psalm 90 *Prayer. Of Moses, the man of God.*

Choir 1 O Lord, you have been a refuge for us
from generation to generation.
Before the mountains were born
and before you formed the earth and the universe,
you are God from eternity to eternity.

Choir 2 You return mortals to dust,
and then you say, "Come back, O humans."
For a thousand years in your eyes
are like the day of yesterday that has gone by,

or like a vigil in the night.
You sweep mortals away in their sleep,
but in the morning they will be
like the grass that flourishes.
In the morning grass is bright and flourishes
but at night it fades and dries out.

Choir 1 For we have been consumed by your anger
and we have been terrified by your zeal.
You have set our iniquities before you,
our hidden sins in the light of your face.
All our days pass away in your anger,
our years end up like a sigh.
The days of our lives are seventy years,
perhaps eighty if we are very strong.
Still most of them are toil and emptiness,
for our lives soon pass away—
quickly we vanish!

Choir 2 Who knows the power of your anger,
and that your wrath equals the reverence due you?
So teach us to count our days
and let wisdom come to our hearts.

Choir 1 Turn back, O LORD! How long?
Bring comfort to your servants.
Fill us in the morning with your steadfast love,
that we may sing and rejoice all our days.
Gladden us as many days as you have humbled us,
those years we experienced evil.

Choir 2 Let your work be visible to your servants,
and your splendor to their offspring.
Let the favor of the Lord our God be over us,
and the work of our hands be a strength over us.

All O may the work of our hands be a strength over us!

Word of God

Benedictus
Blessed be the Lord God of **Israel**,
who visited and redeemed the **people**,

who raised up for us a **mighty** savior
from the house of **ser**vant David.

Just as the Lord spoke through the mouths of the holy prophets of **old**—
salvation comes out of the hands of our enemies and those who **hate** us,
that, with our ancestors, we might perform **works** of mercy,
remembering the holy covenant **sworn** to Abraham—

so does the Lord deliver us from the hands **of** our enemies,
that we might serve without fear before **the** Lord,
worshiping in **ho**liness
and in righteousness **all** our days.

And you also, child, will be called a prophet of God Most **High**:
for you will go before the Lord to prepare a **way**,
bringing people knowledge of salvation by for**giveness** of sins;
because of the deep and tender mercy **of** our God.

Whereby a light rising from on high will **vis**it us
to appear to those in darkness and in a shadow **of** death,
to guide our feet along a **straight**, sure path
into a **way** of peace.

INTERCESSIONS

Invocations

Cantor, then Assembly:

KH
How glo - ri-ous is your name!

Cantor:

Risen **Christ**, you still the enemy and av**enger**,
Risen **Christ**, you care for hu**manity**,
Risen **Christ**, you crown human beings with glory and **radiance**,
Risen **Christ**, you give humans dominion over all **things**,
Risen **Christ**, you are God from eternity to e**ternity**,
Risen **Christ**, you conquer frailty and **weakness**,
Risen **Christ**, you bring wisdom to our **hearts**,

Risen **Christ**, you comfort the **sorrowing**,
Risen **Christ**, you gladden us with your **splendor**,

Our Father ...

Prayer
God of the universe,
you created us in your divine image:
may we respond to your election to be sons and daughters
through the resurrection of Jesus Christ our Savior. **Amen.**

CONCLUSION

Blessing
May the creator God bless us
in the name of the Father, and of the Son, and of the Holy Spirit. **Amen.**

Dismissal
Go forth to be images of God by the power of the resurrection. **Thanks be to God.**

WEDNESDAYS of EASTER Evening Prayer

EASTER EVENING HYMN

PSALMODY

Psalm 139 *To the choirmaster. Of David. Psalm.*

Solo 1 O LORD, you have searched me and you know:
you know when I sit and when I stand,
you discern my thought from a distance,
you search my path and my resting place,
and you are familiar with all my ways.
Even before there is any word on my tongue,
behold, O LORD, you know it completely.
You surround me behind and before,
you set your hand over me.
Such knowledge is too wonderful for me,
so lofty that I cannot reach it.

All Where can I go from your spirit?
And where can I flee from your face?

Solo 2 If I ascend to the heavens, you are there;
if I lie down in Sheol, behold, you are there.
If I rise with the wings of dawn
or lie down in the far end of the sea:
even there, your hand leads me
and your right hand seizes me.
If I say, "Surely darkness
will fall upon me
and night will replace the light around me,"
even darkness is not dark for you:
the night will shine like the day,
and darkness will be like light.

Solo 1 For you formed my inmost parts;
you weaved me in my mother's womb.
I give thanks to you because I was made
in an awesome and wonderful way.
Your works are wonderful,
well known to my soul.
My bones were not hidden from you
when I was made in secret,
woven in the depths of the earth.
Your eyes have seen my unformed matter.
In your book, the days to be formed were all written
before any one of them existed.

All How difficult for me are your thoughts!
How immeasurable, O God, their sum!
Were I to count them, they would be more than the sand.
Were I to end, I would still be with you.

Solo 2 If only, O God, you could kill the wicked,
then the bloodthirsty would turn away from me—
those who have spoken malice against you
and have risen up to destroy your cities.
Should I not, O LORD, hate those who hate you
and loathe those who rise up against you?
With pure hatred I hate them;
they have become my own enemies.

All Search me, O God, and know my heart;
examine me and know my thoughts.
See if any way in me is hurtful
and lead me into the way of eternity.

Psalm 9 *To the choirmaster. Muth lebben. Psalm of David.*

Solo 1 I will give thanks, O LORD, with all my heart.
I will tell of all your wonderful deeds.
I will rejoice, I will exult in you,
and I will play music for your name, O Most High.

Solo 2 When my enemies turned back
they stumbled and perished before you,
for you had taken up my case and my judgment.
You sat on the throne
as the one who judges with justice.
You rebuked nations;
you destroyed the wicked,
erasing their names
forever and ever.
The enemy has vanished
in ruins for eternity.
You destroyed cities—
even their memory has perished.

Choir 1 But the LORD remains enthroned forever,
making firm the throne of judgment.
God judges the world in justice
and the peoples in equity.

Choir 2 The LORD will be
a refuge for the poor,
a refuge in times of distress.
Those who know your name
will trust in you,
for you do not abandon those who seek you, O LORD.

Word of God

Magnificat
My soul does magnify the Lord!

I delight in **God** my savior
who looked kindly **on** lowliness.

Now all ages will **call** me blessed
for the Mighty One **did** great things.
Holy is **God's** name;
mercy is from age to age for **those** in awe!

The Lord's strong arm did **might**y deeds:
confused the proud in **their** smug hearts;
toppled sovereigns **from** their thrones,
and exalted **hum**ble ones;
filled the hungering with **good** things,
and sent the rich **a**way empty.

The Lord helped servant **Is**rael
to re**mem**ber mercy,
as was spoken to Ab**ra**ham
and his descendants for**ev**ermore!

INTERCESSIONS

Petitions

Cantor, then Assembly:

KH
How im - meas- ura - ble are the works of God.

Cantor:

That God may lead us into the way of e**ternity** ...
That God may judge with **justice** ...
That God may rebuke those who do **evil** ...
That God may destroy that which is **harmful** ...
That God may rule equitably for**ever** ...
That God may be a refuge for the **poor** ...
That God may not abandon those who seek **peace** ...
That God may raise the faithful departed to new **life** ...

Our Father ...

Prayer
God of the resurrection,
you have formed us in the hidden womb of your life-giving power:
may we always recognize the wonders of your works
and the splendor of your majesty.
We pray through your risen Son. **Amen.**

CONCLUSION

Blessing
May the God who formed us bless us
in the name of the Father, and of the Son, and of the Holy Spirit. **Amen.**

Dismissal
Go and rest in the life of Christ. **Thanks be to God.**

THURSDAYS of EASTER Morning Praise

EASTER MORNING HYMN

PSALMODY

Psalm 63 *Psalm of David. While he was in the desert of Judah.*

Solo 1 O God, you are my God, I seek you;
my soul thirsts for you.
My flesh longs for you
in a dry and wasted land,
deprived of water.

Solo 2 So in the sanctuary I have contemplated you
to see your might and your glory.
Because your steadfast love is better than life,
my lips will praise you.
So I will bless you all my life;
in your name I will raise my hands.
As with milk and rich food,
my soul is filled;
my mouth gives praise with joyful lips.
I remember you upon my bed,

pondering you throughout the night.
For you were a help for me;
in the shade of your wings I keep singing.
My soul clings to you;
your right hand upholds me.

Solo 1 But let those who seek my destruction
be cast into the depths of the earth.
Let them be given over to the power of the sword;
let them become a prey for jackals.

All Then the king shall rejoice in God.
All those who swear by God will be praised,
for the mouths of liars will be shut.

Psalm 126 *Song of ascents (pilgrimages).*

Choir 1 When the LORD accompanied
those who returned to Zion,
we were like dreamers.
Then our mouth
was filled with laughter
and our tongue with joy.
Then it was said among nations:
"The LORD has done great
deeds among these people."

All The LORD has done great
deeds among us.
Now we rejoice.

Choir 2 Return our captives, O LORD,
like torrents in the Negeb.
Those who sow in tears
harvest with shouts of joy.
Indeed, the one who goes out weeping,
carrying the bag of seed,
comes back joyful,
carrying the sheaves.

Word of God

Benedictus

Blessed be the Lord God of **Israel**,
who visited and redeemed the **people**,
who raised up for us a **mighty** savior
from the house of **ser**vant David.

Just as the Lord spoke through the mouths of the holy prophets of **old**—
salvation comes out of the hands of our enemies and those who **hate** us,
that, with our ancestors, we might perform **works** of mercy,
remembering the holy covenant **sworn** to Abraham—

so does the Lord deliver us from the hands **of** our enemies,
that we might serve without fear before **the** Lord,
worshiping in **ho**liness
and in righteousness **all** our days.

And you also, child, will be called a prophet of God Most **High**:
for you will go before the Lord to prepare a **way**,
bringing people knowledge of salvation by for**giveness** of sins;
because of the deep and tender mercy **of** our God.

Whereby a light rising from on high will **vis**it us
to appear to those in darkness and in a shadow **of** death,
to guide our feet along a **straight**, sure path
into a **way** of peace.

INTERCESSIONS

Invocations

Cantor, then Assembly:
KH
Al - le - lu - ia, al - le - lu - ia, al - le - lu - ia!

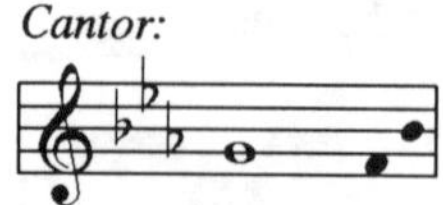

Cantor:

Risen Savior, you have unleashed your might **and** glory,
Risen Savior, you have satisfied us with a **rich** feast,
Risen Savior, you have kept us in the shade of **your** wings,
Risen Savior, you have upheld us by your **right** hand,

Risen Savior, you have con**quered** death,
Risen Savior, you have filled us **with** laughter,
Risen Savior, you have harvested in us **your** joy,
Risen Savior, you have risen to **new** life,

Our Father ...

Prayer
O God of salvation,
you have done great deeds among your people:
as we celebrate the resurrection of your Son,
may we deepen our appreciation of the life you offer us.
We pray through your Son, in the unity of the Holy Spirit,
one God forever and ever. **Amen.**

CONCLUSION

Blessing
May the God of the resurrection bless us
in the name of the Father, and of the Son, and of the Holy Spirit. **Amen.**

Dismissal
Go forth to live God's rich life. **Thanks be to God.**

THURSDAYS of EASTER Evening Prayer

EASTER EVENING HYMN

PSALMODY

Psalm 66 *To the choirmaster. A Song. Psalm.*

Choir 1 Sound the trumpet for God, all the earth!
Make music to the glory of God's name!
Give glory and praise!
Say to God:
"How awesome are your deeds!
At the magnitude of your power,
your enemies cringe before you.
Let all the earth worship you,

let them sing to you,
let them sing to your name."

Selah (pause).

Choir 2 Come and see the accomplishments
of God—
an awesome work
on behalf of mortals.
God turned the sea into dry land,
they crossed through the river on foot.
Therefore let us rejoice in God,
who rules over the world with power
and whose eyes watch over the nations.
Let not the stubborn rise up against God.

Selah (pause).

All All you nations, bless our God!
Let the sound of praise be heard
for the one who gives life to our souls,
and who kept our feet from stumbling.

Choir 1 For you have tested us, O God;
you have tried us like silver is tried.
You have caught us in a net.
You have put a burden on our backs.
You have let mortals enslave us.
We went through fire and water,
but you brought us out to a fertile land.

Solo 1 I shall go into your house with offerings.
I will fulfill my promises to you
which my lips uttered
and my mouth spoke when I was in distress.
I will bring you offerings of fatlings;
along with the smoke of rams
I will offer bulls and goats.

Selah (pause).

Solo 2 Come, listen, all those who revere God,
and I will tell

all that God did for my soul.
I have cried out with my mouth,
extolling God with my tongue.
If I had harbored emptiness in my heart,
the Lord would not have listened.
But truly God has listened,
listened to the voice of my prayer.

Solo 1 Blessed be God
who has not rejected my prayer,
nor taken steadfast love away from me.

Psalm 122 *Song of ascents (pilgrimages). Of David.*

Solo 1 I rejoiced when they said to me,
"We shall go to the house of the LORD."

Choir 1 Our feet are standing
at your gates, O Jerusalem.
Jerusalem, you are built like a city
well-bound together.
There the tribes went up,
the tribes of the LORD,
to give thanks to the name of the LORD,
keeping a precept for Israel.
For there the thrones for judgment were placed,
the thrones for the house of David.

Choir 2 Pray for the peace of Jerusalem:
"May those who love you live in peace.
May peace be within your walls
and tranquility within your palaces."

Solo 1 For the sake of my kindred
and my companions, let me speak:
"Peace be upon you."
For the sake of the house of the LORD our God,
I will seek your prosperity.

Word of God

Magnificat
My soul does magnify the Lord!

I delight in **God** my savior
who looked kindly **on** lowliness.

Now all ages will **call** me blessed
for the Mighty One **did** great things.
Holy is **God's** name;
mercy is from age to age for **those** in awe!

The Lord's strong arm did **mighty** deeds:
confused the proud in **their** smug hearts;
toppled sovereigns **from** their thrones,
and exalted **hum**ble ones;
filled the hungering with **good** things,
and sent the rich **a**way empty.

The Lord helped servant **Is**rael
to re**mem**ber mercy,
as was spoken to Ab**ra**ham
and his descendants for**ev**ermore!

INTERCESSIONS

Petitions

Cantor, then Assembly:

Cantor:

We give glory, praise, **and** thanks,
We rejoice in God's awe**some** works,
We fulfill our promise **of** love,
We revere God for great and won**drous** deeds,
We bless God for **sal**vation,
We thank God for res**ur**rection,
We extoll God for **new** life,
We commend to eternal life those who **have** died,

Our Father ...

Prayer
O redeeming God,
you brought new life to the world
through the death and resurrection of your Son:
nurture us, your holy people,
that we may enter into joy with you forever and ever. **Amen.**

CONCLUSION

Blessing
May our life-giving God bless us
in the name of the Father, and of the Son, and of the Holy Spirit. **Amen.**

Dismissal
Go and rest in the graciousness of our God. **Thanks be to God.**

FRIDAYS of EASTER Morning Praise

EASTER MORNING HYMN

PSALMODY

Psalm 51 *To the choirmaster. Psalm of David. In the coming to him of Nathan the prophet, after David had been with Bathsheba.*

ANTIPHON
KH
Cre- ate in me a pure heart, O God.

Be gracious to **me**, O God,
in your **stead**fast love.
According to the abundance **of** your mercy
blot out my **trans**gressions. ANTIPHON

Cleanse me completely **from** my guilt
and purify me **from** my sin.

For my transgressions I do **rec**ognize,
and my sin stands always **be**fore me.

Against you alone **have** I sinned,
and what is evil in your eyes **I** have done.
Thus you may be declared just in your ways,
  and pure **in** your judgments.
Indeed, I was born guilty,
  already a sinner when my mother **con**ceived me. ANTIPHON

Surely in truth **you** delight,
and deep within my self you will **teach** me wisdom.
Cleanse me from my sin with hyssop and I **will** be pure,
wash me and I shall be brighter **than** snow.

Let me hear glad**ness** and joy,
let the bones you **broke** exult.
Turn your face **from** my sins
and blot out all my iniq**ui**ties. ANTIPHON

Create in me a pure **heart**, O God,
and renew within me **a** firm spirit.
Do not dismiss me **from** your presence,
and do not take away from me your ho**ly** spirit.

Give me back the joy of **your** salvation,
and let a willing spirit lie **o**ver me.
I will teach transgres**sors** your ways,
and sinners will turn back **to** you. ANTIPHON

Deliver me from bloodshed, O God,
  God of **my** salvation,
and my tongue will **sing** your justice.
O Lord, o**pen** my lips,
and my mouth will tell **your** praise.

For you take no pleasure in **sa**crifice,
and you would not accept an offering were **I** to give it.
The perfect sacrifice for God is a **brok**en spirit.
A broken and humble heart,
  O God, you will not **de**spise. ANTIPHON

In your kindness bring prosperi**ty** to Zion;
rebuild the walls of Je**ru**salem.
Then you can delight in sacrifices of justice,
  burnt and complete **of**ferings;
then bulls can be offered on **your** altars. ANTIPHON

Word of God

Benedictus
Blessed be the Lord God of **Israel**,
who visited and redeemed the **people**,
who raised up for us a **mighty** savior
from the house of **ser**vant David.

Just as the Lord spoke through the mouths of the holy prophets of **old**—
salvation comes out of the hands of our enemies and those who **hate** us,
that, with our ancestors, we might perform **works** of mercy,
remembering the holy covenant **sworn** to Abraham—

so does the Lord deliver us from the hands **of** our enemies,
that we might serve without fear before **the** Lord,
worshiping in **ho**liness
and in righteousness **all** our days.

And you also, child, will be called a prophet of God Most **High**:
for you will go before the Lord to prepare a **way**,
bringing people knowledge of salvation by for**giveness** of sins;
because of the deep and tender mercy **of** our God.

Whereby a light rising from on high will **visit** us
to appear to those in darkness and in a shadow **of** death,
to guide our feet along a **straight**, sure path
into a **way** of peace.

INTERCESSIONS

Invocations

Cantor, then Assembly:

Cantor:

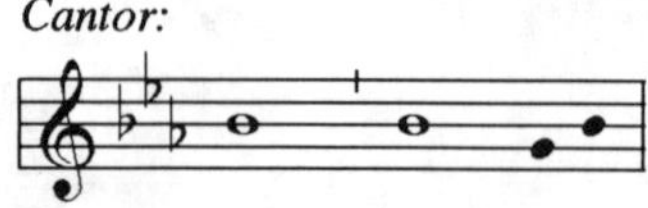

Risen Christ, victor **over** sin,
Risen Christ, victor **over** death,
Risen Christ, victor **over** guilt,
Risen Christ, victor **over** darkness,
Risen Christ, source **of** truth,
Risen Christ, source **of** pure hearts,
Risen Christ, source **of** joy,
Risen Christ, source **of** light,
Risen Christ, source **of** new life,

Our Father ...

Prayer
Loving-kind God,
you bring us salvation through your Son Jesus Christ:
teach us to seek life in you now and always. **Amen.**

CONCLUSION

Blessing
May God, the source of life, bless us
in the name of the Father, and of the Son, and of the Holy Spirit. **Amen.**

Dismissal
Go forth and live the joy of the resurrection. **Thanks be to God.**

FRIDAYS of EASTER Evening Prayer

EASTER EVENING HYMN

PSALMODY

Psalm 85 *To the choirmaster. By the Qorahites. Psalm.*

ANTIPHON

You have **cher**ished your **land**, O LORD;
you have returned the cap**tives** of Jacob.
You have taken away the guilt **of** your people,
forgiving **all** their sins. ANTIPHON

You have **tak**en away **all** your wrath;
you have turned away from the heat **of** your anger.
Bring us back, O God of **our** salvation,
and put away your dis**pleasure** with us. ANTIPHON

Will you be **an**gry with **us** forever?
Will you maintain your anger
  from generation to **gen**eration?
Will you not return **and** revive us
so that your people re**joice** in you? ANTIPHON

Make us **see**, O LORD, your steadfast love
  and give us **your** salvation.
Let me hear what **God** will say.
The LORD speaks words of peace
  to the people and **to** the faithful.
But let them not turn **back** to folly. ANTIPHON

Surely salv**a**tion is near
  for those who revere God,
  that glory may dwell **in** our land.
Steadfast love and **truth** have met;
justice and peace have **kissed** each other.
Truth will spring up from the ground,
  and justice will look **down** from heaven. ANTIPHON

The **LORD** will also **give** prosperity,
and the land will **yield** its fruit.
Justice **will** go forth
to set the way **for** God's steps. ANTIPHON

Psalm Prayer
O mighty God,
you raise all to new life:
bring us to love and truth,
justice and peace
that we may one day live with you
forever and ever. **Amen.**

Psalm 138 *Of David.*

ANTIPHON
KH
I give you thanks, O God; with my
whole heart I sing your praise.

I give you thanks with **all** my heart;
instead of other gods, I **sing** to you.
I bow down toward the **ho**ly sanctuary,
and I give thanks to your name
on account of your steadfast love **and** your truth.

For you have ex**alted** your promise
even a**bove** your name.
On the day I cried, you **an**swered me;
you renewed cour**age** within me. ANTIPHON

Let all the rulers of the earth give thanks to you, O LORD,
for they have heard the **words of** your mouth.
Let them sing about the ways of the LORD,
for great is the **glory of** the LORD.
Although exalted,
the LORD looks up**on** the lowly,
but recognizes the proud only **from** a distance. ANTIPHON

When I walk in the midst of distress,
  you revive me against the **anger of** my enemies.
You stretch out your hand,
  and your **right** hand saves me;
the LORD will do every**thing** for me.
O LORD, your steadfast love is forever.
  Do not forsake the work **of** your hands. ANTIPHON

Psalm Prayer
Exalted God,
your name is above all others:
hear the thanksgiving prayer of your holy people
as we celebrate our salvation
through the life of your risen Son, Jesus Christ. **Amen.**

Word of God

Magnificat
My soul does magni**fy** the Lord!
I delight in **God** my savior
who looked kindly **on** lowliness.

Now all ages will **call** me blessed
for the Mighty One **did** great things.
Holy is **God's** name;
mercy is from age to age for **those** in awe!

The Lord's strong arm did **might**y deeds:
confused the proud in **their** smug hearts;
toppled sovereigns **from** their thrones,
and exalted **hum**ble ones;
filled the hungering with **good** things,
and sent the rich **a**way empty.

The Lord helped servant **Is**rael
to re**mem**ber mercy,
as was spoken to Ab**ra**ham
and his descendants for**e**vermore!

INTERCESSIONS

Petitions

Cantor, then Assembly:

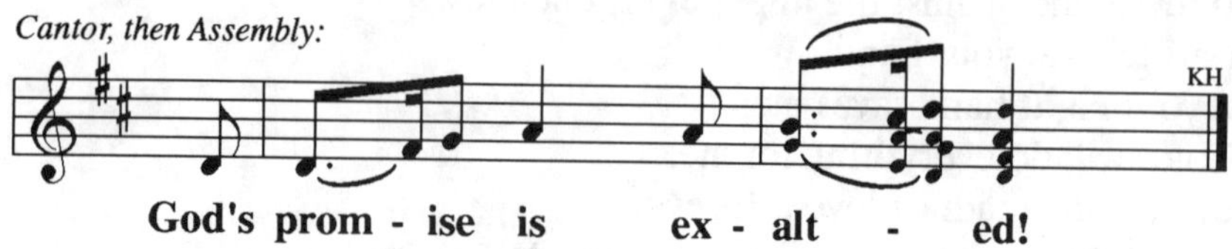

God's prom - ise is ex - alt - ed!
KH

Cantor:

For assured **for**giveness ...
For unwaver**ing** hope ...
For stead**fast** love ...
For unsurpassa**ble** holiness ...
For right**eous** answers ...
For looking kindly on **the** lowly ...
For outstretched **right** hand ...
For not forsaking the faithful **de**parted ...

Our Father ...

Prayer
Exalted God,
you deserve thanks with all our hearts:
may the resurrection of Jesus
bring us salvation and peace now and always. **Amen.**

CONCLUSION

Blessing
May the God who conquered death on a cross bless us
in the name of the Father, and of the Son, and of the Holy Spirit. **Amen.**

Dismissal
Go and rest confidently in our saving God. **Thanks be to God.**

SATURDAYS of EASTER Morning Praise

EASTER MORNING HYMN

PSALMODY

Psalm 65 *To the choirmaster. Psalm of David. Psalm.*

ANTIPHON

KH
You ans- wer us, O God, with awe- some deeds.

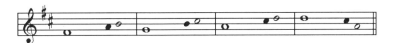

To you praise is due,
  O God **in** Zion,
and for you promises will be **ful**filled.
O you who listen to prayer,
  to you all flesh **shall** come.
When our transgressions—our deeds of iniquity—overcome us,
  you **for**give them. ANTIPHON

Blessed is the one you elect and **bring** near;
that one shall dwell in **your** courts.
Let us be filled with the goodness of **your** house,
the holiness of **your** temple.

With awesome deeds you answer us **in** justice,
O God of our **sal**vation,
protector of all the ends of **the** earth
and of the dis**tant** seas. ANTIPHON

Girded with might,
  you establish mountains **in** strength.
You still the roaring of the seas—
  the roaring of their waves—
  and the clamor **of** nations.
Because of **your** signs,
the inhabitants of the ends of the earth will stand **in** awe. ANTIPHON

You cause the breaking of morning and of evening
  to burst **with** joy.
You visit the earth and give it water;
  abundantly, you **en**rich it:

the river of God
  is replete **with** water.
You provide people with grain,
  for you designed **it** so.

Its furrows you water **a**bundantly,
and you make **them** smooth.
You soften it **with** showers,
and you bless **its** sprout. ANTIPHON

You crown the year with your bounty,
  and fertility springs in the wake of **your** chariot.
The pastures of the wilderness drip with water,
  and the hills are girded **with** joy.
Meadows are clothed with flocks,
  and valleys are covered **with** grain.
They shout, even more, **they** sing. ANTIPHON

Psalm Prayer
O God of creation and salvation,
you provide us with all good things
and sustain us by your care:
receive our morning prayer
celebrating the resurrection
of your Son, Jesus Christ. **Amen.**

Psalm 96

ANTIPHON
KH
Sing a new song, all__ the earth;
sing a new song all the earth.

Sing to the LORD a **new** song.
Sing to the LORD, all **the** earth.

Sing to **the** LORD,
bless **God's** name. ANTIPHON

From day to day proclaim the good news of sal**vation**.
Recount among the nations God's glory,
  God's marvels among **all** peoples.
For great is the LORD, highly to **be** praised
and revered above **all** gods.

For all the gods of the nations are as **nothing**,
but the LORD made **the** heavens.
Honor and splendor stand be**fore** God,
might and glory fill **the** temple. ANTIPHON

Give to the LORD, O families of **peoples**.
Give to the LORD glory **and** might.
Give to **the** LORD
the glory of **God's** name. ANTIPHON

Bring an offering and come into the **courts**.
Worship the LORD with ho**ly** splendor.
Dance in the sac**red** presence,
all **the** earth.

Say among the nations: "The LORD **reigns**."
Surely God formed the universe
  so that it would **not** falter.
God **will** judge
the peoples **in** equity. ANTIPHON

Let the heavens re**joice**
and the earth **ex**ult.
Let the sea and its full**ness** roar.
Let the fields and all within them **be** glad. ANTIPHON

Then all the trees of the forest will shout with **joy**
in the presence of the LORD **who** comes.
For God comes to judge the earth,
  to judge the universe **with** justice
and with fidelity, **the** peoples. ANTIPHON

Psalm Prayer
O glorious and ever living God,

you are worthy of all praise:
we exalt you for raising your Son to life.
Draw us into your presence
so that we may live the Good News now and always. **Amen.**

Word of God

Benedictus
Blessed be the Lord God of **Israel**,
who visited and redeemed the **people**,
who raised up for us a **mighty** savior
from the house of **ser**vant David.

Just as the Lord spoke through the mouths of the holy prophets of **old**—
salvation comes out of the hands of our enemies and those who **hate** us,
that, with our ancestors, we might perform **works** of mercy,
remembering the holy covenant **sworn** to Abraham—

so does the Lord deliver us from the hands **of** our enemies,
that we might serve without fear before **the** Lord,
worshiping in **ho**liness
and in righteousness **all** our days.

And you also, child, will be called a prophet of God Most **High**:
for you will go before the Lord to prepare a **way**,
bringing people knowledge of salvation by for**giveness** of sins;
because of the deep and tender mercy **of** our God.

Whereby a light rising from on high will **vis**it us
to appear to those in darkness and in a shadow **of** death,
to guide our feet along a **straight**, sure path
into a **way** of peace.

INTERCESSIONS

Invocations

Cantor, then Assembly:
KH
Al - le - lu - ia, Al - le - lu - ia!

Cantor:

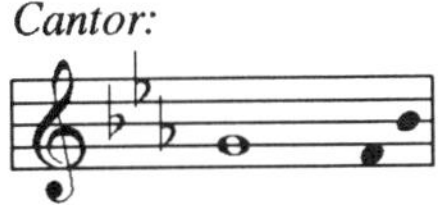

To you, O Risen Christ, praise **is** due,
To you, O Risen Christ, promises are **ful**filled,
To you, O Risen Christ, prayers **are** raised,
To you, O Risen Christ, the elect are **brought** near,
To you, O Risen Christ, goodness is **a**bundant,
To you, O Risen Christ, holiness **is** fitting,
To you, O Risen Christ, blessing **is** given,
To you, O Risen Christ, Good News **is** truth,
To you, O Risen Christ, offering **is** brought,
To you, O Risen Christ, life **is** won,

Our Father ...

Prayer
O redeeming God,
you shine the light of the risen Son upon us:
may that brightness guide us on our way today
as we look to the resurrection of your Son, Jesus Christ. **Amen.**

CONCLUSION

Blessing
Bow your heads and pray for God's blessing.
God of the resurrection, make your face shine on us today. **Amen.**
Son of new life, look upon us with kindness. **Amen.**
Spirit of love, give us peace. **Amen.**
And may God bless us
in the name of the Father, and of the Son, and of the Holy Spirit. **Amen.**

Sign of Peace/Dismissal
In the new life promised by the resurrection, let us offer one another a sign of Christ's peace.

SATURDAYS of EASTER Evening Prayer

LIGHT SERVICE

Proclamation of the Light

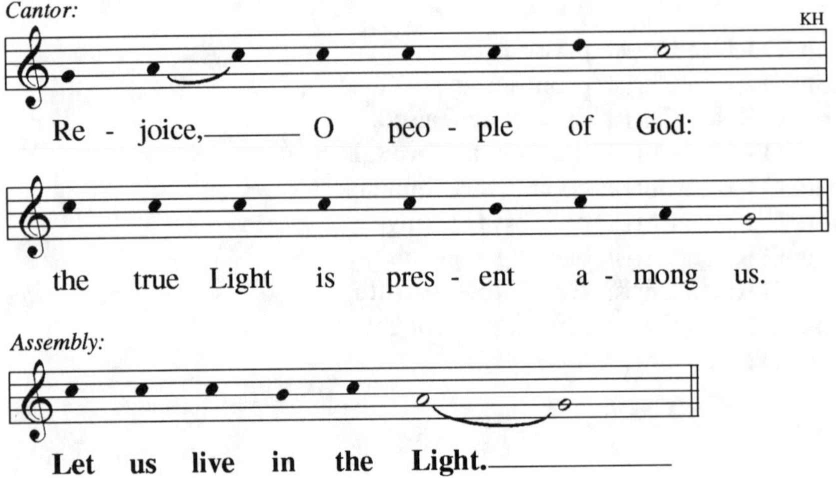
Cantor:
KH
Re - joice, O peo - ple of God:
the true Light is pres - ent a - mong us.
Assembly:
Let us live in the Light.

Easter Evening Hymn

Thanksgiving for the Light

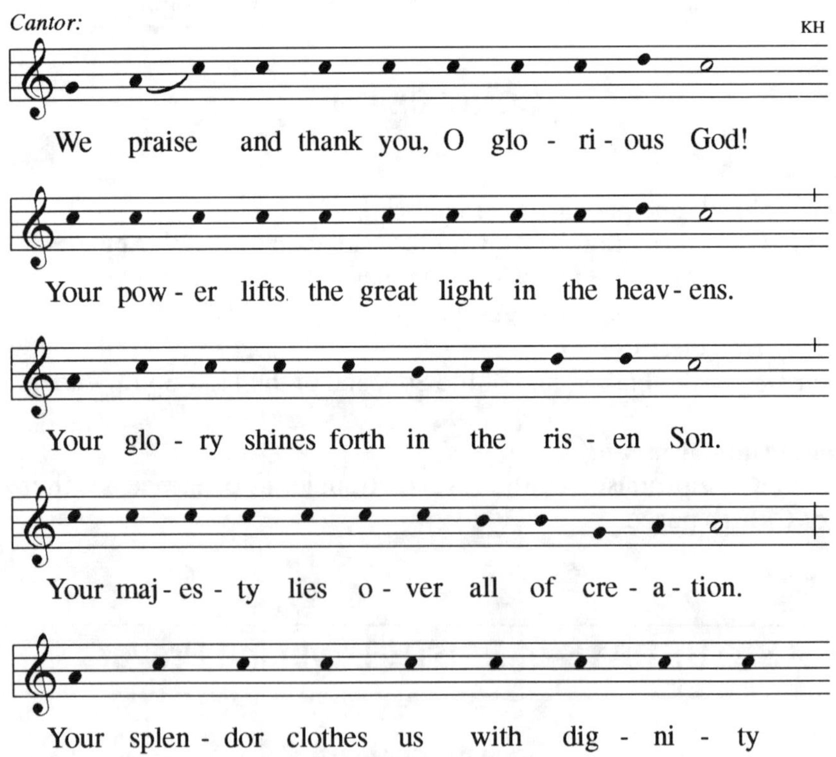
Cantor:
KH
We praise and thank you, O glo - ri - ous God!
Your pow - er lifts the great light in the heav - ens.
Your glo - ry shines forth in the ris - en Son.
Your maj - es - ty lies o - ver all of cre - a - tion.
Your splen - dor clothes us with dig - ni - ty

and hon - or. Your good- ness o - ver-comes an - y
weak - ness. Your boun-ty sat - is- fies all hun- ger.
Your grace pro - claims our des - ti - ny.
Re - joice, O ho - ly peo- ple, in this great Light:
on this day Je - sus was raised from the dead, and now
lives for - ev - er at the right hand of the e - ter -
nal God. As our day draws to a close,
and dark- ness des- cends in qui - et rest, keep us
safe in this Light that nev - er fades. We praise and
thank you for your bless- ings, through the ris - en Christ our

Light for- ev - er and ev - er. A- men.

PSALMODY

Psalm 141 *Psalm of David.*

ANTIPHON
KH
Let my prayer rise like in - cense.

O LORD, I cry **to** you:
"Hasten to me,
listen to my voice
when I cry **to** you."
Let my prayer rise
like incense in **your** presence,
the lifting up of my hands
like an evening **of**fering. ANTIPHON

Set, O LORD,
a guard over **my** mouth,
keep the door of **my** lips.
Do not incline my heart to any evil,
to performing wicked deeds
with those who work **in**iquity;
let me not partake **in** their feasting. ANTIPHON

When a just person strikes me, it is **a** favor;
and when I am corrected, it is like anoin**ting** oil.
May my head never **re**fuse it,
while my prayer stands firm against **e**vil doings.

Let wicked judges be smashed against **the** rock,
and they will understand that my words **were** measured.
Like plowed and broken furrows on **the** land,
their bones are shattered at the **mouth** of Sheol. ANTIPHON

But my eyes look to you,
O LORD, **my** Lord.
In you I take refuge;
do not pour out **my** life.
Keep me from the snare they have prepared for me
and from the traps of those who cre**ate** emptiness.
Let the wicked fall into their nets
while I **alone** escape. ANTIPHON

Psalm Prayer
O merciful God,
you hear the voice of those who call to you:
as our evening prayer rises on incense,
may our gaze turn toward the life
of your risen Son, Jesus Christ forever and ever. **Amen.**

Psalm 30 *Psalm of David. Song for the dedication of the temple.*

ANTIPHON
KH
I will ex- alt you, God: you have set me free.

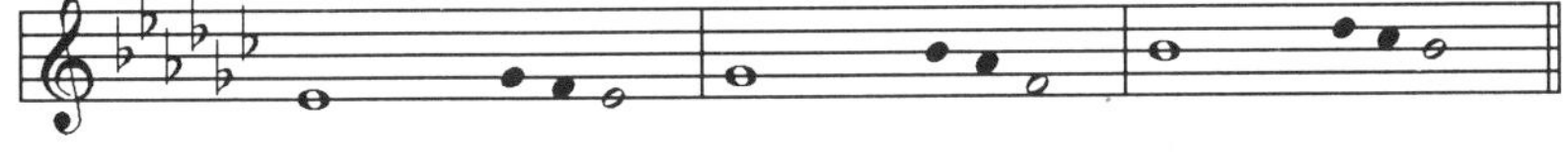

I will **exalt** you, O LORD,
for you have **set** me free
and have not allowed my enemies to re**joice** over me. ANTIPHON

O LORD my God,
I have cried to you
and **you** have healed me.
O LORD, you have brought my soul
up from Sheol.
You have restored me to life,
preventing me from going **down** the Pit. ANTIPHON

Sing to the LORD, O **faith**ful ones;
celebrate a memorial **to** God's holiness.
For we stand only an instant in God's anger,
but a whole lifetime in **God's** delight.

In the evening come tears,
  but in the morning come **shouts** of joy.
So I said in my tranquility,
  "I will not **falter** forever."
O LORD, in your delight
  you have established might **as** my mountain.

When you hid your face,
  I was **ter**rified.
To you, O **LORD**, I cry
and to you, O Lord, I raise my **supp**lication.

What profit is there in my blood,
  in my going down **to** the Pit?
Does dust give you thanks,
  and **tell** your truth?
Listen, O LORD, and have mercy;
  O LORD, be a **help** to me. ANTIPHON

You have changed my **mourning** to dancing;
you have **loosened** my sackcloth
and girded **me** with joy.

So I **sing** your glory;
I **am** not silent.
O LORD my God,
  I will give thanks to **you** forever. ANTIPHON

Psalm Prayer
Glorious God of resurrection,
you overcome darkness and restore us to life:
draw us to your loving presence,
and hear our evening prayer of thanksgiving
for we extol and give thanks to you always and everwhere. **Amen.**

Word of God

Magnificat
My soul does magni**fy** the Lord!
I delight in **God** my savior
who looked kindly **on** lowliness.

Now all ages will **call** me blessed
for the Mighty One **did** great things.
Holy is **God's** name;
mercy is from age to age for **those** in awe!

The Lord's strong arm did **might**y deeds:
confused the proud in **their** smug hearts;
toppled sovereigns **from** their thrones,
and exalted **hum**ble ones;
filled the hungering with **good** things,
and sent the rich **a**way empty.

The Lord helped servant **Is**rael
to re**mem**ber mercy,
as was spoken to Ab**ra**ham
and his descendants for**ev**ermore!

INTERCESSIONS

Petitions

Cantor, then Assembly:

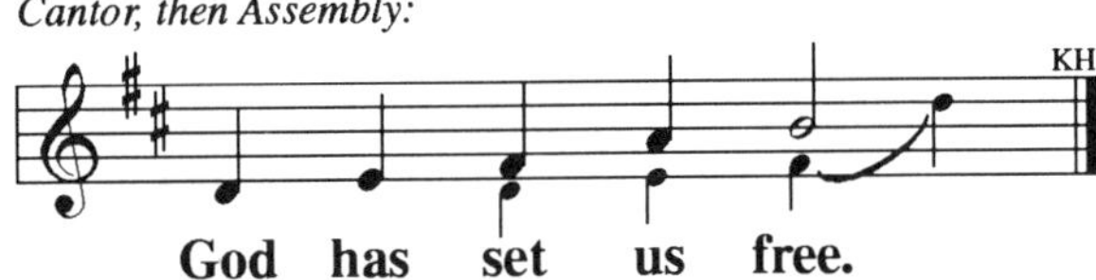

Cantor:

From de**ceit** ...
From all **evil** ...
From **emptiness** ...
From being conquered by **death** ...
From forgetting God's **holiness** ...
From tears of des**pair** ...
From terror during the **night** ...
From everlasting punishment for the faithful de**parted** ...

Our Father ...

Prayer
O God,
you conquer death and restore life:

restore us to your holy courts
that we may praise you forever and ever. **Amen.**

CONCLUSION

Blessing
Bow your heads and pray for God's blessing.
May God give us life. **Amen.**
May Jesus give us salvation. **Amen.**
May the Spirit give us peace. **Amen.**
And may the triune God bless us
in the name of the Father, and of the Son, and of the Holy Spirit. **Amen.**

Sign of Peace/Dismissal
Let us offer a sign of the peace of the risen Christ among us.

SOLEMNITY of the ASCENSION Morning Praise

FESTAL MORNING HYMN

PSALMODY

Psalm 113

ANTIPHON

KH
Who is like our won - drous God, en -

throned in glo - ry? Al - le - lu - ia!

Give praise, servants of **the** LORD;
praise the name of **the** LORD.
Let the name of the LORD **be** blessed
from now on and **for**ever.

From the rising of the sun to **its** setting,
let the name of the LORD **be** praised.
The LORD is exalted above **all** nations;
God's glory is greater than **the** heavens. ANTIPHON

Who looks down to watch over
  the skies and **the** earth?
Who raises the weak from dust
  and the poor **from** ashes,
to return them to the company of nobles,
  the nobles of **the** people?
Who brings home the sterile woman,
  now a rejoicing mother of many children? ANTIPHON

Psalm Prayer
O wondrous God,
your glory is greater than all the heavens
and your light shines brighter than even the sun:
we offer you our morning praise
to celebrate the ascension of your Son
who takes his place at your right hand forever and ever. **Amen.**

Psalm 65 *To the choirmaster. Psalm of David. Psalm.*

ANTIPHON

KH
Blest is the one you choose to bring near.

To you praise is due,
O God **in** Zion,
and for you promises will be **ful**filled.
O you who listen to prayer,
to you all flesh **shall** come.
When our transgressions—our deeds of iniquity—overcome us,
you **for**give them. ANTIPHON

Blessed is the one you elect and **bring** near;
that one shall dwell in **your** courts.
Let us be filled with the goodness of **your** house,
the holiness of **your** temple.

With awesome deeds you answer us **in** justice,
O God of our **sal**vation,
protector of all the ends of **the** earth
and of the dis**tant** seas. ANTIPHON

Girded with might,
you establish mountains **in** strength.
You still the roaring of the seas—
the roaring of their waves—
and the clamor **of** nations.
Because of **your** signs,
the inhabitants of the ends of the earth will stand **in** awe. ANTIPHON

You cause the breaking of morning and of evening
to burst **with** joy.
You visit the earth and give it water;
abundantly, you **en**rich it:
the river of God
is replete **with** water.
You provide people with grain,
for you designed **it** so.

Its furrows you water **a**bundantly,
and you make **them** smooth.
You soften it **with** showers,
and you bless **its** sprout. ANTIPHON

You crown the year with your bounty,
  and fertility springs in the wake of **your** chariot.
The pastures of the wilderness drip with water,
  and the hills are girded **with** joy.
Meadows are clothed with flocks,
  and valleys are covered **with** grain.
They shout, even more, **they** sing. ANTIPHON

Psalm Prayer
O mighty God,
you brought your Son near to sit at your right hand:
hear our morning prayer
for we shout your praises now and always. **Amen.**

Word of God

Benedictus
Blessed be the Lord God of **Israel**,
who visited and redeemed the **people**,
who raised up for us a **mighty** savior
from the house of **ser**vant David.

Just as the Lord spoke through the mouths of the holy prophets of **old**—
salvation comes out of the hands of our enemies and those who **hate** us,
that, with our ancestors, we might perform **works** of mercy,
remembering the holy covenant **sworn** to Abraham—

so does the Lord deliver us from the hands **of** our enemies,
that we might serve without fear before **the** Lord,
worshiping in **ho**liness
and in righteousness **all** our days.

And you also, child, will be called a prophet of God Most **High**:
for you will go before the Lord to prepare a **way**,
bringing people knowledge of salvation by for**giveness** of sins;
because of the deep and tender mercy **of** our God.

Whereby a light rising from on high will **vis**it us
to appear to those in darkness and in a shadow **of** death,
to guide our feet along a **straight**, sure path
into a **way** of peace.

INTERCESSIONS

Invocations

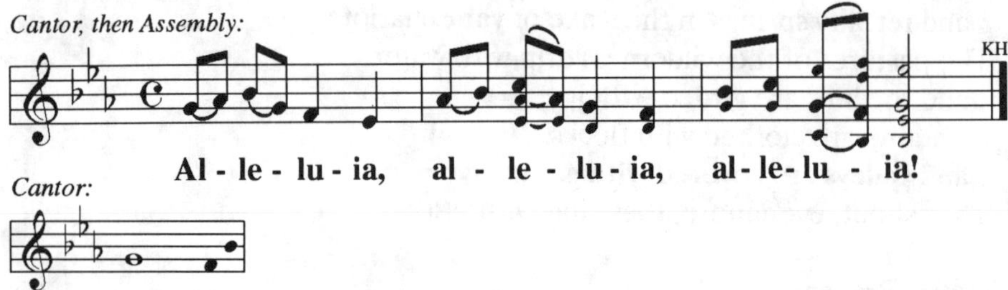

Cantor, then Assembly:
KH
Al - le - lu - ia, al - le - lu - ia, al - le - lu - ia!
Cantor:

O Jesus raised on high, **we** praise you,
O Jesus raised on high, **we** bless you,
O Jesus raised on high, **we ex**alt you,
O Jesus raised on high, **we re**joice with you,
O Jesus raised on high, we are in awe of **your** holiness,
O Jesus raised on high, we are filled with **your** goodness,
O Jesus raised on high, we are bursting **with** joy,
O Jesus raised on high, we are enriched by **your** life,
O Jesus raised on high, we crown you **with** honor,
O Jesus raised on high, we shout and sing on **this** festival,
O Jesus raised on high, we eagerly anticipate **your** Spirit,

Our Father ...

Prayer
God of power and majesty,
you raised your Son to life and
now raise him to sit at your right hand:
keep us always in your loving care
that one day, too, we may join the heavenly choir
to sing your praises forever and ever. **Amen.**

CONCLUSION

Blessing
Bow your heads and pray for God's blessing.
May God who raised Jesus to life grant us new life. **Amen.**
May Jesus who ascended reign forever at God's right hand. **Amen.**
May the Spirit who loves descend upon us with peace. **Amen.**
And may God bless us
in the name of the Father, and of the Son, and of the Holy Spirit. **Amen.**

Sign of Peace/Dismissal
Share with one another a sign of the victorious Christ.

SOLEMNITY of the ASCENSION Evening Prayer

LIGHT SERVICE

Proclamation of the Light

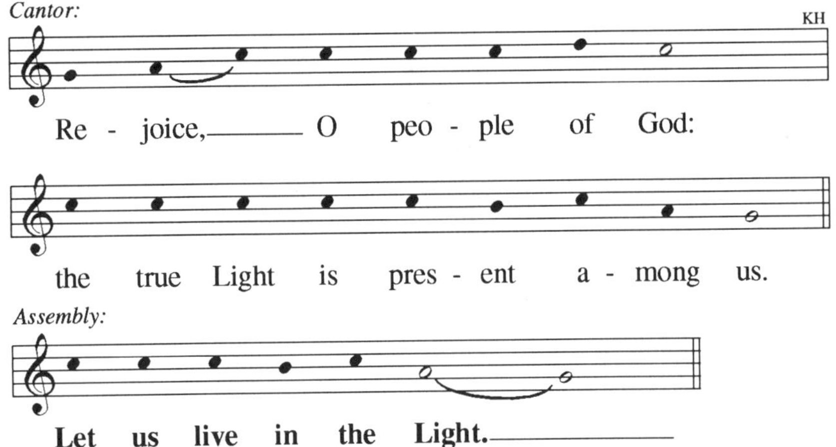
Cantor:
KH
Re - joice, O peo - ple of God:
the true Light is pres - ent a - mong us.
Assembly:
Let us live in the Light.

Festal Evening Hymn

Thanksgiving for the Light

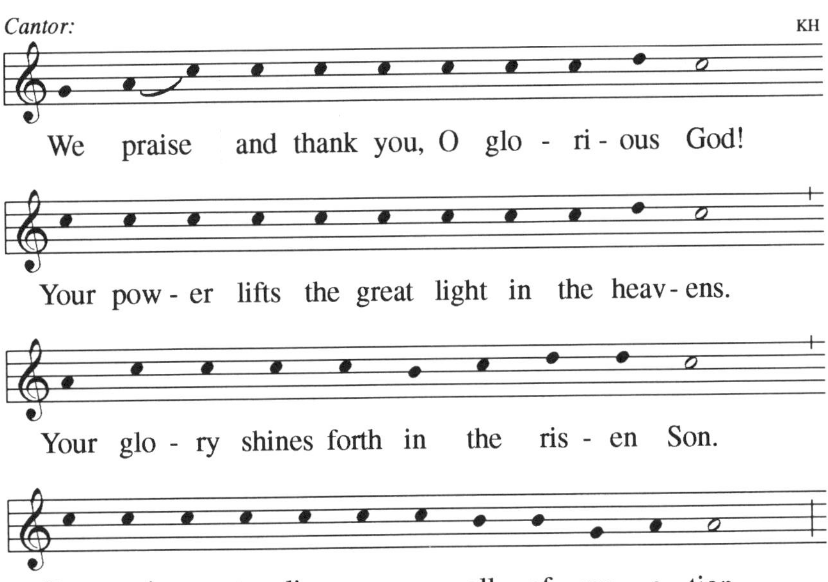
Cantor:
KH
We praise and thank you, O glo - ri - ous God!
Your pow - er lifts the great light in the heav - ens.
Your glo - ry shines forth in the ris - en Son.
Your maj - es - ty lies o - ver all of cre - a - tion.

Your splen - dor clothes us with dig - ni - ty
and hon - or. Your good-ness o - ver-comes an - y
weak - ness. Your boun-ty sat - is - fies all hun - ger.
Your grace pro - claims our des - ti - ny.
Re - joice,___ O ho - ly peo - ple, in this great Light:
on this day Je - sus as - cend - ed in - to the heav - ens,
and now lives for - ev - er at the right hand of the
e - ter - nal God. As our day draws to a close,
and dark - ness des - cends in qui - et rest, keep us
safe in this Light that nev - er fades. We praise and

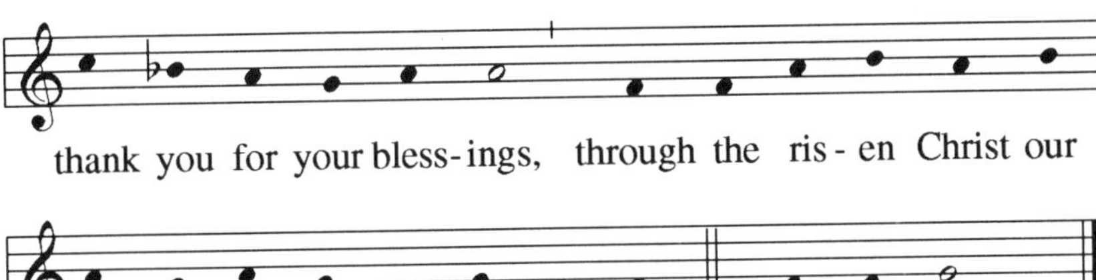
thank you for your bless-ings, through the ris-en Christ our

Light for-ev-er and ev - er. A-men.

PSALMODY

Psalm 110 *Of David. Psalm.*

ANTIPHON

KH
Our Sav-ior sits at the right hand of
God, Al - le - lu - ia!

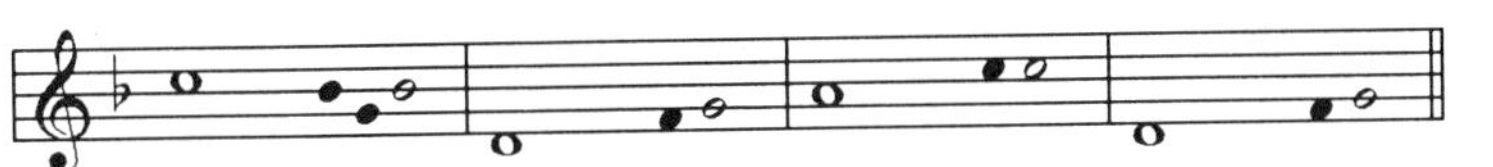

Thus says the LORD **to** my lord:
"Sit on my right
  until I place your enemies
  as a footstool for **your** feet."
Let the LORD send from Zion
  the scepter of **your** strength.
Rule in the midst of **your** enemies. ANTIPHON

Your people bring free **of**ferings
on the day of your might
  in hol**y** splendor.
From the womb **of** dawn,
a dew of rejuvenation comes **to** you. ANTIPHON

The Lord has promised
and will **not** repent:
"According to my word,
you are a priest forever, my king **of** justice."
The Lord is at **your** right,
who has smashed rulers on the day **of** wrath.

The Lord judges a**gainst** the nations,
piling them **with** corpses.
The Lord has smashed heads
all over **the** land.
From a torrent the Lord drinks on the way,
and rises up **in** triumph. ANTIPHON

Psalm Prayer
O gracious God,
you invite us to be near:
call us to your presence
that we may rise up in triumph
with your Son and our brother Jesus Christ forever and ever. **Amen.**

Psalm 111

ANTIPHON

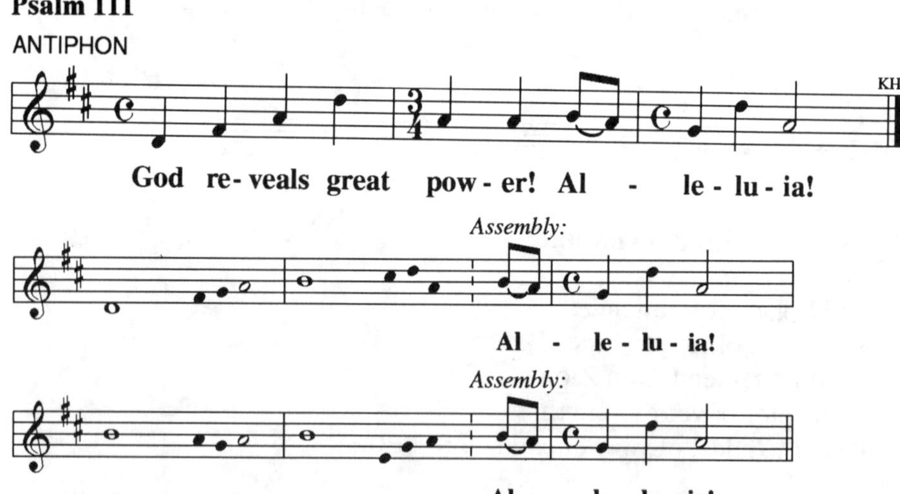
KH
God re- veals great pow - er! Al - le - lu - ia!
Assembly:
Al - le - lu - ia!
Assembly:
Al - le - lu - ia!

I will give thanks to the Lord with **all** my heart
in the council of the righteous and **the** assembly.
Great are the deeds **of** the Lord,
pondered by all who de**light** in them. ANTIPHON

God's work is majes**ty** and splendor,
and justice **stands** forever.
A memorial God has made **of** these wonders;
gracious and merciful **is** the LORD. ANTIPHON

God has given food to those **who** show reverence,
remembering the cove**nant** forever.
God has revealed to the people the power **of** these deeds
in giving them the nations **for** their heritage. ANTIPHON

The deeds of God's hands are **truth** and justice;
the precepts of God **all** are trustworthy.
They are established forev**er** and ever,
wrought in truth and eq**uity**. ANTIPHON

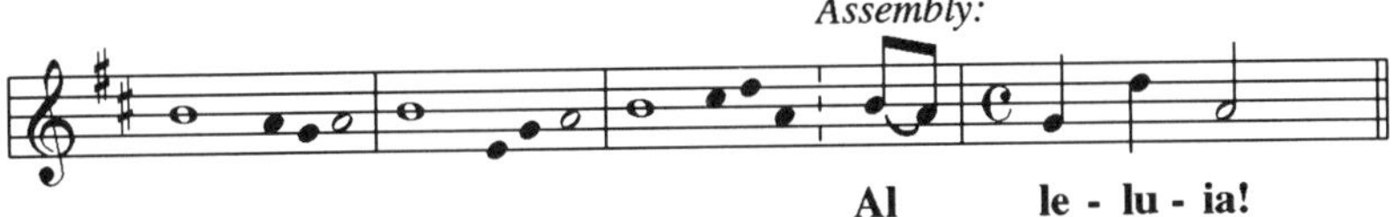

God has sent deliverance **to** the people,
appointing the cove**nant** forever;
holy and to be revered **is** God's name.

The beginning of wisdom is reverence **for** the LORD,
and its practice brings about clear **un**derstanding. ANTIPHON
The praise of God **stands** forever! ANTIPHON

Psalm Prayer
God of majesty and splendor,
you are worthy of all thanks and praise:
hear our evening prayer
that our reverence for you
may bring us wisdom now and always. **Amen.**

Word of God

Magnificat
My soul does magni**fy** the Lord!
I delight in **God** my savior
who looked kindly **on** lowliness.

Now all ages will **call** me blessed
for the Mighty One **did** great things.

Holy is **God's** name;
mercy is from age to age for **those** in awe!

The Lord's strong arm did **might**y deeds:
confused the proud in **their** smug hearts;
toppled sovereigns **from** their thrones,
and exalted **hum**ble ones;
filled the hungering with **good** things,
and sent the rich **a**way empty.

The Lord helped servant **Is**rael
to re**mem**ber mercy,
as was spoken to Ab**ra**ham
and his descendants for**e**vermore!

INTERCESSIONS

Petitions

Cantor, then Assembly:

Cantor:

For God's **great** power ...
For God's heal**ing** strength ...
For God's hol**y** splendor ...
For God's priest**ly** people ...
For God's everlast**ing** triumph ...
For God's right**eous** mercy ...
For God's delight**ful** deeds ...
For God's age**less** covenant ...
For God's bounti**ful** heritage ...
For God's trust**worthy** precepts ...
For God's mighty **de**liverance ...
For God's victorious **right** hand ...
For God's acceptance of the faithful **de**parted ...

Our Father ...

Prayer
O God,
you give us great joy
as we celebrate the festival of the ascension of your Son:
help us to look not in the clouds but
here among us for your presence.
We pray through Jesus Christ in the Spirit,
one God forever and ever. **Amen.**

CONCLUSION

Blessing
Bow your heads and pray for God's blessing.
May the God of the heavens protect us. **Amen.**
May the Son of justice deliver us. **Amen.**
May the Spirit of life be among us. **Amen.**
And may God bless us
in the name of the Father, and of the Son, and of the Holy Spirit. **Amen.**

Sign of Peace/Dismissal
In anticipation of the descent of the Spirit, let us share with one another the peace of the risen, ascended Christ.

SOLEMNITY of PENTECOST Morning Praise

FESTAL MORNING HYMN

PSALMODY

Psalm 113

ANTIPHON

KH
Who is like our won - drous God, en -

throned in glo - ry? Al - le - lu - ia!

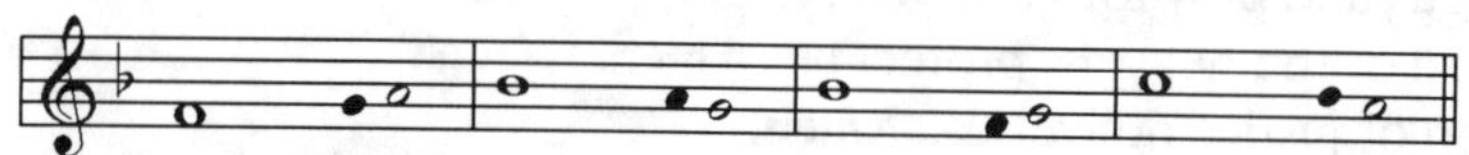

Give praise, servants of **the** LORD;
praise the name of **the** LORD.
Let the name of the LORD **be** blessed
from now on and **for**ever.

From the rising of the sun to **its** setting,
let the name of the LORD **be** praised.
The LORD is exalted above **all** nations;
God's glory is greater than **the** heavens. ANTIPHON

Who looks down to watch over
  the skies and **the** earth?
Who raises the weak from dust
  and the poor **from** ashes,
to return them to the company of nobles,
  the nobles of **the** people?
Who brings home the sterile woman,
  now a rejoicing mother of many children? ANTIPHON

Psalm Prayer
O wondrous God,
your glory is greater than all the heavens
and your Light shines brighter than even the sun:
we offer you our morning praise
to celebrate the descent of your holy Spirit upon us
now and always. **Amen.**

Psalm 65 *To the choirmaster. Psalm of David. Psalm.*

ANTIPHON

KH
Let us be filled with your ho - li- ness, O God.

To you praise is due,
  O God **in** Zion,
and for you promises will be **ful**filled.
O you who listen to prayer,
  to you all flesh **shall** come.
When our transgressions—our deeds of iniquity—overcome us,
  you **for**give them. ANTIPHON

Blessed is the one you elect and **bring** near;
that one shall dwell in **your** courts.
Let us be filled with the goodness of **your** house,
the holiness of **your** temple.

With awesome deeds you answer us **in** justice,
O God of our **sal**vation,
protector of all the ends of **the** earth
and of the dis**tant** seas. ANTIPHON

Girded with might,
  you establish mountains **in** strength.
You still the roaring of the seas—
  the roaring of their waves—
  and the clamor **of** nations.
Because of **your** signs,
the inhabitants of the ends of the earth will stand **in** awe. ANTIPHON

You cause the breaking of morning and of evening
  to burst **with** joy.
You visit the earth and give it water;
  abundantly, you **en**rich it:
the river of God
  is replete **with** water.
You provide people with grain,
  for you designed **it** so.

Its furrows you water **a**bundantly,
and you make **them** smooth.
You soften it **with** showers,
and you bless **its** sprout. ANTIPHON

You crown the year with your bounty,
  and fertility springs in the wake of **your** chariot.
The pastures of the wilderness drip with water,
  and the hills are girded **with** joy.
Meadows are clothed with flocks,
  and valleys are covered **with** grain.
They shout, even more, **they** sing. ANTIPHON

Psalm Prayer
O mighty God,
you sent your Spirit to give strength and courage:
hear our morning prayer
for we celebrate the Good News now and always. **Amen.**

Word of God

Benedictus
Blessed be the Lord God of **Israel**,
who visited and redeemed the **people**,
who raised up for us a **might**y savior
from the house of **ser**vant David.

Just as the Lord spoke through the mouths of the holy prophets of **old**—
salvation comes out of the hands of our enemies and those who **hate** us,
that, with our ancestors, we might perform **works** of mercy,
remembering the holy covenant **sworn** to Abraham—

so does the Lord deliver us from the hands **of** our enemies,
that we might serve without fear before **the** Lord,
worshiping in **ho**liness
and in righteousness **all** our days.

And you also, child, will be called a prophet of God Most **High**:
for you will go before the Lord to prepare a **way**,
bringing people knowledge of salvation by for**giveness** of sins;
because of the deep and tender mercy **of** our God.

Whereby a light rising from on high will **visit** us
to appear to those in darkness and in a shadow **of** death,
to guide our feet along a **straight**, sure path
into a **way** of peace.

INTERCESSIONS

Invocations

Cantor, then Assembly:

Cantor:

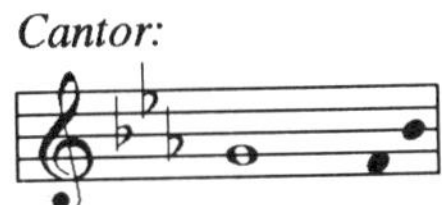

O risen Jesus whose Spirit descended, **we** praise you,
O risen Jesus whose Spirit descended, **we** bless you,
O risen Jesus whose Spirit descended, **we ex**alt you,
O risen Jesus whose Spirit descended, **we re**joice with you,
O risen Jesus whose Spirit descended, we are in awe of **your** holiness,
O risen Jesus whose Spirit descended, we are filled with **your** goodness,
O risen Jesus whose Spirit descended, we are bursting **with** joy,
O risen Jesus whose Spirit descended, we are enriched by **your** life,
O risen Jesus whose Spirit descended, we crown you **with** honor,
O risen Jesus whose Spirit descended, we shout and sing on **this** festival,
O risen Jesus whose Spirit descended, we receive **your** Spirit,

Our Father ...

Prayer
God of power and majesty,
you raised your Son to life and
sent your Spirit to guide us:
keep us always in your loving care
that one day, too, we may join the heavenly choir
to sing your praises forever and ever. **Amen.**

CONCLUSION

Blessing

Bow your heads and pray for God's blessing.

May God who raised Jesus to life grant us new life. **Amen.**

May Jesus who ascended reign forever at God's right hand. **Amen.**

May the Spirit who loves descend upon us with peace. **Amen.**

And may God bless us
in the name of the Father, and of the Son, and of the Holy Spirit. **Amen.**

Sign of Peace/Dismissal

Share with one another a sign of the Spirit's peace.

SOLEMNITY of PENTECOST Evening Prayer

LIGHT SERVICE

Proclamation of the Light

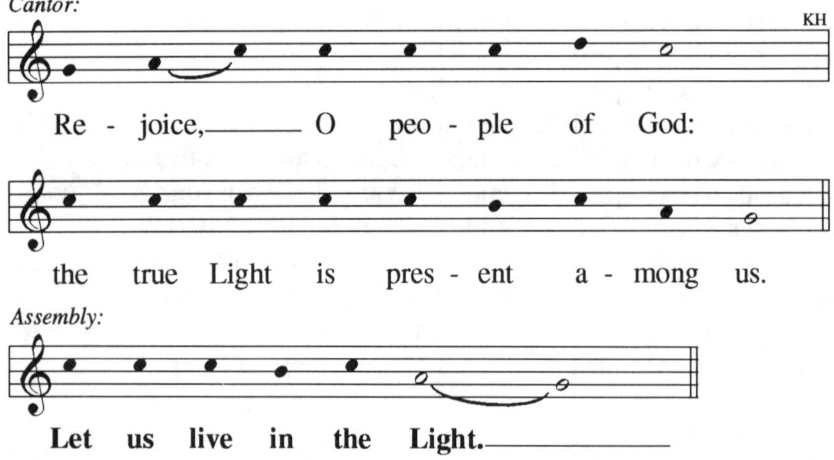

Festal Evening Hymn

Thanksgiving for the Light

Cantor:
KH
We praise and thank you, O glo - ri - ous God!

Your pow - er lifts the great light in the heav - ens.
Your glo - ry shines forth in the ris - en Son.
Your maj - es - ty lies o - ver all of cre - a - tion.
Your splen - dor clothes us with dig - ni - ty
and hon - or. Your good - ness o - ver-comes an - y
weak - ness. Your boun-ty sat - is - fies all hun - ger.
Your grace pro - claims our des - ti - ny.
Re - joice, O ho - ly peo - ple, in this great Light:
on this day the Spir - it de-scend-ed and the pres -
ence of the ris - en Christ is firm - ly es - tab-lished

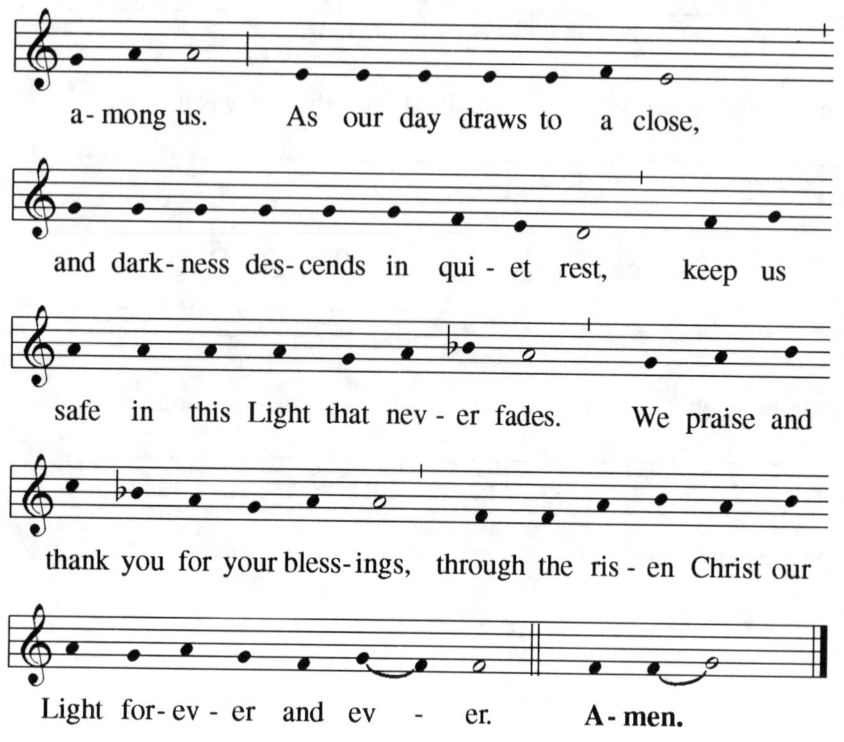
a- mong us. As our day draws to a close,
and dark- ness des- cends in qui - et rest, keep us
safe in this Light that nev - er fades. We praise and
thank you for your bless- ings, through the ris - en Christ our
Light for- ev - er and ev - er. A- men.

PSALMODY

Psalm 110 *Of David. Psalm.*

ANTIPHON

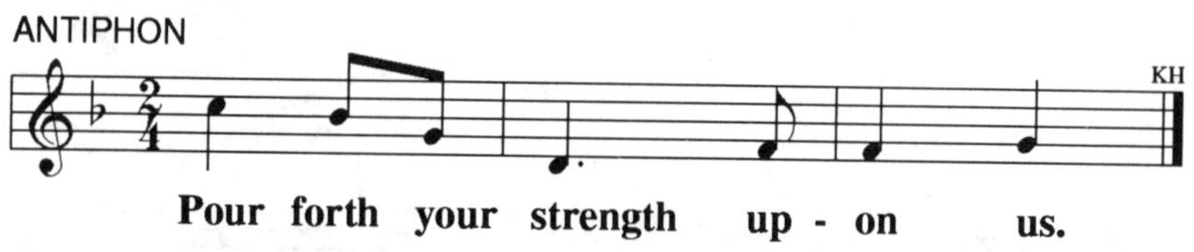
KH
Pour forth your strength up - on us.

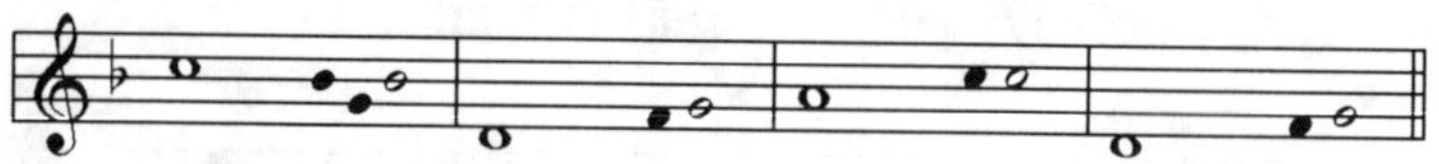

Thus says the LORD **to** my lord:
"Sit on my right
 until I place your enemies
 as a footstool for **your** feet."
Let the LORD send from Zion
 the scepter of **your** strength.
Rule in the midst of **your** enemies. ANTIPHON

Your people bring free **offerings**
on the day of your might
  in ho**ly** splendor.
From the womb **of** dawn,
a dew of rejuvenation comes **to** you. ANTIPHON

The LORD has promised
  and will **not** repent:
"According to my word,
  you are a priest forever, my king **of** justice."
The Lord is at **your** right,
who has smashed rulers on the day **of** wrath.

The Lord judges a**gainst** the nations,
piling them **with** corpses.
The Lord has smashed heads
  all over **the** land.
From a torrent the Lord drinks on the way,
  and rises up **in** triumph. ANTIPHON

Psalm Prayer
O gracious God,
you invite us to be near:
call us to your presence
in the Spirit and
with your Son and our brother Jesus Christ forever and ever. **Amen.**

Psalm 111

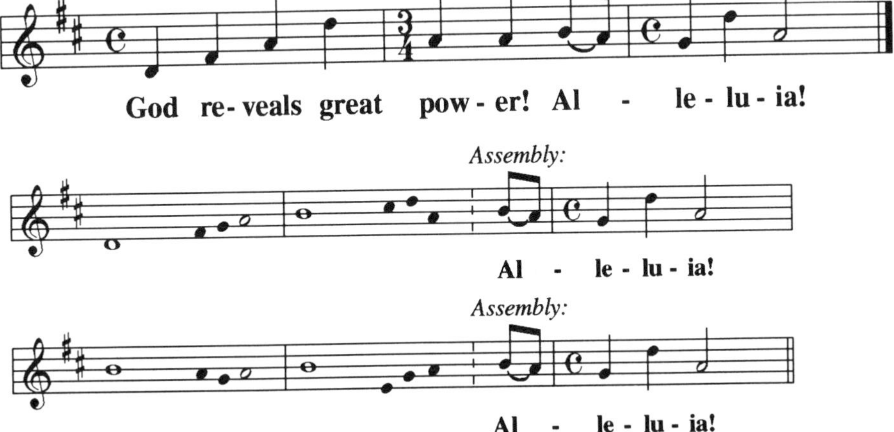
ANTIPHON
KH
God re- veals great pow - er! Al - le - lu - ia!
Assembly:
Al - le - lu - ia!
Assembly:
Al - le - lu - ia!

I will give thanks to the LORD with **all** my heart
in the council of the righteous and **the** assembly.
Great are the deeds **of** the LORD,
pondered by all who de**light** in them. ANTIPHON

God's work is majes**ty** and splendor,
and justice **stands** forever.
A memorial God has made **of** these wonders;
gracious and merciful **is** the LORD. ANTIPHON

God has given food to those **who** show reverence,
remembering the cove**nant** forever.
God has revealed to the people the power **of** these deeds
in giving them the nations **for** their heritage. ANTIPHON

The deeds of God's hands are **truth** and justice;
the precepts of God **all** are trustworthy.
They are established forev**er** and ever,
wrought in truth and eq**uity**. ANTIPHON

God has sent deliverance **to** the people,
appointing the cove**nant** forever;
holy and to be revered **is** God's name.

The beginning of wisdom is reverence **for** the LORD,
and its practice brings about clear **un**derstanding. ANTIPHON
The praise of God **stands** forever! ANTIPHON

Psalm Prayer
God of majesty and splendor,
you are worthy of all thanks and praise:
hear our evening prayer
that our reverence for you
may bring us wisdom now and always. **Amen.**

Word of God

Magnificat
My soul does magni**fy** the Lord!

I delight in **God** my savior
who looked kindly **on** lowliness.

Now all ages will **call** me blessed
for the Mighty One **did** great things.
Holy is **God's** name;
mercy is from age to age for **those** in awe!

The Lord's strong arm did **might**y deeds:
confused the proud in **their** smug hearts;
toppled sovereigns **from** their thrones,
and exalted **hum**ble ones;
filled the hungering with **good** things,
and sent the rich **a**way empty.

The Lord helped servant **Is**rael
to re**mem**ber mercy,
as was spoken to Ab**ra**ham
and his descendants for**e**vermore!

INTERCESSIONS

Petitions

Cantor, then Assembly:

Cantor:

With **wis**dom ...
With under**stan**ding ...
With **coun**sel ...
With **strength** ...
With **know**ledge ...
With **rever**ence ...
With **awe** ...
With **love** ...
With **joy** ...
With **peace** ...
With **pa**tience ...

With **kind**ness ...
With gener**os**ity ...
With **faithful**ness ...
With **gentle**ness ...
With **self-con**trol ...
For the faithful de**part**ed ...

Our Father ...

Prayer
O God,
you give us great joy
as we celebrate the festival of the descent of your Spirit:
give us courage to live the Good News.
We pray through Jesus Christ in the Spirit,
one God forever and ever. **Amen.**

CONCLUSION

Blessing
Bow your heads and pray for God's blessing.
May the strength of God be upon us. **Amen.**
May the salvation of the Son renew us. **Amen.**
May the gifts of the Spirit make our lives fruitful. **Amen.**
And may God bless us
in the name of the Father, and of the Son, and of the Holy Spirit. **Amen.**

Sign of Peace/Dismissal
Let us share with one another the Spirit's peace.

Solemnities
Feasts
Holidays

January 25
Feast of the CONVERSION OF PAUL, Apostle
Morning Praise

FESTAL MORNING HYMN

PSALMODY

Psalm 63 *Psalm of David. While he was in the desert of Judah.*

Solo 1 O God, you are my God, I seek you;
my soul thirsts for you.
My flesh longs for you
in a dry and wasted land,
deprived of water.

Solo 2 So in the sanctuary I have contemplated you
to see your might and your glory.
Because your steadfast love is better than life,
my lips will praise you.
So I will bless you all my life;
in your name I will raise my hands.
As with milk and rich food,
my soul is filled;
my mouth gives praise with joyful lips.
I remember you upon my bed,
pondering you throughout the night.
For you were a help for me;
in the shade of your wings I keep singing.
My soul clings to you;
your right hand upholds me.

Solo 1 But let those who seek my destruction
be cast into the depths of the earth.
Let them be given over to the power of the sword;
let them become a prey for jackals.

All Then the king shall rejoice in God.
All those who swear by God will be praised,
for the mouths of liars will be shut.

Psalm 149

All Alleluia!

Choir 1 Sing a new song to the LORD,
God's praise in the assembly of the faithful.
Let Israel rejoice in its Creator,
the children of Zion exult in their Sovereign.
Let them praise God's name with dancing;
with drums and harp, let them play music for God.

Choir 2 For the LORD takes delight in the people,
adorning the poor with salvation.
Let the faithful exult with glory,
let them ring out joy on their couches,
and cry out the great deeds of God from their throats.

Choir 1 With two-edged swords in their hands,
let them do vengeance against peoples
and rebuke nations;
let them tie their rulers with fetters
and their nobles with chains of bronze,
in order to accomplish judgment against them as written.
This is honor for all the faithful.

All Alleluia!

Word of God

Benedictus

Blessed be the Lord God of **Israel**,
who visited and redeemed the **people**,
who raised up for us a **mighty** savior
from the house of **ser**vant David.

Just as the Lord spoke through the mouths of the holy prophets of **old**—
salvation comes out of the hands of our enemies and those who **hate** us,
that, with our ancestors, we might perform **works** of mercy,
remembering the holy covenant **sworn** to Abraham—

so does the Lord deliver us from the hands **of** our enemies,
that we might serve without fear before **the** Lord,

worshiping in **ho**liness
and in righteousness **all** our days.

And you also, child, will be called a prophet of God Most **High**:
for you will go before the Lord to prepare a **way**,
bringing people knowledge of salvation by for**giveness** of sins;
because of the deep and tender mercy **of** our God.

Whereby a light rising from on high will **vis**it us
to appear to those in darkness and in a shadow **of** death,
to guide our feet along a **straight**, sure path
into a **way** of peace.

INTERCESSIONS

Invocations

Cantor, then Assembly:

KH
Your stead-fast love is bet - ter than life.

Cantor:

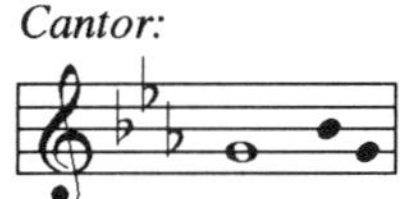

O Son of God, you seek us for **your** service ...
O Son of God, you draw us to **your**self ...
O Son of God, you help us spread the **Good** News ...
O Son of God, you shade us from **dis**couragement ...
O Son of God, you keep **us** faithful ...
O Son of God, you rejoice in your **dis**ciples ...
O Son of God, you adorn your disciples **with** glory ...
O Son of God, you honor all **your** faithful ...

Our Father ...

Prayer
Gracious God,
you blinded Paul so that he might see your Light more clearly:
open our eyes to the splendor of the resurrection
that we might seek only you now and always. **Amen.**

CONCLUSION

Blessing
May the God of salvation bless us
in the name of the Father, and of the Son, and of the Holy Spirit. **Amen.**

Dismissal
Go forth to be disciples of Christ. **Thanks be to God.**

Feast of the CONVERSION OF PAUL, Apostle
Evening Prayer

FESTAL EVENING HYMN

PSALMODY

Psalm 116

Solo 1 I love the LORD
who has heard
the voice of my supplications.
For God has turned an ear to me
as I cry all my days.

Solo 2 Deadly chains have fettered me,
and the anguish of Sheol has reached up to me.
Distress and terror, I have encountered;
but I have called on the name of the LORD.
How long, O LORD?
Deliver my soul.

All The LORD is gracious and just;
our God is merciful.

Solo 1 The LORD is the protector of the innocent;
I was poor and God brought salvation to me.
Return, O my soul, to your rest,
for the LORD has done good to you.

Solo 2 For you have delivered my soul from death,
my eye from tears
and my foot from stumbling,
that I may walk in the presence of the LORD
in the lands of the living.

Solo 1 Yes, I was right in saying,
"I am greatly afflicted."
In my agitation, I have said,
"Every human being is a liar."

Solo 2 What shall I return to the LORD
for all the bounty in my favor?
I will lift up the cup of salvation
and I will call on the name of the LORD.
Indeed, I will fulfill my promises to the LORD
in the presence of all the people.

All Precious in the eyes of the LORD
is the death of the faithful ones.

Solo 1 How long, O LORD?
For I am your servant,
I am your servant, the offspring of your handmaid.
You have loosened my bonds.

Solo 2 To you I will offer a sacrifice of thanksgiving
and I will call on the name of the LORD.
Indeed, I will fulfill my promises to the LORD
in the presence of all the people,
in the courts of the house of the LORD,
in your midst, O Jerusalem.

All Alleluia!

Psalm 126 *Song of ascents (pilgrimages).*

Choir 1 When the LORD accompanied
those who returned to Zion,
we were like dreamers.
Then our mouth
was filled with laughter
and our tongue with joy.

Then it was said among nations:
"The LORD has done great
deeds among these people."

All The LORD has done great
deeds among us.
Now we rejoice.

Choir 2 Return our captives, O LORD,
like torrents in the Negeb.
Those who sow in tears
harvest with shouts of joy.
Indeed, one goes out weeping,
carrying the bag of seed,
and comes back joyful,
carrying the sheaves.

Word of God

Magnificat
My soul does magni**fy** the Lord!
I delight in **God** my savior
who looked kindly **on** lowliness.

Now all ages will **call** me blessed
for the Mighty One **did** great things.
Holy is **God's** name;
mercy is from age to age for **those** in awe!

The Lord's strong arm did **might**y deeds:
confused the proud in **their** smug hearts;
toppled sovereigns **from** their thrones,
and exalted **hum**ble ones;
filled the hungering with **good** things,
and sent the rich **a**way empty.

The Lord helped servant **Is**rael
to re**mem**ber mercy,
as was spoken to Ab**ra**ham
and his descendants for**e**vermore!

INTERCESSIONS

Petitions

Cantor, then Assembly:

Cantor:

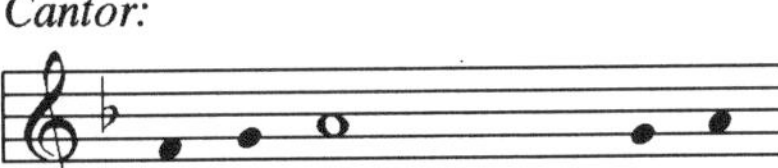

Who has **turned** an ear **to** us? ...
Who has **broken** the chains **of** bondage? ...
Who has **de**livered us **from** death? ...
Who has **pro**tected **the** innocent? ...
Who has **brought** salvation **to** us? ...
Who has **called us** precious? ...
Who has **ac**companied us during **our** service? ...
Who has **done** great deeds among **the** people? ...
Who has **called** the dead to **new** life? ...

Our Father ...

Prayer
O God,
your Son calls disciples to be his followers:
protect us and encourage us
that we might spread the Good News of salvation
and enjoy life everlasting. **Amen.**

CONCLUSION

Blessing
May the God who calls followers bless us
in the name of the Father, and of the Son, and of the Holy Spirit. **Amen.**

Dismissal
Go and rest peacefully, comforted by the nearness of God. **Thanks be to God.**

February 2
Feast of the PRESENTATION OF THE LORD
Morning Praise

FESTAL MORNING HYMN

PSALMODY

Psalm 63 *Psalm of David. While he was in the desert of Judah.*

Solo 1 O God, you are my God, I seek you;
my soul thirsts for you.
My flesh longs for you
in a dry and wasted land,
deprived of water.

Solo 2 So in the sanctuary I have contemplated you
to see your might and your glory.
Because your steadfast love is better than life,
my lips will praise you.
So I will bless you all my life;
in your name I will raise my hands.
As with milk and rich food,
my soul is filled;
my mouth gives praise with joyful lips.
I remember you upon my bed,
pondering you throughout the night.
For you were a help for me;
in the shade of your wings I keep singing.
My soul clings to you;
your right hand upholds me.

Solo 1 But let those who seek my destruction
be cast into the depths of the earth.
Let them be given over to the power of the sword;
let them become a prey for jackals.

All Then the king shall rejoice in God.
All those who swear by God will be praised,
for the mouths of liars will be shut.

Psalm 113

All Alleluia!

Choir 1 Give praise, servants of the LORD;
praise the name of the LORD.

Let the name of the LORD be blessed
from now on and forever.
From the rising of the sun to its setting,
let the name of the LORD be praised.
The LORD is exalted above all nations;
God's glory is greater than the heavens.

All Who is like the LORD our God,
enthroned above?

Choir 2 Who looks down to watch over
the skies and the earth?
Who raises the weak from dust
and the poor from ashes,
to return them to the company of nobles,
the nobles of the people?
Who brings home the sterile woman,
now a rejoicing mother of many children?

All Alleluia!

Word of God

Benedictus
Blessed be the Lord God of **Israel**,
who visited and redeemed the **people**,
who raised up for us a **mighty** savior
from the house of **ser**vant David.

Just as the Lord spoke through the mouths of the holy prophets of **old**—
salvation comes out of the hands of our enemies and those who **hate** us,
that, with our ancestors, we might perform **works** of mercy,
remembering the holy covenant **sworn** to Abraham—

so does the Lord deliver us from the hands **of** our enemies,
that we might serve without fear before **the** Lord,
worshiping in **ho**liness
and in righteousness **all** our days.

And you also, child, will be called a prophet of God Most **High**:
for you will go before the Lord to prepare a **way**,
bringing people knowledge of salvation by for**giveness** of sins;
because of the deep and tender mercy **of** our God.

Whereby a light rising from on high will **visit** us
to appear to those in darkness and in a shadow **of** death,
to guide our feet along a **straight**, sure path
into a **way** of peace.

INTERCESSIONS

Invocations

Cantor, then Assembly:

KH
Our eyes have seen your sal - va - tion.

Cantor:

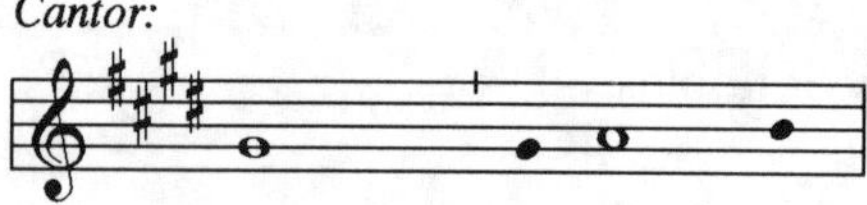

Messiah God, **we** seek you ...
Messiah God, **we** long for you ...
Messiah God, **we** contemplate you ...
Messiah God, **we** praise you ...
Messiah God, **we** bless you ...
Messiah God, **we** cling to you ...
Messiah God, **we re**joice in you ...
Messiah God, **we exalt** you ...

Our Father ...

Prayer
God of our salvation,
you allowed Simeon and Anna to
behold your Son, the Messiah God:
as Mary and Joseph offered Jesus
who is their firstborn to you as a fitting sacrifice,
so do we offer ourselves to you
now and forever. **Amen.**

CONCLUSION

Blessing
May God save us and bless us
in the name of the Father, and of the Son, and of the Holy Spirit. **Amen.**

Dismissal
Go forth to live this festival
as those who have seen the Light of salvation. **Thanks be to God.**

Feast of the PRESENTATION OF THE LORD Evening Prayer

FESTAL EVENING HYMN

PSALMODY

Psalm 43

Solo 1 Judge me, O God,
and plead my trial
against a nation unfaithful.
From people of deceit and iniquity, deliver me.

Solo 2 Since you are the God who is my fortress,
Why did you reject me?
Why should I wander in darkness,
hard pressed by the enemy?

Solo 1 Send your light and your truth;
they will guide me.
They will lead me to your holy mountain
and to your tents.

Solo 2 So I will come to the altar of God,
to God who makes me rejoice and dance;
with harp I will praise
God my God.

All Why are you cast down my soul
and disturbed within me?
Put your hope in God—
my salvation and my God—
whom I will praise again.

Psalm 27 *Of David.*

Solo 1 The LORD is my light and my salvation;
whom shall I fear?
The LORD is the stronghold of my life,
of whom shall I be afraid?

Solo 2 When evildoers approached
to devour me—
my adversaries and my enemies—
they stumbled and fell.
If an army encamps against me,
my heart shall not fear.
If war rises against me,
in this I trust:
One thing I ask from the LORD,
this only I will seek,
to dwell in the house of the LORD
all the days of my life,
to contemplate the favor of the LORD
and to meditate in God's sanctuary.

Solo 1 For God will hide me
in a shelter in the day of evil.
God will hide me in a secret chamber.
Upon a rock God will lift me up.

Solo 2 And now my head will be lifted above
my enemies who surround me.
And I will offer sacrifices in God's chamber,
sacrifices with wild jubilation.
I will sing and play music for the LORD.

Solo 1 Listen to my voice, O LORD, when I cry.
Have pity on me and answer me.
About you my heart has said:
"Seek God's face."
Your face, O LORD, I shall seek.

Solo 2 Do not hide your face from me;
do not send your servant back in anger.
You are my help.
Do not let me go, do not abandon me,

O God of my salvation.
Even if my father and my mother abandon me,
the LORD will receive me.

Solo 1 Teach me your way, O LORD,
and lead me on an upright path
because of my enemies.
Do not give me over to the their wiles,
for false witnesses have risen against me,
breathing out violence.

Solo 2 If only I could be proved right
by seeing the goodness of the LORD
in the land of the living.

All Hope in the LORD!
Let your heart be strong and firm,
and hope in the LORD.

Word of God

Magnificat
My soul does magni**fy** the Lord!
I delight in **God** my savior
who looked kindly **on** lowliness.

Now all ages will **call** me blessed
for the Mighty One **did** great things.
Holy is **God's** name;
mercy is from age to age for **those** in awe!

The Lord's strong arm did **might**y deeds:
confused the proud in **their** smug hearts;
toppled sovereigns **from** their thrones,
and exalted **hum**ble ones;
filled the hungering with **good** things,
and sent the rich **a**way empty.

The Lord helped servant **Is**rael
to re**mem**ber mercy,
as was spoken to Ab**ra**ham
and his descendants for**ev**ermore!

INTERCESSIONS

Petitions

Cantor, then Assembly:

Cantor:

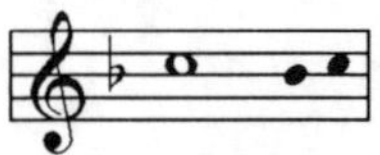

When God is **my** judge,
When God is **my** fortress,
When God is **my** guide,
When God is **my** ruler,
When God is **my** joy,
When God is **my** hope,
When God is **my** light,
When God is my **sal**vation,
When God is **my** stronghold,
When God is my dwell**ing** place,
When God is **my** answer,
When God is **my** help,
When God is **my** path,
When God is **my** goodness,
When God calls **the** dead,

Our Father ...

Prayer

O God of salvation,
just as Mary and Joseph offered
your only-begotten Son Jesus in the temple,
so do we offer ourselves to you:
receive us as a fitting sacrifice for others
that your goodness may be known throughout the world.
We pray through your Son Jesus Christ. **Amen.**

CONCLUSION

Blessing

May the God who received the offering of Mary and Joseph,

receive us and bless us
in the name of the Father, and of the Son, and of the Holy Spirit. **Amen.**

Dismissal
Go and rest as servants of God, for you have seen the gift of salvation.
Thanks be to God.

February 22
Feast of the CHAIR OF PETER, Apostle
Morning Praise

FESTAL MORNING HYMN

PSALMODY

Psalm 63 *Psalm of David. While he was in the desert of Judah.*

Solo 1 O God, you are my God, I seek you;
my soul thirsts for you.
My flesh longs for you
in a dry and wasted land,
deprived of water.

Solo 2 So in the sanctuary I have contemplated you
to see your might and your glory.
Because your steadfast love is better than life,
my lips will praise you.
So I will bless you all my life;
in your name I will raise my hands.
As with milk and rich food,
my soul is filled;
my mouth gives praise with joyful lips.
I remember you upon my bed,
pondering you throughout the night.
For you were a help for me;
in the shade of your wings I keep singing.
My soul clings to you;
your right hand upholds me.

Solo 1 But let those who seek my destruction
be cast into the depths of the earth.
Let them be given over to the power of the sword;
let them become a prey for jackals.

All Then the king shall rejoice in God.
All those who swear by God will be praised,
for the mouths of liars will be shut.

Psalm 149

All Alleluia!

Choir 1 Sing a new song to the LORD,
God's praise in the assembly of the faithful.
Let Israel rejoice in its Creator,
the children of Zion exult in their Sovereign.
Let them praise God's name with dancing;
with drums and harp, let them play music for God.

Choir 2 For the LORD takes delight in the people,
adorning the poor with salvation.
Let the faithful exult with glory,
let them ring out joy on their couches,
and cry out the great deeds of God from their throats.

Choir 1 With two-edged swords in their hands,
let them do vengeance against peoples
and rebuke nations;
let them tie their rulers with fetters
and their nobles with chains of bronze,
in order to accomplish judgment against them as written.
This is honor for all the faithful.

All Alleluia!

Word of God

Benedictus
Blessed be the Lord God of **Israel**,
who visited and redeemed the **people**,
who raised up for us a **mighty** savior
from the house of **ser**vant David.

Just as the Lord spoke through the mouths of the holy prophets of **old**—
salvation comes out of the hands of our enemies and those who **hate** us,
that, with our ancestors, we might perform **works** of mercy,
remembering the holy covenant **sworn** to Abraham—

so does the Lord deliver us from the hands **of** our enemies,
that we might serve without fear before **the** Lord,
worshiping in **ho**liness
and in righteousness **all** our days.

And you also, child, will be called a prophet of God Most **High**:
for you will go before the Lord to prepare a **way**,
bringing people knowledge of salvation by for**giveness** of sins;
because of the deep and tender mercy **of** our God.

Whereby a light rising from on high will **vis**it us
to appear to those in darkness and in a shadow **of** death,
to guide our feet along a **straight**, sure path
into a **way** of peace.

INTERCESSIONS

Invocations

Cantor, then Assembly:

KH
Your stead- fast love is bet - ter than life.

Cantor:

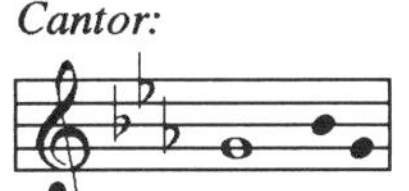

O Son of God, you seek us for **your** service ...
O Son of God, you draw us to **your**self ...
O Son of God, you help us spread the **Good** News ...
O Son of God, you shade us from **dis**couragement ...
O Son of God, you keep **us** faithful ...
O Son of God, you rejoice in your **dis**ciples ...
O Son of God, you adorn your disciples **with** glory ...
O Son of God, you honor all **your** faithful ...

Our Father ...

Prayer
O God,
you are our rock and our stronghold:
you called Peter your rock and built your Church upon him.
As Peter's love spread the Gospel,
so may our love bring unity and peace
to the Church and world now and always. **Amen.**

CONCLUSION

Blessing
May the God of salvation bless us
in the name of the Father, and of the Son, and of the Holy Spirit. **Amen.**

Dismissal
Go forth to be disciples of Christ. **Thanks be to God.**

Feast of the CHAIR OF PETER, Apostle
Evening Prayer

FESTAL EVENING HYMN

PSALMODY

Psalm 116

Solo 1 I love the LORD
who has heard
the voice of my supplications.
For God has turned an ear to me
as I cry all my days.

Solo 2 Deadly chains have fettered me,
and the anguish of Sheol has reached up to me.
Distress and terror, I have encountered;
but I have called on the name of the LORD.
How long, O LORD?
Deliver my soul.

All The LORD is gracious and just;
our God is merciful.

Solo 1 The LORD is the protector of the innocent;
I was poor and God brought salvation to me.
Return, O my soul, to your rest,
for the LORD has done good to you.

Solo 2 For you have delivered my soul from death,
my eye from tears
and my foot from stumbling,
that I may walk in the presence of the LORD
in the land of the living.

Solo 1 Yes, I was right in saying,
"I am greatly afflicted."
In my agitation, I have said,
"Every human being is a liar."

Solo 2 What shall I return to the LORD
for all the bounty in my favor?
I will lift up the cup of salvation
and I will call on the name of the LORD.
Indeed, I will fulfill my promises to the LORD
in the presence of all the people.

All Precious in the eyes of the LORD
is the death of the faithful ones.

Solo 1 How long, O LORD?
For I am your servant,
I am your servant, the offspring of your handmaid.
You have loosened my bonds.

Solo 2 To you I will offer a sacrifice of thanksgiving
and I will call on the name of the LORD.
Indeed, I will fulfill my promises to the LORD
in the presence of all the people,
in the courts of the house of the LORD,
in your midst, O Jerusalem.

All Alleluia!

Psalm 126 *Song of ascents (pilgrimages).*

Choir 1 When the LORD accompanied
those who returned to Zion,
we were like dreamers.
Then our mouth
was filled with laughter
and our tongue with joy.
Then it was said among nations:
"The LORD has done great
deeds among these people."

All The LORD has done great
deeds among us.
Now we rejoice.

Choir 2 Return our captives, O LORD,
like torrents in the Negeb.
Those who sow in tears
harvest with shouts of joy.
Indeed, one goes out weeping,
carrying the bag of seed,
and comes back joyful,
carrying the sheaves.

Word of God

Magnificat
My soul does magni**fy** the Lord!
I delight in **God** my savior
who looked kindly **on** lowliness.

Now all ages will **call** me blessed
for the Mighty One **did** great things.
Holy is **God's** name;
mercy is from age to age for **those** in awe!

The Lord's strong arm did **migh**ty deeds:
confused the proud in **their** smug hearts;
toppled sovereigns **from** their thrones,
and exalted **hum**ble ones;
filled the hungering with **good** things,
and sent the rich **a**way empty.

The Lord helped servant **Is**rael
to re**mem**ber mercy,
as was spoken to Ab**ra**ham
and his descendants for**e**vermore!

INTERCESSIONS

Petitions

Cantor, then Assembly:

Who has **turned** an ear **to** us? ...
Who has **broken** the chains **of** bondage? ...
Who has **de**livered us **from** death? ...
Who has **pro**tected **the** innocent? ...
Who has **brought** salvation **to** us? ...
Who has **called us** precious? ...
Who has **ac**companied us during **our** service? ...
Who has **done** great deeds among **the** people? ...
Who has **fed his** sheep? ...
Who has **called** the dead to **new** life? ...

Our Father ...

Prayer
O God,
your Son calls disciples to be his followers:
protect us and encourage us
that we might spread the Good News
of salvation and life everlasting. **Amen.**

CONCLUSION

Blessing
May the God who calls followers bless us
in the name of the Father, and of the Son, and of the Holy Spirit. **Amen.**

Dismissal
Rest peacefully, comforted by the nearness of God. **Thanks be to God.**

March 19
Solemnity of JOSEPH, Husband of Mary
Morning Praise

FESTAL MORNING HYMN

PSALMODY

Psalm 63 *Psalm of David. While he was in the desert of Judah.*

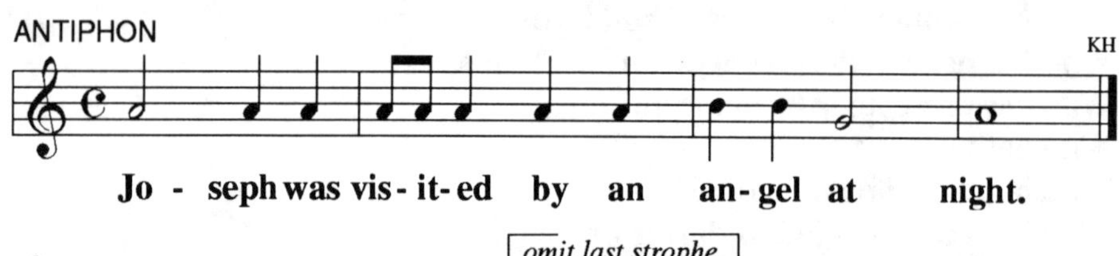
ANTIPHON
KH
Jo - seph was vis - it - ed by an an - gel at night.

omit last strophe

O God, you are my God, **I** seek you;
my **soul** thirsts **for** you.
My flesh longs for you
  in a dry and **wast**ed land,
deprived **of** water. ANTIPHON

So in the sanctuary I have contemplated you
  to see your might and your **glo**ry.
Because your **stead**fast love is better than life,
  my lips will **praise** you.
So I will bless you **all** my life;
in your name I will raise **my** hands.

As with milk and rich food,
  my soul **is** filled;
my **mouth** gives praise with joy**ful** lips.
I remember you up**on** my bed,
pondering you throughout **the** night.

For you were a help **for** me;
in the **shade** of your wings I **keep** singing.
My soul **clings** to you;
your right hand **up**holds me. ANTIPHON

But let those who seek my des**truc**tion
be **cast** into the depths of **the** earth.
Let them be given over to the power **of** the sword;
let them become a prey **for** jackals. ANTIPHON

Then the king shall rejoice **in** God.
All **those** who swear by God will **be** praised,
for the mouths of liars will **be** shut. ANTIPHON

Psalm Prayer
O God,
you sent an angel to Joseph to announce your will:
as Joseph pondered your ways and remained always faithful,
so may we know and follow your will all the days of our lives.
We pray through Jesus Christ. **Amen.**

Psalm 150

ANTIPHON
KH
Just and ho - ly is Jo - seph.

Praise God for **ho**liness;
praise God for the firmament **of** might.

Praise God for the mighty **deeds**;
praise God for unlimit**ed** greatness. ANTIPHON

Praise God with blast of **trumpet**;
praise God with lyre **and** harp.

Praise God with cymbal and **dance**;
praise God with strings **and** pipes. ANTIPHON

Praise God with resounding **drums**;
praise God with clamor**ous** drums.

Let all living **creatures**
praise **the** LORD. ANTIPHON

Psalm Prayer
Mighty God,
you are worthy of all praise:
Joseph honored you by the work of his hands.
May we also honor you by all we do.
We pray through Jesus Christ. **Amen.**

Word of God

Benedictus
Blessed be the Lord God of **Israel**,
who visited and redeemed the **people**,
who raised up for us a **might**y savior
from the house of **ser**vant David.

Just as the Lord spoke through the mouths of the holy prophets of **old**—
salvation comes out of the hands of our enemies and those who **hate** us,
that, with our ancestors, we might perform **works** of mercy,
remembering the holy covenant **sworn** to Abraham—

so does the Lord deliver us from the hands **of** our enemies,
that we might serve without fear before **the** Lord,
worshiping in **ho**liness
in righteousness **all** our days.

And you also, child, will be called a prophet of God Most **High**:
for you will go before the Lord to prepare a **way**,
bringing people knowledge of salvation by for**giveness** of sins;
because of the deep and tender mercy **of** our God.

Whereby a light rising from on high will **vis**it us
to appear to those in darkness and in a shadow **of** death,
to guide our feet along a **straight**, sure path
into a **way** of peace.

INTERCESSIONS

Invocations

Cantor, then Assembly:
KH
Your stead-fast love is bet-ter than life.

Cantor:

O Son of God and of Joseph, you seek us to do **your** will ...
O Son of God and of Joseph, you draw us to **your**self ...
O Son of God and of Joseph, you help us spread the **Good** News ...
O Son of God and of Joseph, you shade us from unright**eous** paths ...
O Son of God and of Joseph, you keep **us** faithful ...
O Son of God and of Joseph, you rejoice in **just** people ...
O Son of God and of Joseph, you adorn your children **with** glory ...
O Son of God and of Joseph, you honor all **your** faithful ...

Our Father ...

Prayer
O God,
you called Joseph to guide quietly
your Son on the path of life:
may he faithfully intercede for us
that we may hear your call and
lead others to know your Son, Jesus Christ. **Amen.**

CONCLUSION

Blessing
Bow your heads and pray for God's blessing.
May the Creator bless us. **Amen.**
May the Son protect us. **Amen.**
May the Spirit love us. **Amen.**
And may God bless us
in the name of the Father, and of the Son, and of the Holy Spirit. **Amen.**

Sign of Peace/Dismissal
Share with one another a sign of the peace of Christ,
knowing that we live our day under the protection of Joseph.

Solemnity of JOSEPH, Husband of Mary
Evening Prayer

LIGHT SERVICE

Proclamation of the Light

Cantor:

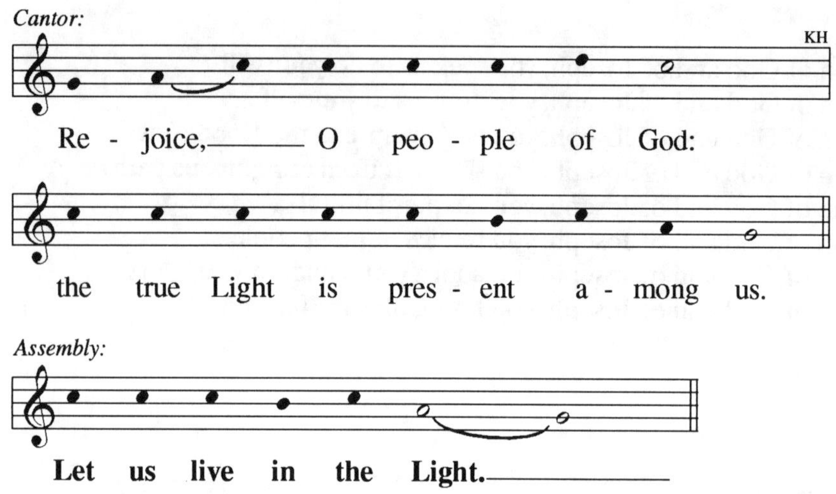
KH
Re - joice, O peo - ple of God:
the true Light is pres - ent a - mong us.
Assembly:
Let us live in the Light.

Festal Evening Hymn

Thanksgiving for the Light

Cantor:

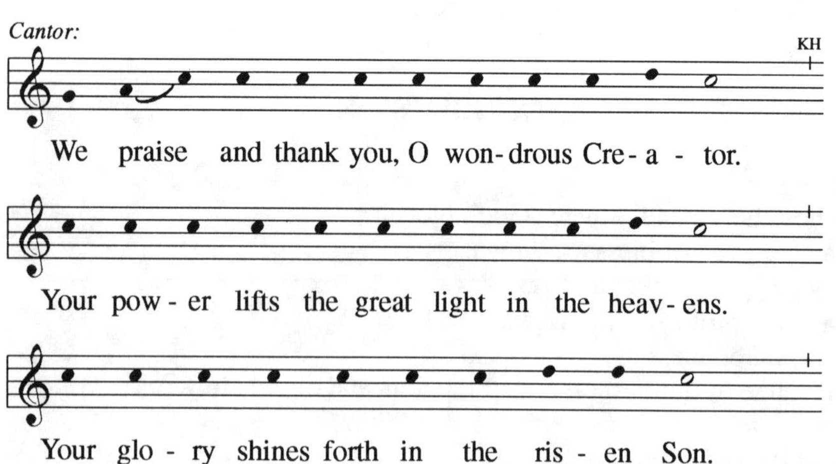
KH
We praise and thank you, O won-drous Cre - a - tor.
Your pow - er lifts the great light in the heav - ens.
Your glo - ry shines forth in the ris - en Son.

Your maj - es - ty lies o - ver all of cre - a - tion.
Your splen - dor clothes us with dig - ni - ty
and hon - or. Your good- ness o - ver-comes an - y
weak - ness. Your boun-ty sat - is - fies all hun - ger.
Your grace pro - claims our des - ti - ny.
Re - joice,___ O ho - ly peo - ple, in this great Light:
it is our sure sal - va - tion and glo - rious free - dom.
As we cel - e - brate this fes - ti - val in hon - or
of Jo - seph, guard us from all harm. Keep us
safe in this Light that nev - er fades. We praise and

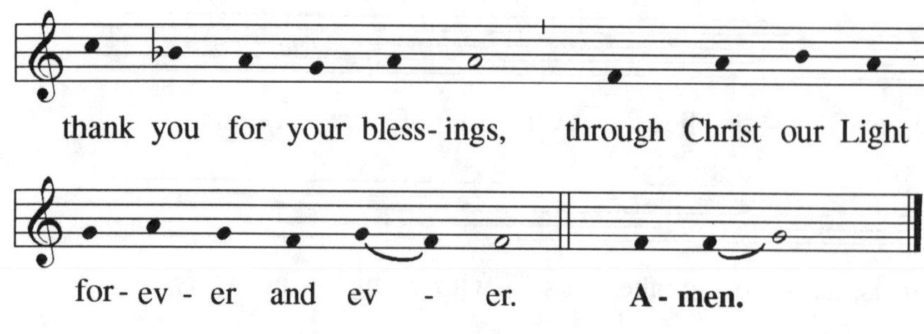

PSALMODY

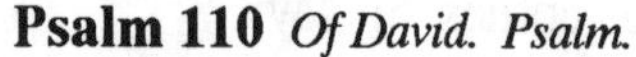
Psalm 110 *Of David. Psalm.*

ANTIPHON
KH
Qui-et gen-tle-ness is Jo-seph's strength.

Thus says the LORD **to** my lord:
"Sit on my right
  until I place your enemies
  as a footstool for **your** feet."
Let the LORD send from Zion
  the scepter of **your** strength.
Rule in the midst of **your** enemies. ANTIPHON

Your people bring free **of**ferings
on the day of your might
  in ho**ly** splendor.
From the womb **of** dawn,
a dew of rejuvenation comes **to** you. ANTIPHON

The LORD has promised
  and will **not** repent:
"According to my word,
  you are a priest forever, my king **of** justice."
The Lord is at **your** right,
who has smashed rulers on the day **of** wrath.

The Lord judges **against** the nations,
piling them **with** corpses.

The Lord has smashed heads
all over **the** land.
From a torrent the Lord drinks on the way,
and rises up **in** triumph. ANTIPHON

Psalm Prayer
God of might and splendor,
you brought forth Joseph to
protect and guide your only Son, Jesus Christ:
may he intercede for us
and bring us life and peace.
We pray through Jesus Christ. **Amen.**

Psalm 111

ANTIPHON
KH
God re- veals great pow - er! Al - le - lu - ia!
Assembly:
Al - le - lu - ia!
Assembly:
Al - le - lu - ia!

I will give thanks to the LORD with **all** my heart
in the council of the righteous and **the** assembly.
Great are the deeds **of** the LORD,
pondered by all who de**light** in them. ANTIPHON

God's work is majes**ty** and splendor,
and justice **stands** forever.
A memorial God has made **of** these wonders;
gracious and merciful **is** the LORD. ANTIPHON

God has given food to those **who** show reverence,
remembering the cove**nant** forever.
God has revealed to the people the power **of** these deeds
in giving them the nations **for** their heritage. ANTIPHON

The deeds of God's hands are **truth** and justice;
the precepts of God **all** are trustworthy.
They are established forev**er** and ever,
wrought in truth and eq**uity**. ANTIPHON

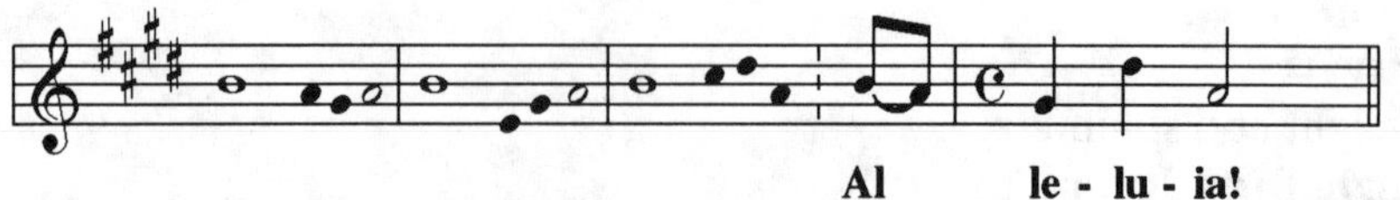

God has sent deliverance **to** the people,
appointing the cove**nant** forever;
holy and to be revered **is** God's name.

The beginning of wisdom is reverence **for** the LORD,
and its practice brings about clear **un**derstanding. ANTIPHON
The praise of God **stands** forever! ANTIPHON

Psalm Prayer
God of majesty and splendor,
you are worthy of all thanks and praise:
hear our evening prayer in honor of Joseph
that our reverence for you
may bring us justice and righteousness now and always. **Amen.**

Word of God

Magnificat
My soul does magni**fy** the Lord!
I delight in **God** my savior
who looked kindly **on** lowliness.

Now all ages will **call** me blessed
for the Mighty One **did** great things.
Holy is **God's** name;
mercy is from age to age for **those** in awe!

The Lord's strong arm did **mighty** deeds:
confused the proud in **their** smug hearts;
toppled sovereigns **from** their thrones,
and exalted **hum**ble ones;
filled the hungering with **good** things,
and sent the rich **a**way empty.

The Lord helped servant **Is**rael
to re**mem**ber mercy,
as was spoken to Ab**ra**ham
and his descendants for**ev**ermore!

INTERCESSIONS

Petitions

Cantor, then Assembly:

Cantor:

For God's great **pow**er ...
For God's heal**ing** strength ...
For God's holy **splen**dor ...
For God's priestly **peo**ple ...
For God's everlasting **tri**umph ...
For God's righteous **mer**cy ...
For God's delight**ful** deeds ...
For God's ageless **cov**enant ...
For God's bountiful **herit**age ...
For God's trustworthy **pre**cepts ...
For God's mighty de**liver**ance ...
For God's victorious **right** hand ...
For God's acceptance of the faithful de**part**ed ...

Our Father ...

Prayer
O God,
you give us great joy
as we celebrate this festival honoring Saint Joseph:
help us to imitate Joseph
who is a model of virtue and justice,
patience and goodness.
We pray through Jesus Christ. **Amen.**

CONCLUSION

Blessing

Bow your heads and pray for God's blessing.
May the Creator bless us. **Amen.**
May the Son protect us. **Amen.**
May the Spirit love us. **Amen.**
And may God bless us
in the name of the Father, and of the Son, and of the Holy Spirit. **Amen.**

Sign of Peace/Dismissal

Share with one another a sign of the peace of Christ,
knowing that we rest this night under the protection of Saint Joseph.

March 25
Solemnity of the ANNUNCIATION
Morning Praise

FESTAL MORNING HYMN

PSALMODY

Psalm 63 *Psalm of David. While he was in the desert of Judah.*

ANTIPHON

KH
Hail Ma - ry, who con - ceived by the Ho - ly Spir - it.

omit last strophe

O God, you are my God, **I** seek you;
my **soul** thirsts **for** you.
My flesh longs for you
  in a dry and **wast**ed land,
deprived **of** water. ANTIPHON

So in the sanctuary I have contemplated you
  to see your might and your **glo**ry.
Because your **stead**fast love is better than life,
  my lips will **praise** you.
So I will bless you **all** my life;
in your name I will raise **my** hands.

As with milk and rich food,
  my soul **is** filled;
my **mouth** gives praise with joy**ful** lips.
I remember you up**on** my bed,
pondering you throughout **the** night.

For you were a help **for** me;
in the **shade** of your wings I **keep** singing.
My soul **clings** to you;
your right hand **up**holds me. ANTIPHON

But let those who seek my des**truc**tion
be **cast** into the depths of **the** earth.
Let them be given over to the power **of** the sword;
let them become a prey **for** jackals. ANTIPHON

Then the king shall rejoice **in** God.
All **those** who swear by God will **be** praised,
for the mouths of liars will **be** shut. ANTIPHON

Psalm Prayer
O God,
you sent an angel to Mary to announce your will:
as Mary pondered your ways and remained always faithful,
so may we know and follow your will all the days of our lives.
We pray through Jesus Christ. **Amen.**

Psalm 113

ANTIPHON

KH
Who is like our won - drous God, en -

throned in glo - ry? Al - le - lu - ia!

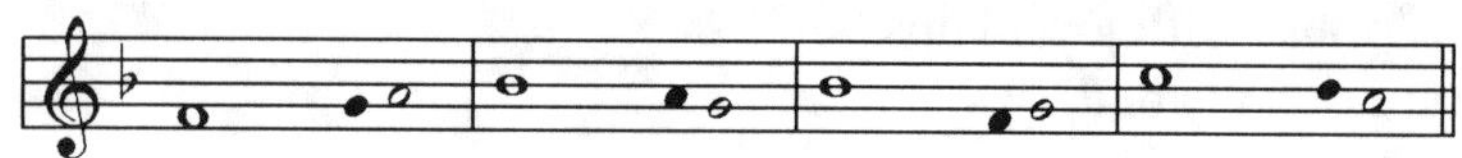

Give praise, servants of **the** Lord;
praise the name of **the** Lord.
Let the name of the Lord **be** blessed
from now on and **for**ever.

From the rising of the sun to **its** setting,
let the name of the Lord **be** praised.
The Lord is exalted above **all** nations;
God's glory is greater than **the** heavens. ANTIPHON

Who looks down to watch over
  the skies and **the** earth?
Who raises the weak from dust
  and the poor **from** ashes,
to return them to the company of nobles,
  the nobles of **the** people?
Who brings home the sterile woman,
  now a rejoicing mother of many children? ANTIPHON

Psalm Prayer
Praiseworthy God,
you made Mary the rejoicing mother of your Son:
may she always look down and watch over us
in the name of her Son, Jesus Christ. **Amen.**

Word of God

Benedictus
Blessed be the Lord God of **Israel**,
who visited and redeemed the **people**,
who raised up for us a **mighty** savior
from the house of **ser**vant David.

Just as the Lord spoke through the mouths of the holy prophets of **old**—
salvation comes out of the hands of our enemies and those who **hate** us,
that, with our ancestors, we might perform **works** of mercy,
remembering the holy covenant **sworn** to Abraham—

so does the Lord deliver us from the hands **of** our enemies,
that we might serve without fear before **the** Lord,
worshiping in **ho**liness
and in righteousness **all** our days.

And you also, child, will be called a prophet of God Most **High**:
for you will go before the Lord to prepare a **way**,
bringing people knowledge of salvation by for**giveness** of sins;
because of the deep and tender mercy **of** our God.

Whereby a light rising from on high will **visit** us
to appear to those in darkness and in a shadow **of** death,
to guide our feet along a **straight**, sure path
into a **way** of peace.

INTERCESSIONS

Invocations

Cantor, then Assembly:

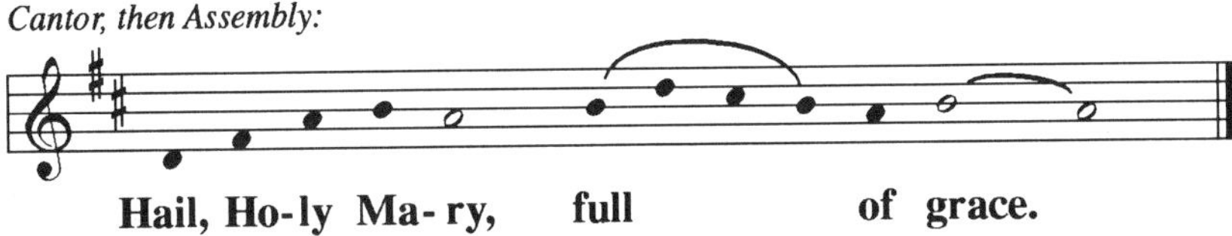
Hail, Ho-ly Ma- ry, full of grace.

Cantor:

O divine Son, your mother pon**dered** God's will ...
O divine Son, your mother saw your **might** and glory ...
O divine Son, your mother **prais**es you ...

O divine Son, your mother blesses your name ...
O divine Son, your mother remained in the shade of your wings ...
O divine Son, your mother rejoices in you ...
O divine Son, your mother is exalted above all others ...
O divine Son, your mother watches over us ...
O divine Son, your mother cares for us as her beloved children ...

Our Father ...

Prayer
O God of our salvation,
your Son's mother bowed to your holy will:
may we, too, say with Mary,
"Here are we, God's servants;
let it be with us according to God's word."
We pray through the divine Son Jesus Christ. **Amen.**

CONCLUSION

Blessing
Bow your heads and pray for God's blessing.
May God almighty call us. **Amen.**
May the divine Son be with us. **Amen.**
May the Spirit overshadow us. **Amen.**
And may God bless us
in the name of the Father, and of the Son, and of the Holy Spirit. **Amen.**

Sign of Peace/Dismissal
Share with one another a sign of the peace of the divine Son.

Solemnity of the ANNUNCIATION Evening Prayer

LIGHT SERVICE

Proclamation of the Light

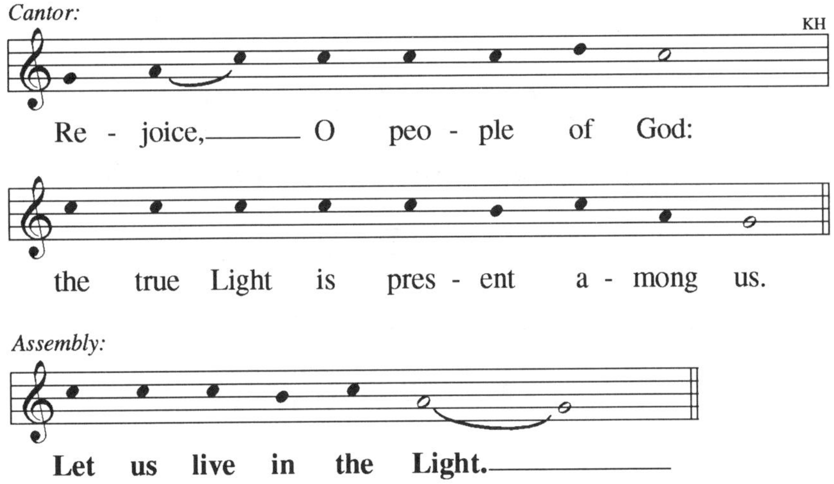

Festal Evening Hymn

Thanksgiving for the Light

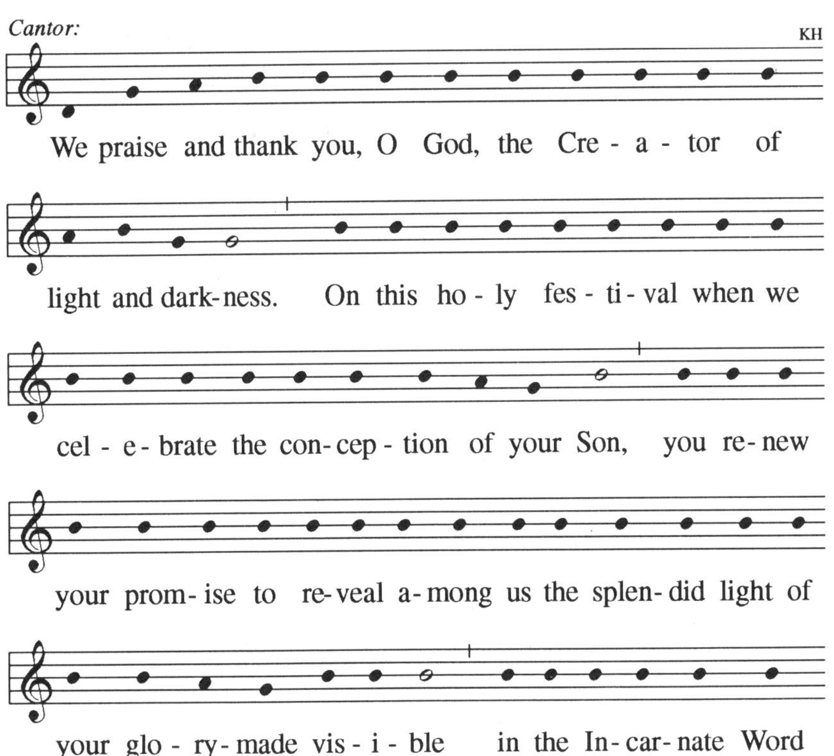

Cantor:
KH
We praise and thank you, O God, the Cre - a - tor of
light and dark-ness. On this ho - ly fes - ti - val when we
cel - e - brate the con - cep - tion of your Son, you re - new
your prom - ise to re - veal a - mong us the splen - did light of
your glo - ry - made vis - i - ble in the In - car - nate Word

Je- sus Christ. Through the proph-ets of old you call us

to your cov- e- nant of love. Now through the Spir- it you

o - pen our eyes to the peace of Christ's pres- ence.

So with the ho - ly an- gels on high we sing out:

Glo- ry to God in the high- est, to whom we of - fer

praise, hon- or and bless- ing, now and al - ways and

for - ev - er and ev - er. **A - men.**

PSALMODY

Psalm 130 *Song of ascents (pilgrimages).*

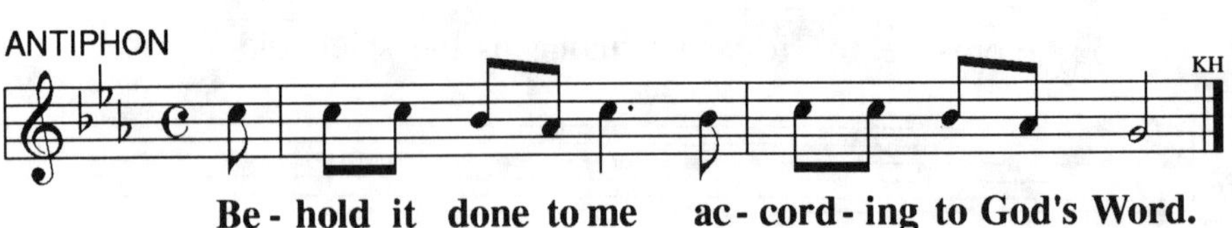

ANTIPHON
KH
Be - hold it done to me ac - cord - ing to God's Word.

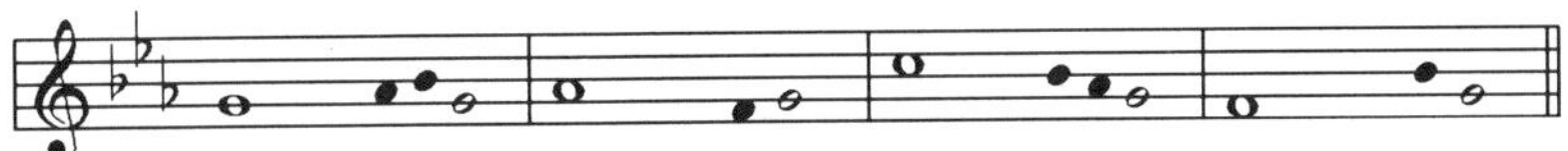

Out of the depths, I cry to **you**, O LORD.
Lord, listen to **my** voice;
let your ears **be** attentive
to the voice of my sup**pli**cations. ANTIPHON

If you, O LORD, were to keep in**iquities** in mind,
Lord, who **could** stand?
But with you **is** forgiveness,
and for that you are **re**vered. ANTIPHON

I wait for the LORD;
my soul waits, and for God's **word** I hope.
My soul waits for **the** Lord
more than watchers **of** the morning
watch for **the** dawn. ANTIPHON

Let Israel hope **in** the LORD,
for steadfast love is found with the LORD
and abundance of **re**demption.
It is the LORD who shall redeem **Is**rael
from all iniq**ui**ties. ANTIPHON

Psalm Prayer
O God who listens to our voices,
you are steadfast in love and sure in forgiveness:
speak your Word to us
that we may know and revere you
now and always. **Amen.**

Psalm 67 *To the choirmaster. With stringed instruments. Psalm. Song.*

ANTIPHON

KH
Let the peo - ples give you thanks, O God; let
all the peo - ples give you thanks.

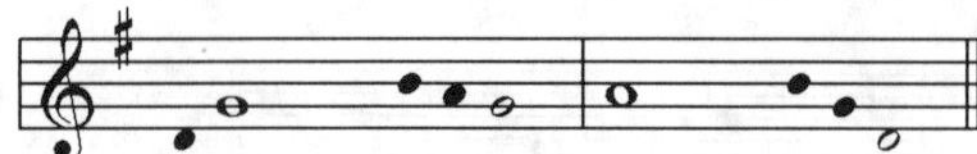

May God have mercy on us and **bless** us.
May God's face **shine** among us.

For your way is known **over** the earth,
and your salvation is known a**mong** all nations. ANTIPHON

May the nations rejoice and **shout** with joy,
for you judge the peoples rightly
  and the nations on the **earth** you guide. ANTIPHON

The earth has **given** its fruit.
May God, our God, **bless** us.

May God **bless** us,
and let all ends of the **earth** show reverence. ANTIPHON

Psalm Prayer
God of all blessings,
you are worthy of all thanksgiving:
by giving us Mary our Mother as a model,
guide us to do your holy will
so that we may be fruitful all our lives.
We pray through Jesus Christ. **Amen.**

Word of God

Magnificat
My soul does magni**fy** the Lord!
I delight in **God** my savior
who looked kindly **on** lowliness.

Now all ages will **call** me blessed
for the Mighty One **did** great things.
Holy is **God's** name;
mercy is from age to age for **those** in awe!

The Lord's strong arm did **migh**ty deeds:
confused the proud in **their** smug hearts;
toppled sovereigns **from** their thrones,
and exalted **hum**ble ones;

filled the hungering with **good** things,
and sent the rich **a**way empty.

The Lord helped servant **Is**rael
to re**mem**ber mercy,
as was spoken to Ab**ra**ham
and his descendants for**e**vermore!

INTERCESSIONS

Petitions

Cantor, then Assembly:

Cantor:

We cry **out** to God ...
We listen **to** God's voice ...
We are attentive **to** God's deeds ...
We are forgiven **our** iniquities ...
We revere God's **ho**ly name ...
We hope **in** God's Word ...
We greet God's **stead**fast love ...
We enjoy abun**dant** redemption ...
We make **known** God's ways ...
We give **thanks** forever ...
We rejoice and **shout** with joy ...
We honor Ma**ry** our mother ...
We commend the faithful departed **to** God's love ...

Our Father ...

Prayer
O wondrous God,
your face shines on us
and we receive Life:
may we always open ourselves to your message of love
through the intercession of Mary our Mother
and her divine Son Jesus Christ. **Amen.**

CONCLUSION

Blessing
Bow your heads and pray for God's blessing.
May the Creator God make the divine face to shine upon us. **Amen.**
May the Redeemer Son look upon us kindly. **Amen.**
May the Sanctifying Spirit give us peace. **Amen.**
And may God bless us
in the name of the Father, and of the Son, and of the Holy Spirit. **Amen.**

Sign of Peace/Dismissal
Share with one another the peace of the divine Son,
that we may rest confidently under the protection of Mary our Mother.

April 25
Feast of MARK, Evangelist
Morning Praise

FESTAL MORNING HYMN

PSALMODY

Psalm 63 *Psalm of David. While he was in the desert of Judah.*

Solo 1 O God, you are my God, I seek you;
my soul thirsts for you.
My flesh longs for you
in a dry and wasted land,
deprived of water.

Solo 2 So in the sanctuary I have contemplated you
to see your might and your glory.
Because your steadfast love is better than life,
my lips will praise you.
So I will bless you all my life;
in your name I will raise my hands.
As with milk and rich food,
my soul is filled;
my mouth gives praise with joyful lips.
I remember you upon my bed,

pondering you throughout the night.
For you were a help for me;
in the shade of your wings I keep singing.
My soul clings to you;
your right hand upholds me.

Solo 1 But let those who seek my destruction
be cast into the depths of the earth.
Let them be given over to the power of the sword;
let them become a prey for jackals.

All Then the king shall rejoice in God.
All those who swear by God will be praised,
for the mouths of liars will be shut.

Psalm 149

All Alleluia!

Choir 1 Sing a new song to the LORD,
God's praise in the assembly of the faithful.
Let Israel rejoice in its Creator,
the children of Zion exult in their Sovereign.
Let them praise God's name with dancing;
with drums and harp, let them play music for God.

Choir 2 For the LORD takes delight in the people,
adorning the poor with salvation.
Let the faithful exult with glory,
let them ring out joy on their couches,
and cry out the great deeds of God from their throats.

Choir 1 With two-edged swords in their hands,
let them do vengeance against peoples
and rebuke nations;
let them tie their rulers with fetters
and their nobles with chains of bronze,
in order to accomplish judgment against them as written.
This is honor for all the faithful.

All Alleluia!

Word of God

Benedictus
Blessed be the Lord God of **Israel**,
who visited and redeemed the **people**,
who raised up for us a **mighty** savior
from the house of **ser**vant David.

Just as the Lord spoke through the mouths of the holy prophets of **old**—
salvation comes out of the hands of our enemies and those who **hate** us,
that, with our ancestors, we might perform **works** of mercy,
remembering the holy covenant **sworn** to Abraham—

so does the Lord deliver us from the hands **of** our enemies,
that we might serve without fear before **the** Lord,
worshiping in **ho**liness
and in righteousness **all** our days.

And you also, child, will be called a prophet of God Most **High**:
for you will go before the Lord to prepare a **way**,
bringing people knowledge of salvation by for**giveness** of sins;
because of the deep and tender mercy **of** our God.

Whereby a light rising from on high will **vis**it us
to appear to those in darkness and in a shadow **of** death,
to guide our feet along a **straight**, sure path
into a **way** of peace.

INTERCESSIONS

Invocations

Cantor, then Assembly:

KH
Your stead- fast love is bet - ter than life.

Cantor:

O risen Christ, you seek us for **your** service ...
O risen Christ, you draw us to **your**self ...
O risen Christ, you help us spread the **Good** News ...
O risen Christ, you shade us from **dis**couragement ...
O risen Christ, you keep **us** faithful ...

O risen Christ, you rejoice in your **disciples** ...
O risen Christ, you adorn your disciples **with** glory ...
O risen Christ, you honor all **your** faithful ...

Our Father ...

Prayer
Gracious God,
you enlightened Mark to record
the Good News of the Messiah:
open our eyes to the splendor of the resurrection
that we might seek you now and always. **Amen.**

CONCLUSION

Blessing
May the God of salvation bless us
in the name of the Father, and of the Son, and of the Holy Spirit. **Amen.**

Dismissal
Go forth to be disciples of Christ. **Thanks be to God.**

Feast of MARK, Evangelist
Evening Prayer

FESTAL EVENING HYMN

PSALMODY

Psalm 116

Solo 1 I love the LORD
who has heard
the voice of my supplications.
For God has turned an ear to me
as I cry all my days.

Solo 2 Deadly chains have fettered me,
and the anguish of Sheol has reached up to me.

Distress and terror, I have encountered;
but I have called on the name of the LORD.
How long, O LORD?
Deliver my soul.

All The LORD is gracious and just;
our God is merciful.

Solo 1 The LORD is the protector of the innocent;
I was poor and God brought salvation to me.
Return, O my soul, to your rest,
for the LORD has done good to you.

Solo 2 For you have delivered my soul from death,
my eye from tears
and my foot from stumbling,
that I may walk in the presence of the LORD
in the land of the living.

Solo 1 Yes, I was right in saying,
"I am greatly afflicted."
In my agitation, I have said,
"Every human being is a liar."

Solo 2 What shall I return to the LORD
for all the bounty in my favor?
I will lift up the cup of salvation
and I will call on the name of the LORD.
Indeed, I will fulfill my promises to the LORD
in the presence of all the people.

All Precious in the eyes of the LORD
is the death of the faithful ones.

Solo 1 How long, O LORD?
For I am your servant,
I am your servant, the offspring of your handmaid.
You have loosened my bonds.

Solo 2 To you I will offer a sacrifice of thanksgiving
and I will call on the name of the LORD.
Indeed, I will fulfill my promises to the LORD
in the presence of all the people,

in the courts of the house of the LORD,
in your midst, O Jerusalem.

All Alleluia!

Psalm 126 *Song of ascents (pilgrimages).*

Choir 1 When the LORD accompanied
those who returned to Zion,
we were like dreamers.
Then our mouth
was filled with laughter
and our tongue with joy.
Then it was said among nations:
"The LORD has done great
deeds among these people."

All The LORD has done great
deeds among us.
Now we rejoice.

Choir 2 Return our captives, O LORD,
like torrents in the Negeb.
Those who sow in tears
harvest with shouts of joy.
Indeed, one goes out weeping,
carrying the bag of seed,
and comes back joyful,
carrying the sheaves.

Word of God

Magnificat
My soul does magni**fy** the Lord!
I delight in **God** my savior
who looked kindly **on** lowliness.

Now all ages will **call** me blessed
for the Mighty One **did** great things.
Holy is **God's** name;
mercy is from age to age for **those** in awe!

The Lord's strong arm did **mighty** deeds:
confused the proud in **their** smug hearts;
toppled sovereigns **from** their thrones,
and exalted **hum**ble ones;
filled the hungering with **good** things,
and sent the rich **a**way empty.

The Lord helped servant **Is**rael
to re**mem**ber mercy,
as was spoken to Ab**ra**ham
and his descendants for**ev**ermore!

INTERCESSIONS

Petitions

Cantor, then Assembly:

Cantor:

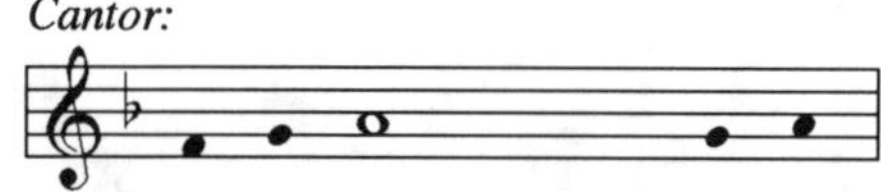

Who has **turned** an ear **to** us? ...
Who has **broken** the chains **of** bondage? ...
Who has **de**livered us **from** death? ...
Who has **pro**tected **the** innocent? ...
Who has **brought** salvation **to** us? ...
Who has **called us** precious? ...
Who has **ac**companied us during **our** service? ...
Who has **done** great deeds among **the** people? ...
Who has **called** the dead to **new** life? ...

Our Father ...

Prayer
O God,
your Son called Mark to be his evangelist:
protect us and encourage us
that we, too, might spread the Good News
of salvation and life everlasting. **Amen.**

CONCLUSION

Blessing
May the God who calls followers bless us
in the name of the Father, and of the Son, and of the Holy Spirit. **Amen.**

Dismissal
Go and rest peacefully, comforted by the nearness of God. **Thanks be to God.**

Sunday after Pentecost
Solemnity of the HOLY TRINITY
Morning Praise

FESTAL MORNING HYMN

PSALMODY

Psalm 63 *Psalm of David. While he was in the desert of Judah.*

ANTIPHON

KH
Ho- ly, ho - ly, ho- ly is the Tri- une God.

omit last strophe

O God, you are my God, I seek you;
my **soul** thirsts **for** you.
My flesh longs for you
  in a dry and **wast**ed land,
deprived **of** water. ANTIPHON

So in the sanctuary I have contemplated you
  to see your might and your **glo**ry.
Because your **stead**fast love is better than life,
  my lips will **praise** you.
So I will bless you **all** my life;
in your name I will raise **my** hands.

As with milk and rich food,
my soul **is** filled;
my **mouth** gives praise with joy**ful** lips.
I remember you up**on** my bed,
pondering you throughout **the** night.

For you were a help **for** me;
in the **shade** of your wings I **keep** singing.
My soul **clings** to you;
your right hand **up**holds me. ANTIPHON

But let those who seek my de**struc**tion
be **cast** into the depths of **the** earth.
Let them be given over to the power **of** the sword;
let them become a prey **for** jackals. ANTIPHON

Then the king shall rejoice **in** God.
All **those** who swear by God will **be** praised,
for the mouths of liars will **be** shut. ANTIPHON

Psalm Prayer
O God,
you reveal yourself in might and glory:
help us to know you, the triune God,
and ponder your great mystery.
We pray through Jesus Christ. **Amen.**

Psalm 150

ANTIPHON
KH
Al - le - lu - ia, al - le - lu - ia!

Praise God for **ho**liness;
praise God for the firmament **of** might.

Praise God for the mighty **deeds**;
praise God for unlimit**ed** greatness. ANTIPHON

Praise God with blast of **trumpet**;
praise God with lyre **and** harp.

Praise God with cymbal and **dance**;
praise God with strings **and** pipes. ANTIPHON

Praise God with resounding **drums**;
praise God with clamor**ous** drums.

Let all living **creatures**
praise **the** LORD. ANTIPHON

Psalm Prayer
Mighty God,
you are worthy of all praise and
all the heavens and all on the earth honor you:
help us to see your presence everywhere
as a sign of unity, for you are one God forever and ever. **Amen.**

Word of God

Benedictus
Blessed be the Lord God of **Israel**,
who visited and redeemed the **people**,
who raised up for us a **mighty** savior
from the house of **ser**vant David.

Just as the Lord spoke through the mouths of the holy prophets of **old**—
salvation comes out of the hands of our enemies and those who **hate** us,
that, with our ancestors, we might perform **works** of mercy,
remembering the holy covenant **sworn** to Abraham—

so does the Lord deliver us from the hands **of** our enemies,
that we might serve without fear before **the** Lord,
worshiping in **ho**liness
in righteousness **all** our days.

And you also, child, will be called a prophet of God Most **High**:
for you will go before the Lord to prepare a **way**,
bringing people knowledge of salvation by for**giveness** of sins;
because of the deep and tender mercy **of** our God.

Whereby a light rising from on high will **visit** us
to appear to those in darkness and in a shadow **of** death,
to guide our feet along a **straight**, sure path
into a **way** of peace.

INTERCESSIONS

Invocations

Cantor, then Assembly:

KH
Your stead - fast love is bet - ter than life.

Cantor:

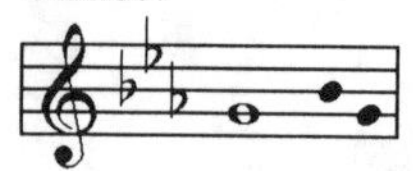

O triune God, you seek us to do **your** will ...
O triune God, you draw us to **your**self ...
O triune God, you help us spread the **Good** News ...
O triune God, you shade us from unright**eous** paths ...
O triune God, you keep **us** faithful ...
O triune God, you rejoice in **just** people ...
O triune God, you adorn your children **with** glory ...
O triune God, you honor all **your** faithful ...
O triune God, you reveal to us the strength **of** unity ...
O triune God, you bring **us** peace ...

Our Father ...

Prayer
O triune God,
your mystery is ineffable and
your majesty is glorious:
increase our faith and love
that we might one day live with you
in everlasting happiness. **Amen.**

CONCLUSION

Blessing
Bow your heads and pray for God's blessing.
May the Creator bless us. **Amen.**

May the Son protect us. **Amen.**
May the Spirit love us. **Amen.**
And may God bless us
in the name of the Father, and of the Son, and of the Holy Spirit. **Amen.**

Sign of Peace/Dismissal
Share with one another a sign of the peace and unity of the triune God.

Solemnity of the HOLY TRINITY Evening Prayer

LIGHT SERVICE

Proclamation of the Light

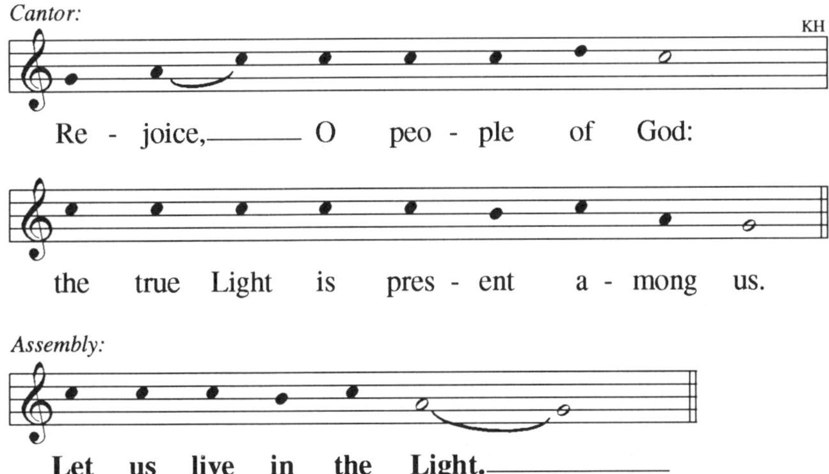
Cantor:
KH
Re - joice, O peo - ple of God:
the true Light is pres - ent a - mong us.
Assembly:
Let us live in the Light.

Festal Evening Hymn

Thanksgiving for the Light

Cantor:
KH
We praise and thank you, O won- drous Cre - a - tor.

Your pow - er lifts the great light in the heav - ens.
Your glo - ry shines forth in the ris - en Son.
Your maj - es - ty lies o - ver all of cre - a - tion.
Your splen - dor clothes us with dig - ni - ty
and hon - or. Your good - ness o - ver-comes an - y
weak - ness. Your boun-ty sat - is - fies all hun - ger.
Your grace pro - claims our des - ti - ny.
Re - joice, O ho - ly peo - ple, in this great Light:
it is our sure sal - va - tion and glo - rious free - dom.
As we cel - e - brate this fes - ti - val in hon - or of God's

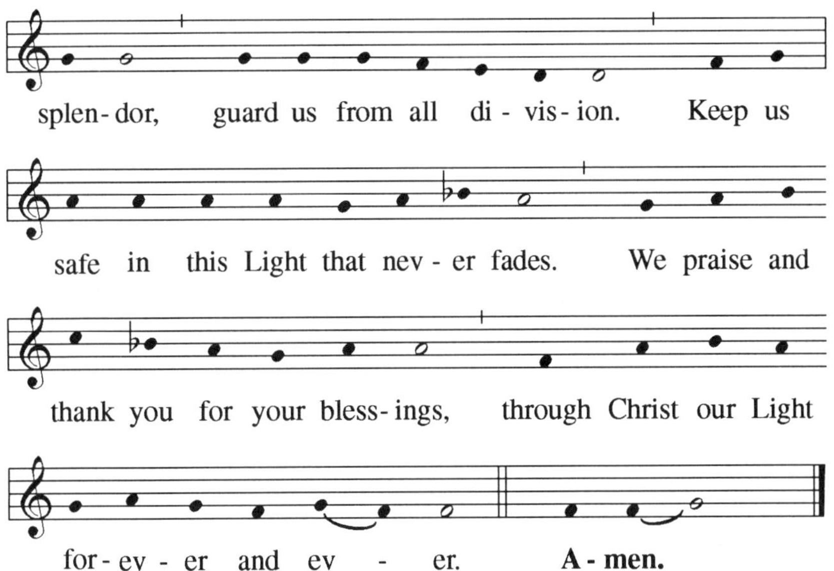
splen-dor, guard us from all di - vis - ion. Keep us
safe in this Light that nev - er fades. We praise and
thank you for your bless-ings, through Christ our Light
for - ev - er and ev - er. A - men.

PSALMODY

Psalm 110 *Of David. Psalm.*

ANTIPHON
KH
God rules in all and o - ver all.

Thus says the LORD **to** my lord:
"Sit on my right
  until I place your enemies
  as a footstool for **your** feet."
Let the LORD send from Zion
  the scepter of **your** strength.
Rule in the midst of **your** enemies. ANTIPHON

Your people bring free **of**ferings
on the day of your might
  in **holy** splendor.

From the womb **of** dawn,
a dew of rejuvenation comes **to** you. ANTIPHON

The LORD has promised
  and will **not** repent:
"According to my word,
  you are a priest forever, my king **of** justice."
The Lord is at **your** right,
who has smashed rulers on the day **of** wrath.

The Lord judges a**gainst** the nations,
piling them **with** corpses.
The Lord has smashed heads
  all over **the** land.
From a torrent the Lord drinks on the way,
  and rises up **in** triumph. ANTIPHON

Psalm Prayer
God of might and splendor,
you reveal the scepter of your strength to those who believe in you:
rise up in triumph and draw us in faith to you.
We pray through Jesus Christ
in the unity of the Holy Spirit, one God forever and ever. **Amen.**

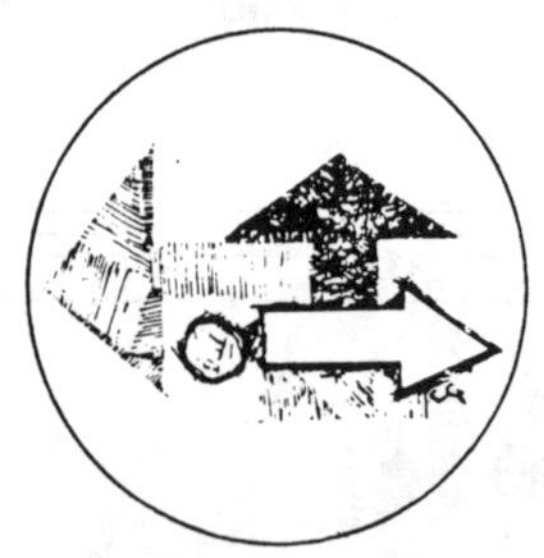

Psalm 111

ANTIPHON

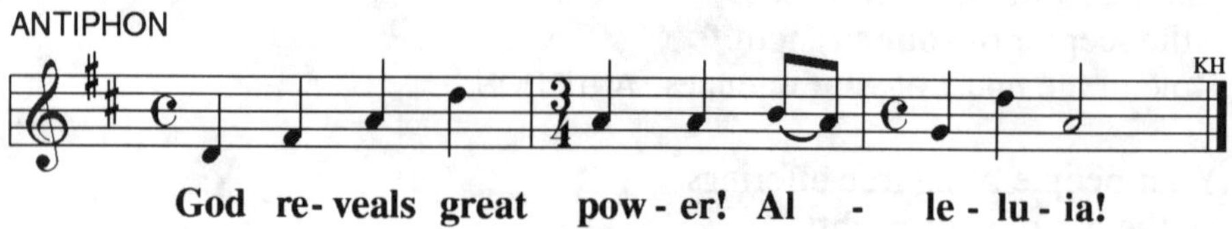

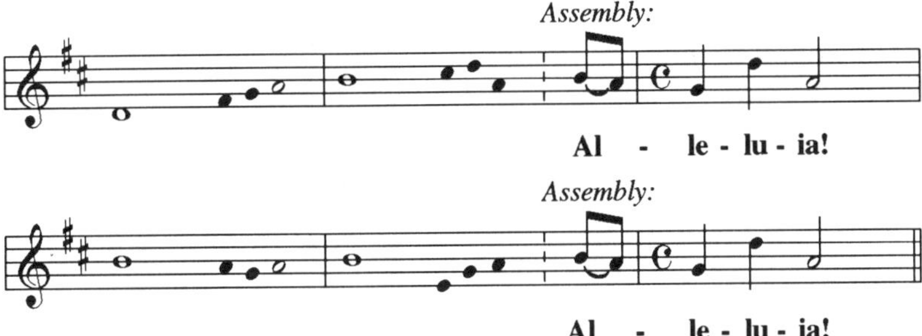
Assembly:
Al - le - lu - ia!
Assembly:
Al - le - lu - ia!

I will give thanks to the Lord with **all** my heart
in the council of the righteous and **the** assembly.
Great are the deeds **of** the Lord,
pondered by all who de**light** in them. ANTIPHON

God's work is majes**ty** and splendor,
and justice **stands** forever.
A memorial God has made **of** these wonders;
gracious and merciful **is** the Lord. ANTIPHON

God has given food to those **who** show reverence,
remembering the cove**nant** forever.
God has revealed to the people the power **of** these deeds
in giving them the nations **for** their heritage. ANTIPHON

The deeds of God's hands are **truth** and justice;
the precepts of God **all** are trustworthy.
They are established forev**er** and ever,
wrought in truth and eq**ui**ty. ANTIPHON

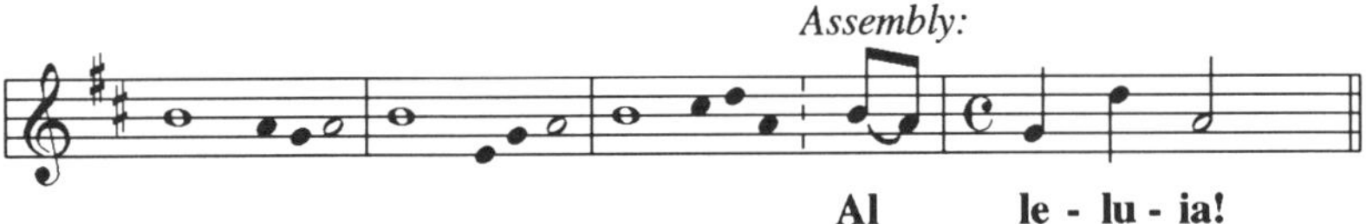
Assembly:
Al le - lu - ia!

God has sent deliverance **to** the people,
appointing the cove**nant** forever;
holy and to be revered **is** God's name.

The beginning of wisdom is reverence **for** the Lord,
and its practice brings about clear **un**derstanding. ANTIPHON
The praise of God **stands** forever! ANTIPHON

Psalm Prayer
God of majesty and splendor,

you are worthy of all thanks and praise:
hear our evening prayer in honor of your unity in diversity
so that our reverence for you
may bring us increased faith now and always. **Amen.**

Word of God

Magnificat
My soul does magni**fy** the Lord!
I delight in **God** my savior
who looked kindly **on** lowliness.

Now all ages will **call** me blessed
for the Mighty One **did** great things.
Holy is **God's** name;
mercy is from age to age for **those** in awe!

The Lord's strong arm did **might**y deeds:
confused the proud in **their** smug hearts;
toppled sovereigns **from** their thrones,
and exalted **hum**ble ones;
filled the hungering with **good** things,
and sent the rich **a**way empty.

The Lord helped servant **Is**rael
to re**mem**ber mercy,
as was spoken to Ab**ra**ham
and his descendants for**e**vermore!

INTERCESSIONS

Petitions

Cantor, then Assembly:

KH
Praise and thanks- giv - ing to our Tri- une God.

Cantor:

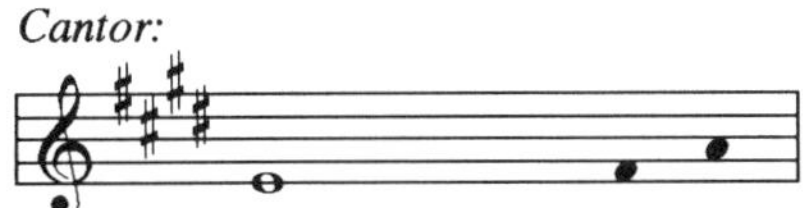

For **great** power,
For heal**ing** strength,
For ho**ly** splendor,
For creating a priest**ly** people,
For everlast**ing** triumph,
For right**eous** mercy,
For delight**ful** deeds,
For age**less** covenant,
For a bounti**ful** heritage,
For trustwor**thy** precepts,
For mighty **de**liverance,
For a victorious **right** hand,
For acceptance of the faithful **de**parted,

Our Father ...

Prayer
O God,
you give us great joy
as we celebrate the festival of your triune majesty:
help us to recognize your presence in diverse ways
and to protect us from all that may lead us astray.
We pray through Jesus Christ
in the unity of the Holy Spirit, one God forever and ever. **Amen.**

CONCLUSION

Blessing
Bow your heads and pray for God's blessing.
May the Creator bless us. **Amen.**
May the Son protect us. **Amen.**
May the Spirit love us. **Amen.**
And may God bless us
in the name of the Father, and of the Son, and of the Holy Spirit. **Amen.**

Sign of Peace/Dismissal
Share with one another a sign of the peace and unity of our triune God.

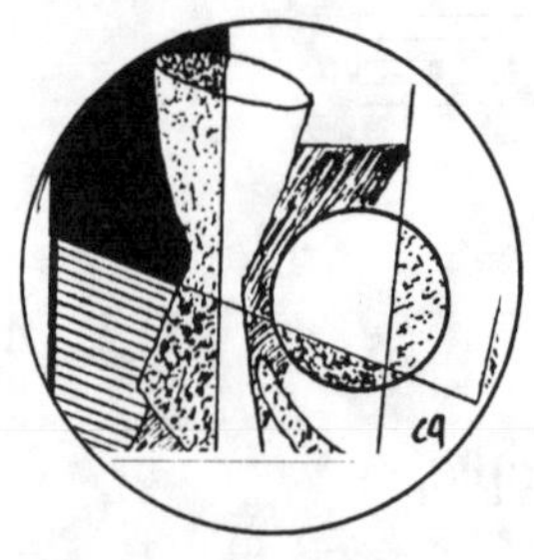
cg

Second Sunday after Pentecost

Solemnity of the BODY AND BLOOD OF CHRIST Morning Praise

FESTAL MORNING HYMN

PSALMODY

Psalm 126 *Song of ascents (pilgrimages).*

ANTIPHON

KH
God's boun - ty is lav - ish.

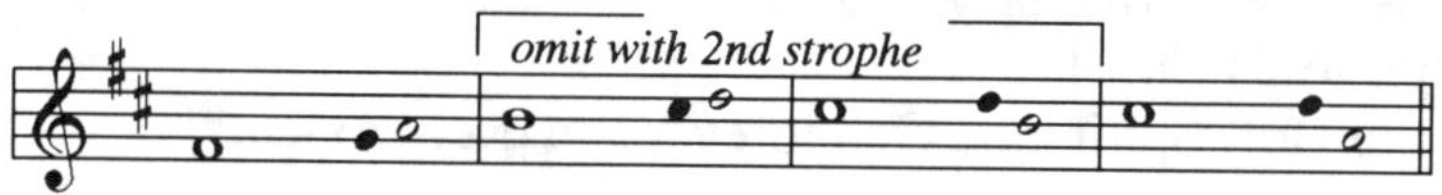
omit with 2nd strophe

When the LORD accompanied
those who returned to Zion,
we were **like** dreamers.
Then our mouth
was filled with laughter
and our tongue **with** joy.
Then it was said a**mong** nations:
"The LORD has done great
deeds among **these** people." ANTIPHON

The LORD has done great
deeds **among** us.
Now we **re**joice. ANTIPHON

Return our captives, O LORD,
  like torrents in **the** Negeb.
Those who sow in tears
  harvest with shouts **of** joy.
Indeed, the one who goes out weeping,
  carrying the bag **of** seed,
comes back joyful,
  carrying **the** sheaves. ANTIPHON

Psalm Prayer
God our refreshment and nourishment,
you accompany our journey as your pilgrim people:
sow in us the seeds of rejoicing and
harvest in us the promise of everlasting life.
We pray through Jesus Christ, the Bread of Life. **Amen.**

Psalm 148

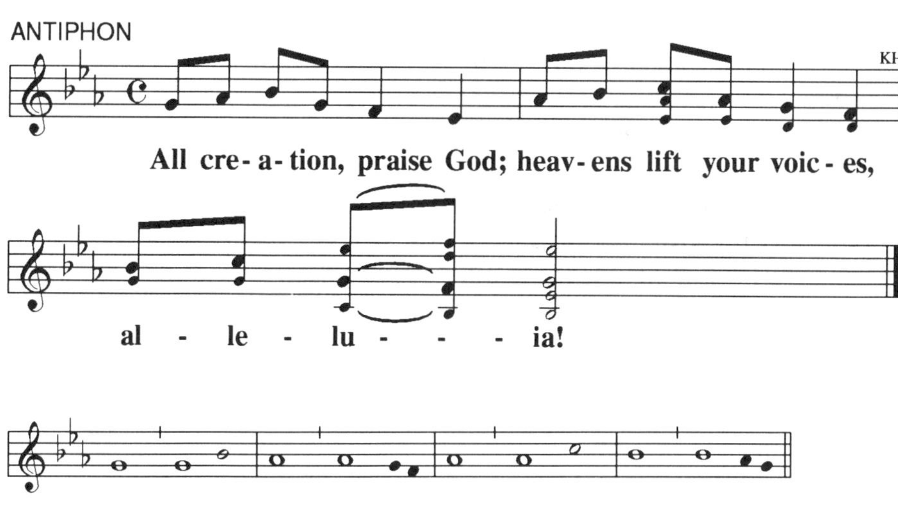

ANTIPHON
KH
All cre- a- tion, praise God; heav- ens lift your voic - es,
al - le - lu - - - ia!

Praise the LORD from the heavens:
  praise God in the **highest**,
praise God, O you messengers,
  praise God, O **you** hosts,
praise God, sun and moon,
  praise God, all shining **stars**
praise God, farthest heavens
  and waters from above **the** heavens. ANTIPHON

Let them praise the name of the **Lord**,
who commanded and they were **cre**ated,
who established them forever and **ever**,
fixing a limit that they can**not** cross. ANTIPHON

Praise the Lord from the earth:
  sea monsters and all deep **waters**,
fire and hail,
  snow and frost,
  stormy winds fulfilling **God's** word,
mountains and all hills,
  fruit trees and all **cedars**,
living creatures and all cattle,
  reptiles and fly**ing** birds. ANTIPHON

Rulers of the earth and all nations,
  nobles and all judges of the **earth**,
youthful men and women,
  elderly and **young** people:
let them praise the Lord,
  for God's name only is most **high**.
God's glory is above earth and heaven;
  God will act mightily for **the** people. ANTIPHON

Praise from all the **faithful**,
from the children of Is**ra**el,
the people close to **God**!
Alle**lu**ia!

Psalm Prayer

O God,
you are worthy of all praise from the heavens and all the earth:
hear our prayer of jubilation
that we may rejoice in your Son's gift of his Body and Blood
now and always. **Amen.**

Word of God

Benedictus
Blessed be the Lord God of **Israel**,
who visited and redeemed the **people**,
who raised up for us a **mighty** savior
from the house of **ser**vant David.

Just as the Lord spoke through the mouths of the holy prophets of **old**—
salvation comes out of the hands of our enemies and those who **hate** us,
that, with our ancestors, we might perform **works** of mercy,
remembering the holy covenant **sworn** to Abraham—

so does the Lord deliver us from the hands **of** our enemies,
that we might serve without fear before **the** Lord,
worshiping in **ho**liness
and in righteousness **all** our days.

And you also, child, will be called a prophet of God Most **High**:
for you will go before the Lord to prepare a **way**,
bringing people knowledge of salvation by for**giveness** of sins;
because of the deep and tender mercy **of** our God.

Whereby a light rising from on high will **vis**it us
to appear to those in darkness and in a shadow **of** death,
to guide our feet along a **straight**, sure path
into a **way** of peace.

INTERCESSIONS

Invocations

Cantor, then Assembly:

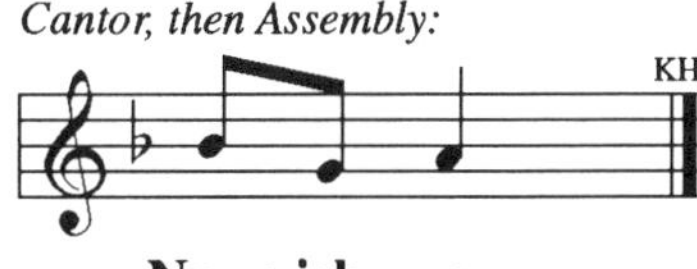

Cantor:

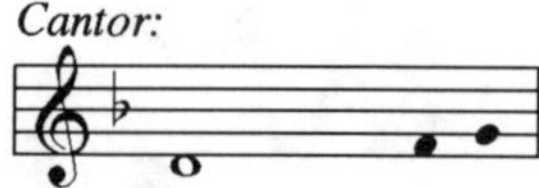

Jesus, origin **of** Life ...
Jesus, source of **re**joicing ...
Jesus, font **of** holiness ...
Jesus, refuge **of** captives ...
Jesus, protector of **the** poor ...
Jesus, sower of seeds **of** hope ...
Jesus, justice for **the** nations ...
Jesus, hope for **the** world ...
Jesus, feast for **our** souls ...

Our Father ...

Prayer
O God,
your Son gave us his Body and Blood
to eat and drink as everlasting nourishment:
grant us fullness of your Life and presence
now and forever. **Amen.**

CONCLUSION

Blessing
Bow your heads and pray for God's blessing.
May the God of abundance satisfy all hunger. **Amen.**
May the Christ of salvation anoint us with compassion. **Amen.**
May the Spirit of love fill us with peace. **Amen.**
And may God bless us
in the name of the Father, and of the Son, and of the Holy Spirit. **Amen.**

Sign of Peace/Dismissal
Share with one another a sign of the peace and love of God.

Solemnity of the BODY AND BLOOD OF CHRIST Evening Prayer

LIGHT SERVICE

Proclamation of the Light

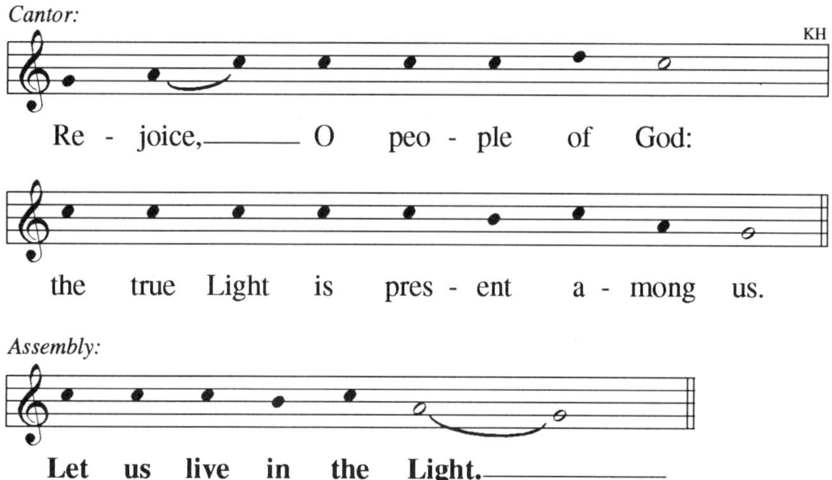
Cantor:
KH
Re - joice, O peo - ple of God:
the true Light is pres - ent a - mong us.
Assembly:
Let us live in the Light.

Festal Evening Hymn

Thanksgiving for the Light

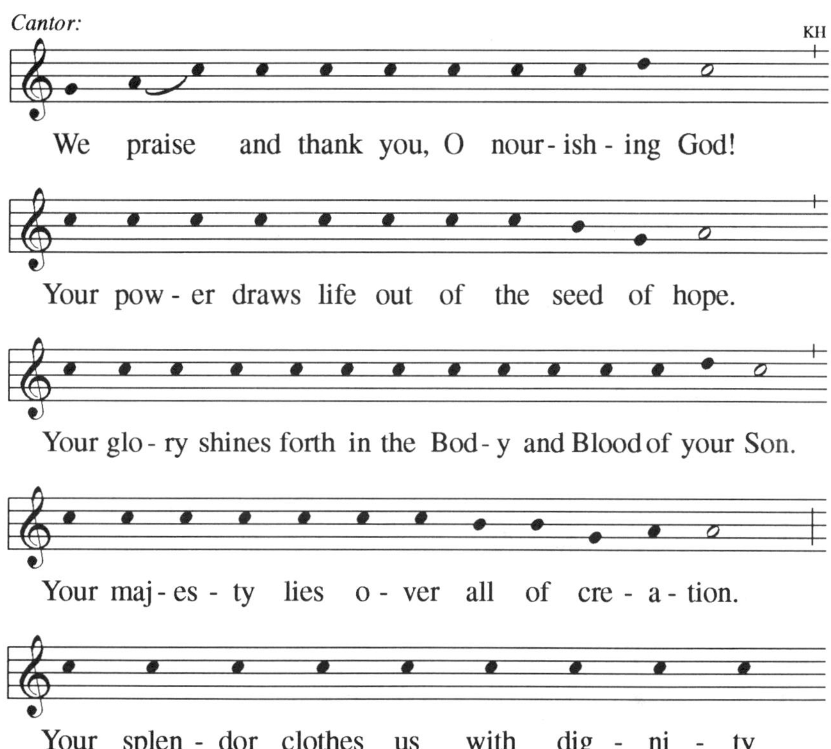
Cantor:
KH
We praise and thank you, O nour - ish - ing God!
Your pow - er draws life out of the seed of hope.
Your glo - ry shines forth in the Bod - y and Blood of your Son.
Your maj - es - ty lies o - ver all of cre - a - tion.
Your splen - dor clothes us with dig - ni - ty

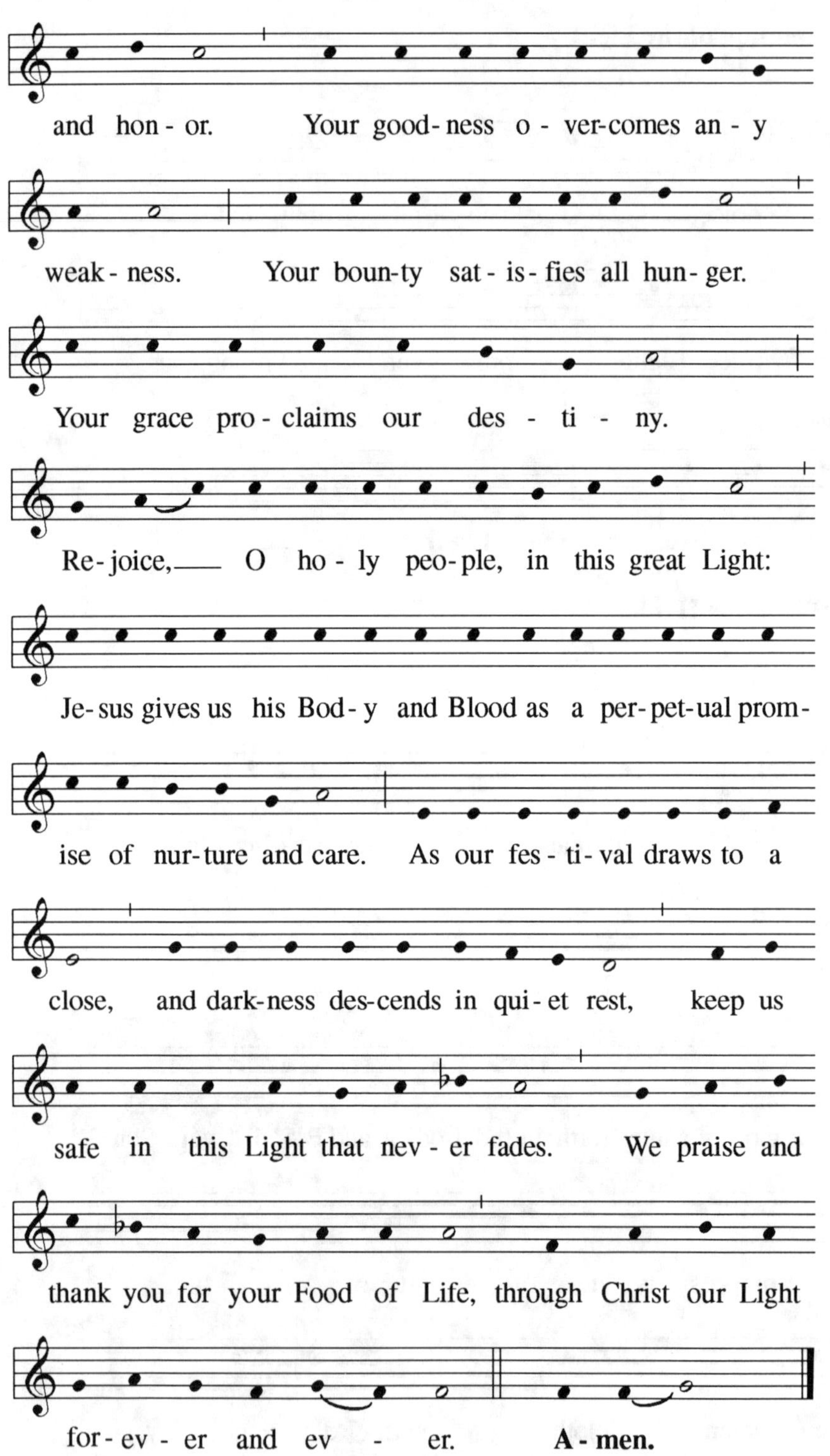
and hon - or. Your good - ness o - ver-comes an - y
weak - ness. Your boun-ty sat - is - fies all hun - ger.
Your grace pro - claims our des - ti - ny.
Re - joice, O ho - ly peo - ple, in this great Light:
Je - sus gives us his Bod - y and Blood as a per - pet - ual prom -
ise of nur - ture and care. As our fes - ti - val draws to a
close, and dark - ness des - cends in qui - et rest, keep us
safe in this Light that nev - er fades. We praise and
thank you for your Food of Life, through Christ our Light
for - ev - er and ev - er. A - men.

PSALMODY

Psalm 80 *To the choirmaster. "On lilies." Testimony. Of Asaf. Psalm.*

ANTIPHON
KH
Let your face shine that we may be saved.

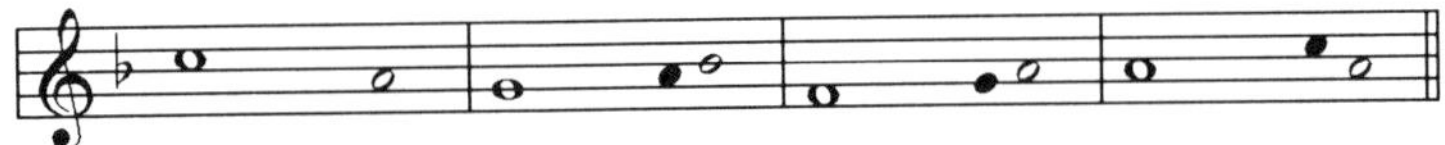

Give ear, O Shepherd of Israel,
 you who lead Joseph like a **flock**;
you who are enthroned on the cherubim,
 shine forth.
Before Ephraim, Benjamin and **Ma**nasseh,
arouse your strength
 and come to **save** us!

Cantor:
to Ant.
Bring us back, O God:

O LORD God of hosts,
 how long will you be angry
 in spite of the prayer of your **peo**ple?
You feed them with the bread of tears;
 you give them tears to drink in tri**ple** measure.
You set us up as an object of contention for **our** neighbors,
and our enemies have reasons to laugh among **them**selves.

Cantor:
to Ant.
Bring us back, O God of hosts:

You have plucked out a vine from **Egypt**.
You have expelled nations and plant**ed** it.
You have cleared the ground **for** it
so that it may take root
 and fill **the** land.

The mountains are covered with its **shade**
and the highest cedars with **its** branches.

It sends its branches to **the** sea
and its shoots to **the** river.

Why did you break down its **fences**
so that those who pass by on the way **can** pluck it?
The boar from the forest **de**vours it
and the animals of the fields eat **it** up.

Turn back, O God of hosts;
  look down from heaven and **see.**
Look after this vine,
  the stock your right hand has planted,
  on account of the one you made strong for **your**self.
Like filth, they burned it **with** fire;
let them perish by the rebuke of **your** face.

Let your hand be on the one at your right **hand**,
the one you made strong for **your**self.
Then we will not depart **from** you.
Give us life, and in your name we **shall** pray.

Cantor:
to Ant.
Bring us back, O Lord God of hosts:

Psalm Prayer
Tender God,
you plant a vine and nurture it with your own Son's Blood:
let your hand be upon us that we may be strong
in faith and steadfast in love.
We pray through Jesus Christ. **Amen.**

Psalm 116

ANTIPHON
KH
We take up the cup of sal - va - tion.

I love the LORD
  who **has** heard
the voice of my supplic**a**tions.
For God has turned an ear **to** me
as I cry all **my** days. ANTIPHON

Deadly chains have fettered me,
  and the anguish of Sheol has reached up **to** me.
Distress and terror, I have en**countered**;
but I have called on the name of **the** LORD.
How long, O LORD?
  Deliver **my** soul. ANTIPHON

The LORD is gracious and just;
  our God **is** merciful.
The LORD is the protector of the **innocent**;
I was poor and God brought salvation **to** me.
Return, O my soul, to your rest,
  for the LORD has done good **to** you. ANTIPHON

For you have delivered my soul **from** death,
my eye from tears and my foot from **stumbling**,
that I may walk in the presence of **the** LORD
in the land of **the** living. ANTIPHON

Yes, I was right **in** saying,
"I am greatly af**flicted**."
In my agitation, I **have** said,
"Every human being is **a** liar." ANTIPHON

What shall I return to the LORD
  for all the bounty in **my** favor?
I will lift up the cup of salvation
  and I will call on the name of the **LORD**.
Indeed, I will fulfill my promises to **the** LORD
in the presence of all **the** people. ANTIPHON

Precious in the eyes of the LORD
  is the death of **the** faithful ones.
How long, O **LORD**?
For I am your servant,
  I am your servant, the offspring of **your** handmaid.
You have loosened **my** bonds. ANTIPHON

To you I will offer a sacrifice of thanksgiving
and I will call on the name of **the** LORD.
Indeed, I will fulfill my promises to the LORD
in the presence of all the **people**,
in the courts of the house of **the** LORD,
in your midst, O Jerusalem.
Alle**lu**ia! ANTIPHON

Psalm Prayer
O God,
you offer us the cup of salvation:
receive our thanksgiving sacrifice
that we may stand in your courts
now and forever. **Amen.**

Word of God

Magnificat
My soul does magni**fy** the Lord!
I delight in **God** my savior
who looked kindly **on** lowliness.

Now all ages will **call** me blessed
for the Mighty One **did** great things.
Holy is **God's** name;
mercy is from age to age for **those** in awe!

The Lord's strong arm did **might**y deeds:
confused the proud in **their** smug hearts;
toppled sovereigns **from** their thrones,
and exalted **hum**ble ones;
filled the hungering with **good** things,
and sent the rich **a**way empty.

The Lord helped servant **Is**rael
to re**mem**ber mercy,
as was spoken to Ab**ra**ham
and his descendants for**e**vermore!

INTERCESSIONS

Petitions

Cantor, then Assembly:

Bod - y and Blood of Christ, save us.

Cantor:

Jesus shep**herds** his people ...
Jesus shines his **face** upon us ...
Jesus **is** the true vine ...
Jesus **is** the leavened wheat ...
Jesus strengthens **those** who call on him ...
Jesus gives **Life** as nourishment ...
Jesus **breaks** the chains of death ...
Jesus delivers us from dis**tress** and terror ...
Jesus **is** the Bread of Life ...
Jesus is the Cup **of** Salvation ...
Jesus receives the faith**ful** departed ...

Our Father ...

Prayer

O God of redemption,
your Son's sacred Body and precious Blood
is our strength and our nourishment:
help us to remain faithful to our baptismal promises
and to live in the unity of the Body of Christ now and always. **Amen.**

CONCLUSION

Blessing

Bow your heads and pray for God's blessing.
May the Body of Christ nourish us. **Amen.**
May the Blood of Christ refresh us. **Amen.**
And may God bless us
in the name of the Father, and of the Son, and of the Holy Spirit. **Amen.**

Sign of Peace/Dismissal

Turn to one another as members of the one Body of Christ
and offer a sign of peace.

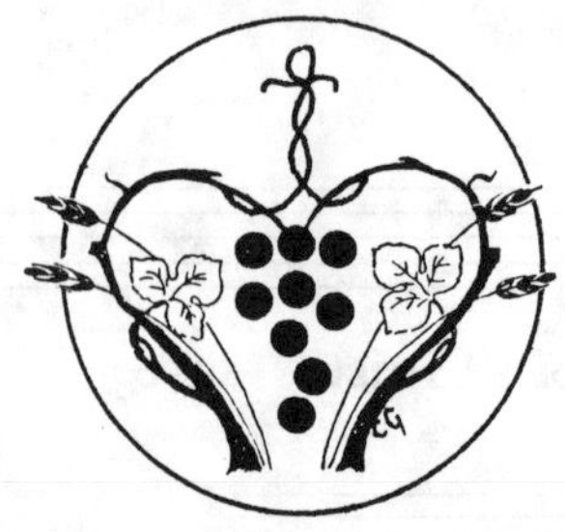

Friday after the Second Sunday after Pentecost
Solemnity of the SACRED HEART
Morning Praise

FESTAL MORNING HYMN

PSALMODY

Psalm 51 *To the choirmaster. Psalm of David. In the coming to him of Nathan the prophet, after David had been with Bathsheba.*

Be gracious to **me**, O God,
in your **stead**fast love.
According to the abundance **of** your mercy
blot out my **trans**gressions. ANTIPHON

Cleanse me completely **from** my guilt
and purify me **from** my sin.
For my transgressions I do **rec**ognize,
and my sin stands always **be**fore me.

Against you alone **have** I sinned,
and what is evil in your eyes **I** have done.
Thus you may be declared just in your ways,
  and pure **in** your judgments.
Indeed, I was born guilty,
  already a sinner when my mother **con**ceived me. ANTIPHON

Surely in truth **you** delight,
and deep within my self you will **teach** me wisdom.
Cleanse me from my sin with hyssop and I **will** be pure,
wash me and I shall be brighter **than** snow.

Let me hear glad**ness** and joy,
let the bones you **broke** exult.
Turn your face **from** my sins
and blot out all my iniq**ui**ties. ANTIPHON

Create in me a pure **heart**, O God,
and renew within me **a** firm spirit.
Do not dismiss me **from** your presence,
and do not take away from me your ho**ly** spirit.

Give me back the joy of **your** salvation,
and let a willing spirit lie **o**ver me.
I will teach transgres**sors** your ways,
and sinners will turn back **to** you. ANTIPHON

Deliver me from bloodshed, O God,
  God of **my** salvation,
and my tongue will **sing** your justice.
O Lord, o**pen** my lips,
and my mouth will tell **your** praise.

For you take no pleasure in **sac**rifice,
and you would not accept an offering were **I** to give it.
The perfect sacrifice for God is a **brok**en spirit.
A broken and humble heart,
  O God, you will not **de**spise. ANTIPHON

In your kindness bring prosperi**ty** to Zion;
rebuild the walls of Je**ru**salem.
Then you can delight in sacrifices of justice,
  burnt and complete **of**ferings;
then bulls can be offered on **your** altars. ANTIPHON

Psalm Prayer
O Sacred Heart of Jesus,
your love sustains us even in our transgressions:
wash us brighter than snow
and restore us to your favor now and forever. **Amen.**

Word of God

Benedictus
Blessed be the Lord God of **Israel**,
who visited and redeemed the **people**,
who raised up for us a **mighty** savior
from the house of **ser**vant David.

Just as the Lord spoke through the mouths of the holy prophets of **old**—
salvation comes out of the hands of our enemies and those who **hate** us,
that, with our ancestors, we might perform **works** of mercy,
remembering the holy covenant **sworn** to Abraham—

so does the Lord deliver us from the hands **of** our enemies,
that we might serve without fear before **the** Lord,
worshiping in **ho**liness
and in righteousness **all** our days.

And you also, child, will be called a prophet of God Most **High**:
for you will go before the Lord to prepare a **way**,
bringing people knowledge of salvation by for**giveness** of sins;
because of the deep and tender mercy **of** our God.

Whereby a light rising from on high will **vis**it us
to appear to those in darkness and in a shadow **of** death,
to guide our feet along a **straight**, sure path
into a **way** of peace.

INTERCESSIONS

Invocations

Cantor, then Assembly in canon:

1.
2.
KH
Hear___ our prayer, O God.___
one or two voices
Hear,___ O God.

Cantor:

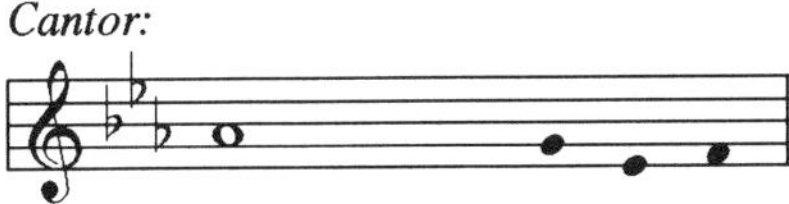

O Sacred Heart, **source** of mercy ...
O Sacred Heart, **source** of forgiveness ...
O Sacred Heart, **source** of compassion ...
O Sacred Heart, **source** of healing ...
O Sacred Heart, **source** of strength ...
O Sacred Heart, **source** of courage ...
O Sacred Heart, **source** of light ...
O Sacred Heart, **source** of life ...
O Sacred Heart, **source** of tenderness ...
O Sacred Heart, **source** of peace ...

Our Father ...

Prayer
Loving-kind God,
you show us mercy and compassion, truth and wisdom:
help us to receive the depths of your great love.
May our festival honoring your Sacred Heart
restore to us a clean heart now and always. **Amen.**

CONCLUSION

Blessing
Bow your heads and pray for God's blessing.
May God, the source of love, bless us. **Amen.**
May the Son, the source of tenderness, bless us. **Amen.**
May the Spirit, the source of gentleness, bless us. **Amen.**
And may God bless us
in the name of the Father, and of the Son, and of the Holy Spirit. **Amen.**

Sign of Peace/Dismissal
Let us share a sign of peace that we might go forth hand-in-hand with our loving God.

Solemnity of the SACRED HEART Evening Prayer

LIGHT SERVICE

Proclamation of the Light

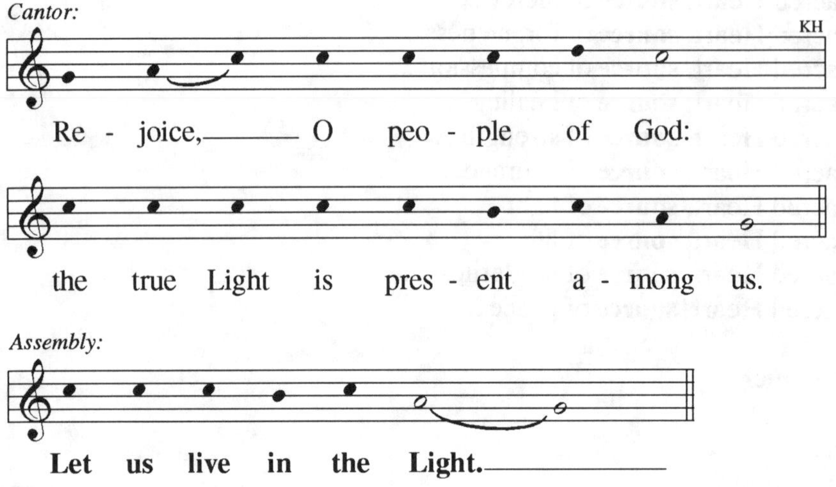
Cantor:
KH
Re - joice, O peo - ple of God:
the true Light is pres - ent a - mong us.
Assembly:
Let us live in the Light.

Festal Evening Hymn

Thanksgiving for the Light

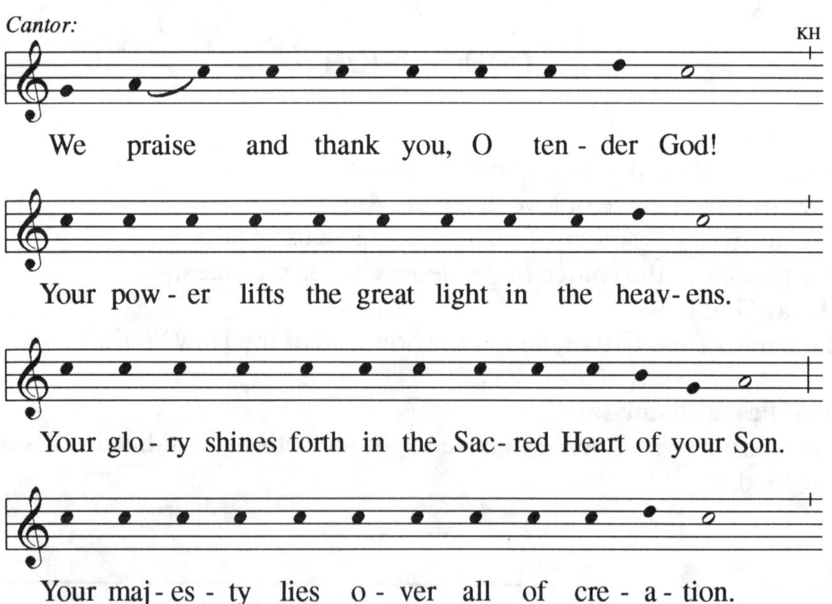
Cantor:
KH
We praise and thank you, O ten - der God!
Your pow - er lifts the great light in the heav - ens.
Your glo - ry shines forth in the Sac - red Heart of your Son.
Your maj - es - ty lies o - ver all of cre - a - tion.

Your splen - dor clothes us with dig - ni - ty
and hon - or. Your good- ness o - ver- comes an - y
weak - ness. Your boun-ty sat - is- fies all hun- ger.
Your grace pro - claims our des - ti - ny.
Re- joice, O ho - ly peo- ple, in this great Light:
God's ten - der mer - cy en - a - bles it to shine al-ways
and ev - 'ry - where. As our fes - ti - val draws to a
close, and dark-ness des-cends in qui - et rest, keep us
safe in this Light that nev - er fades. We praise and
thank you for your bless- ings, through the Heart of your Son

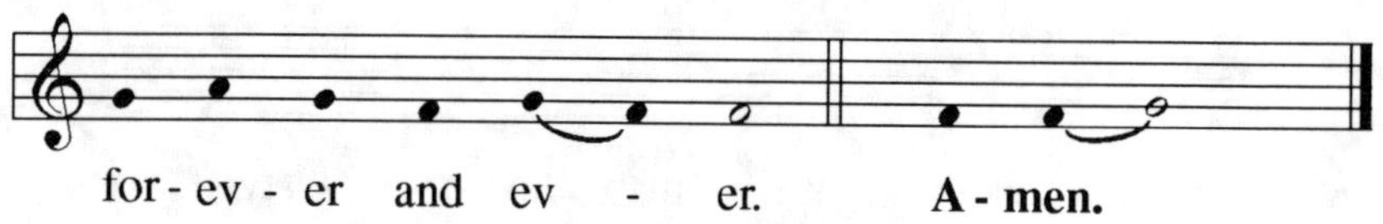
for - ev - er and ev - er.
A - men.

PSALMODY

Psalm 110 *Of David. Psalm.*

ANTIPHON

KH
From the womb of dawn God's love o - ver - flows.

Thus says the LORD **to** my lord:
"Sit on my right
  until I place your enemies
  as a footstool for **your** feet."
Let the LORD send from Zion
  the scepter of **your** strength.
Rule in the midst of **your** enemies. ANTIPHON

Your people bring free **of**ferings
on the day of your might
  in ho**ly** splendor.
From the womb **of** dawn,
a dew of rejuvenation comes **to** you. ANTIPHON

The LORD has promised
  and will **not** repent:
"According to my word,
  you are a priest forever, my king **of** justice."
The Lord is at **your** right,
who has smashed rulers on the day **of** wrath.

The Lord judges a**gainst** the nations,
piling them **with** corpses.
The Lord has smashed heads
  all over **the** land.
From a torrent the Lord drinks on the way,
  and rises up **in** triumph. ANTIPHON

Psalm Prayer
God of might and splendor,
you reveal your great love to those who believe in you:
draw us to your Son's Sacred Heart
that we may pour forth your gentle tenderness on others.
We pray through Jesus Christ
in the unity of the Holy Spirit, one God forever and ever. **Amen.**

Psalm 111

ANTIPHON

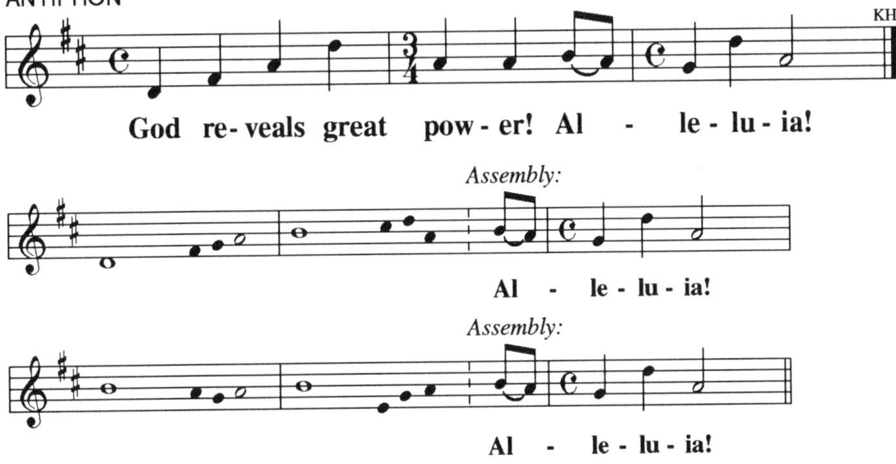
KH
God re- veals great pow - er! Al - le - lu - ia!
Assembly:
Al - le - lu - ia!
Assembly:
Al - le - lu - ia!

I will give thanks to the LORD with **all** my heart
in the council of the righteous and **the** assembly.
Great are the deeds **of** the LORD,
pondered by all who de**light** in them. ANTIPHON

God's work is majes**ty** and splendor,
and justice **stands** forever.
A memorial God has made **of** these wonders;
gracious and merciful **is** the LORD. ANTIPHON

God has given food to those **who** show reverence,
remembering the cove**nant** forever.
God has revealed to the people the power **of** these deeds
in giving them the nations **for** their heritage. ANTIPHON

The deeds of God's hands are **truth** and justice;
the precepts of God **all** are trustworthy.
They are established fore**ver** and ever,
wrought in truth and eq**uity**. ANTIPHON

God has sent deliverance **to** the people,
appointing the cove**nant** forever;
holy and to be revered **is** God's name.

The beginning of wisdom is reverence **for** the LORD,
and its practice brings about clear **un**derstanding. ANTIPHON
The praise of God **stands** forever! ANTIPHON

Psalm Prayer
God of majesty and splendor,
you are worthy of all thanks and praise:
hear our evening prayer in honor of your Son's Sacred Heart
so that our reverence for you
may bring us increased faith now and always. **Amen.**

Word of God

Magnificat
My soul does magni**fy** the Lord!
I delight in **God** my savior
who looked kindly **on** lowliness.

Now all ages will **call** me blessed
for the Mighty One **did** great things.
Holy is **God's** name;
mercy is from age to age for **those** in awe!

The Lord's strong arm did **might**y deeds:
confused the proud in **their** smug hearts;
toppled sovereigns **from** their thrones,
and exalted **hum**ble ones;
filled the hungering with **good** things,
and sent the rich **a**way empty.

The Lord helped servant **Is**rael
to re**mem**ber mercy,
as was spoken to Abra**ham**
and his descendants fore**ver**more!

INTERCESSIONS

Petitions

Cantor, then Assembly:

Cantor:

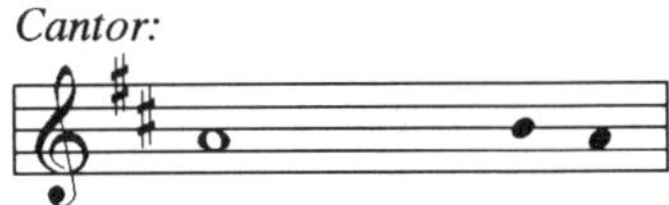

For great **pow**er,
For **heal**ing strength,
For holy **splen**dor,
For creating a priestly **peo**ple,
For everlasting **tri**umph,
For right**eous** mercy,
For de**light**ful deeds,
For ageless **cove**nant,
For a bountiful **herit**age,
For trustworthy **pre**cepts,
For mighty de**liver**ance,
For a victorious **right** hand,
For acceptance of the faithful de**part**ed,

Our Father ...

Prayer
O God,
you give us great joy
as we celebrate the festival of your Son's Sacred Heart:
help us to recognize your presence in the tender love you show
and to protect us from all that may lead us astray.
We pray through Jesus Christ. **Amen.**

CONCLUSION

Blessing
Bow your heads and pray for God's blessing.
May the Creator bless us. **Amen.**
May the Son protect us. **Amen.**
May the Spirit love us. **Amen.**

And may God bless us
in the name of the Father, and of the Son, and of the Holy Spirit. **Amen.**

Sign of Peace/Dismissal
Share with one another a sign of the peace and love of the heart of Christ.

May 3
Feast of PHILIP & JAMES, Apostles
Morning Praise

FESTAL MORNING HYMN

PSALMODY

Psalm 63 *Psalm of David. While he was in the desert of Judah.*

Solo 1 O God, you are my God, I seek you;
my soul thirsts for you.
My flesh longs for you
in a dry and wasted land,
deprived of water.

Solo 2 So in the sanctuary I have contemplated you
to see your might and your glory.
Because your steadfast love is better than life,
my lips will praise you.
So I will bless you all my life;
in your name I will raise my hands.
As with milk and rich food,
my soul is filled;
my mouth gives praise with joyful lips.
I remember you upon my bed,
pondering you throughout the night.
For you were a help for me;
in the shade of your wings I keep singing.
My soul clings to you;
your right hand upholds me.

Solo 1 But let those who seek my destruction
be cast into the depths of the earth.

Let them be given over to the power of the sword;
let them become a prey for jackals.

All Then the king shall rejoice in God.
All those who swear by God will be praised,
for the mouths of liars will be shut.

Psalm 149

All Alleluia!

Choir 1 Sing a new song to the LORD,
God's praise in the assembly of the faithful.
Let Israel rejoice in its Creator,
the children of Zion exult in their Sovereign.
Let them praise God's name with dancing;
with drums and harp, let them play music for God.

Choir 2 For the LORD takes delight in the people,
adorning the poor with salvation.
Let the faithful exult with glory,
let them ring out joy on their couches,
and cry out the great deeds of God from their throats.

Choir 1 With two-edged swords in their hands,
let them do vengeance against peoples
and rebuke nations;
let them tie their rulers with fetters
and their nobles with chains of bronze,
in order to accomplish judgment against them as written.
This is honor for all the faithful.

All Alleluia!

Word of God

Benedictus
Blessed be the Lord God of **Israel**,
who visited and redeemed the **people**,
who raised up for us a **mighty** savior
from the house of **ser**vant David.

Just as the Lord spoke through the mouths of the holy prophets of **old**—
salvation comes out of the hands of our enemies and those who **hate** us,
that, with our ancestors, we might perform **works** of mercy,
remembering the holy covenant **sworn** to Abraham—

so does the Lord deliver us from the hands **of** our enemies,
that we might serve without fear before **the** Lord,
worshiping in **ho**liness
and in righteousness **all** our days.

And you also, child, will be called a prophet of God Most **High**:
for you will go before the Lord to prepare a **way**,
bringing people knowledge of salvation by for**giveness** of sins;
because of the deep and tender mercy **of** our God.

Whereby a light rising from on high will **vis**it us
to appear to those in darkness and in a shadow **of** death,
to guide our feet along a **straight**, sure path
into a **way** of peace.

INTERCESSIONS

Invocations

Cantor, then Assembly:

KH
Your stead - fast love is bet - ter than life.

Cantor:

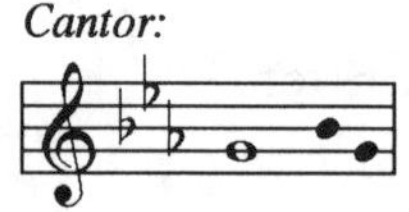

O risen Christ, you seek us for **your** service ...
O risen Christ, you draw us to **your**self ...
O risen Christ, you help us spread the **Good** News ...
O risen Christ, you shade us from **dis**couragement ...
O risen Christ, you keep **us** faithful ...
O risen Christ, you rejoice in your **dis**ciples ...
O risen Christ, you adorn your disciples **with** glory ...
O risen Christ, you honor all **your** faithful ...

Our Father ...

Prayer
Gracious God,
you called Philip and James to be in the company of your apostles:
as they looked upon your Son with faith,
open our eyes to the splendor of the resurrection
that we might seek you now and always. **Amen.**

CONCLUSION

Blessing
May the God of salvation bless us
in the name of the Father, and of the Son, and of the Holy Spirit. **Amen.**

Dismissal
Go forth to be disciples of Christ. **Thanks be to God.**

Feast of PHILIP & JAMES, Apostles Evening Prayer

FESTAL EVENING HYMN

PSALMODY

Psalm 116

Solo 1 I love the LORD
who has heard
the voice of my supplications.
For God has turned an ear to me
as I cry all my days.

Solo 2 Deadly chains have fettered me,
and the anguish of Sheol has reached up to me.
Distress and terror, I have encountered;
but I have called on the name of the LORD.
How long, O LORD?
Deliver my soul.

All The LORD is gracious and just;
our God is merciful.

Solo 1 The LORD is the protector of the innocent;
I was poor and God brought salvation to me.
Return, O my soul, to your rest,
for the LORD has done good to you.

Solo 2 For you have delivered my soul from death,
my eye from tears
and my foot from stumbling,
that I may walk in the presence of the LORD
in the land of the living.

Solo 1 Yes, I was right in saying,
"I am greatly afflicted."
In my agitation, I have said,
"Every human being is a liar."

Solo 2 What shall I return to the LORD
for all the bounty in my favor?
I will lift up the cup of salvation
and I will call on the name of the LORD.
Indeed, I will fulfill my promises to the LORD
in the presence of all the people.

All Precious in the eyes of the LORD
is the death of the faithful ones.

Solo 1 How long, O LORD?
For I am your servant,
I am your servant, the offspring of your handmaid.
You have loosened my bonds.

Solo 2 To you I will offer a sacrifice of thanksgiving
and I will call on the name of the LORD.
Indeed, I will fulfill my promises to the LORD
in the presence of all the people,
in the courts of the house of the LORD,
in your midst, O Jerusalem.

All Alleluia!

Psalm 126 *Song of ascents (pilgrimages).*

Choir 1 When the LORD accompanied

those who returned to Zion,
we were like dreamers.
Then our mouth
was filled with laughter
and our tongue with joy.
Then it was said among nations:
"The LORD has done great
deeds among these people."

All The LORD has done great
deeds among us.
Now we rejoice.

Choir 2 Return our captives, O LORD,
like torrents in the Negeb.
Those who sow in tears
harvest with shouts of joy.
Indeed, one goes out weeping,
carrying the bag of seed,
and comes back joyful,
carrying the sheaves.

Word of God

Magnificat
My soul does magni**fy** the Lord!
I delight in **God** my savior
who looked kindly **on** lowliness.

Now all ages will **call** me blessed
for the Mighty One **did** great things.
Holy is **God's** name;
mercy is from age to age for **those** in awe!

The Lord's strong arm did **migh**ty deeds:
confused the proud in **their** smug hearts;
toppled sovereigns **from** their thrones,
and exalted **hum**ble ones;
filled the hungering with **good** things,
and sent the rich **a**way empty.

The Lord helped servant **Is**rael
to re**mem**ber mercy,

as was spoken to Abra**ha**m
and his descendants for**e**vermore!

INTERCESSIONS

Petitions

Cantor, then Assembly:

KH
What shall we re- turn to God?

Cantor:

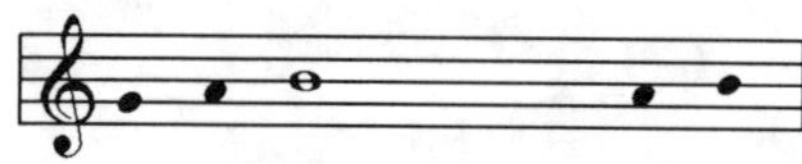

Who has **turned** an ear **to** us? ...
Who has **broken** the chains **of** bondage? ...
Who has **de**livered us **from** death? ...
Who has **pro**tected **the** innocent? ...
Who has **brought** salvation **to** us? ...
Who has **called us** precious? ...
Who has **ac**companied us during **our** service? ...
Who has **done** great deeds among **the** people? ...
Who has **called** the dead to **new** life? ...

Our Father ...

Prayer
O God,
your Son called Philip and James to be his apostles:
help us to believe in the Good News of Jesus Christ
that we may also do the works
that lead to salvation and life everlasting. **Amen.**

CONCLUSION

Blessing
May the God who calls followers bless us
in the name of the Father, and of the Son, and of the Holy Spirit. **Amen.**

Dismissal
Go and rest peacefully, comforted by the nearness of God. **Thanks be to God.**

May 14
Feast of MATTHIAS, Apostle
Morning Praise

From the Feast of PHILIP & JAMES, Apostles, p. 534.

Prayer
Gracious God,
you chose Matthias to be numbered among the apostles
because he had been with your Son from the beginning
even to witnessing the resurrection:
open our eyes to the splendor of the resurrection
that we might seek you now and always. **Amen.**

Feast of MATTHIAS, Apostle
Evening Prayer

From the Feast of PHILIP & JAMES, Apostles, p. 537.

Prayer
O God,
you called Matthias to be an apostle:
protect us and encourage us
that we, too, might witness to the resurrection
and come to salvation and life everlasting. **Amen.**

May 31
Feast of the VISITATION
Morning Praise

FESTAL MORNING HYMN

PSALMODY

Psalm 63 *Psalm of David. While he was in the desert of Judah.*

Solo 1 O God, you are my God, I seek you;
my soul thirsts for you.
My flesh longs for you
in a dry and wasted land,
deprived of water.

Solo 2 So in the sanctuary I have contemplated you
to see your might and your glory.
Because your steadfast love is better than life,
my lips will praise you.
So I will bless you all my life;
in your name I will raise my hands.
As with milk and rich food,
my soul is filled;
my mouth gives praise with joyful lips.
I remember you upon my bed,
pondering you throughout the night.
For you were a help for me;
in the shade of your wings I keep singing.
My soul clings to you;
your right hand upholds me.

Solo 1 But let those who seek my destruction
be cast into the depths of the earth.
Let them be given over to the power of the sword;
let them become a prey for jackals.

All Then the king shall rejoice in God.
All those who swear by God will be praised,
for the mouths of liars will be shut.

Psalm 113

All Alleluia!

Choir 1 Give praise, servants of the LORD;
praise the name of the LORD.
Let the name of the LORD be blessed
from now on and forever.
From the rising of the sun to its setting,
let the name of the LORD be praised.
The LORD is exalted above all nations;
God's glory is greater than the heavens.

All Who is like the LORD our God,
enthroned above?

Choir 2 Who looks down to watch over
the skies and the earth?
Who raises the weak from dust
and the poor from ashes,
to return them to the company of nobles,
the nobles of the people?
Who brings home the sterile woman,
now a rejoicing mother of many children?

All Alleluia!

Word of God

Benedictus
Blessed be the Lord God of **Israel**,
who visited and redeemed the **people**,
who raised up for us a **mighty** savior
from the house of **ser**vant David.

Just as the Lord spoke through the mouths of the holy prophets of **old**—
salvation comes out of the hands of our enemies and those who **hate** us,
that, with our ancestors, we might perform **works** of mercy,
remembering the holy covenant **sworn** to Abraham—

so does the Lord deliver us from the hands **of** our enemies,
that we might serve without fear before **the** Lord,
worshiping in **ho**liness
and in righteousness **all** our days.

And you also, child, will be called a prophet of God Most **High**:
for you will go before the Lord to prepare a **way**,
bringing people knowledge of salvation by for**giveness** of sins;
because of the deep and tender mercy **of** our God.

Whereby a light rising from on high will **visit** us
to appear to those in darkness and in a shadow **of** death,
to guide our feet along a **straight**, sure path
into a **way** of peace.

INTERCESSIONS

Invocations

Cantor, then Assembly:

Hail, Ho-ly Ma- ry, full of grace.

Cantor:

O divine Son, your mother **pondered** God's will ...
O divine Son, your mother saw your **might** and glory ...
O divine Son, your mother **prais**es you ...
O divine Son, your mother bless**es** your name ...
O divine Son, your mother remains in the shade **of** your wings ...
O divine Son, your mother rejoi**ces** in you ...
O divine Son, your mother is exalted a**bove** all others ...
O divine Son, your mother watches **o**ver us ...
O divine Son, your mother cares for us as her be**lo**ved children ...

Our Father ...

Prayer
O God of our salvation,
John leapt in Elizabeth's womb
when Mary visited her cousin:
may we always rejoice in the gift of salvation
and honor Mary, the mother of your divine Son Jesus Christ. **Amen.**

CONCLUSION

Blessing
May God bless us
in the name of the Father, and of the Son, and of the Holy Spirit. **Amen.**

Dismissal
Go forth to live under the watchful eye of Mary our mother. **Thanks be to God.**

Feast of the VISITATION
Evening Prayer

FESTAL EVENING HYMN

PSALMODY

Psalm 130 *Song of ascents (pilgrimages).*

Solo 1 Out of the depths, I cry to you, O Lord.
Lord, listen to my voice;
let your ears be attentive
to the voice of my supplications.

All If you, O Lord, were to keep iniquities in mind,
Lord, who could stand?
But with you is forgiveness,
and for that you are revered.

Solo 1 I wait for the Lord;
my soul waits,
and for God's word I hope.
My soul waits for the Lord
more than watchers of the morning
watch for the dawn.

All Let Israel hope in the Lord,
for steadfast love is found with the Lord
and abundance of redemption.
It is the Lord who shall redeem Israel
from all iniquities.

Psalm 67 *To the choirmaster. With stringed instruments. Psalm. Song.*

Choir 1 May God have mercy on us and bless us.
May God's face shine among us.

Selah (pause).

Choir 2 For your way is known over the earth,
and your salvation is known among all nations.

All Let the peoples give you thanks, O God,
let all the peoples give you thanks.

Choir 1 May the nations rejoice and shout with joy,
for you judge the peoples rightly
and the nations on the earth you guide.

Selah (pause).

All Let the peoples give you thanks, O God,
let all the peoples give you thanks.

Choir 2 The earth has given its fruit.
May God, our God, bless us.
May God bless us,
and let all ends of the earth
show reverence.

Word of God

Magnificat
My soul does magni**fy** the Lord!
I delight in **God** my savior
who looked kindly **on** lowliness.

Now all ages will **call** me blessed
for the Mighty One **did** great things.
Holy is **God's** name;
mercy is from age to age for **those** in awe!

The Lord's strong arm did **mighty** deeds:
confused the proud in **their** smug hearts;
toppled sovereigns **from** their thrones,
and exalted **hum**ble ones;
filled the hungering with **good** things,
and sent the rich **a**way empty.

The Lord helped servant **Is**rael
to re**mem**ber mercy,
as was spoken to Ab**ra**ham
and his descendants for**e**vermore!

INTERCESSIONS

Petitions

Cantor, then Assembly:

Cantor:

We cry **out** to God ...
We listen **to** God's voice ...
We are attentive **to** God's deeds ...
We are forgiven **our** iniquities ...
We revere God's **ho**ly name ...
We hope **in** God's Word ...
We greet God's **stead**fast love ...
We enjoy abun**dant** redemption ...
We make **known** God's ways ...
We give **thanks** forever ...
We rejoice and **shout** with joy ...
We honor Ma**ry** our mother ...
We commend the faithful departed **to** God's love ...

Our Father ...

Prayer
O wondrous God,
your face shines on us
and we receive Life:
may we always open ourselves to your message of love
through the intercession of Mary our Mother
and her divine Son Jesus Christ. **Amen.**

CONCLUSION

Blessing
May God bless us
in the name of the Father, and of the Son, and of the Holy Spirit. **Amen.**

Dismissal
Go and rest confidently under the protection of Mary our Mother.
Thanks be to God.

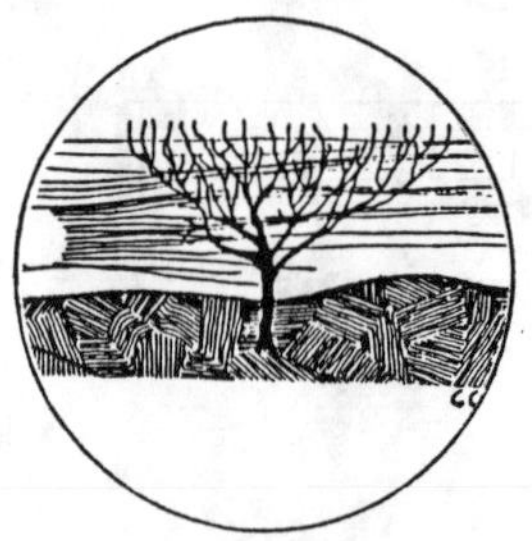

June 24
Solemnity of the BIRTH OF JOHN THE BAPTIST
Morning Praise

FESTAL MORNING HYMN

PSALMODY

Psalm 96

ANTIPHON

KH
John pre- pared the way for the Good News.

Sing to the LORD a **new** song.
Sing to the LORD, all **the** earth.
Sing to **the** LORD,
bless **God's** name. ANTIPHON

From day to day proclaim the good news of sal**vation**.
Recount among the nations God's glory,
  God's marvels among **all** peoples.
For great is the LORD, highly to **be** praised
and revered above **all** gods.

For all the gods of the nations are as **nothing**,
but the LORD made **the** heavens.
Honor and splendor stand be**fore** God,
might and glory fill **the** temple. ANTIPHON

Give to the LORD, O families of **peoples**.
Give to the LORD glory **and** might.
Give to **the** LORD
the glory of **God's** name. ANTIPHON

Bring an offering and come into the **courts**.
Worship the LORD with ho**ly** splendor.
Dance in the sac**red** presence,
all **the** earth.

Say among the nations: "The LORD **reigns**."
Surely God formed the universe
  so that it would **not** falter.
God **will** judge
the peoples **in** equity. ANTIPHON

Let the heavens re**joice**
and the earth **ex**ult.
Let the sea and its full**ness** roar.
Let the fields and all within them **be** glad. ANTIPHON

Then all the trees of the forest will shout with **joy**
in the presence of the LORD **who** comes.
For God comes to judge the earth,
  to judge the universe **with** justice
and with fidelity, **the** peoples. ANTIPHON

Psalm Prayer
O mighty God,
you announced the coming of your Son
through the prophet John:
open our eyes to a straight path
that we may journey toward you without faltering.
We pray through Jesus Christ. **Amen.**

Psalm 65 *To the choirmaster. Psalm of David. Psalm.*

ANTIPHON

KH
Bless- ed is the One who is to come!

To you praise is due,
  O God **in** Zion,
and for you promises will be **ful**filled.
O you who listen to prayer,
  to you all flesh **shall** come.
When our transgressions—our deeds of iniquity—overcome us,
  you **for**give them. ANTIPHON

Blessed is the one you elect and **bring** near;
that one shall dwell in **your** courts.
Let us be filled with the goodness of **your** house,
the holiness of **your** temple.

With awesome deeds you answer us **in** justice,
O God of our **sal**vation,
protector of all the ends of **the** earth
and of the dis**tant** seas. ANTIPHON

Girded with might,
  you establish mountains **in** strength.
You still the roaring of the seas—
  the roaring of their waves—
  and the clamor **of** nations.
Because of **your** signs,
the inhabitants of the ends of the earth will stand **in** awe. ANTIPHON

You cause the breaking of morning and of evening
  to burst **with** joy.
You visit the earth and give it water;
  abundantly, you **en**rich it:
the river of God
  is replete **with** water.
You provide people with grain,
  for you designed **it** so.

Its furrows you water **a**bundantly,
and you make **them** smooth.
You soften it **with** showers,
and you bless **its** sprout. ANTIPHON

You crown the year with your bounty,
  and fertility springs in the wake of **your** chariot.
The pastures of the wilderness drip with water,
  and the hills are girded **with** joy.
Meadows are clothed with flocks,
  and valleys are covered **with** grain.
They shout, even more, **they** sing. ANTIPHON

Psalm Prayer
O God of promises,
you girded John the Baptist with might:
fulfill in us the Good News
of our Savior Jesus Christ
through whom we pray in the unity of the Holy Spirit,
one God forever and ever. **Amen.**

Word of God

Benedictus
Blessed be the Lord God of **Israel**,
who visited and redeemed the **people**,
who raised up for us a **mighty** savior
from the house of **ser**vant David.

Just as the Lord spoke through the mouths of the holy prophets of **old**—
salvation comes out of the hands of our enemies and those who **hate** us,
that, with our ancestors, we might perform **works** of mercy,
remembering the holy covenant **sworn** to Abraham—

so does the Lord deliver us from the hands **of** our enemies,
that we might serve without fear before **the** Lord,
worshiping in **ho**liness
and in righteousness **all** our days.

And you also, child, will be called a prophet of God Most **High**:
for you will go before the Lord to prepare a **way**,
bringing people knowledge of salvation by for**giveness** of sins;
because of the deep and tender mercy **of** our God.

Whereby a light rising from on high will **vis**it us
to appear to those in darkness and in a shadow **of** death,
to guide our feet along a **straight**, sure path
into a **way** of peace.

INTERCESSIONS

Invocations

Cantor, then Assembly:

Cantor:

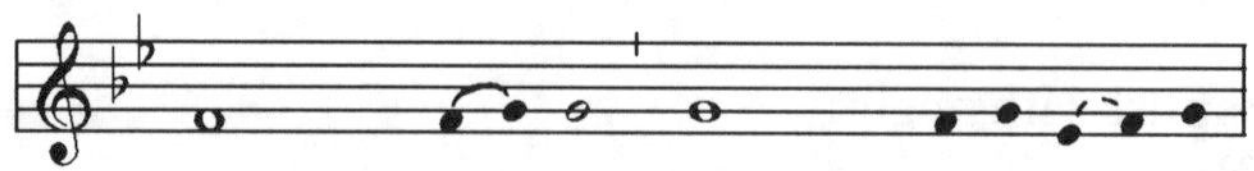

Jesus our Messiah, you **are** the Good News,
Jesus our Messiah, you are great a**mong** all creatures,
Jesus our Messiah, you are filled with **might** and glory,
Jesus our Messiah, you are ruler o**ver** the universe,
Jesus our Messiah, you are the elect **who** is brought near,
Jesus our Messiah, you are our good**ness** and holiness,
Jesus our Messiah, you are an abun**dance** of blessings,

Our Father ...

Prayer
Mighty God,
you raised up John to be the herald of your Son's presence:
may we speak your Good News boldly and with humility,
never losing sight of the One who is greater than all,
Jesus Christ through whom we pray. **Amen.**

CONCLUSION

Blessing
Bow your heads and pray for God's blessing.
May God grant us courage. **Amen.**
May Jesus open us to the Good News. **Amen.**
May the Spirit make straight our way. **Amen.**
And may God bless us
in the name of the Father, and of the Son, and of the Holy Spirit. **Amen.**

Sign of Peace/Dismissal
Let us recognize Christ in the other
by sharing a sign of peace.

Solemnity of the BIRTH OF JOHN THE BAPTIST Evening Prayer

LIGHT SERVICE

Proclamation of the Light

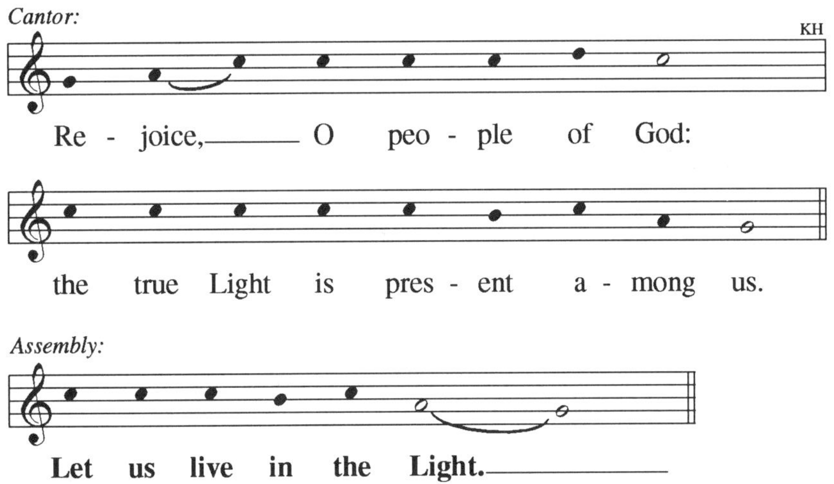

Festal Evening Hymn

Thanksgiving for the Light

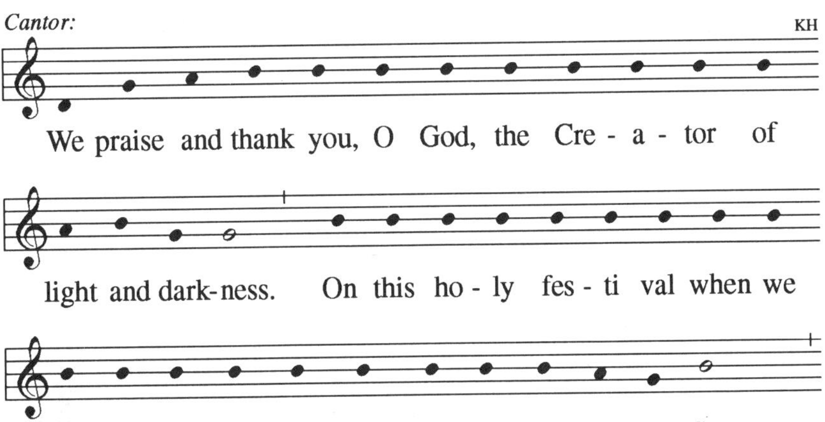

Cantor:
KH
We praise and thank you, O God, the Cre - a - tor of
light and dark-ness. On this ho - ly fes - ti val when we
hon- or John who an-nounced the com-ing of your Son,

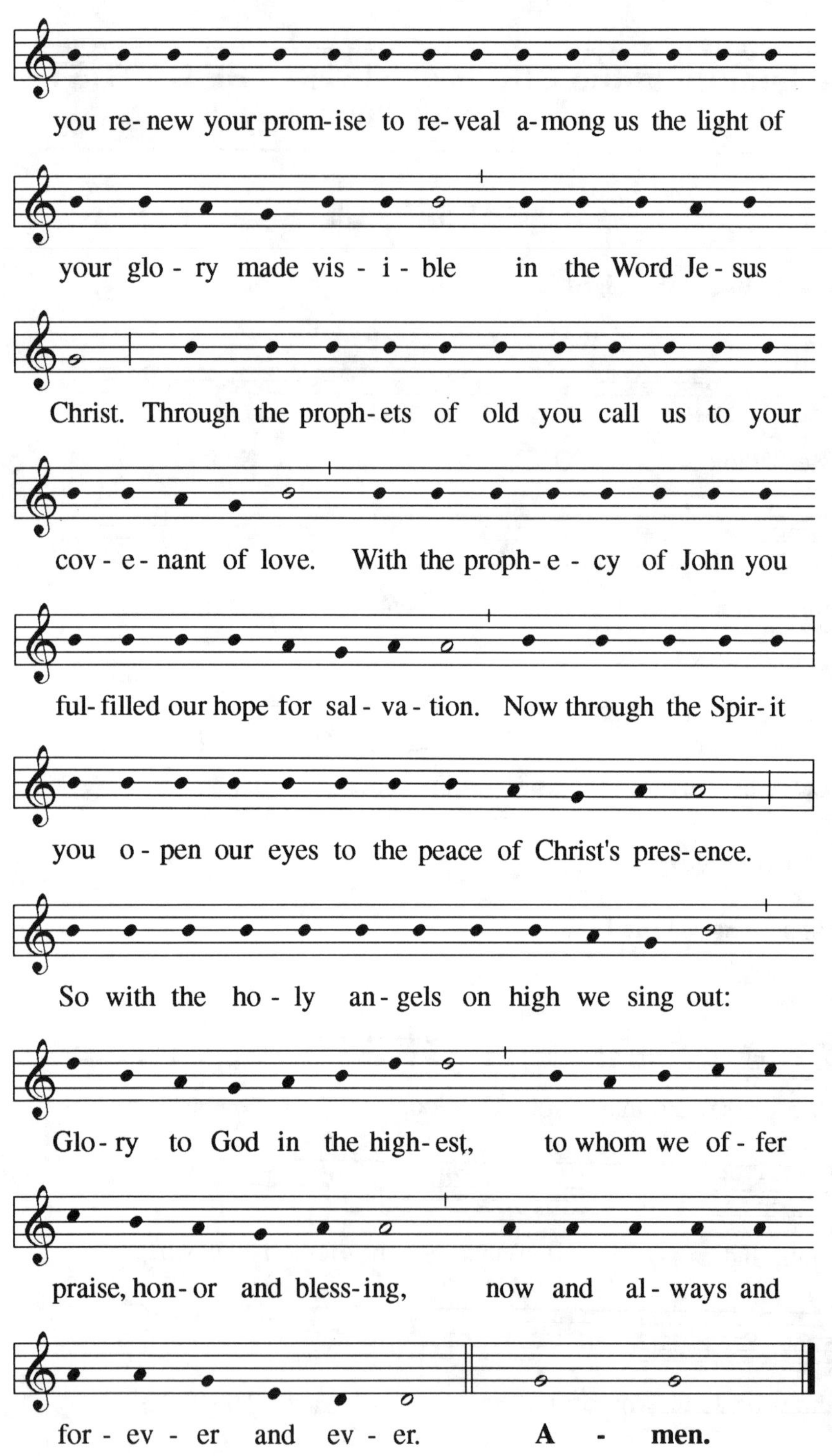
you re- new your prom- ise to re- veal a- mong us the light of
your glo - ry made vis - i - ble in the Word Je - sus
Christ. Through the proph- ets of old you call us to your
cov - e - nant of love. With the proph- e - cy of John you
ful- filled our hope for sal - va - tion. Now through the Spir- it
you o - pen our eyes to the peace of Christ's pres- ence.
So with the ho - ly an- gels on high we sing out:
Glo- ry to God in the high- est, to whom we of - fer
praise, hon- or and bless- ing, now and al - ways and
for - ev - er and ev - er. A - men.

PSALMODY

Psalm 30 *Psalm of David. Song for the dedication of the temple.*

ANTIPHON

KH
John won the crown of life; you have raised him up.

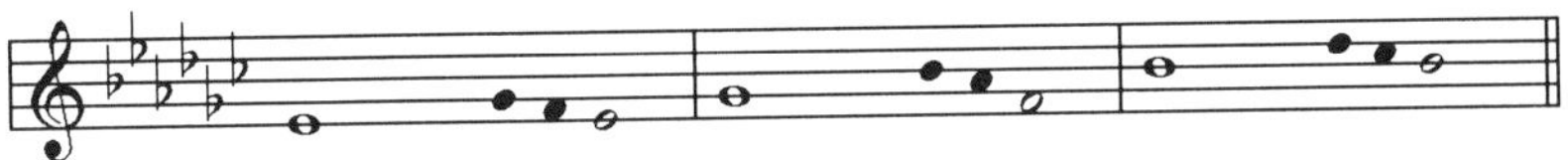

I will **exalt** you, O LORD,
for you have **set** me free
and have not allowed my enemies to re**joice** over me. ANTIPHON

O LORD my God,
  I have cried to you
  and **you** have healed me.
O LORD, you have brought my soul
  up from Sheol.
You have restored me to life,
  preventing me from going **down** the Pit. ANTIPHON

Sing to the LORD, O **faith**ful ones;
celebrate a memorial **to** God's holiness.
For we stand only an instant in God's anger,
  but a whole lifetime in **God's** delight.

In the evening come tears,
  but in the morning come **shouts** of joy.
So I said in my tranquility,
  "I will not **falter** forever."
O LORD, in your delight
  you have established might **as** my mountain.

When you hid your face,
  I was **ter**rified.
To you, O **LORD**, I cry
and to you, O Lord, I raise my **sup**plication.

What profit is there in my blood,
  in my going down **to** the Pit?

Does dust give you thanks,
  and **tell** your truth?
Listen, O LORD, and have mercy;
  O LORD, be a **help** to me. ANTIPHON

You have changed my **mourning** to dancing;
you have **loosened** my sackcloth
and girded **me** with joy.

So I **sing** your glory;
I **am** not silent.
O LORD my God,
  I will give thanks to **you** forever. ANTIPHON

Psalm Prayer
Exalted God,
you have restored us to life in Christ:
give us the courage and strength of John
to live in your presence now and always. **Amen.**

Psalm 138 *Of David.*

ANTIPHON
KH
I give you thanks, O God; with my
whole heart I sing your praise.

I give you thanks with **all** my heart;
instead of other gods, I **sing** to you.
I bow down toward the **ho**ly sanctuary,
and I give thanks to your name
  on account of your steadfast love **and** your truth.

For you have ex**alted** your promise
even a**bove** your name.
On the day I cried, you **ans**wered me;
you renewed cour**age** within me. ANTIPHON

Let all the rulers of the earth give thanks to you, O LORD,
for they have heard the **words of** your mouth.
Let them sing about the ways of the LORD,
for great is the **glory of** the LORD.
Although exalted,
the LORD looks up**on** the lowly,
but recognizes the proud only **from** a distance. ANTIPHON

When I walk in the midst of distress,
you revive me against the **anger of** my enemies.
You stretch out your hand,
and your **right** hand saves me;
the LORD will do every**thing** for me.
O LORD, your steadfast love is forever.
Do not forsake the work **of** your hands. ANTIPHON

Psalm Prayer
God of salvation,
you stretch out your right hand and save us from all evil:
do not forsake us
but draw us to your presence now and always. **Amen.**

Word of God

Magnificat
My soul does magni**fy** the Lord!
I delight in **God** my savior
who looked kindly **on** lowliness.

Now all ages will **call** me blessed
for the Mighty One **did** great things.
Holy is **God's** name;
mercy is from age to age for **those** in awe!

The Lord's strong arm did **might**y deeds:
confused the proud in **their** smug hearts;
toppled sovereigns **from** their thrones,
and exalted **hum**ble ones;

filled the hungering with **good** things,
and sent the rich **a**way empty.

The Lord helped servant **Is**rael
to re**mem**ber mercy,
as was spoken to Ab**ra**ham
and his descendants for**e**vermore!

INTERCESSIONS

Petitions

Cantor, then Assembly:

Make straight our paths.

Cantor:

With stead**fast** love,
With unwav**ering** truth,
With re**newed** courage,
With **sure** words,
With promised **sal**vation,
With undaunt**ed** freedom,
With peace**ful** healing,
With **restored** life,
With unbound**ed** holiness,
With quiet **tran**quility,
With song-filled **de**light,
With mercy for the faithful **de**parted,

Our Father ...

Prayer
God of salvation,
you sent John to prepare the way for your Son:
may we, too, humble ourselves by acknowledging
the truth before us and
thereby win exaltation with Jesus Christ forever and ever. **Amen.**

CONCLUSION

Blessing
Bow your heads and pray for God's blessing.
May God grant us courage. **Amen.**
May Jesus open us to the Good News. **Amen.**
May the Spirit make straight our way. **Amen.**
And may God bless us
in the name of the Father, and of the Son, and of the Holy Spirit. **Amen.**

Sign of Peace/Dismissal
Let us recognize Christ in the other
by sharing a sign of peace.

June 29
Solemnity of PETER & PAUL, Apostles
Morning Praise

FESTAL MORNING HYMN

PSALMODY

Psalm 63 *Psalm of David. While he was in the desert of Judah.*

ANTIPHON

O God, you are my God, **I** seek you;
my **soul** thirsts **for** you.
My flesh longs for you
in a dry and **wast**ed land,
deprived **of** water. ANTIPHON

So in the sanctuary I have contemplated you
to see your might and your **glory**.
Because your **stead**fast love is better than life,
my lips will **praise** you.
So I will bless you **all** my life;
in your name I will raise **my** hands.

As with milk and rich food,
my soul **is** filled;
my **mouth** gives praise with joy**ful** lips.
I remember you up**on** my bed,
pondering you throughout **the** night.

For you were a help **for** me;
in the **shade** of your wings I **keep** singing.
My soul **clings** to you;
your right hand **up**holds me. ANTIPHON

But let those who seek my de**struc**tion
be **cast** into the depths of **the** earth.
Let them be given over to the power **of** the sword;
let them become a prey **for** jackals. ANTIPHON

Then the king shall rejoice **in** God.
All **those** who swear by God will **be** praised,
for the mouths of liars will **be** shut. ANTIPHON

Psalm Prayer
O God,
your Son said to Peter,
"Feed my lambs; tend my sheep":
help us to continue Peter's ministry
that no one become a prey for jackals.
We pray through Jesus Christ. **Amen.**

Psalm 149

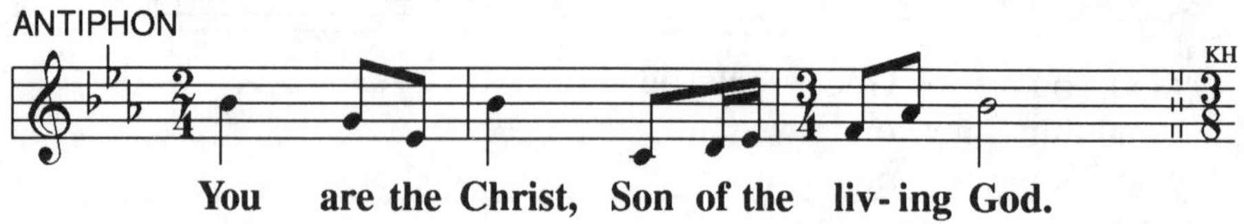
ANTIPHON
KH
You are the Christ, Son of the liv-ing God.

sing with first and final antiphon ♩. = ♩

Al - le - lu - ia! Al - le - lu - ia!

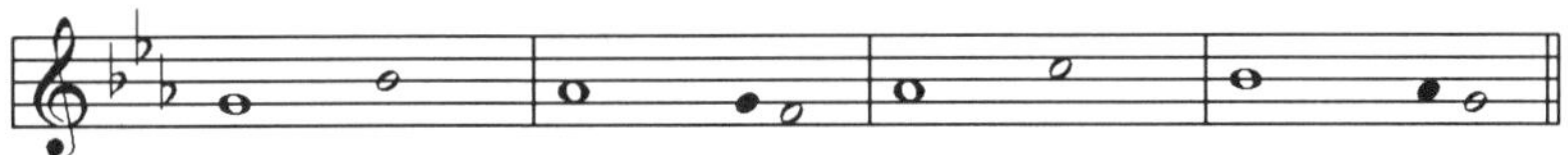

Sing a new song to the LORD,
  God's praise in the assembly of the **faith**ful.
Let Israel rejoice in its Creator,
  the children of Zion exult in **their** Sovereign.
Let them praise God's name with **danc**ing;
with drums and harp, let them play music **for** God. ANTIPHON

For the LORD takes delight in the people,
  adorning the poor with sal**va**tion.
Let the faithful exult **with** glory,
let them ring out joy on their **couch**es,
and cry out the great deeds of God from **their** throats. ANTIPHON

With two-edged swords in their hands,
  let them do vengeance against peoples
  and rebuke **na**tions;
let them tie their rulers with fetters
  and their nobles with chains **of** bronze,
in order to accomplish judgment against them as **writ**ten.
This is honor for all **the** faithful. ANTIPHON

Psalm Prayer
Mighty God,
Peter acknowledged the mightiest of your works
when he acclaimed your Son as Messiah:
help us to honor you
by spreading the Good News of salvation.
We pray through your Son, Jesus Christ. **Amen.**

Word of God

Benedictus
Blessed be the Lord God of **Israel**,
who visited and redeemed the **people**,

who raised up for us a **mighty** savior
from the house of **ser**vant David.

Just as the Lord spoke through the mouths of the holy prophets of **old**—
salvation comes out of the hands of our enemies and those who **hate** us,
that, with our ancestors, we might perform **works** of mercy,
remembering the holy covenant **sworn** to Abraham—

so does the Lord deliver us from the hands **of** our enemies,
that we might serve without fear before **the** Lord,
worshiping in **ho**liness
and in righteousness **all** our days.

And you also, child, will be called a prophet of God Most **High**:
for you will go before the Lord to prepare a **way**,
bringing people knowledge of salvation by for**giveness** of sins;
because of the deep and tender mercy **of** our God.

Whereby a light rising from on high will **vis**it us
to appear to those in darkness and in a shadow **of** death,
to guide our feet along a **straight**, sure path
into a **way** of peace.

INTERCESSIONS

Invocations

Cantor, then Assembly:
KH
Your stead - fast love is bet - ter than life.

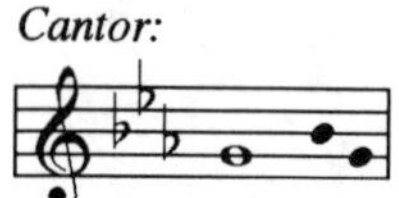
Cantor:

O Messiah God, you seek us for **your** service ...
O Messiah God, you draw us to **your**self ...
O Messiah God, you help us spread the **Good** News ...
O Messiah God, you shade us from **dis**couragement ...
O Messiah God, you keep **us** faithful ...
O Messiah God, you rejoice in your **dis**ciples ...
O Messiah God, you adorn your disciples **with** glory ...
O Messiah God, you honor all **your** faithful ...

Our Father ...

Prayer
Gracious God,
you called Peter and Paul
to be first among the apostles:
keep us faithful to the Good News
that we might honor you by serving you diligently.
We pray through Jesus Christ. **Amen.**

CONCLUSION

Blessing
Bow your heads and pray for God's blessing.
May the Creator bless us. **Amen.**
May the Messiah anoint us. **Amen.**
May the Spirit love us. **Amen.**
And may God bless us
in the name of the Father, and of the Son, and of the Holy Spirit. **Amen.**

Sign of Peace/Dismissal
As you go forth to spread the Good News,
strengthen one another with a sign of peace.

Solemnity of PETER & PAUL, Apostles
Evening Prayer

LIGHT SERVICE

Proclamation of the Light

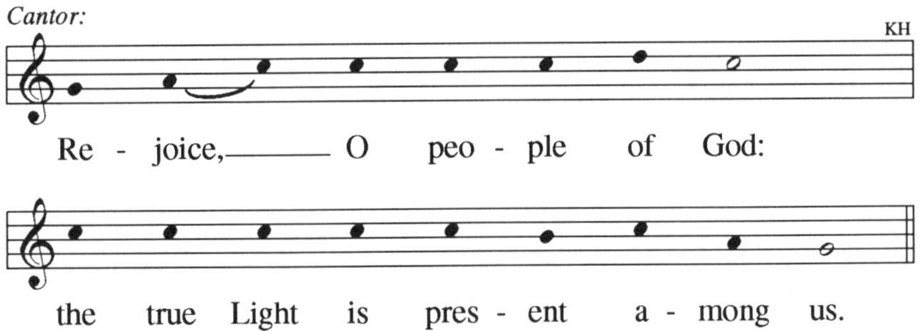

Cantor:
KH
Re - joice,—— O peo - ple of God:
the true Light is pres - ent a - mong us.

Assembly:

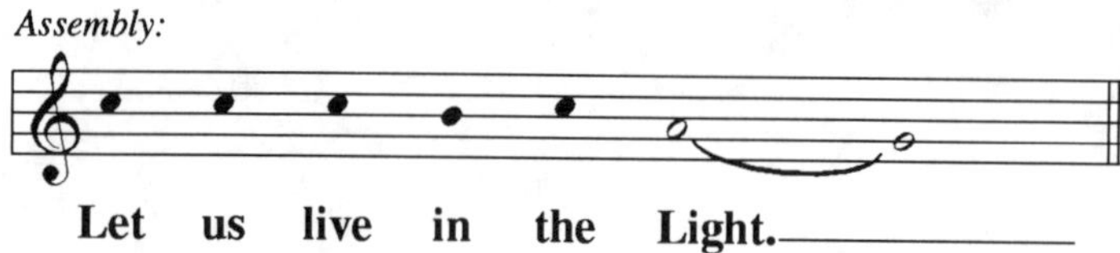

Festal Evening Hymn

Thanksgiving for the Light

Cantor:

KH

We praise and thank you, O God, the Cre - a - tor of

light and dark-ness. On this ho - ly fes - ti val when we

hon - or Pe - ter and Paul, those who first spread the Good News,

you re - new your prom - ise to re - veal a - mong us the light of

your glo - ry made vis - i - ble in the Word Je - sus Christ.

Through the proph - ets of old you call us to your cov - e -

nant of love. With the reign of the Mes - si - ah you ful -

filled our hope for sal - va - tion. Now through the Spir - it

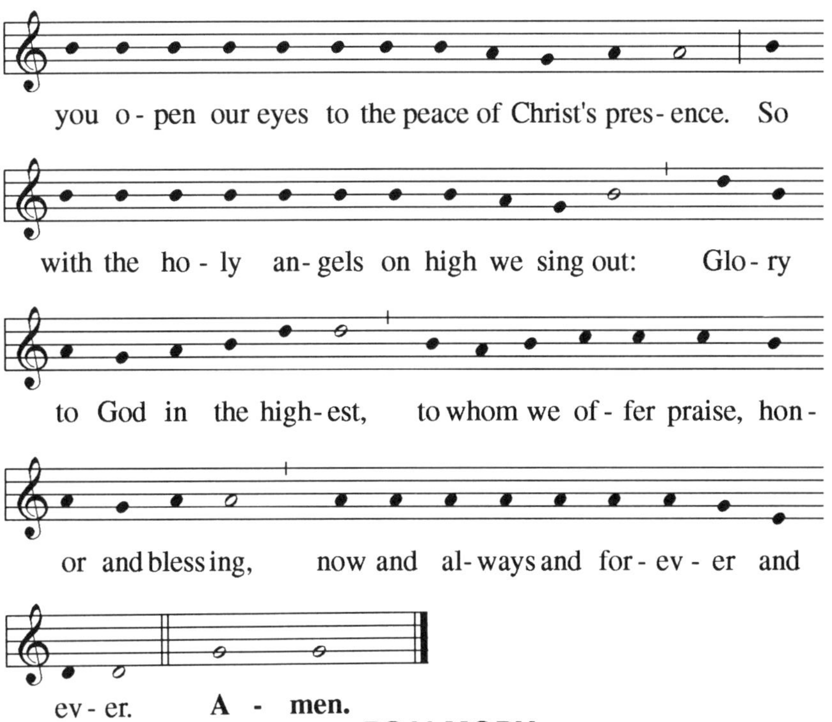

PSALMODY

Psalm 116

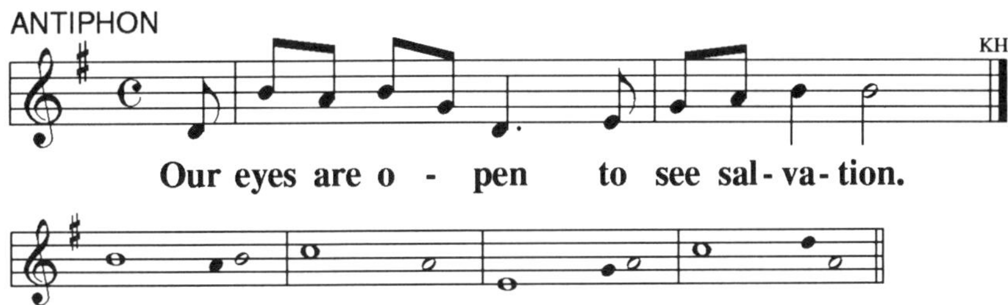

ANTIPHON
KH
Our eyes are o - pen to see sal - va - tion.

I love the LORD
  who **has** heard
the voice of my suppli**ca**tions.
For God has turned an ear **to** me
as I cry all **my** days. ANTIPHON

Deadly chains have fettered me,
  and the anguish of Sheol has reached up **to** me.
Distress and terror, I have en**countered**;
but I have called on the name of **the** LORD.
How long, O LORD?
  Deliver **my** soul. ANTIPHON

The LORD is gracious and just;
  our God **is** merciful.
The LORD is the protector of the **innocent**;
I was poor and God brought salvation **to** me.
Return, O my soul, to your rest,
  for the LORD has done good **to** you. ANTIPHON

For you have delivered my soul **from** death,
my eye from tears
  and my foot from **stumbling**,
that I may walk in the presence of **the** LORD
in the land of **the** living. ANTIPHON

Yes, I was right **in** saying,
"I am greatly af**flicted**."
In my agitation, I **have** said,
"Every human being is **a** liar." ANTIPHON

What shall I return to the LORD
  for all the bounty in **my** favor?
I will lift up the cup of salvation
  and I will call on the name of the **LORD**.
Indeed, I will fulfill my promises to **the** LORD
in the presence of all **the** people. ANTIPHON

Precious in the eyes of the LORD
  is the death of **the** faithful ones.
How long, O **LORD**?
For I am your servant,
  I am your servant, the offspring of **your** handmaid.
You have loosened **my** bonds. ANTIPHON

To you I will offer a sacrifice of thanksgiving
  and I will call on the name of **the** LORD.
Indeed, I will fulfill my promises to the LORD
  in the presence of all the **people**,
in the courts of the house of **the** LORD,
in your midst, O Jerusalem.
  Alle**lu**ia! ANTIPHON

Psalm Prayer
Faithful God,
you called Paul to spread the Good News:

as he remained faithful to his death,
so may we be constant in our commitment.
We pray through Jesus Christ. **Amen.**

Psalm 126 *Song of ascents (pilgrimages).*
ANTIPHON

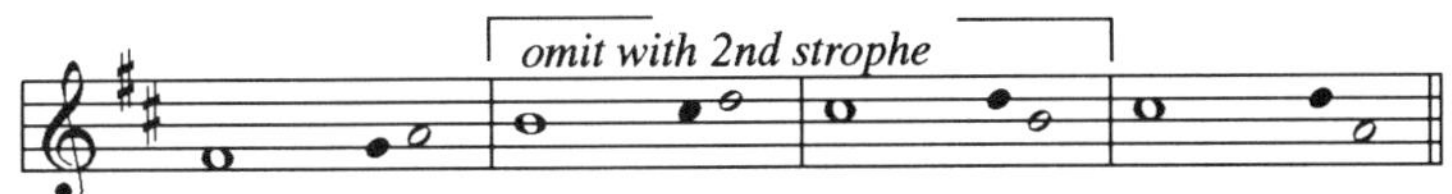

When the LORD accompanied
  those who returned to Zion,
  we were **like** dreamers.
Then our mouth
  was filled with laughter
  and our tongue **with** joy.
Then it was said a**mong** nations:
"The LORD has done great
  deeds among **these** people." ANTIPHON

The LORD has done great
  deeds **among** us.
Now we **re**joice. ANTIPHON

Return our captives, O LORD,
  like torrents in **the** Negeb.
Those who sow in tears
  harvest with shouts **of** joy.
Indeed, the one who goes out weeping,
  carrying the bag **of** seed,
comes back joyful,
  carrying **the** sheaves. ANTIPHON

Psalm Prayer
Gracious God,
you did great things for Paul:
be with us as we spend our lives
in service of your Son, Jesus Christ. **Amen.**

Word of God

Magnificat
My soul does magni**fy** the Lord!
I delight in **God** my savior
who looked kindly **on** lowliness.

Now all ages will **call** me blessed
for the Mighty One **did** great things.
Holy is **God's** name;
mercy is from age to age for **those** in awe!

The Lord's strong arm did **mighty** deeds:
confused the proud in **their** smug hearts;
toppled sovereigns **from** their thrones,
and exalted **hum**ble ones;
filled the hungering with **good** things,
and sent the rich **a**way empty.

The Lord helped servant **Is**rael
to re**mem**ber mercy,
as was spoken to Abra**ha**m
and his descendants for**e**vermore!

INTERCESSIONS

Petitions

Cantor, then Assembly:

Cantor:

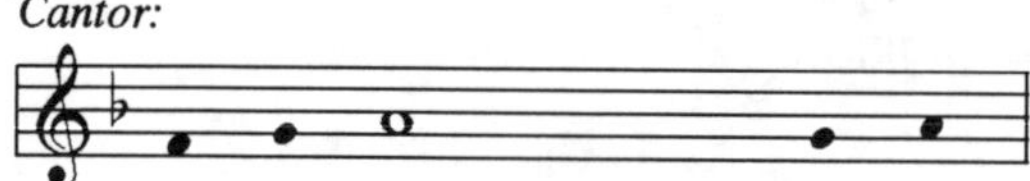

Who has **turned** an ear **to** us? ...
Who has **broken** the chains **of** bondage? ...
Who has **delivered** us **from** death? ...
Who has **protected the** innocent? ...
Who has **brought** salvation **to** us? ...
Who has **called us** precious? ...
Who has **accompanied** us during **our** service? ...

Who has **done** great deeds among **the** people? ...
Who has **called** the dead to **new** life? ...

Our Father ...

Prayer
O God,
your Son calls disciples to be his followers:
protect us and encourage us
that we might spread the Good News
of salvation and enjoy life everlasting. **Amen.**

CONCLUSION

Blessing
Bow your heads and pray for God's blessing.
May Peter be a rock for us. **Amen.**
May Paul lead us to truth and wisdom. **Amen.**
May their Messiah Teacher open us to God's Word. **Amen.**
And may God bless us
in the name of the Father, and of the Son, and of the Holy Spirit. **Amen.**

Sign of Peace/Dismissal
As disciples of Christ, share with one another a sign of peace.

July 3
Feast of THOMAS, Apostle
Morning Praise

From the Feast of PHILIP & JAMES, Apostles, Morning Praise, p. 534.

Prayer
Patient God,
you brought forth belief from Thomas' doubt:
increase our faith
that we may be worthy disciples
of your Son, Jesus Christ. **Amen.**

Feast of THOMAS, Apostle
Evening Prayer

From the Feast of PHILIP & JAMES, Apostles, Evening Prayer, p. 537.

Prayer
Loving God,
your Son invited Thomas to touch his wounds:
help us to reach out to those in need of healing
so that we are fitting witnesses to the power of the resurrection.
We pray through Jesus Christ. **Amen.**

July 25
Feast of JAMES, Apostle
Morning Praise

From the Feast of PHILIP & JAMES, Apostles, Morning Praise, p. 534.

Prayer
God who calls,
your Son invited James to leave his fishing
and follow him:
may we follow your call without hesitation
and be fruitful in all we do.
We pray through Jesus Christ. **Amen.**

Feast of JAMES, Apostle
Evening Prayer

From the Feast of PHILIP & JAMES, Apostles, Evening Prayer, p. 537.

Prayer
Gracious God,
James was privileged to witness
the miracles and glory of your Son:
open us to your overtures of presence
that we may spread your salvific love now and always. **Amen.**

August 6
Feast of the TRANSFIGURATION
Morning Praise

FESTAL MORNING HYMN

PSALMODY

Psalm 63 *Psalm of David. While he was in the desert of Judah.*

Solo 1 O God, you are my God, I seek you;
my soul thirsts for you.
My flesh longs for you
in a dry and wasted land,
deprived of water.

Solo 2 So in the sanctuary I have contemplated you
to see your might and your glory.
Because your steadfast love is better than life,
my lips will praise you.
So I will bless you all my life;
in your name I will raise my hands.
As with milk and rich food,
my soul is filled;
my mouth gives praise with joyful lips.
I remember you upon my bed,
pondering you throughout the night.
For you were a help for me;
in the shade of your wings I keep singing.
My soul clings to you;
your right hand upholds me.

Solo 1 But let those who seek my destruction
be cast into the depths of the earth.
Let them be given over to the power of the sword;
let them become a prey for jackals.

All Then the king shall rejoice in God.
All those who swear by God will be praised,
for the mouths of liars will be shut.

Psalm 149

All Alleluia!

Choir 1 Sing a new song to the LORD,
God's praise in the assembly of the faithful.
Let Israel rejoice in its Creator,
the children of Zion exult in their Sovereign.
Let them praise God's name with dancing;
with drums and harp, let them play music for God.

Choir 2 For the LORD takes delight in the people,
adorning the poor with salvation.
Let the faithful exult with glory,
let them ring out joy on their couches,
and cry out the great deeds of God from their throats.

Choir 1 With two-edged swords in their hands,
let them do vengeance against peoples
and rebuke nations;
let them tie their rulers with fetters
and their nobles with chains of bronze,
in order to accomplish judgment against them as written.
This is honor for all the faithful.

All Alleluia!

Word of God

Benedictus

Blessed be the Lord God of **Israel**,
who visited and redeemed the **people**,
who raised up for us a **mighty** savior
from the house of **ser**vant David.

Just as the Lord spoke through the mouths of the holy prophets of **old**—
salvation comes out of the hands of our enemies and those who **hate** us,
that, with our ancestors, we might perform **works** of mercy,
remembering the holy covenant **sworn** to Abraham—

so does the Lord deliver us from the hands **of** our enemies,
that we might serve without fear before **the** Lord,

worshiping in **ho**liness
and in righteousness **all** our days.

And you also, child, will be called a prophet of God Most **High**:
for you will go before the Lord to prepare a **way**,
bringing people knowledge of salvation by for**giveness** of sins;
because of the deep and tender mercy **of** our God.

Whereby a light rising from on high will **vis**it us
to appear to those in darkness and in a shadow **of** death,
to guide our feet along a **straight**, sure path
into a **way** of peace.

INTERCESSIONS

Invocations

Cantor, then Assembly:

KH
You are our light and glo - ry!

Cantor:

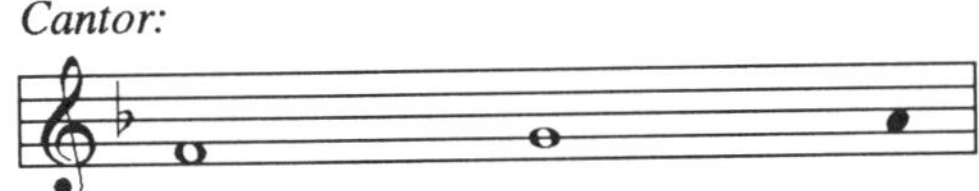

Jesus, you as**cend**ed a high **moun**tain,
Jesus, you re**vealed** the power of **God**,
Jesus, you foreshadowed the **glo**ry of the resur**rec**tion,
Jesus, you re**mem**bered the prophets of **old**,
Jesus, you **shone** with dazzling **light**,
Jesus, you **prom**ised everlasting **glo**ry,
Jesus, you disclosed the **pres**ence of **God**,

Our Father

Prayer
Glorious God,
you declared pleasure in your Son, Jesus Christ:
may we be willing
to go the length and breadth,
the height and depth for the glory of your name.
We pray through Jesus Christ. **Amen.**

CONCLUSION

Blessing
May God dazzle us with pure light and bless us
in the name of the Father, and of the Son, and of the Holy Spirit. **Amen.**

Dismissal
Go forth to live this day in the Light of Christ. **Thanks be to God.**

Feast of the TRANSFIGURATION
Evening Prayer

FESTAL EVENING HYMN

PSALMODY

Psalm 122 *Song of ascents (pilgrimages). Of David.*

Solo 1 I rejoiced when they said to me,
"We shall go to the house of the LORD."

Choir 1 Our feet are standing
at your gates, O Jerusalem.
Jerusalem, you are built like a city
well-bound together.
There the tribes went up,
the tribes of the LORD,
to give thanks to the name of the LORD,
keeping a precept for Israel.
For there the thrones for judgment were placed,
the thrones for the house of David.

Choir 2 Pray for the peace of Jerusalem:
"May those who love you live in peace.
May peace be within your walls
and tranquility within your palaces."

Solo 1 For the sake of my kindred
and my companions, let me speak:
"Peace be upon you."

For the sake of the house of the LORD our God,
I will seek your prosperity.

Psalm 67 *To the choirmaster. With stringed instruments. Psalm. Song.*

Choir 1 May God have mercy on us and bless us.
May God's face shine among us.

Selah (pause).

Choir 2 For your way is known over the earth,
and your salvation is known among all nations.

All Let the peoples give you thanks, O God,
let all the peoples give you thanks.

Choir 1 May the nations rejoice and shout with joy,
for you judge the peoples rightly
and the nations on the earth you guide.

Selah (pause).

All Let the peoples give you thanks, O God,
let all the peoples give you thanks.

Choir 2 The earth has given its fruit.
May God, our God, bless us.
May God bless us,
and let all ends of the earth
show reverence.

Word of God

Magnificat
My soul does magni**fy** the Lord!
I delight in **God** my savior
who looked kindly **on** lowliness.

Now all ages will **call** me blessed
for the Mighty One **did** great things.
Holy is **God's** name;
mercy is from age to age for **those** in awe!

The Lord's strong arm did **mighty** deeds:
confused the proud in **their** smug hearts;
toppled sovereigns **from** their thrones,
and exalted **hum**ble ones;
filled the hungering with **good** things,
and sent the rich **a**way empty.

The Lord helped servant **Is**rael
to re**mem**ber mercy,
as was spoken to Ab**ra**ham
and his descendants for**e**vermore!

INTERCESSIONS

Petitions

Cantor, then Assembly:

Cantor:

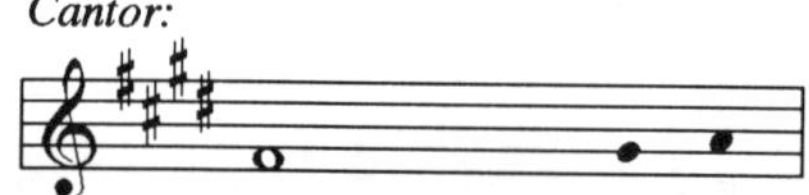

That we seek always the presence **of** God ...
That we give thanks continually for **God's** name ...
That we keep faithfully **God's** precepts ...
That we live resolutely **in** peace ...
That we pursue diligently prosperity **for** all ...
That we remain evermore sons and daughters **of** God ...
That the faithful departed enjoy life **ever**lasting ...

Our Father ...

Prayer
Loving God,
you found favor with your beloved Son:
keep us constantly in your presence
that we may fruitfully witness
to the resurrection of Jesus Christ,
your Son and our brother. **Amen.**

CONCLUSION

Blessing
May God open the heavens to us and bless us
in the name of the Father, and of the Son, and of the Holy Spirit. **Amen.**

Dismissal
Go and rest in the loving-kindness of our God. **Thanks be to God.**

August 10
Feast of LAWRENCE, Deacon and Martyr
Morning Praise

From the Feast of STEPHEN, First Martyr, Morning Praise, p. 204.

Prayer
O mighty God,
you received Lawrence into your heavenly court:
as Lawrence spent his life serving others
as a deacon of the Church,
help us to give of ourselves tirelessly
for the good of others and the salvation of all
so that we might also enjoy everlasting life with you. **Amen.**

Feast of LAWRENCE, Deacon and Martyr
Evening Prayer

From the Feast of STEPHEN, First Martyr, Evening Prayer, p. 207.

Prayer
O gracious God,
you receive the souls of the just who cry out to you:
as Lawrence was given strength even to the point of death
in order to witness to your steadfast love,
so also strengthen us to live faithfully in Jesus' name
now and always. **Amen.**

August 15
Solemnity of the ASSUMPTION
Morning Praise

FESTAL MORNING HYMN

PSALMODY

Psalm 63 *Psalm of David. While he was in the desert of Judah.*

ANTIPHON

KH
Ho-ly Ma-ry was as - sumed in - to the heav - ens.

omit last strophe

O God, you are my God, **I** seek you;
my **soul** thirsts **for** you.
My flesh longs for you
  in a dry and **wast**ed land,
deprived **of** water. ANTIPHON

So in the sanctuary I have contemplated you
  to see your might and your **glor**y.
Because your **stead**fast love is better than life,
  my lips will **praise** you.
So I will bless you **all** my life;
in your name I will raise **my** hands.

As with milk and rich food,
  my soul **is** filled;
my **mouth** gives praise with joy**ful** lips.
I remember you up**on** my bed,
pondering you throughout **the** night.

For you were a help **for** me;
in the **shade** of your wings I **keep** singing.
My soul **clings** to you;
your right hand **up**holds me. ANTIPHON

But let those who seek my des**truc**tion
be **cast** into the depths of **the** earth.
Let them be given over to the power **of** the sword;
let them become a prey **for** jackals. ANTIPHON

Then the king shall rejoice **in** God.
All **those** who swear by God will **be** praised,
for the mouths of liars will **be** shut. ANTIPHON

Psalm Prayer
O God,
you received Mary into heaven to reign as our mother:
as Mary pondered your ways and always remained faithful,
so may we know and follow your will all the days of our lives.
We pray through Jesus Christ. **Amen.**

Psalm 113

ANTIPHON

KH
Who is like our won - drous God, en -

throned in glo - ry? Al - le - lu - ia!

Give praise, servants of **the** LORD;
praise the name of **the** LORD.
Let the name of the LORD **be** blessed
from now on and **for**ever.

From the rising of the sun to **its** setting,
let the name of the LORD **be** praised.
The LORD is exalted above **all** nations;
God's glory is greater than **the** heavens. ANTIPHON

Who looks down to watch over
  the skies and **the** earth?
Who raises the weak from dust
  and the poor **from** ashes,
to return them to the company of nobles,
  the nobles of **the** people?
Who brings home the sterile woman,
  now a rejoicing mother of many children? ANTIPHON

Psalm Prayer
Praiseworthy God,
you made Mary the rejoicing mother of your Son:
may she always look down and watch over us
in the name of her Son, Jesus Christ. **Amen.**

Word of God

Benedictus
Blessed be the Lord God of **Israel**,
who visited and redeemed the **people**,
who raised up for us a **mighty** savior
from the house of **ser**vant David.

Just as the Lord spoke through the mouths of the holy prophets of **old**—
salvation comes out of the hands of our enemies and those who **hate** us,
that, with our ancestors, we might perform **works** of mercy,
remembering the holy covenant **sworn** to Abraham—

so does the Lord deliver us from the hands **of** our enemies,
that we might serve without fear before **the** Lord,

worshiping in **ho**liness
and in righteousness **all** our days.

And you also, child, will be called a prophet of God Most **High**:
for you will go before the Lord to prepare a **way**,
bringing people knowledge of salvation by for**giveness** of sins;
because of the deep and tender mercy **of** our God.

Whereby a light rising from on high will **vis**it us
to appear to those in darkness and in a shadow **of** death,
to guide our feet along a **straight**, sure path
into a **way** of peace.

INTERCESSIONS

Invocations

Cantor, then Assembly:

Hail, Ho-ly Ma- ry, full of grace.

Cantor:

O divine Son, your mother pon**dered** God's will ...
O divine Son, your mother saw your **might** and glory ...
O divine Son, your mother **prais**es you ...
O divine Son, your mother bless**es** your name ...
O divine Son, your mother remains in the shade **of** your wings ...
O divine Son, your mother rejoic**es** in you ...
O divine Son, your mother is exalted a**bove** all others ...
O divine Son, your mother watches **o**ver us ...
O divine Son, your mother cares for us as her be**lo**ved children ...

Our Father ...

Prayer
O God of our salvation,
your Son's mother remained faithful to your holy will:
keep us faithful to your commandments.
We place ourselves under Mary's loving care
just as her Son placed her under the beloved apostle's care.
We pray through the divine Son Jesus Christ. **Amen.**

CONCLUSION

Blessing

Bow your heads and pray for God's blessing.
May God almighty raise us up. **Amen.**
May the divine Son be with us. **Amen.**
May the Spirit overshadow us. **Amen.**
And may God bless us
in the name of the Father, and of the Son, and of the Holy Spirit. **Amen.**

Sign of Peace/Dismissal

Share with one another a sign of the peace of the divine Son.

Solemnity of the ASSUMPTION Evening Prayer

LIGHT SERVICE

Proclamation of the Light

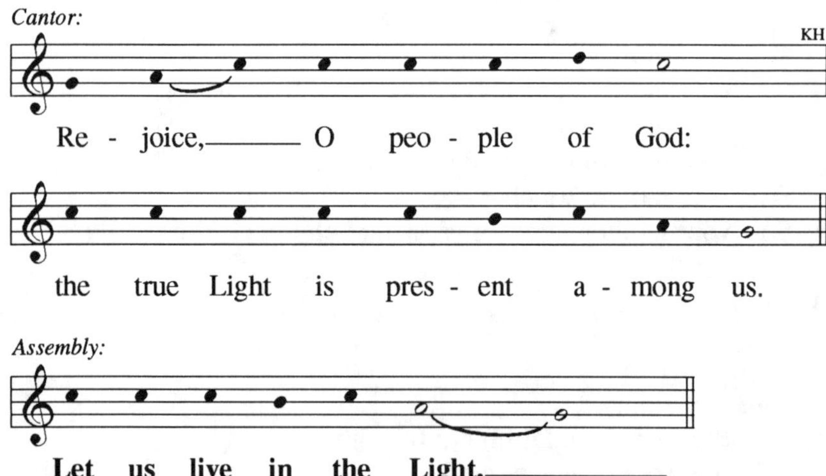
Cantor:
KH
Re - joice, O peo - ple of God:
the true Light is pres - ent a - mong us.
Assembly:
Let us live in the Light.

Festal Evening Hymn

Thanksgiving for the Light

Cantor:
KH
We praise and thank you, O God, the Cre - a - tor of
light and dark-ness. On this fes - ti - val when we cel - e - brate
the as - sump - tion of Ma - ry in - to heav-en, you re - new
your prom - ise to re - veal a - mong us the splen - did light of
your glo - ry - made vis - i - ble in the In - car - nate Word
Je - sus Christ. Through the proph-ets of old you call us
to your cov - e - nant of love. Now through the Spir - it you
o - pen our eyes to the peace of Christ's pres - ence.
So with the ho - ly an - gels on high we sing out:

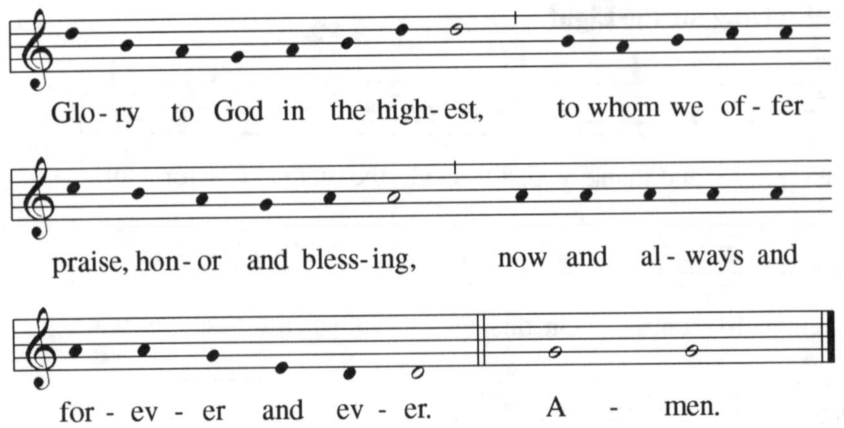

PSALMODY

Psalm 130 *Song of ascents (pilgrimages).*

ANTIPHON

KH
Al-le-lu-ia! Ma-ry lis-tened to your Word!

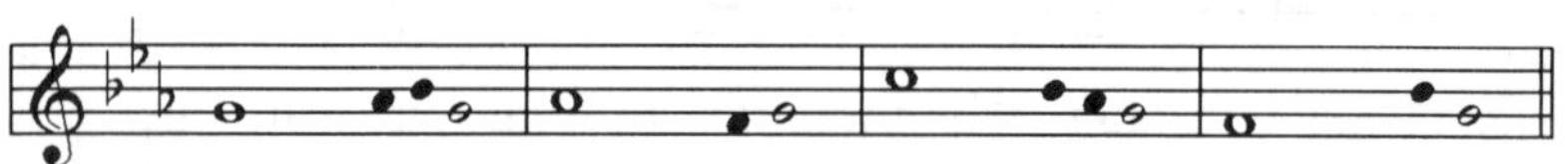

Out of the depths, I cry to **you**, O LORD.
Lord, listen to **my** voice;
let your ears **be** attentive
to the voice of my sup**pli**cations. ANTIPHON

If you, O LORD, were to keep in**iquities** in mind,
Lord, who **could** stand?
But with you **is** forgiveness,
and for that you are **re**vered. ANTIPHON

I wait for the LORD;
  my soul waits, and for God's **word** I hope.
My soul waits for **the** Lord
more than watchers **of** the morning
watch for **the** dawn. ANTIPHON

Let Israel hope **in** the LORD,
for steadfast love is found with the LORD
  and abundance of **re**demption.
It is the LORD who shall redeem **Is**rael
from all iniq**ui**ties. ANTIPHON

Psalm Prayer
O God who listens to our voices,
you are steadfast in love and sure in forgiveness:
speak your Word to us
that we may know and revere you
now and always. **Amen.**

Psalm 67 *To the choirmaster. With stringed instruments. Psalm. Song.*

ANTIPHON
KH
Let the peo - ples give you thanks, O God; let
all the peo - ples give you thanks.

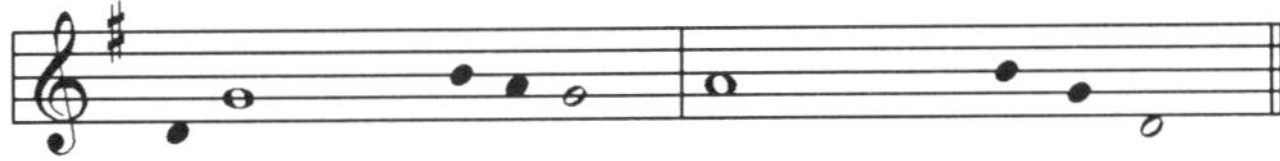

May God have mercy on us and **bless** us.
May God's face **shine** among us.

For your way is known **over** the earth,
and your salvation is known a**mong** all nations. ANTIPHON

May the nations rejoice and **shout** with joy,
for you judge the peoples rightly
  and the nations on the **earth** you guide. ANTIPHON

The earth has **given** its fruit.
May God, our God, **bless** us.

May God **bless** us,
and let all ends of the **earth** show reverence. ANTIPHON

Psalm Prayer
God of all blessings,
you are worthy of all thanksgiving:
by giving us Mary our Mother as a model,
guide us to do your holy will
so that we may be fruitful all our lives.
We pray through Jesus Christ. **Amen.**

Word of God

Magnificat
My soul does magni**fy** the Lord!
I delight in **God** my savior
who looked kindly **on** lowliness.

Now all ages will **call** me blessed
for the Mighty One **did** great things.
Holy is **God's** name;
mercy is from age to age for **those** in awe!

The Lord's strong arm did **might**y deeds:
confused the proud in **their** smug hearts;
toppled sovereigns **from** their thrones,
and exalted **hum**ble ones;
filled the hungering with **good** things,
and sent the rich **a**way empty.

The Lord helped servant **Is**rael
to re**mem**ber mercy,
as was spoken to Ab**ra**ham
and his descendants for**e**vermore!

INTERCESSIONS

Petitions

Cantor, then Assembly:

Cantor:

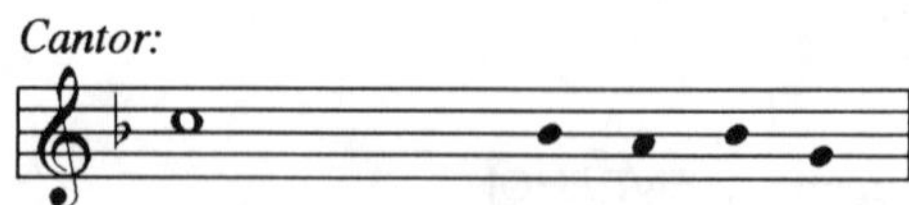

We **cry** out to God ...
We lis**ten** to God's voice ...
We are atten**tive** to God's deeds ...
We are forgiv**en** our iniquities ...
We revere **God's** holy name ...
We **hope** in God's Word ...
We greet **God's** steadfast love ...
We enjoy abun**dant** redemption ...
We **make** known God's ways ...
We **give** thanks forever ...
We rejoice **and** shout with joy ...
We honor **Ma**ry our mother ...
We commend the faithful depart**ed** to God's love ...

Our Father ...

Prayer
O wondrous God,
your face shines on us
and we receive Life:
may we always open ourselves to your message of love
through the intercession of Mary our Mother
and her divine Son Jesus Christ. **Amen.**

CONCLUSION

Blessing
Bow your heads and pray for God's blessing.
May the Creator God make the divine face to shine upon us. **Amen.**
May the Redeemer Son look upon us kindly. **Amen.**
May the Sanctifying Spirit give us peace. **Amen.**
And may God bless us
in the name of the Father, and of the Son, and of the Holy Spirit. **Amen.**

Sign of Peace/Dismissal
Share with one another the peace of the divine Son,
that we may rest confidently under the protection of Mary our Mother.

August 24
Feast of BARTHOLOMEW, Apostle
Morning Praise

From the Feast of PHILIP & JAMES, Apostles, Morning Praise, p. 534.

Prayer
O God,
you called Bartholomew to be your follower
through the apostle Philip:
open us to hear always your voice through others.
We pray through Jesus Christ. **Amen.**

Feast of BARTHOLOMEW, Apostle
Evening Prayer

From the Feast of PHILIP & JAMES, Apostles, Evening Prayer, p. 537.

Prayer
O God,
the apostles witnessed to the resurrection
of your Son Jesus Christ, the Messiah:
help us to be witnesses of the Good News
and to remain loyal to Jesus Christ now and always. **Amen.**

September 8
Feast of the BIRTH OF MARY
Morning Praise

From the Feast of the VISITATION Morning Praise, p. 541.

Prayer
Gracious God,
you brought forth Mary from the shoot of Jesse
and destined her to be the Mother of your divine Son:
may our celebration of her birth
increase in us your life and
bring us hope and peace.
We pray through Jesus Christ. **Amen.**

Feast of the BIRTH OF MARY
Evening Prayer

From the Feast of the VISITATION Evening Prayer, p. 544.

Prayer
O God of redemption,
through Mary you brought salvation to the whole world:
as we celebrate the birth of her earthly life
may we also look to joining her among the heavenly choir
where we may sing your praise and thanksgiving forever and ever. **Amen.**

September 14
Feast of the TRIUMPH OF THE CROSS
Morning Praise

FESTAL MORNING HYMN

PSALMODY

Psalm 3 *Psalm of David. In his flight from Absalom his son.*

Solo 1 O LORD, how many are my adversaries!
Many are rising against me;
many are saying to my soul:
"There is no salvation
for you in God."

Selah (pause).

Solo 2 But you, O LORD,
are a shield over me,
my glory and the one lifting my head.
With my voice to the LORD I will cry,
and God will answer me from the holy mountain.

Selah (pause).

Solo 1 I lie down and sleep;
I wake up
for the LORD sustains me.
I shall not fear the multitudes of people
positioning themselves
around and against me.

Solo 2 Arise, O LORD;
save me, my God,
for you strike all my enemies on the cheek
and you shatter the teeth of the wicked.

All From the LORD, salvation!
Upon your people, blessing!

Selah (pause).

Psalm 96

Choir 1 Sing to the LORD a new song.
Sing to the LORD, all the earth.
Sing to the LORD, bless God's name.

Choir 2 From day to day proclaim the good news of salvation.
Recount among the nations God's glory,
God's marvels among all peoples.
For great is the LORD, highly to be praised
and revered above all gods.
For all the gods of the nations are as nothing,
but the LORD made the heavens.
Honor and splendor stand before God,
might and glory fill the temple.

Choir 1 Give to the LORD, O families of peoples.
Give to the LORD glory and might.
Give to the LORD the glory of God's name.

Choir 2 Bring an offering and come into the courts.
Worship the LORD with holy splendor.
Dance in the sacred presence, all the earth.
Say among the nations: "The LORD reigns."
Surely God formed the universe

so that it would not falter.
God will judge the peoples in equity.

Choir 1 Let the heavens rejoice and the earth exult.
Let the sea and its fullness roar.
Let the fields and all within them be glad.

Choir 2 Then all the trees of the forest will shout with joy
in the presence of the LORD who comes.
For God comes to judge the earth,
to judge the universe with justice
and with fidelity, the peoples.

Word of God

Benedictus
Blessed be the Lord God of **Israel**,
who visited and redeemed the **people**,
who raised up for us a **might**y savior
from the house of **ser**vant David.

Just as the Lord spoke through the mouths of the holy prophets of **old**—
salvation comes out of the hands of our enemies and those who **hate** us,
that, with our ancestors, we might perform **works** of mercy,
remembering the holy covenant **sworn** to Abraham—

so does the Lord deliver us from the hands **of** our enemies,
that we might serve without fear before **the** Lord,
worshiping in **ho**liness
and in righteousness **all** our days.

And you also, child, will be called a prophet of God Most **High**:
for you will go before the Lord to prepare a **way**,
bringing people knowledge of salvation by for**giveness** of sins;
because of the deep and tender mercy **of** our God.

Whereby a light rising from on high will **vis**it us
to appear to those in darkness and in a shadow **of** death,
to guide our feet along a **straight**, sure path
into a **way** of peace.

INTERCESSIONS

Invocations

Cantor, then Assembly:

O won - drous Cross of sal - va - tion.

Cantor:

Jesus our Savior, your adversaries nailed **you** to a cross,
Jesus our Savior, many rose **up** against you,
Jesus our Savior, you cried aloud **in** desolation,
Jesus our Savior, you slept **the** sleep of death,
Jesus our Savior, your **death** brought salvation,
Jesus our Savior, you judge the **uni**verse with justice,
Jesus our Savior, you stand with **hon**or and splendor,
Jesus our Savior, you are filled **with** might and glory,

Our Father ...

Prayer
O gentle God,
the cross of your Son brought salvation to the world:
help us to take up our daily crosses
that we might bring hope and consolation to all in need.
We pray through Jesus Christ. **Amen.**

CONCLUSION

Blessing
May the God of the cross bless us
in the name of the Father, and of the Son, and of the Holy Spirit. **Amen.**

Dismissal
Go forth to live your day under the banner of the cross. **Thanks be to God.**

Feast of the TRIUMPH OF THE CROSS
Evening Prayer

FESTAL EVENING HYMN

PSALMODY

Psalm 130 *Song of ascents (pilgrimages).*

Solo 1 Out of the depths, I cry to you, O LORD.
Lord, listen to my voice;
let your ears be attentive
to the voice of my supplications.

All If you, O LORD, were to keep iniquities in mind,
Lord, who could stand?
But with you is forgiveness,
and for that you are revered.

Solo 1 I wait for the LORD;
my soul waits,
and for God's word I hope.
My soul waits for the Lord
more than watchers of the morning
watch for the dawn.

All Let Israel hope in the LORD,
for steadfast love is found with the LORD
and abundance of redemption.
It is the LORD who shall redeem Israel
from all iniquities.

Psalm 138 *Of David.*

Solo 1 I give you thanks with all my heart;
instead of other gods, I sing to you.
I bow down toward the holy sanctuary,
and I give thanks to your name
on account of your steadfast love and your truth.
For you have exalted your promise
even above your name.
On the day I cried, you answered me;
you renewed courage within me.

All Let all the rulers of the earth give thanks to you, O LORD,
for they have heard the words of your mouth.

Let them sing about the ways of the LORD,
for great is the glory of the LORD.
Although exalted,
the LORD looks upon the lowly,
but recognizes the proud only from a distance.

Solo 1 When I walk in the midst of distress,
you revive me against the anger of my enemies.
You stretch out your hand,
and your right hand saves me;
the LORD will do everything for me.

All O LORD, your steadfast love is forever.
Do not forsake the work of your hands.

INTERCESSIONS

Petitions

Cantor, then Assembly:

O how sweet is the wood of sal - va - tion.

Cantor:

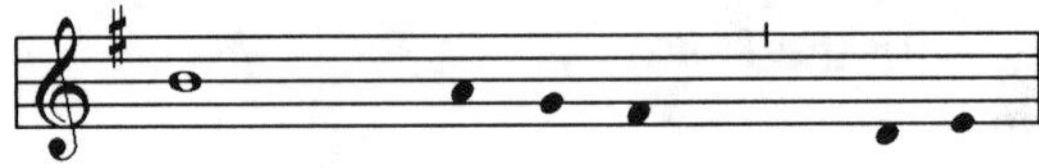

Out **of** the depths ... **we** cry,
Desiring at**ten**tive ears ... **we** cry,
Seek**ing** forgiveness ... **we** cry,
Wait**ing** for hope ... **we** cry,
Assured of **stead**fast love ... **we** cry,
Promised an abundance **of** redemption ... **we** cry,
Bowing **down** in worship ... **we** cry,
Re**newed** in courage ... **we** cry,
Revived **a**gainst anger ... **we** cry,
Saved **from** all harm ... **we** cry,
Forsaking not the faith**ful** departed ... **we** cry,

Our Father ...

Prayer
O tender God,
an instrument of pain

was the means to overcome death and bring new life:
may the Blood of the cross
fill us with renewed strength
to live as your sons and daughters now and always. **Amen.**

CONCLUSION

Blessing
May the God of salvation bless us
in the name of the Father, and of the Son, and of the Holy Spirit. **Amen.**

Dismissal
Go and rest in the victory of the cross. **Thanks be to God.**

September 21
Feast of MATTHEW, Apostle and Evangelist
Morning Praise

From the Feast of PHILIP & JAMES, Apostles, Morning Praise, p. 534.

Prayer
God of surprises,
you chose a tax collector to be
numbered among the apostles:
deliver us from judging others
so that we might break down the barriers
that still separate us one from another.
We pray through Jesus Christ. **Amen.**

Feast of MATTHEW, Apostle and Evangelist
Evening Prayer

From the Feast of PHILIP & JAMES, Apostles, Evening Prayer, p. 537.

Prayer
O God,
you speak words of love and tenderness,

strength and covenant:
help us to love and reverence the Good News as did Matthew,
that we might draw others to your saving grace.
We pray through Jesus Christ. **Amen.**

September 29
Feast of
MICHAEL, GABRIEL, & RAPHAEL, Archangels
Morning Praise

FESTAL MORNING HYMN

PSALMODY

Psalm 8 *To the choirmaster. On the gittith. Of David.*

All O LORD our Lord,
how magnificent is your name
over all the earth!

Choir 1 You set your glory above the skies.
From the mouths of babes and infants,
you have established strength against your adversaries
to still the enemy and avenger.

Solo 1 If I look at your skies,
the work of your fingers,
the moon and stars that you have set in place,
What are mortals that you remember them?
And human beings that you care for them?

Choir 2 But you have made them slightly less than a god,
and with glory and radiance you crown them.
You made them rule over the work of your hands.
You have placed everything under their feet—
sheep and cattle, all together,
and even the beasts from the fields,
the birds of heaven
and the fish from the sea,
all that crosses along the paths of the seas.

All O LORD our Lord,
how magnificent is your name
over all the earth!

Psalm 148

All Alleluia!

Choir 1 Praise the LORD from the heavens:
praise God in the highest,
praise God, O you messengers,
praise God, O you hosts,
praise God, sun and moon,
praise God, all shining stars
praise God, farthest heavens
and waters from above the heavens.

Choir 2 Let them praise the name of the LORD,
who commanded and they were created,
who established them forever and ever,
fixing a limit that they cannot cross.

Choir 1 Praise the LORD from the earth:
sea monsters and all deep waters,
fire and hail,
snow and frost,
stormy winds fulfilling God's word,
mountains and all hills,
fruit trees and all cedars,
living creatures and all cattle,
reptiles and flying birds.

Choir 2 Rulers of the earth and all nations,
nobles and all judges of the earth,
youthful men and women,
elderly and young people:
let them praise the LORD,
for God's name only is most high.
God's glory is above earth and heaven;
God will act mightily for the people.

All Praise from all the faithful,
from the children of Israel,

the people close to God!

Alleluia!

Word of God

Benedictus

Blessed be the Lord God of **Israel**,
who visited and redeemed the **people**,
who raised up for us a **mighty** savior
from the house of **ser**vant David.

Just as the Lord spoke through the mouths of the holy prophets of **old**—
salvation comes out of the hands of our enemies and those who **hate** us,
that, with our ancestors, we might perform **works** of mercy,
remembering the holy covenant **sworn** to Abraham—

so does the Lord deliver us from the hands **of** our enemies,
that we might serve without fear before **the** Lord,
worshiping in **ho**liness
and in righteousness **all** our days.

And you also, child, will be called a prophet of God Most **High**:
for you will go before the Lord to prepare a **way**,
bringing people knowledge of salvation by for**giveness** of sins;
because of the deep and tender mercy **of** our God.

Whereby a light rising from on high will **visit** us
to appear to those in darkness and in a shadow **of** death,
to guide our feet along a **straight**, sure path
into a **way** of peace.

INTERCESSIONS

Invocations

Cantor, then Assembly:

Cantor:

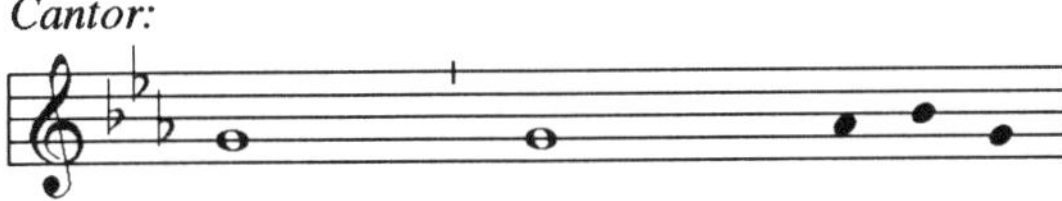

Lamb of God, an angel hailed **your** conception,
Lamb of God, angels an**nounced** your birth,
Lamb of God, an angel warned Joseph in his **sleep** to flee,
Lamb of God, angels ministered to you **in** the desert,
Lamb of God, angels stood guard **at** your tomb,
Lamb of God, angelic choirs sur**round** your throne,
Lamb of God, angels sing your **praises** forever,

Our Father ...

Prayer
O heavenly God,
you have sent angels even from the time of old
to convey your holy will to humanity:
open our eyes to be attentive to your divine messages
that with the angels we may praise you forever and ever. **Amen.**

CONCLUSION

Blessing
May the God of the heavenly court bless us
in the name of the Father, and of the Son, and of the Holy Spirit. **Amen.**

Dismissal
Go forth this day to serve others,
confident of the protection of God's holy angels. **Thanks be to God.**

Feast of MICHAEL, GABRIEL, & RAPHAEL, Archangels Evening Prayer

---

FESTAL EVENING HYMN

PSALMODY

Psalm 16 *A poem. Of David.*

Solo 1 Keep me, O God,
for I take refuge in you.
I say to the LORD:
"You are my Lord,
my happiness is only in you."

All As for idols in the land,
they are mighty only for those who delight in them.
People multiply these idols
after which they hurry.

Solo 2 But I will not offer them sacrifices of blood,
nor will I raise their names to my lips.
O LORD, my given portion and my cup,
you support my destiny
which has fallen for me in pleasant places,
nothing but a goodly heritage.

Solo 1 I bless the LORD who gives me counsel.
Even at night my heart instructs me.
I keep the LORD always before me.
Because God is at my right hand,
I shall not be moved.

Solo 2 Hence my heart rejoices
and my soul exults.
Even my body rests secure
because you do not abandon me to Sheol.
You do not allow your faithful
to experience the Pit.
You teach me the path of life.

All In your presence there is fullness of joy;
in your right hand, pleasures for eternity.

Psalm 138 *Of David.*

Solo 1 I give you thanks with all my heart;
instead of other gods, I sing to you.
I bow down toward the holy sanctuary,
and I give thanks to your name
on account of your steadfast love and your truth.
For you have exalted your promise

even above your name.
On the day I cried, you answered me;
you renewed courage within me.

All Let all the rulers of the earth give thanks to you, O LORD,
for they have heard the words of your mouth.
Let them sing about the ways of the LORD,
for great is the glory of the LORD.
Although exalted,
the LORD looks upon the lowly,
but recognizes the proud only from a distance.

Solo 1 When I walk in the midst of distress,
you revive me against the anger of my enemies.
You stretch out your hand,
and your right hand saves me;
the LORD will do everything for me.

All O LORD, your steadfast love is forever.
Do not forsake the work of your hands.

Word of God

Magnificat
My soul does magni**fy** the Lord!
I delight in **God** my savior
who looked kindly **on** lowliness.

Now all ages will **call** me blessed
for the Mighty One **did** great things.
Holy is **God's** name;
mercy is from age to age for **those** in awe!

The Lord's strong arm did **migh**ty deeds:
confused the proud in **their** smug hearts;
toppled sovereigns **from** their thrones,
and exalted **hum**ble ones;
filled the hungering with **good** things,
and sent the rich **a**way empty.

The Lord helped servant **Is**rael
to re**mem**ber mercy,

as was spoken to Abr**a**ham
and his descendants for**e**vermore!

INTERCESSIONS

Petitions

Cantor, then Assembly:

Cantor:

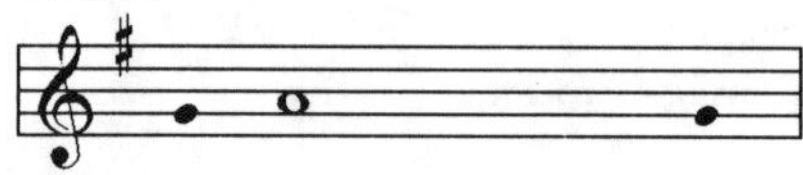

From **all** idols ...
From **false** pre**ten**ses ...
From **mis**guided **wis**dom ...
From **de**ceiving **coun**sel ...
From **bro**ken **prom**ises ...
From **para**lyzing dis**cour**agement ...
From **de**vastating **pride** ...
From **o**verwhelming dis**tress** ...
From **un**founded **an**ger ...
From **e**verlasting punishment for those who have **died** ...

Our Father ...

Prayer
Attentive God,
you never abandon us to the power of darkness:
may your angels keep us safe and
walk with us as we journey toward life with you now and forever. **Amen.**

CONCLUSION

Blessing
May the God of the heavenly courts bless us
in the name of the Father, and of the Son, and of the Holy Spirit. **Amen.**

Dismissal
Go and rest, accompanied by the angels. **Thanks be to God.**

October 18
Feast of LUKE, Evangelist
Morning Praise

From the Feast of MARK, Evangelist, Morning Praise, p. 494.

Prayer
O God who speaks a mighty Word,
you chose Luke to record the message of your Good News:
keep us open to the truth
that we, too, might proclaim your love now and always. **Amen.**

Feast of LUKE, Evangelist
Evening Prayer

From the Feast of MARK, Evangelist, Evening Prayer, p. 497.

Prayer
Tender and gentle God,
you inspired Luke to write a Gospel
sensitive to prayer, and to the poor and lowly:
break down any barriers that divide us and
help us to reach out to all others in need.
We pray through Jesus Christ. **Amen.**

October 28
Feast of SIMON & JUDE, Apostles
Morning Praise

From the Feast of PHILIP & JAMES, Apostles, Morning Praise, p. 534.

Prayer
O God,
you reveal yourself to those who love you:
by the example of the apostles Simon and Jude,
may we ever spread your Good News throughout the world.
We pray through Jesus Christ. **Amen.**

Feast of SIMON & JUDE, Apostles
Evening Prayer

From the Feast of PHILIP & JAMES, Apostles, Evening Prayer, p. 537.

Prayer
O God who calls followers,
your Son called Simon and Jude
to be numbered among his apostles:
keep us faithful to our baptismal call
to serve you in the Body of Christ.
We pray through Jesus Christ. **Amen.**

C.G.

November 1
Solemnity of ALL SAINTS
Morning Praise

FESTAL MORNING HYMN

PSALMODY

Psalm 63 *Psalm of David. While he was in the desert of Judah.*

ANTIPHON
3
KH
In your sanc- tu - a - ry we bless___ you.

omit last strophe

O God, you are my God, **I** seek you;
my **soul** thirsts **for** you.
My flesh longs for you
  in a dry and **wast**ed land,
deprived **of** water. ANTIPHON

So in the sanctuary I have contemplated you
  to see your might and your **glo**ry.
Because your **stead**fast love is better than life,
  my lips will **praise** you.
So I will bless you **all** my life;
in your name I will raise **my** hands.

As with milk and rich food,
  my soul **is** filled;
my **mouth** gives praise with joy**ful** lips.
I remember you up**on** my bed,
pondering you throughout **the** night.

For you were a help **for** me;
in the **shade** of your wings I **keep** singing.
My soul **clings** to you;
your right hand **up**holds me. ANTIPHON

But let those who seek my de**struc**tion
be **cast** into the depths of **the** earth.
Let them be given over to the power **of** the sword;
let them become a prey **for** jackals. ANTIPHON

Then the king shall rejoice **in** God.
All **those** who swear by God will **be** praised,
for the mouths of liars will **be** shut. ANTIPHON

Psalm Prayer
God of blessings,
you have raised up holy men and women
to inspire us to increase our love and fidelity to you:
help us to remember your presence always
that we may sing your praises forever and ever. **Amen.**

Psalm 148

ANTIPHON
KH
All you faith - ful, praise God; heav - ens lift your voic - es,
al - le - lu - - - ia!

Praise the LORD from the heavens:
  praise God in the **highest**,
praise God, O you messengers,
  praise God, O **you** hosts,
praise God, sun and moon,
  praise God, all shining **stars**
praise God, farthest heavens
  and waters from above **the** heavens. ANTIPHON

Let them praise the name of the **LORD**,
who commanded and they were **cre**ated,
who established them forever and **ever**,
fixing a limit that they can**not** cross. ANTIPHON

Praise the LORD from the earth:
  sea monsters and all deep **waters**,
fire and hail,
  snow and frost,
  stormy winds fulfilling **God's** word,

mountains and all hills,
  fruit trees and all **cedars**,
living creatures and all cattle,
  reptiles and fly**ing** birds. ANTIPHON

Rulers of the earth and all nations,
  nobles and all judges of the **earth**,
youthful men and women,
  elderly and **young** people:
let them praise the LORD,
  for God's name only is most **high**.
God's glory is above earth and heaven;
  God will act mightily for **the** people. ANTIPHON

Praise from all the **faithful**,
from the children of Isr**a**el,
the people close to **God**!
Alle**lu**ia!

Psalm Prayer
Wondrous God,
you are worthy of all praise:
hear the morning prayer of your holy people,
for we join the saints in heaven
to proclaim your wonderful deeds.
We pray through your Son, Jesus Christ,
in the unity of the Holy Spirit, one God, forever and ever. **Amen.**

Word of God

Benedictus
Blessed be the Lord God of **Israel**,
who visited and redeemed the **people**,
who raised up for us a **mighty** savior
from the house of **ser**vant David.

Just as the Lord spoke through the mouths of the holy prophets of **old**—
salvation comes out of the hands of our enemies and those who **hate** us,

that, with our ancestors, we might perform **works** of mercy,
remembering the holy covenant **sworn** to Abraham—

so does the Lord deliver us from the hands **of** our enemies,
that we might serve without fear before **the** Lord,
worshiping in **ho**liness
and in righteousness **all** our days.

And you also, child, will be called a prophet of God Most **High**:
for you will go before the Lord to prepare a **way**,
bringing people knowledge of salvation by for**giveness** of sins;
because of the deep and tender mercy **of** our God.

Whereby a light rising from on high will **vis**it us
to appear to those in darkness and in a shadow **of** death,
to guide our feet along a **straight**, sure path
into a **way** of peace.

INTERCESSIONS

Invocations

Cantor, then Assembly:
KH
All your saints praise___ you!

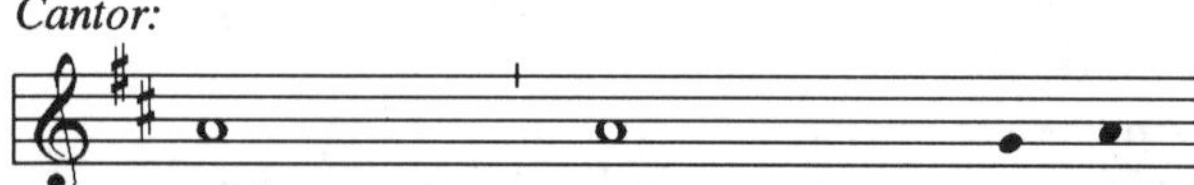
Cantor:

O risen Christ, you are the Lamb that **was** slain,
O risen Christ, you are filled with might **and** glory,
O risen Christ, you are surrounded by the Saints with gold**en** crowns,
O risen Christ, you are worthy to open the seals of **the** scroll,
O risen Christ, you ransomed for God saints from every tribe and language and people **and** nation,
O risen Christ, you washed the robes of the saints and made them white in **your** blood,
O risen Christ, you mark the foreheads of your saints with **your** seal,
O risen Christ, in your saints the mystery of God is **ful**filled,

Our Father ...

Prayer
O mighty God,
you were, and are, and always will be:
the saints are the blessed ones
who heard the Good News and
kept it faithfully until death.
May they accompany us on our journey toward you and
by their example of holiness encourage us
to stray not from the path of Life.
We pray through the Lamb who was slain, Jesus Christ. **Amen.**

CONCLUSION

Blessing
Bow your heads and pray for God's blessing.
May the God who is the source of all holiness bless us. **Amen.**
May the Son who is the Lamb slain for us keep us. **Amen.**
May the Spirit who is Love made present shine upon us. **Amen.**
And may God bless us
in the name of the Father, and of the Son, and of the Holy Spirit. **Amen.**

Sign of Peace/Dismissal
Share with the saints of God near you a sign of Christ's peace.

Solemnity of ALL SAINTS
Evening Prayer

LIGHT SERVICE

Proclamation of the Light

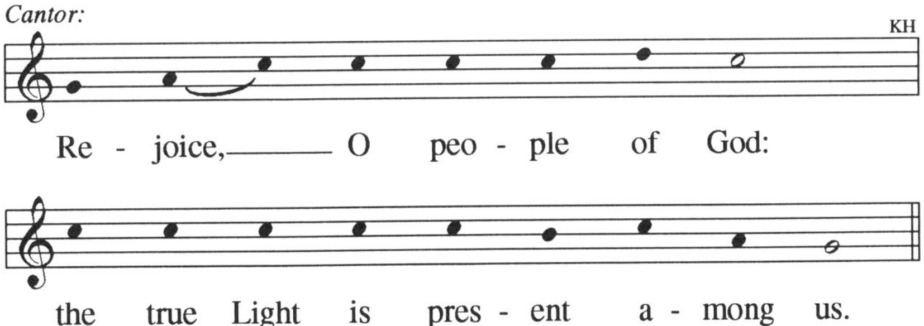
Cantor:
KH
Re - joice, O peo - ple of God:
the true Light is pres - ent a - mong us.

Assembly:

Festal Evening Hymn

Thanksgiving for the Light

Cantor:

KH

We praise and thank you, O ho - ly God!

Your pow - er lifts the great light in the heav - ens.

Your glo - ry shines forth in the ris - en Son.

Your ho - li - ness is poured up - on us by your Spir - it.

Your splen - dor clothes us with dig - ni - ty

and hon - or. Your good - ness o - ver - comes an - y

weak - ness. Your boun - ty sat - is - fies all hun - ger.

Your grace pro - claims our des - ti - ny.

Re-joice, O ho-ly peo-ple, in this great Light:

on this day we cel-e-brate the saints who live with

you now and al-ways. As our fes-ti-val draws to a

close, and dark-ness des-cends in qui-et rest, keep us

safe in this Light that nev-er fades. We praise and

thank you for your bless-ings, through Christ our Light

for-ev-er and ev-er. **A-men.**

PSALMODY

Psalm 110 *Of David. Psalm.*

ANTIPHON
KH
Raise high the scep-ter of strength.

Thus says the LORD **to** my lord:
"Sit on my right
  until I place your enemies
  as a footstool for **your** feet."
Let the LORD send from Zion
  the scepter of **your** strength.
Rule in the midst of **your** enemies. ANTIPHON

Your people bring free **of**ferings
on the day of your might
  in ho**ly** splendor.
From the womb **of** dawn,
a dew of rejuvenation comes **to** you. ANTIPHON

The LORD has promised
  and will **not** repent:
"According to my word,
  you are a priest forever, my king **of** justice."
The Lord is at **your** right,
who has smashed rulers on the day **of** wrath.

The Lord judges a**gainst** the nations,
piling them **with** corpses.
The Lord has smashed heads
  all over **the** land.
From a torrent the Lord drinks on the way,
  and rises up **in** triumph. ANTIPHON

Psalm Prayer
Gracious God,
you have raised up holy men and women from all corners of the earth
to aid us in our weakness:
on this day of splendor receive our free offering—
an evening sacrifice of thanksgiving for your honor and glory.
May your saints inspire us and lead us to life everlasting. **Amen.**

Psalm 116

ANTIPHON

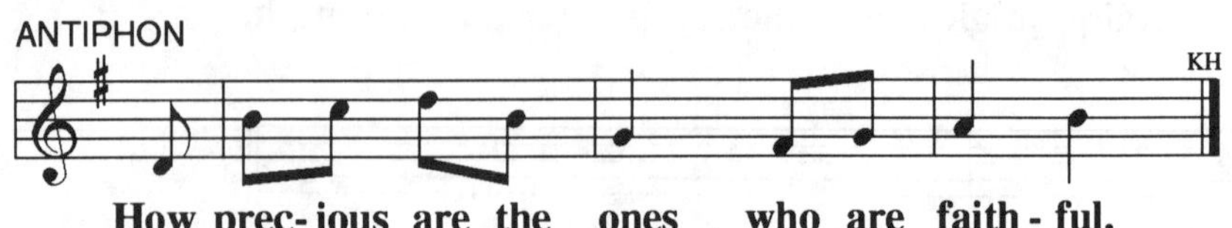

KH
How prec- ious are the ones who are faith - ful.

I love the Lord
 who **has** heard
the voice of my suppli**ca**tions.
For God has turned an ear **to** me
as I cry all **my** days. ANTIPHON

Deadly chains have fettered me,
 and the anguish of Sheol has reached up **to** me.
Distress and terror, I have en**countered**;
but I have called on the name of **the** Lord.
How long, O Lord?
 Deliver **my** soul. ANTIPHON

The Lord is gracious and just;
 our God **is** merciful.
The Lord is the protector of the **innocent**;
I was poor and God brought salvation **to** me.
Return, O my soul, to your rest,
 for the Lord has done good **to** you. ANTIPHON

For you have delivered my soul **from** death,
my eye from tears
 and my foot from **stumbling**,
that I may walk in the presence of **the** Lord
in the land of **the** living. ANTIPHON

Yes, I was right **in** saying,
"I am greatly af**flicted**."
In my agitation, I **have** said,
"Every human being is **a** liar." ANTIPHON

What shall I return to the Lord
 for all the bounty in **my** favor?
I will lift up the cup of salvation
 and I will call on the name of the **Lord**.
Indeed, I will fulfill my promises to **the** Lord
in the presence of all **the** people. ANTIPHON

Precious in the eyes of the LORD
  is the death of **the** faithful ones.
How long, O **LORD**?
For I am your servant,
  I am your servant, the offspring of **your** handmaid.
You have loosened **my** bonds. ANTIPHON

To you I will offer a sacrifice of thanksgiving
  and I will call on the name of **the** LORD.
Indeed, I will fulfill my promises to the LORD
  in the presence of all the **people**,
in the courts of the house of **the** LORD,
in your midst, O Jerusalem.
  Alle**lu**ia! ANTIPHON

Psalm Prayer
Attentive God,
today we join our voices
with all holy men and women
in a ceaseless chorus of joyful thanksgiving:
may this festival in honor of the saints
remind us that we join them
when our mouths offer praise,
when our works proclaim your Good News, and
when our lives celebrate your holiness forever and ever. **Amen.**

Word of God

Magnificat
My soul does magni**fy** the Lord!
I delight in **God** my savior
who looked kindly **on** lowliness.

Now all ages will **call** me blessed
for the Mighty One **did** great things.
Holy is **God's** name;
mercy is from age to age for **those** in awe!

The Lord's strong arm did **mighty** deeds:
confused the proud in **their** smug hearts;
toppled sovereigns **from** their thrones,
and exalted **hum**ble ones;

filled the hungering with **good** things,
and sent the rich **a**way empty.

The Lord helped servant **Is**rael
to re**mem**ber mercy,
as was spoken to Ab**ra**ham
and his descendants for**e**vermore!

INTERCESSIONS

Petitions
(For music, see the Litany for the Liturgy of Baptism at the Easter Vigil in the Sacramentary*).*

Lord, have mercy. **Lord, have mercy.**
Christ, have mercy. **Christ, have mercy.**
Lord, have mercy. **Lord, have mercy.**
Holy Adam and **Eve**, **Pray for us!**
Holy Noah and **fam**ily, "
Holy Abraham and **S**arah,
Holy Isaac and Re**be**kah,
Holy Jacob and **Ra**chel,
Holy Joseph and **A**senath,
Holy Moses and **Zip**porah,
Holy Boaz and **Ruth**,
Holy David and Bath**she**ba,
Holy prophets and **sa**ges,
Saint John the **Bap**tist,
Holy Mary, Mother of **God**,
Saint **Jo**seph,
Saint **Pe**ter,
Saint **Paul**,
Holy martyrs and con**fess**ors,

[add other saints of choice]

Holy angels of **God**,
All holy mothers and **fa**thers,
All members of our holy **fam**ilies,
All holy men and **wo**men,
All holy faithful de**part**ed,

Our Father ...

Prayer
Blessed God,
source of all holiness,
your work is manifest in the saints and
the beauty of your truth is reflected in their faith:
may we who aspire to have part in their joy
be filled with the Spirit that blessed their lives,
so that having shared their faith on earth
we may also know their peace in your heavenly court.
Grant this through Jesus Christ. **Amen.**

CONCLUSION

Blessing
Bow your heads and pray for God's blessing.
May God, the creator of all that is good and source of all holiness, bless us and keep us. **Amen.**
May Jesus Christ, the revelation of God's love, graciously smile upon us. **Amen.**
May the Holy Spirit, the presence of the Risen Christ in the holy people of God, grant us peace. **Amen.**
And may God bless us
in the name of the Father, and of the Son, and of the Holy Spirit. **Amen.**

Sign of Peace/Dismissal
Share with one another a sign of peace, that we may rest in the company of all the saints. **Thanks be to God.**

November 2
ALL SOULS
Morning Praise

FESTAL MORNING HYMN

PSALMODY

Psalm 51 *To the choirmaster. Psalm of David. In the coming to him of Nathan the prophet, after David had been with Bathsheba.*

November 2 ALL SOULS Morning Praise

ANTIPHON
KH
The souls of the just cry out.

Be gracious to **me**, O God,
in your **stead**fast love.
According to the abundance **of** your mercy
blot out my **trans**gressions. ANTIPHON

Cleanse me completely **from** my guilt
and purify me **from** my sin.
For my transgressions I do **rec**ognize,
and my sin stands always **be**fore me.

Against you alone **have** I sinned,
and what is evil in your eyes **I** have done.
Thus you may be declared just in your ways,
  and pure **in** your judgments.
Indeed, I was born guilty,
  already a sinner when my mother **con**ceived me. ANTIPHON

Surely in truth **you** delight,
and deep within my self you will **teach** me wisdom.
Cleanse me from my sin with hyssop and I **will** be pure,
wash me and I shall be brighter **than** snow.

Let me hear glad**ness** and joy,
let the bones you **broke** exult.
Turn your face **from** my sins
and blot out all my iniq**ui**ties. ANTIPHON

Create in me a pure **heart**, O God,
and renew within me **a** firm spirit.
Do not dismiss me **from** your presence,
and do not take away from me your ho**ly** spirit.

Give me back the joy of **your** salvation,
and let a willing spirit lie **o**ver me.
I will teach transgres**sors** your ways,
and sinners will turn back **to** you. ANTIPHON

Deliver me from bloodshed, O God,
  God of **my** salvation,
and my tongue will **sing** your justice.
O Lord, **open** my lips,
and my mouth will tell **your** praise.

For you take no pleasure in **sac**rifice,
and you would not accept an offering were **I** to give it.
The perfect sacrifice for God is a **brok**en spirit.
A broken and humble heart,
  O God, you will not **des**pise. ANTIPHON

In your kindness bring prosperi**ty** to Zion;
rebuild the walls of Je**ru**salem.
Then you can delight in sacrifices of justice,
  burnt and complete **of**ferings;
then bulls can be offered on **your** altars. ANTIPHON

Psalm Prayer
Merciful God,
your steadfast love sustains the faithful departed:
wash us brighter than snow
and restore us, with them, to your favor now and forever. **Amen.**

Psalm 149

ANTIPHON
KH
Let us re- joice in God, our Sav - ior!
sing with first and final antiphon
Al - le - lu - ia! Al - le - lu - ia!

Sing a new song to the LORD,
  God's praise in the assembly of the **faith**ful.
Let Israel rejoice in its Creator,
  the children of Zion exult in **their** Sovereign.
Let them praise God's name with **danc**ing;
with drums and harp, let them play music **for** God. ANTIPHON

For the LORD takes delight in the people,
  adorning the poor with sal**va**tion.
Let the faithful exult **with** glory,
let them ring out joy on their **couch**es,
and cry out the great deeds of God from **their** throats. ANTIPHON

With two-edged swords in their hands,
  let them do vengeance against peoples
  and rebuke **na**tions;
let them tie their rulers with fetters
  and their nobles with chains **of** bronze,
in order to accomplish judgment against them as **writ**ten.
This is honor for all **the** faithful. ANTIPHON

Psalm Prayer
Creator God,
you adorn all your works with hope for salvation:
receive the faithful departed into your gentle care
that they may praise you now and always. **Amen.**

Word of God

Benedictus
Blessed be the Lord God of **Israel**,
who visited and redeemed the **people**,
who raised up for us a **mighty** savior
from the house of **ser**vant David.

Just as the Lord spoke through the mouths of the holy prophets of **old**—
salvation comes out of the hands of our enemies and those who **hate** us,
that, with our ancestors, we might perform **works** of mercy,
remembering the holy covenant **sworn** to Abraham—

so does the Lord deliver us from the hands **of** our enemies,
that we might serve without fear before **the** Lord,
worshiping in **ho**liness
and in righteousness **all** our days.

And you also, child, will be called a prophet of God Most **High**:
for you will go before the Lord to prepare a **way**,
bringing people knowledge of salvation by for**giveness** of sins;
because of the deep and tender mercy **of** our God.

Whereby a light rising from on high will **visit** us
to appear to those in darkness and in a shadow **of** death,
to guide our feet along a **straight**, sure path
into a **way** of peace.

INTERCESSIONS

Invocations

Cantor, then Assembly in canon:

1.
2.
KH
Hear our prayer, O God.
one or two voices
Hear, O God.

Cantor:

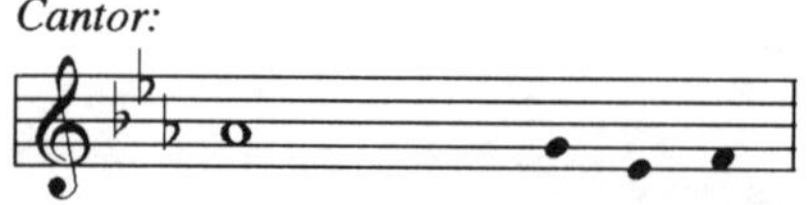

Jesus our Savior, **source** of mercy ...
Jesus our Savior, **source** of forgiveness ...
Jesus our Savior, **source** of compassion ...
Jesus our Savior, **source** of healing ...

Jesus our Savior, **source** of hope ...
Jesus our Savior, **source** of just judgment ...
Jesus our Savior, **source** of eternal life ...
Jesus our Savior, **source** of peace ...

Our Father ...

Prayer
Loving-kind God,
you show mercy and compassion to the faithful departed:
receive into your everlasting life
all those who have died faithful to your covenant.
We pray through Jesus Christ. **Amen.**

CONCLUSION

Blessing
May God, the source of mercy, bless us now and always
in the name of the Father, and of the Son, and of the Holy Spirit. **Amen.**

Dismissal
Go forth to remember the faithful departed. **Thanks be to God.**

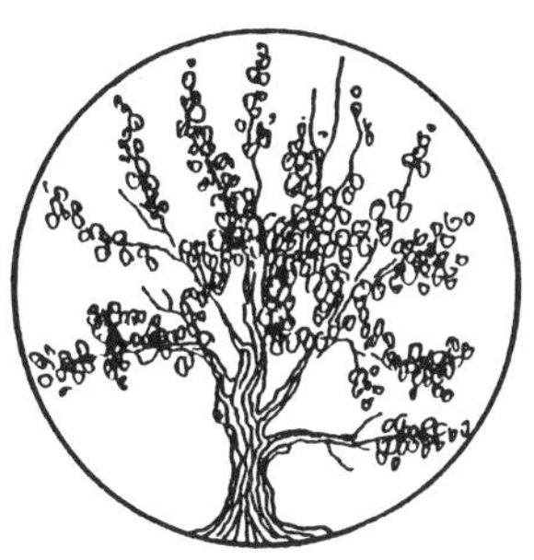

ALL SOULS
Evening Prayer

FESTAL EVENING HYMN

PSALMODY

Psalm 130 *Song of ascents (pilgrimages).*

ANTIPHON
KH
Out of the depths I cry to you, O God.

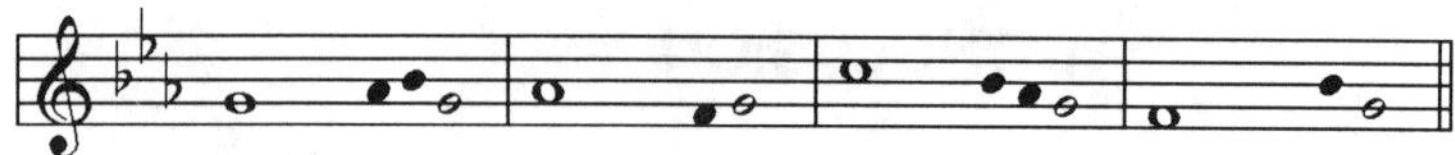

Out of the depths, I cry to **you**, O LORD.
Lord, listen to **my** voice;
let your ears **be** attentive
to the voice of my sup**pli**cations. ANTIPHON

If you, O LORD, were to keep in**iquities** in mind,
Lord, who **could** stand?
But with you **is** forgiveness,
and for that you are **re**vered. ANTIPHON

I wait for the LORD;
my soul waits, and for God's **word** I hope.
My soul waits for **the** Lord
more than watchers **of** the morning
watch for **the** dawn. ANTIPHON

Let Israel hope **in** the LORD,
for steadfast love is found with the LORD
and abundance of **re**demption.
It is the LORD who shall redeem **Is**rael
from all iniq**ui**ties. ANTIPHON

Psalm Prayer
Attentive God,
you hear our voice with unfailing kindness:
we cry out to you for the faithful departed,
that you forgive any transgressions and
draw them to your redeeming love now and always. **Amen.**

Psalm 138 *Of David.*

ANTIPHON

KH
I give you thanks, O God; with my
whole heart I sing your praise.

I give you thanks with **all** my heart;
instead of other gods, I **sing** to you.
I bow down toward the **ho**ly sanctuary,
and I give thanks to your name
 on account of your steadfast love **and** your truth.

For you have ex**alted** your promise
even a**bove** your name.
On the day I cried, you **an**swered me;
you renewed cour**age** within me. ANTIPHON

Let all the rulers of the earth give thanks to you, O LORD,
 for they have heard the **words of** your mouth.
Let them sing about the ways of the LORD,
 for great is the **glory of** the LORD.
Although exalted,
 the LORD looks up**on** the lowly,
but recognizes the proud only **from** a distance. ANTIPHON

When I walk in the midst of distress,
 you revive me against the **anger of** my enemies.
You stretch out your hand,
 and your **right** hand saves me;
the LORD will do every**thing** for me.
O LORD, your steadfast love is forever.
 Do not forsake the work **of** your hands. ANTIPHON

Psalm Prayer
Exalted God,
your name is above all others:
hear the thanksgiving prayer of your humble people
on behalf of the faithful departed.
Increase our strength of soul
that we may one day enjoy with you life everlasting. **Amen.**

Word of God

Magnificat
My soul does magni**fy** the Lord!
I delight in **God** my savior
who looked kindly **on** lowliness.

Now all ages will **call** me blessed
for the Mighty One **did** great things.
Holy is **God's** name;
mercy is from age to age for **those** in awe!

The Lord's strong arm did **mighty** deeds:
confused the proud in **their** smug hearts;
toppled sovereigns **from** their thrones,
and exalted **hum**ble ones;
filled the hungering with **good** things,
and sent the rich **a**way empty.

The Lord helped servant **Is**rael
to re**mem**ber mercy,
as was spoken to Ab**ra**ham
and his descendants for**e**vermore!

INTERCESSIONS

Petitions

Cantor, then Assembly in canon:

1.
2.
KH
Hear___ our prayer, O God.___
one or two voices
Hear,__ O God.

Cantor:

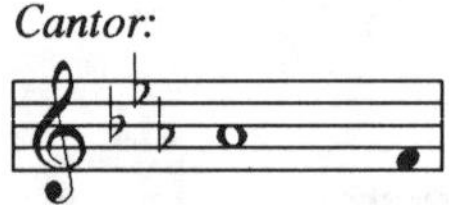

For **help** ...
For for**giveness** ...
For **patience** ...
For en**durance** ...
For re**freshment** ...
For **hope** ...
For re**demption** ...

For **mercy** ...
For de**liverance** ...
For sal**vation** ...
For the faithful de**parted** ...

Our Father ...

Prayer
Merciful God,
you are full of steadfast love
and ever faithful to your word of truth:
receive the souls of the faithful departed
that they may enjoy with you life everlasting. **Amen.**

CONCLUSION

Blessing
May the God of mercy bless us
in the name of the Father, and of the Son, and of the Holy Spirit. **Amen.**

Dismissal
Go and rest, comforted by our tender God. **Thanks be to God.**

November 9
Feast of the DEDICATION OF ST. JOHN LATERAN
Morning Praise

FESTAL MORNING HYMN

PSALMODY

Psalm 65 *To the choirmaster. Psalm of David. Psalm.*

Choir 1 To you praise is due,
O God in Zion,
and for you promises will be fulfilled.
O you who listen to prayer,
to you all flesh shall come.
When our transgressions—deeds of iniquity—overcome us,
you forgive them.

Choir 2 Blessed is the one you elect and bring near;
that one shall dwell in your courts.
Let us be filled with the goodness of your house,
the holiness of your temple.
With awesome deeds you answer us in justice,
O God of our salvation and
protector of all the ends of the earth
and of remote seas.

Choir 1 Girded with might,
you establish mountains in strength.
You still the roaring of the seas—
the roaring of their waves—
and the clamor of nations.
Because of your signs,
the inhabitants of the ends of the earth will stand in awe.

Choir 2 You cause the breaking of morning and of evening
to burst with joy.
You visit the earth and give it water;
abundantly, you enrich it:
the river of God
is replete with water.
You provide people with grain,
for you designed it so.
Its furrows you water abundantly,
and you make them smooth.
You soften it with showers,
and you bless its sprout.

All You crown the year with your bounty,
and fertility springs in the wake of your chariot.
The pastures of the wilderness drip with water,
and the hills are girded with joy.
Meadows are clothed with flocks,
and valleys are covered with grain.
They shout, even more, they sing.

Psalm 84 *To the choirmaster. On the gittith. By the Qorahites. Psalm.*

Solo 1 How lovable are your tents,
O LORD of hosts.
My soul longs—indeed faints—

for the courts of the LORD.
My heart and my flesh sing for joy
to the living God.
Even the sparrow finds a home
and the swallow a nest for herself
where she sets her young
next to your altars,
O LORD of hosts,
my Sovereign and my God.
Blessed are those who dwell in your house;
they will continue to praise you.

Selah (pause).

All Blessed is the one whose strength resides in you.
Those whose hearts are set on pilgrimage
make the valley of tears a place of fountains
as they travel through it.
Even the early rain covers it with blessings.
They walk with ever greater strength:
the God of gods will be seen in Zion.

Solo 1 O LORD God of hosts,
hear my prayer;
listen, O God of Jacob.

Selah (pause).

All See our shield, O God,
and consider the face of your Messiah.
For one day in your courts is better
than a thousand elsewhere.

Solo 1 I would rather stand at the threshold
of the house of my God,
than live in the tents of the wicked.
For the LORD is a sun and a shield;
God is grace and glory.
The LORD gives,
and does not refuse any good
to those who walk in integrity.

All O LORD of hosts,

blessed is the one
who trusts in you.

Word of God

Benedictus

Blessed be the Lord God of **Israel**,
who visited and redeemed the **people**,
who raised up for us a **mighty** savior
from the house of **servant** David.

Just as the Lord spoke through the mouths of the holy prophets of **old**—
salvation comes out of the hands of our enemies and those who **hate** us,
that, with our ancestors, we might perform **works** of mercy,
remembering the holy covenant **sworn** to Abraham—

so does the Lord deliver us from the hands **of** our enemies,
that we might serve without fear before **the** Lord,
worshiping in **ho**liness
and in righteousness **all** our days.

And you also, child, will be called a prophet of God Most **High**:
for you will go before the Lord to prepare a **way**,
bringing people knowledge of salvation by for**giveness** of sins;
because of the deep and tender mercy **of** our God.

Whereby a light rising from on high will **visit** us
to appear to those in darkness and in a shadow **of** death,
to guide our feet along a **straight**, sure path
into a **way** of peace.

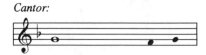

INTERCESSIONS

Invocations

Cantor, then Assembly:

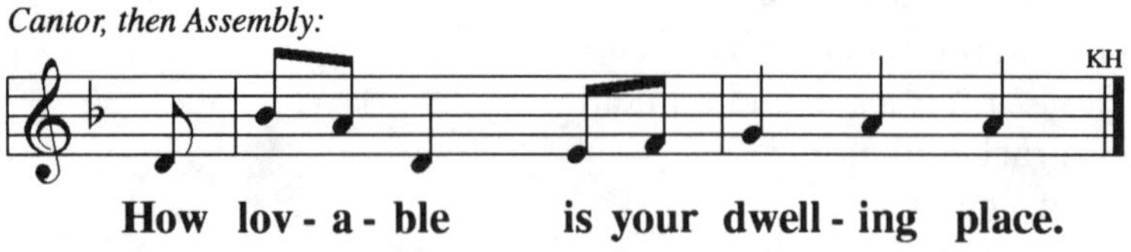

KH
How lov - a - ble is your dwell - ing place.

Cantor:

O risen Christ, you listen **to** prayer ...
O risen Christ, you bring near the **e**lect ...
O risen Christ, you fill us **with** goodness ...
O risen Christ, you inebriate us **with** holiness ...
O risen Christ, you bless those who dwell **in** you ...
O risen Christ, you satisfying our longing **for** you ...
O risen Christ, your temple is a sign of unity **and** strength ...

Our Father ...

Prayer
God of holiness,
your dwelling place is filled with peace and tranquility:
draw us to your presence
that we may dwell in unity with Jesus Christ
and the Holy Spirit, one God forever and ever. **Amen.**

CONCLUSION

Blessing
May the God of holiness bless us
in the name of the Father, and of the Son, and of the Holy Spirit. **Amen.**

Dismissal
Go forth as temples of the Holy Spirit to be a sign of unity. **Thanks be to God.**

Feast of the DEDICATION OF ST. JOHN LATERAN Evening Prayer

FESTAL EVENING HYMN

PSALMODY

Psalm 122 *Song of ascents (pilgrimages). Of David.*

Solo 1 I rejoiced when they said to me,
"We shall go to the house of the LORD."

Choir 1 Our feet are standing
at your gates, O Jerusalem.
Jerusalem, you are built like a city
well-bound together.
There the tribes went up,
the tribes of the LORD,
to give thanks to the name of the LORD,
keeping a precept for Israel.
For there the thrones for judgment were placed,
the thrones for the house of David.

Choir 2 Pray for the peace of Jerusalem:
"May those who love you live in peace.
May peace be within your walls
and tranquility within your palaces."

Solo 1 For the sake of my kindred
and my companions, let me speak:
"Peace be upon you."
For the sake of the house of the LORD our God,
I will seek your prosperity.

Psalm 30 *Psalm of David. Song for the dedication of the temple.*

Solo 1 I will exalt you, O LORD,
for you have set me free
and have not allowed my enemies to rejoice over me.

Solo 2 O LORD my God,
I have cried to you
and you have healed me.
O LORD, you have brought my soul
up from Sheol.
You have restored me to life,
preventing me from going down the Pit.

All Sing to the LORD, O faithful ones;
celebrate a memorial to God's holiness.
For we stand only an instant in God's anger,
but a whole lifetime in God's delight.
In the evening come tears,
but in the morning come shouts of joy.

Solo 1 So I said in my tranquility,
"I will not falter forever."
O LORD, in your delight
you have established might as my mountain.

Solo 2 When you hid your face,
I was terrified.
To you, O LORD, I cry
and to you, O Lord, I raise my supplication.
What profit is there in my blood,
in my going down to the Pit?
Does dust give you thanks,
and tell your truth?
Listen, O LORD, and have mercy;
O LORD, be a help to me.

Solo 1 You have changed my mourning to dancing;
you have loosened my sackcloth
and girded me with joy.
So I sing your glory;
I am not silent.
O LORD my God,
I will give thanks to you forever.

Word of God

Magnificat
My soul does magni**fy** the Lord!
I delight in **God** my savior
who looked kindly **on** lowliness.

Now all ages will **call** me blessed
for the Mighty One **did** great things.
Holy is **God's** name;
mercy is from age to age for **those** in awe!

The Lord's strong arm did **mighty** deeds:
confused the proud in **their** smug hearts;
toppled sovereigns **from** their thrones,
and exalted **hum**ble ones;
filled the hungering with **good** things,
and sent the rich **a**way empty.

The Lord helped servant **Is**rael
to re**mem**ber mercy,
as was spoken to Ab**ra**ham
and his descendants for**ev**ermore!

INTERCESSIONS

Petitions
Cantor, then Assembly:

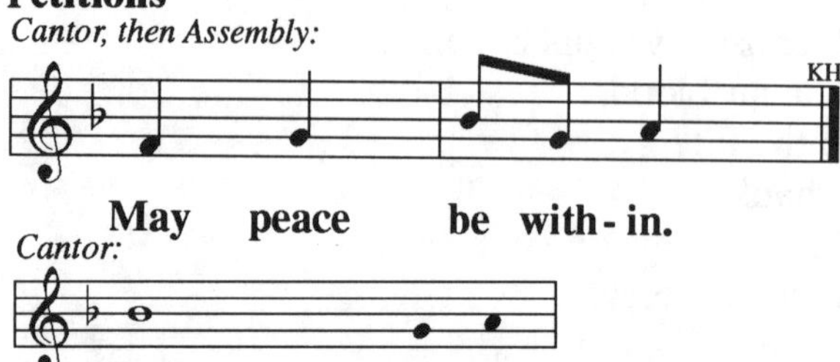

Cantor:

As we celebrate a memorial of **God's** holiness ...
As we reverence a sign **of** unity ...
As we seek **pros**perity ...
As we pray for **tran**quility ...
As we stand well-bound **to**gether ...
As we abide at **God's** threshold ...
As the faithful departed approach the throne **of** judgment ...

Our Father ...

Prayer
Holy God,
you are present in majesty and splendor:
as we celebrate this festival in honor of
our mother church,
may we always seek unity above diversity,
desire holiness beyond the ordinary, and
acknowledge Christ as our true cornerstone.
We pray through Jesus Christ. **Amen.**

CONCLUSION

Blessing
May God bless us
in the name of the Father, and of the Son, and of the Holy Spirit. **Amen.**

Dismissal
Go and rest in the peace of Christ. **Thanks be to God.**

November 30
Feast of ANDREW, Apostle
Morning Praise

From the Feast of PHILIP & JAMES, Apostles, Morning Praise, p. 534.

Prayer
O God,
Andrew asked of the Messiah,
"What are these loaves and fishes
among so many people?":
help us to see your great power and
to believe in your abundant love and care for us.
We pray through Jesus Christ. **Amen.**

Feast of ANDREW, Apostle
Evening Prayer

From the Feast of PHILIP & JAMES, Apostles, Evening Prayer, p. 537.

Prayer
O God who calls followers,
you invited Andrew, the brother of Peter,
to witness your divine Son's glory:
may we acknowledge our election
as your sons and daughters and
live faithfully your blessings.
We pray through Jesus Christ. **Amen.**

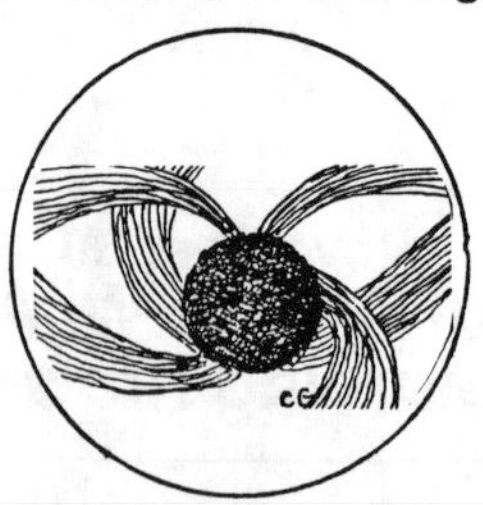

Last Sunday of Ordinary Time
Solemnity of CHRIST THE KING
Morning Praise

FESTAL MORNING HYMN

PSALMODY

Psalm 63 *Psalm of David. While he was in the desert of Judah.*

ANTIPHON

KH
We re- joice in our Sav - ior, who reigns.
omit last strophe

O God, you are my God, **I** seek you;
my **soul** thirsts **for** you.
My flesh longs for you
  in a dry and **wast**ed land,
deprived **of** water. ANTIPHON

So in the sanctuary I have contemplated you
  to see your might and your **glo**ry.
Because your **stead**fast love is better than life,
  my lips will **praise** you.
So I will bless you **all** my life;
in your name I will raise **my** hands.

As with milk and rich food,
  my soul **is** filled;
my **mouth** gives praise with joy**ful** lips.
I remember you up**on** my bed,
pondering you throughout **the** night.

For you were a help **for** me;
in the **shade** of your wings I **keep** singing.
My soul **clings** to you;
your right hand **up**holds me. ANTIPHON

But let those who seek my de**struc**tion
be **cast** into the depths of **the** earth.
Let them be given over to the power **of** the sword;
let them become a prey **for** jackals. ANTIPHON

Then the king shall rejoice **in** God.
All **those** who swear by God will **be** praised,
for the mouths of liars will **be** shut. ANTIPHON

Psalm Prayer
O God,
you exalted your Messiah Son to reign at your right hand:
as Jesus always followed faithfully your holy will,
so may we know and follow your will all the days of our lives.
We pray through Jesus Christ. **Amen.**

Psalm 113

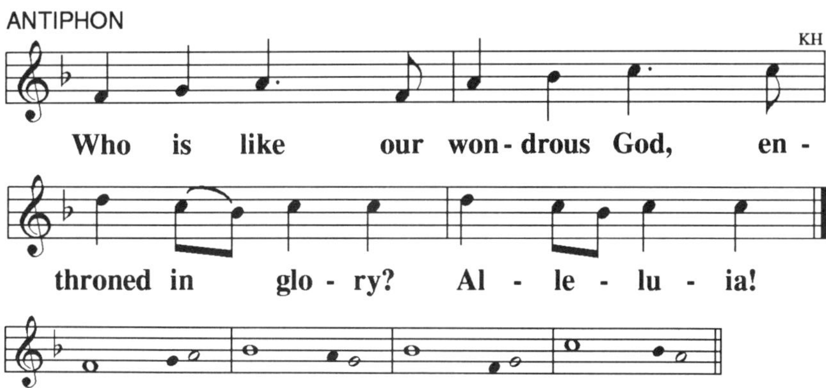
ANTIPHON
KH
Who is like our won - drous God, en -
throned in glo - ry? Al - le - lu - ia!

Give praise, servants of **the** LORD;
praise the name of **the** LORD.
Let the name of the LORD **be** blessed
from now on and **for**ever.

From the rising of the sun to **its** setting,
let the name of the LORD **be** praised.
The LORD is exalted above **all** nations;
God's glory is greater than **the** heavens. ANTIPHON

Who looks down to watch over
  the skies and **the** earth?
Who raises the weak from dust
  and the poor **from** ashes,
to return them to the company of nobles,
  the nobles of **the** people?
Who brings home the sterile woman,
  now a rejoicing mother of many children? ANTIPHON

Psalm Prayer
Praiseworthy God,
your Son fashioned a realm of truth that will never end:
may he always look down and watch over us,
for he reigns with you in the unity of the Holy Spirit,
one God forever and ever. **Amen.**

Word of God

Benedictus
Blessed be the Lord God of **Israel**,
who visited and redeemed the **people**,
who raised up for us a **might**y savior
from the house of **ser**vant David.

Just as the Lord spoke through the mouths of the holy prophets of **old**—
salvation comes out of the hands of our enemies and those who **hate** us,
that, with our ancestors, we might perform **works** of mercy,
remembering the holy covenant **sworn** to Abraham—

so does the Lord deliver us from the hands **of** our enemies,
that we might serve without fear before **the** Lord,
worshiping in **ho**liness
and in righteousness **all** our days.

And you also, child, will be called a prophet of God Most **High**:
for you will go before the Lord to prepare a **way**,
bringing people knowledge of salvation by for**giveness** of sins;
because of the deep and tender mercy **of** our God.

Whereby a light rising from on high will **vis**it us
to appear to those in darkness and in a shadow **of** death,
to guide our feet along a **straight**, sure path
into a **way** of peace.

INTERCESSIONS

Invocations

Cantor, then Assembly:

KH
We ex - ult our Mes- si - ah King!

Cantor:

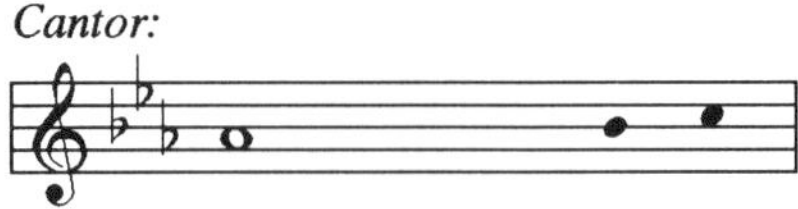

Who reigns at God's **right** hand?
Who is enthroned **in** glory?
Who rules with justice **and** truth?
Who sustains the weak **and** poor?
Who humbles **the** proud-hearted?
Who nourishes with the Food **of** Life?
Who protects us in the shade **of** wings?
Who upholds us in all **we** do?

Our Father ...

Prayer
O God of our salvation,
your Son fulfilled perfectly your holy will:
may we, too, say with Jesus,
"Yet not my will but yours be done."
We pray through the divine Son Jesus Christ. **Amen.**

CONCLUSION

Blessing
Bow your heads and pray for God's blessing.
May God almighty call us. **Amen.**
May the divine Son be with us. **Amen.**
May the Spirit overshadow us. **Amen.**
And may God bless us
in the name of the Father, and of the Son, and of the Holy Spirit. **Amen.**

Sign of Peace/Dismissal
Share with one another a sign of the peace of the Divine Son.

Solemnity of the CHRIST THE KING Evening Prayer

LIGHT SERVICE

Proclamation of the Light

Cantor:

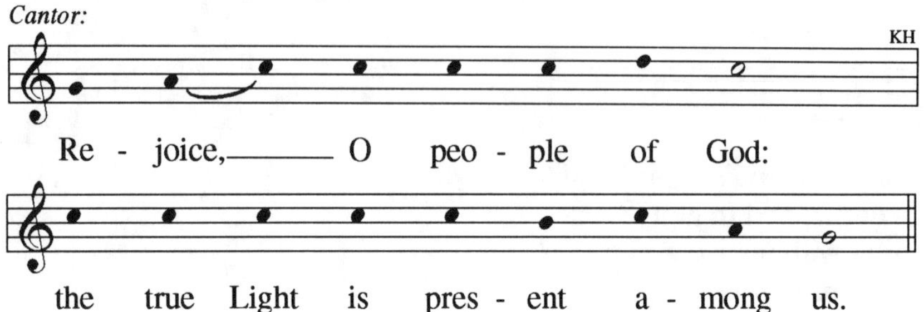

Assembly:

Festal Evening Hymn

Thanksgiving for the Light

Cantor:

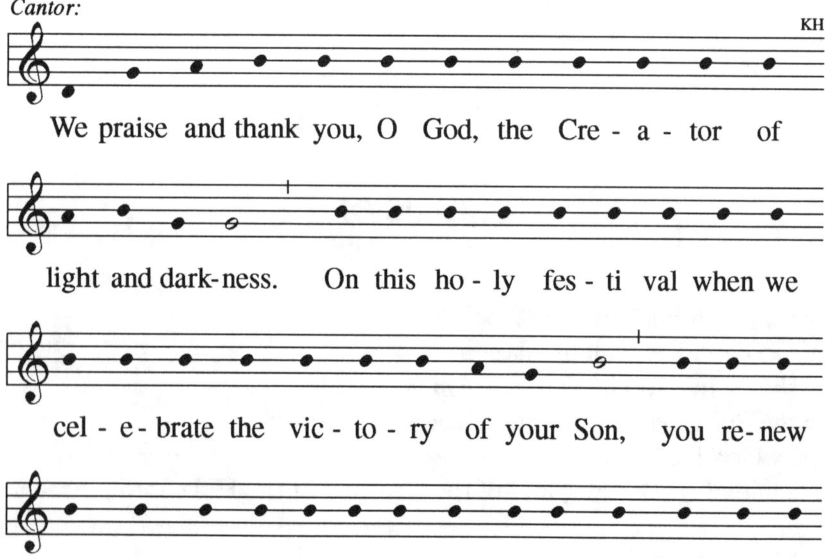

KH
We praise and thank you, O God, the Cre - a - tor of
light and dark-ness. On this ho - ly fes - ti val when we
cel - e - brate the vic - to - ry of your Son, you re- new
your prom- ise to re- veal a- mong us the splen- did light of

your glo - ry- made vis - i - ble in the In- car- nate Word

Je- sus Christ. Through the proph-ets of old you call us

to your cov- e- nant of love. Now through the Spir- it you

o - pen our eyes to the peace of Christ's pres- ence.

So with the ho - ly an- gels on high we sing out:

Glo- ry to God in the high- est, to whom we of - fer

praise, hon- or and bless- ing, now and al- ways and

for - ev - er and ev - er. **A - men.**

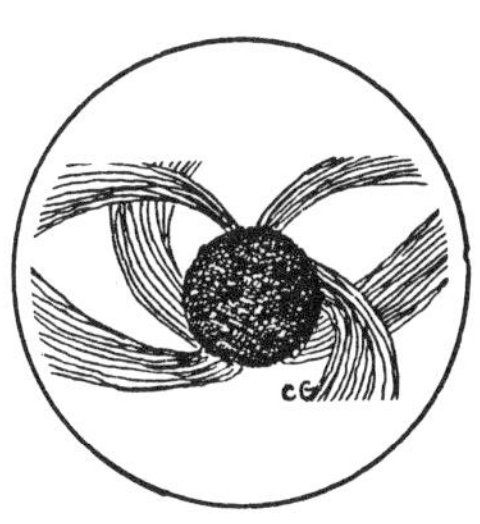

PSALMODY

Psalm 110 *Of David. Psalm.*

ANTIPHON

KH
Our Sav-ior sits at the right hand of
God, Al - le - lu - ia!

Thus says the LORD **to** my lord:
"Sit on my right
until I place your enemies
as a footstool for **your** feet."
Let the LORD send from Zion
the scepter of **your** strength.
Rule in the midst of **your** enemies. ANTIPHON

Your people bring free **of**ferings
on the day of your might
in holy splendor.
From the womb **of** dawn,
a dew of rejuvenation comes **to** you. ANTIPHON

The LORD has promised
and will **not** repent:
"According to my word,
you are a priest forever, my king **of** justice."
The Lord is at **your** right,
who has smashed rulers on the day **of** wrath.

The Lord judges **against** the nations,
piling them **with** corpses.
The Lord has smashed heads
all over **the** land.
From a torrent the Lord drinks on the way,
and rises up **in** triumph. ANTIPHON

Psalm Prayer
O mighty God,
you reign over all peoples and nations forever:
open us to your truth and justice
that we might be worthy to receive
the reward of eternal life
and dwell with you forever and ever. **Amen.**

Psalm 9 *To the choirmaster. Muth lebben. Psalm of David.*

ANTIPHON
KH
You are God Most High, Al - le - lu - ia!

I will give thanks, O LORD, with **all** my heart.
I will tell of all your won**der**ful deeds.
I will rejoice, I will ex**ult** in you,
and I will play music for your name, **O** Most High. ANTIPHON

When my enemies turned back
  they stumbled and per**ished** before you,
for you had taken up my case **and** my judgment.
You sat **on** the throne
as the one who judg**es** with justice.

You re**buked** nations;
you destroyed the wicked,
  erasing their names
  forev**er** and ever.
The enemy has vanished
  in ruins **for** eternity.
You destroyed cities—
  even their memo**ry** has perished. ANTIPHON

But the LORD remains en**throned** forever,
making firm the **throne** of judgment.
God judges the **world** in justice
and the peoples in eq**ui**ty. ANTIPHON

The LORD will be
  a refuge **for** the poor,
a refuge in times **of** distress.
Those who know your name
  will **trust** in you,
for you do not abandon those who seek **you**, O LORD. ANTIPHON

Psalm Prayer
O God,
you are a refuge for those who call out to you:
judge us mercifully and draw us to your majesty
that we may know your name above all others
now and always. **Amen.**

Word of God

Magnificat
My soul does magni**fy** the Lord!
I delight in **God** my savior
who looked kindly **on** lowliness.

Now all ages will **call** me blessed
for the Mighty One **did** great things.
Holy is **God's** name;
mercy is from age to age for **those** in awe!

The Lord's strong arm did **mighty** deeds:
confused the proud in **their** smug hearts;
toppled sovereigns **from** their thrones,
and exalted **hum**ble ones;
filled the hungering with **good** things,
and sent the rich **a**way empty.

The Lord helped servant **Is**rael
to re**mem**ber mercy,
as was spoken to Ab**ra**ham
and his descendants for**e**vermore!

INTERCESSIONS

Petitions

Cantor, then Assembly:

KH
God ris - es up in tri-umph!

Cantor:

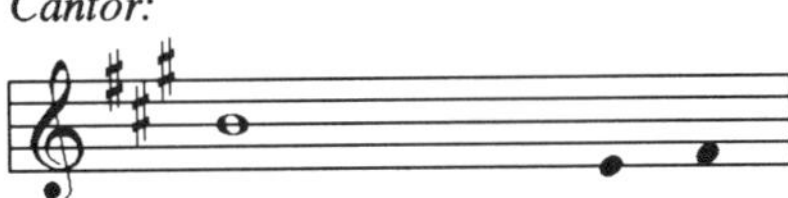

We see **God's** strength ...
We accept **God's** reign...
We offer ourselves **to** God ...
We live our priestly **i**dentity ...
We give thanks **for**ever ...
We rejoice **in** victory ...
We are glad for **God's** equity ...
We salute God as refuge for **the** poor ...
We trust **God's** mercy ...
We commend the faithful departed to **God's** love ...

Our Father ...

Prayer
O wondrous God,
your realm is not of this world:
help us to seek truth unfailingly and
to acclaim your victory over death.
Lead us to eternal life in your Son, Jesus Christ. **Amen.**

CONCLUSION

Blessing
Bow your heads and pray for God's blessing.
  May the Creator God make the divine face to shine upon us. **Amen.**
  May the Redeemer Son look upon us kindly. **Amen.**
  May the Sanctifying Spirit give us peace. **Amen.**
And may God bless us
in the name of the Father, and of the Son, and of the Holy Spirit. **Amen.**

Sign of Peace/Dismissal
Share with one another the peace of the divine Son,
that we may rest confidently in the justice of God's reign.

December 8
Solemnity of the IMMACULATE CONCEPTION
Morning Praise

FESTAL MORNING HYMN

PSALMODY

Psalm 63 *Psalm of David. While he was in the desert of Judah.*

ANTIPHON

O God, you are my God, **I** seek you;
my **soul** thirsts **for** you.
My flesh longs for you
  in a dry and **wast**ed land,
deprived **of** water. ANTIPHON

So in the sanctuary I have contemplated you
  to see your might and your **glo**ry.
Because your **stead**fast love is better than life,
  my lips will **praise** you.
So I will bless you **all** my life;
in your name I will raise **my** hands.

As with milk and rich food,
  my soul **is** filled;
my **mouth** gives praise with joy**ful** lips.
I remember you up**on** my bed,
pondering you throughout **the** night.

For you were a help **for** me;
in the **shade** of your wings I **keep** singing.
My soul **clings** to you;
your right hand **up**holds me. ANTIPHON

But let those who seek my de**struc**tion
be **cast** into the depths of **the** earth.
Let them be given over to the power **of** the sword;
let them become a prey **for** jackals. ANTIPHON

Then the king shall rejoice **in** God.
All **those** who swear by God will **be** praised,
for the mouths of liars will **be** shut. ANTIPHON

Psalm Prayer
O saving God,
you prepared Mary
as a pure and holy sanctuary
for your Son Jesus Christ.
Fill us with your grace and blessings
that we may come blameless into your presence
to sing your praises forever and ever. **Amen**

Psalm 113

ANTIPHON

KH
Who is like our won - drous God, en -

throned in glo - ry? Al - le - lu - ia!

Give praise, servants of **the** LORD;
praise the name of **the** LORD.
Let the name of the LORD **be** blessed
from now on and **for**ever.

From the rising of the sun to **its** setting,
let the name of the LORD **be** praised.
The LORD is exalted above **all** nations;
God's glory is greater than **the** heavens. ANTIPHON

Who looks down to watch over
  the skies and **the** earth?
Who raises the weak from dust
  and the poor **from** ashes,
to return them to the company of nobles,
  the nobles of **the** people?
Who brings home the sterile woman,
  now a rejoicing mother of many children? ANTIPHON

Psalm Prayer
O good and gracious God,
from the rising of the sun to its setting
you favor us with the example of Mary our Mother:
as she rejoiced to be the mother of your only Son,
may we rejoice in Jesus Christ our savior. **Amen.**

Word of God

Benedictus
Blessed be the Lord God of **Israel**,
who visited and redeemed the **people**,
who raised up for us a **mighty** savior
from the house of **ser**vant David.

Just as the Lord spoke through the mouths of the holy prophets of **old**—
salvation comes out of the hands of our enemies and those who **hate** us,
that, with our ancestors, we might perform **works** of mercy,
remembering the holy covenant **sworn** to Abraham—

so does the Lord deliver us from the hands **of** our enemies,
that we might serve without fear before **the** Lord,
worshiping in **ho**liness
and in righteousness **all** our days.

And you also, child, will be called a prophet of God Most **High**:
for you will go before the Lord to prepare a **way**,
bringing people knowledge of salvation by for**giveness** of sins;
because of the deep and tender mercy **of** our God.

Whereby a light rising from on high will **visit** us
to appear to those in darkness and in a shadow **of** death,
to guide our feet along a **straight**, sure path
into a **way** of peace.

INTERCESSIONS

Invocations

Cantor, then Assembly:

Cantor:

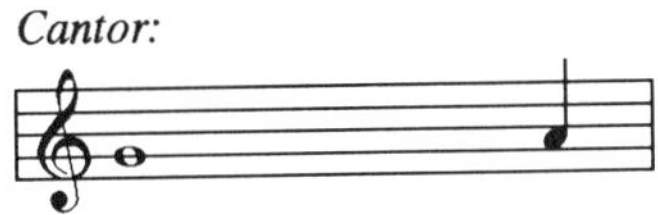

We seek **you** ...
We long for **you** ...
We contemplate **you** ...
We praise **you** ...
We bless **you** ...
Fill **us** ...
Uphold **us** ...
Lift **us** ...
Return to **us** ...
Rejoice with **us** ...

Our Father ...

Prayer
O God,
you protect and save with unfailing love:
keep us safe and blameless in your sight
just as you preserved Mary from all taint of sin.
We pray in the name of Jesus, your Son. **Amen.**

CONCLUSION

Blessing
May the God who deigned the Son to be born of a virgin
pure, spotless, and holy bless us
in the name of the Father, and of the Son, and of the Holy Spirit. **Amen.**

Sign of Peace/Dismissal
Share a sign of peace as you go and rejoice on this festival honoring the holiness of Mary. **Thanks be to God.**

Solemnity of the IMMACULATE CONCEPTION
Evening Prayer

LIGHT SERVICE

Proclamation of the Light

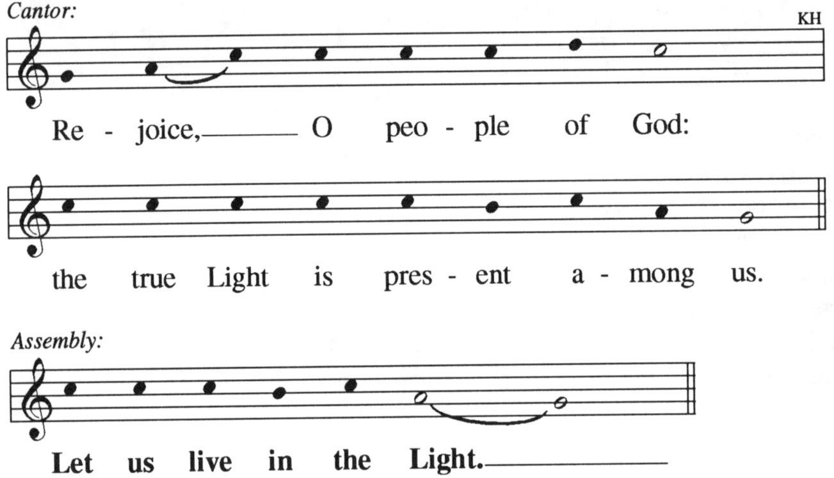
Cantor:
KH
Re - joice, O peo - ple of God:
the true Light is pres - ent a - mong us.
Assembly:
Let us live in the Light.

Festal Evening Hymn

Thanksgiving for the Light

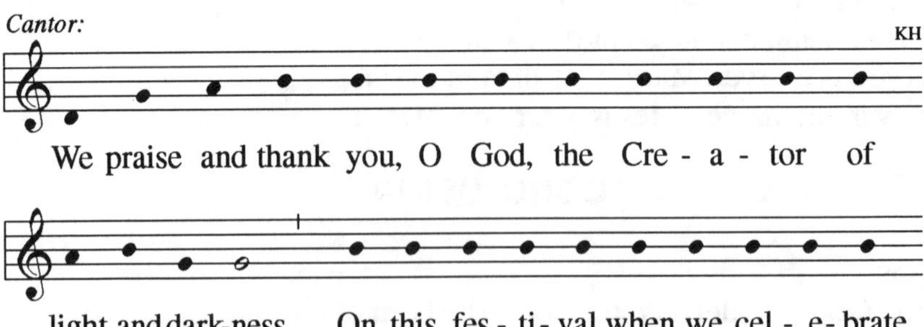
Cantor:
KH
We praise and thank you, O God, the Cre - a - tor of
light and dark-ness. On this fes - ti - val when we cel - e - brate

the con-cep-tion of Ma-ry, our Moth-er, you re-new
your prom-ise to re-veal a-mong us the splen-did light of
your glo-ry-made vis-i-ble in the In-car-nate Word
Je-sus Christ. Through the proph-ets of old you call us
to your cov-e-nant of love. Now through the Spir-it you
o-pen our eyes to the peace of Christ's pres-ence.
So with the ho-ly an-gels on high we sing out:
Glo-ry to God in the high-est, to whom we of-fer
praise, hon-or and bless-ing, now and al-ways and
for-ev-er and ev-er. A-men.

PSALMODY

Psalm 123 *Song of ascents (pilgrimages).*

ANTIPHON
KH
Be- hold the spot- less Vir- gin, God's chos- en hand - maid.

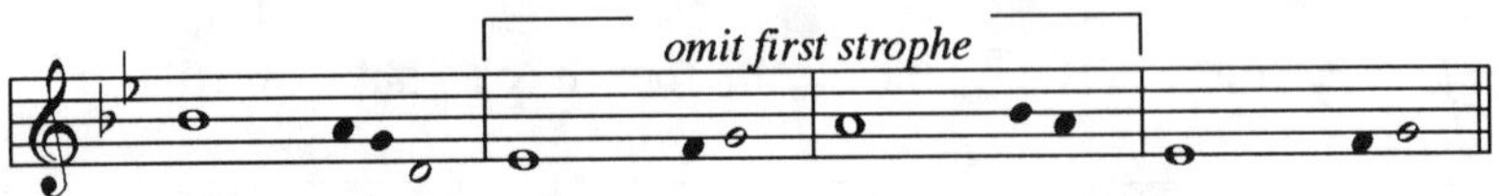

omit first strophe

To you I lift **up** my eyes,
who dwell **in** heaven. ANTIPHON

Behold, like the eyes of servants
  look to the hand **of** their master,
like the eyes of a maid
  look to the hand of **her** mistress,
so our eyes are lifted to the LORD **our** God
until mercy is bestowed **up**on us. ANTIPHON

Have mercy on us, O LORD,
  have mer**cy** on us,
for we have been overwhelmed by **con**tempt.
Our soul has been utterly filled
  with the mockery of the **in**different
and the contempt of **the** arrogant. ANTIPHON

Psalm Prayer
O loving God,
you favored Mary with endless grace and blessing:
keep our eyes ever turned to you
that we may know your mercy
through Jesus Christ. **Amen.**

Psalm 67 *To the choirmaster. With stringed instruments. Psalm. Song.*

ANTIPHON
KH
Let the peo - ples give you thanks, O God; let
all the peo - ples give you thanks.

May God have mercy on us and **bless** us.
May God's face shine among us.

For your way is known **over** the earth,
and your salvation is known a**mong** all nations. ANTIPHON

May the nations rejoice and **shout** with joy,
for you judge the peoples rightly
and the nations on the **earth** you guide. ANTIPHON

The earth has **given** its fruit.
May God, our God, **bless** us.

May God **bless** us,
and let all ends of the **earth** show reverence. ANTIPHON

Psalm Prayer
O gracious God,
we give you thanks
on this festival honoring the holiness of Mary our mother:
as she brought forth the fruit of your only Son Jesus Christ,
make his Life fruitful in our own.
We pray through that same Jesus Christ. **Amen.**

Word of God

Magnificat
My soul does magni**fy** the Lord!
I delight in **God** my savior
who looked kindly **on** lowliness.

Now all ages will **call** me blessed
for the Mighty One **did** great things.
Holy is **God's** name;
mercy is from age to age for **those** in awe!

The Lord's strong arm did **might**y deeds:
confused the proud in **their** smug hearts;
toppled sovereigns **from** their thrones,
and exalted **hum**ble ones;
filled the hungering with **good** things,
and sent the rich **a**way empty.

The Lord helped servant **Is**rael
to re**mem**ber mercy,
as was spoken to Ab**ra**ham
and his descendants for**ev**ermore!

INTERCESSIONS

Petitions

Cantor, then Assembly:

KH
Have mer - cy on us and bless us.

Cantor:

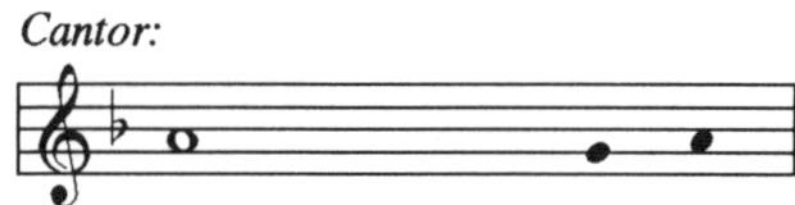

We lift up **our** eyes ...
We cast off carelessness **and** arrogance ...
We **seek** guidance ...
We long for **sal**vation ...
We rejoice **with** Mary ...
We sing **her** praises ...
We venerate **her** fruit ...
We imitate **her** holiness ...
We send forth those who have died **this** day ...

Our Father ...

Prayer

O God,
from all eternity you prepared Mary
to be the pure and blameless temple for your Son:
as we celebrate the spotless conception of Mary,
guide us in sure ways for ever and ever. **Amen.**

CONCLUSION

Blessing
May the God who preserved Mary as one pure and spotless
protect us and bless us
in the name of the Father, and of the Son, and of the Holy Spirit.
Amen.

Sign of Peace/Dismissal
Share a sign of Christ's peace
as you go to rest this night,
confident of the protection of Mary, our Mother most holy.
Thanks be to God.

THANKSGIVING DAY
Morning Praise

FESTAL MORNING HYMN

PSALMODY

Psalm 85 *To the choirmaster. By the Qorahites. Psalm.*

Choir 1 You have cherished your land, O LORD;
you have returned the captives of Jacob.
You have taken away the guilt of your people,
forgiving all their sins.

Selah (pause).

Choir 2 You have taken away all your wrath;
you have turned away from the heat of your anger.

All Bring us back, O God of our salvation,
and put away your displeasure with us.

Choir 1 Will you be angry with us forever?
Will you maintain your anger
from generation to generation?
Will you not return and revive us
so that your people rejoice in you?

All Make us see, O LORD, your steadfast love
and give us your salvation.

Solo 1 Let me hear what God will say.
The LORD speaks words of peace
to the people and to the faithful.
But let them not turn back to folly.

Choir 2 Surely salvation is near
for those who revere God,
that glory may dwell in our land.
Steadfast love and truth have met;
justice and peace have kissed each other.
Truth will spring up from the ground,
and justice will look down from heaven.

All The LORD will also give prosperity,
and the land will yield its fruit.
Justice will go forth
to set the way for God's steps.

Psalm 57 *To the choirmaster. "Do not destroy." Of David. Poem.*
When he flew from the presence of Saul in the cave.

Solo 1 Have pity on me, O God,
have pity on me; for in you
my soul has taken refuge.
In the shade of your wings I will take refuge
until destruction passes away.

Solo 2 I keep crying to God the Most High,
to God who acts in my favor.
May God send from heaven my salvation
and put to shame the one who entraps me.

Selah (pause).

Solo 1 May God send out steadfast love and truth.
I am in the midst of lions,
lying among people who are like burning flames,
their teeth like spears and arrows,
their tongues like sharp swords.

All Rise up, O God, above the heavens;
let your glory be over all the earth!

Solo 2 They have prepared a trap for my steps;
my soul is fearful.
In my presence they have dug a pit,
but then they fell into it.

Selah (pause).

Solo 1 My heart is firm, O God,
my heart is firm.
I will sing, I will play music.
Awake, my soul!
Awake, O harp and lyre!
I will awake the dawn.
I will praise you among peoples, my Lord,
I will play music for you among nations.
For your steadfast love reaches to the skies,
and to the firmaments, your truth.

All Rise up, O God, above the heavens;
let your glory be over all the earth!

Word of God

Benedictus
Blessed be the Lord God of **Israel**,
who visited and redeemed the **people**,

who raised up for us a **mighty** savior
from the house of **ser**vant David.

Just as the Lord spoke through the mouths of the holy prophets of **old**—
salvation comes out of the hands of our enemies and those who **hate** us,
that, with our ancestors, we might perform **works** of mercy,
remembering the holy covenant **sworn** to Abraham—

so does the Lord deliver us from the hands **of** our enemies,
that we might serve without fear before **the** Lord,
worshiping in **ho**liness
and in righteousness **all** our days.

And you also, child, will be called a prophet of God Most **High**:
for you will go before the Lord to prepare a **way**,
bringing people knowledge of salvation by for**giveness** of sins;
because of the deep and tender mercy **of** our God.

Whereby a light rising from on high will **vis**it us
to appear to those in darkness and in a shadow **of** death,
to guide our feet along a **straight**, sure path
into a **way** of peace.

INTERCESSIONS

Invocations

Cantor, then Assembly:

Cantor:

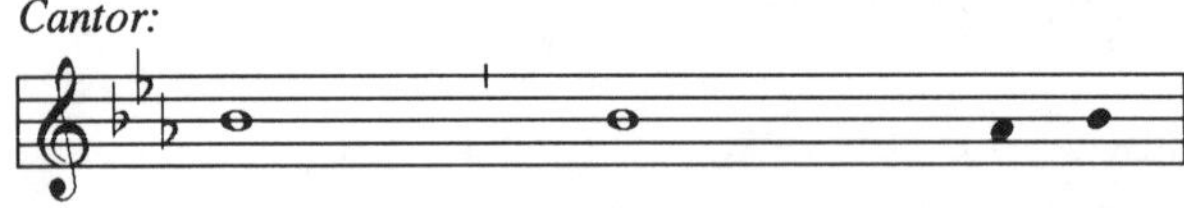

Bounteous Savior, you have cherished **your** land ...
Bounteous Savior, you have turned away **your** wrath ...
Bounteous Savior, you have revived **our** spirits ...
Bounteous Savior, you have spoken words **of** peace ...
Bounteous Savior, you have let jus**tice and peace** kiss ...
Bounteous Savior, you have let truth spring up from **the** earth ...
Bounteous Savior, you have let your glory lie over all **the** earth ...

Our Father ...

Prayer
Bounteous God,
you have favored us with an abundance beyond compare:
help us to be mindful of those in need and
to seek justice for all peoples now and always. **Amen.**

CONCLUSION

Blessing
May the God who shows us favor bless us
in the name of the Father, and of the Son, and of the Holy Spirit. **Amen.**

Dismissal
Be thankful for God's blessings and go forth, mindful of others. **Thanks be to God.**

THANKSGIVING DAY
Evening Prayer

FESTAL EVENING HYMN

PSALMODY

Psalm 122 *Song of ascents (pilgrimages). Of David.*

Solo 1 I rejoiced when they said to me,
"We shall go to the house of the LORD."

Choir 1 Our feet are standing
at your gates, O Jerusalem.
Jerusalem, you are built like a city
well-bound together.
There the tribes went up,
the tribes of the LORD,
to give thanks to the name of the LORD,
keeping a precept for Israel.
For there the thrones for judgment were placed,
the thrones for the house of David.

Choir 2 Pray for the peace of Jerusalem:
"May those who love you live in peace.
May peace be within your walls
and tranquility within your palaces."

Solo 1 For the sake of my kindred
and my companions, let me speak:
"Peace be upon you."
For the sake of the house of the LORD our God,
I will seek your prosperity.

Psalm 67 *To the choirmaster. With stringed instruments. Psalm. Song.*

Choir 1 May God have mercy on us and bless us.
May God's face shine among us.

Selah (pause).

Choir 2 For your way is known over the earth,
and your salvation is known among all nations.

All Let the peoples give you thanks, O God,
let all the peoples give you thanks.

Choir 1 May the nations rejoice and shout with joy,
for you judge the peoples rightly
and the nations on the earth you guide.

Selah (pause).

All Let the peoples give you thanks, O God,
let all the peoples give you thanks.

Choir 2 The earth has given its fruit.
May God, our God, bless us.
May God bless us,
and let all ends of the earth
show reverence.

Word of God

Magnificat
My soul does magni**fy** the Lord!
I delight in **God** my savior
who looked kindly **on** lowliness.

Now all ages will **call** me blessed
for the Mighty One **did** great things.
Holy is **God's** name;
mercy is from age to age for **those** in awe!

The Lord's strong arm did **mighty** deeds:
confused the proud in **their** smug hearts;
toppled sovereigns **from** their thrones,
and exalted **hum**ble ones;
filled the hungering with **good** things,
and sent the rich **a**way empty.

The Lord helped servant **Is**rael
to re**mem**ber mercy,
as was spoken to Ab**ra**ham
and his descendants for**e**vermore!

INTERCESSIONS

Petitions

Cantor, then Assembly:

Cantor:

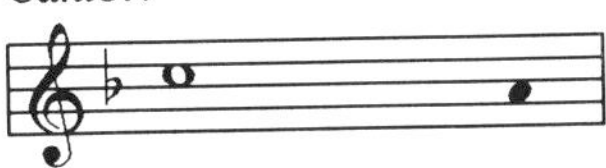

For **guidance** ...
For good **laws** ...
For **peace** ...
For tran**quility** ...
For pros**perity** ...
For **health** ...
For just **judgment** ...
For an abundance of fruits of the **earth** ...
For everlasting life for the faithful de**parted** ...

Our Father ...

Prayer
O God,
you have created the earth with an abundance for all:
we give you thanks for your care and protection,
for your nourishment and bounty.
Help us to be mindful of others,
to preserve the goods of this earth,
and to use them wisely for the good of all.
We pray through Jesus Christ. **Amen.**

CONCLUSION

Blessing
May God continue to grant us peace and prosperity and bless us
in the name of the Father, and of the Son, and of the Holy Spirit. **Amen.**

Dismissal
Go and rest in the gracious care of our God. **Thanks be to God.**

NATIONAL HOLIDAYS
Morning Praise

FESTAL MORNING HYMN

PSALMODY

Psalm 66 *To the choirmaster. A Song. Psalm.*

Choir 1 Sound the trumpet for God, all the earth!
Make music to the glory of God's name!
Give glory and praise!
Say to God:
"How awesome are your deeds!
At the magnitude of your power,
your enemies cringe before you.
Let all the earth worship you,
let them sing to you,
let them sing to your name."

Selah (pause).

Choir 2 Come and see the accomplishments
of God—
an awesome work
on behalf of mortals.
God turned the sea into dry land,
they crossed through the river on foot.
Therefore let us rejoice in God,
who rules over the world with power
and whose eyes watch over the nations.
Let not the stubborn rise up against God.

Selah (pause).

All All you nations, bless our God!
Let the sound of praise be heard
for the one who gives life to our souls,
and who kept our feet from stumbling.

Choir 1 For you have tested us, O God;
you have tried us like silver is tried.
You have caught us in a net.
You have put a burden on our backs.
You have let mortals enslave us.
We went through fire and water,
but you brought us out to a fertile land.

Solo 1 I shall go into your house with offerings.
I will fulfill my promises to you
which my lips uttered
and my mouth spoke when I was in distress.
I will bring you offerings of fatlings;
along with the smoke of rams
I will offer bulls and goats.

Selah (pause).

Solo 2 Come, listen, all those who revere God,
and I will tell
all that God did for my soul.
I have cried out with my mouth,
extolling God with my tongue.

If I had harbored emptiness in my heart,
the Lord would not have listened.
But truly God has listened,
listened to the voice of my prayer.

Solo 1 Blessed be God
who has not rejected my prayer,
nor taken steadfast love away from me.

Psalm 125 *Song of ascents (pilgrimages).*

Choir 1 Those who trust in the LORD are like Mount Zion:
It will not fail; forever it will remain.

Choir 2 As Jerusalem is surrounded by mountains
so does the LORD surround the people,
from now and forever.
For the rule of the wicked will not weigh
upon the fate of the righteous,
because the righteous will not extend
their hands to crime.

Choir 1 Give prosperity, O LORD, to those who are good
and to those who are upright of heart.
But may the LORD drive away
those who turn aside to crooked ways,
the makers of emptiness.

All Peace be upon Israel!

Word of God

Benedictus
Blessed be the Lord God of **Israel**,
who visited and redeemed the **people**,
who raised up for us a **mighty** savior
from the house of **servant** David.

Just as the Lord spoke through the mouths of the holy prophets of **old**—
salvation comes out of the hands of our enemies and those who **hate** us,
that, with our ancestors, we might perform **works** of mercy,
remembering the holy covenant **sworn** to Abraham—

so does the Lord deliver us from the hands **of** our enemies,
that we might serve without fear before **the** Lord,
worshiping in **ho**liness
and in righteousness **all** our days.

And you also, child, will be called a prophet of God Most **High**:
for you will go before the Lord to prepare a **way**,
bringing people knowledge of salvation by for**giveness** of sins;
because of the deep and tender mercy **of** our God.

Whereby a light rising from on high will **vis**it us
to appear to those in darkness and in a shadow **of** death,
to guide our feet along a **straight**, sure path
into a **way** of peace.

INTERCESSIONS

Invocations

Cantor, then Assembly:

KH
We glo - ri - fy and praise you.

Cantor:

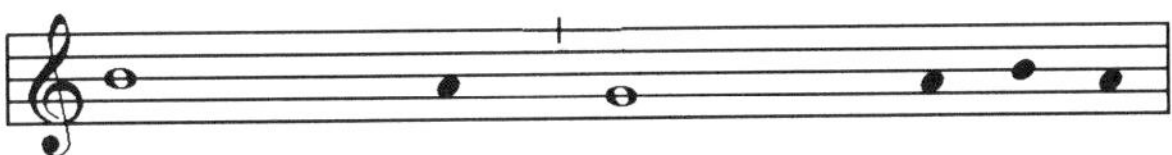

O risen **Christ**, how awesome **are** your deeds ...
O risen **Christ**, the nations **bow** before you ...
O risen **Christ**, you give life **to** all peoples ...
O risen **Christ**, you keep **us** from stumbling ...
O risen **Christ**, you guide us **in** just ways ...
O risen **Christ**, you show us the true **source** of greatness ...
O risen **Christ**, you manifest right **use** of power ...
O risen **Christ**, you give **us** prosperity ...

Our Father ...

Prayer
O God of all nations,
you watch over us with great care:
protect us from evil;
help us to use wealth and might justly;

encourage in us compassion and mercy.
May our nation be strong but caring,
esteemed but humble,
and prosperous but generous
so that we might bring all to enjoy fullness of life
in Christ Jesus now and always. **Amen.**

CONCLUSION

Blessing
May the God who reigns from above bless us
in the name of the Father, and of the Son, and of the Holy Spirit. **Amen.**

Dismissal
Go forth to enjoy the fruits of our nation, mindful of their source in our generous God. **Thanks be to God.**

NATIONAL HOLIDAYS Evening Prayer

FESTAL EVENING HYMN

PSALMODY

Psalm 79 *Psalm of Asaf.*

Choir 1 O God, nations have invaded your heritage.
They have profaned your holy temple;
they have reduced Jerusalem to ruins.
They have given the corpses of your servants
as food for the birds of the skies;
the flesh of your faithful, to the beasts of the land.
They have poured out their blood like water
all around Jerusalem,
and there is no one to bury them.
We are the laughingstock of our neighbors,
the mockery and the scorn of those around us.

All Until when, O LORD?
Will you be angry forever?
Will your indignation burn like fire?

Choir 2 Pour out your anger onto the nations
who have not recognized you,
and against empires
who have not prayed in your name.
For they have eaten up Jacob,
they have destroyed your pasture.

Choir 1 Do not remember against us our sins of the past.
Quickly, let your mercy come to meet us,
for we have grown extremely weak.
Help us, O God of our salvation,
on account of the glory of your name.

Choir 2 Why would the nations say,
"Where is their God?"
Make clear among the nations and to us
the vindication of the blood of your servants that was shed.
Let the groaning of captives come before you;
by your strong arm,
preserve those doomed to death.
Let the disdain by which our neighbors
have scorned you, O Lord,
turn against them deep in their hearts,
seven times over.

All But we are your people,
your flock, and your pasture.
We will give thanks to you forever;
from age to age,
we will tell your praise.

Psalm 67 *To the choirmaster. With stringed instruments. Psalm. Song.*

Choir 1 May God have mercy on us and bless us.
May God's face shine among us.

Selah (pause).

Choir 2 For your way is known over the earth,
and your salvation is known among all nations.

All Let the peoples give you thanks, O God,
let all the peoples give you thanks.

Choir 1 May the nations rejoice and shout with joy,
for you judge the peoples rightly
and the nations on the earth you guide.

Selah (pause).

All Let the peoples give you thanks, O God,
let all the peoples give you thanks.

Choir 2 The earth has given its fruit.
May God, our God, bless us.
May God bless us,
and let all ends of the earth
show reverence.

Word of God

Magnificat
My soul does magni**fy** the Lord!
I delight in **God** my savior
who looked kindly **on** lowliness.

Now all ages will **call** me blessed
for the Mighty One **did** great things.
Holy is **God's** name;
mercy is from age to age for **those** in awe!

The Lord's strong arm did **mighty** deeds:
confused the proud in **their** smug hearts;
toppled sovereigns **from** their thrones,
and exalted **hum**ble ones;
filled the hungering with **good** things,
and sent the rich **a**way empty.

The Lord helped servant **Is**rael
to re**mem**ber mercy,

as was spoken to Ab**ra**ham
and his descendants for**e**vermore!

INTERCESSIONS

Petitions

Cantor, then Assembly:

Cantor:

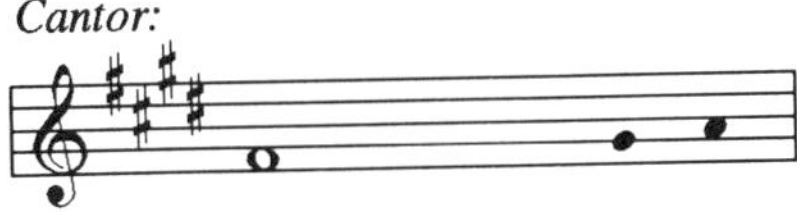

For **the** Church ...
For the people of **this** country ...
For govern**ment** leaders ...
For inhabitants **of** cities ...
For caretakers **of** farmlands ...
For users of natural **re**sources ...
For **our** children ...
For **our** youth ...
For **the** aged ...
For mili**tary** veterans ...
For **the** homeless ...
For the **op**pressed ...
For the **im**prisoned ...
For victims **of** violence ...
For all who died **this** day ...

Our Father ...

Prayer
O mighty God,
your realm is not of this world:
help us always to turn our eyes to you.
May our nation be just and sure,
that all our people may enjoy life and prosperity,
health and freedom.
We pray through Jesus Christ. **Amen.**

CONCLUSION

Blessing
May God bless us and our nation
in the name of the Father, and of the Son, and of the Holy Spirit. **Amen.**

Dismissal
Go and rest, resolved to be citizens of justice and mercy. **Thanks be to God.**

INDEX OF PSALMS*

****Bold** page numbers denote sung text.*

CONTRIBUTORS

JOYCE ANN ZIMMERMAN, C.PP.S. completed her doctoral studies at St. Paul University, Ottawa, Ontario. She is a university/college professor of liturgy, researcher, author, liturgical consultant, and frequent facilitator of workshops on liturgy. She is the founder and director of the INSTITUTE *for* LITURGICAL MINISTRY at Maria Stein Center. Its periodical, *liturgical ministry*, is in its second year of publication. Her most recent work is *Liturgy as Living Faith: A Liturgical Spirituality* (Scranton: University of Scranton Press/Associated University Presses, 1993).

KATHLEEN HARMON, S.N.D.de N. has a Masters degree in religious education from Fordham University and is presently pursuing graduate studies in Church Music at Westminster Choir College, Princeton, New Jersey. She is a parish liturgical musician, voice teacher, and cantor trainer. She directs the music for programs of the INSTITUTE *for* LITURGICAL MINISTRY at Maria Stein Center.

JEAN-PIERRE PRÉVOST, S.M.M. holds an S.S.L. from the Pontifical Biblical Institute and completed his doctoral studies at the Gregorianum. He is professor of Old Testament studies and Hebrew at St. Paul University in Ottawa. His most recent work on the Apocalypse has been translated into English and is published by Crossroads.

DELPHINE KOLKER, C.PP.S. holds a doctorate in literature from Catholic University of America. She is professor of English and literature at Cleveland State University. Her published book of poetry is entitled *Aspects and Attitudes*.